Lawrence Fawcett, a UFO investigator for twenty years, has held memberships in the National Investigations Committee on Aerial Phenomena (NICAP) and the Aerial Phenomena Research Organization (APRO) and has also served as the Early Warning Coordinator in New England for the Air Force–sponsored "Condon Committee" UFO study. Currently, he is on the National Board of Directors for the Center for UFO studies (CUFOS) and is the assistant director and chief investigator for Citizens Against UFO Secrecy (CAUS).

Barry J. Greenwood, involved in UFO research since 1964, is currently the historian, archivist, and Middlesex County director for the Massachusetts Chapter of the Mutual UFO Network (MUFON). He also serves on the Board of Advisors of Citizens Against UFO Secrecy (CAUS) and is a member of the Center for UFO Studies (CUFOS), the Aerial Phenomena Research Organization (APRO), and the British UFO Research Association (BUFORA). He holds associate memberships in the American Association for the Advancement of Science and the American Astronomical Society.

D0111358

The UFO Cover-Up

What the Government Won't Say

Lawrence Fawcett &
Barry J. Greenwood

Foreword by Dr. J. Allen Hynek

PRENTICE
HALL
PRESS

New York   London   Toronto   Sydney   Tokyo   Singapore

PRENTICE HALL PRESS
15 Columbus Circle
New York, NY 10023

Copyright © 1984 by Prentice-Hall, Inc.

All rights reserved,
including the right of reproduction
in whole or in part in any form.

Originally published as *Clear Intent*.

PRENTICE HALL PRESS and colophons are registered trademarks
of Simon & Schuster, Inc.

Library of Congress Cataloging-in-Publication Data
Fawcett, Lawrence.
  The UFO Cover-Up.

  Bibliography: p.
  Includes index.
    1. Unidentified flying objects—Sightings and
encounters—United States.   2. Government information—
United States.   I. Greenwood, Barry J.   II. Title.
TL789.F34   1984   001.9′42   84-9818

ISBN 0-13-137712-4

Manufactured in the United States of America

10 9 8 7 6 5 4 3 2 1

First Prentice Hall Press Edition

To Attorney Peter Gersten,
Director of Citizens Against UFO Secrecy.
The results of his quest for truth
have enriched our knowledge of the UFO subject.

Acknowledgments

Robert Todd, whose voluminous files on government UFO interest was of immense help to us. His research is a model of careful investigation and is much appreciated.

Tom Adams, for documentation on mystery helicopters and the animal mutilation phenomenon.

Linda Moulton Howe, for permission to use the "K-7" story.

Betty and Bob Luca, for firsthand experiences with strange helicopters.

Captain Keith Wolverton, for reports on UFO activity in Montana.

Dean Rhodes, for filling in gaps in the Loring AFB story.

Steven Eichner, Robert Mark, and Franklin Youri, for their firsthand UFO experiences.

The Center for UFO Studies and the Mutual UFO Network, for contributions of information.

Paul Norman and James R. Sullivan for important contributions on our overseas data.

The British UFO Research Association, Dot Street, Jenny Randles, and Brenda Butler for their part in bringing the Rendlesham Forest affair to light. We can never express enough gratitude for their efforts.

Dr. J. Allen Hynek and Raymond Fowler, for assessment and commentary on our work and for technical assistance on several matters.

For typing, proofreading, comment, and evaluation, many thanks to Marge Christensen, Marion Mardem, Claire Rouillard, Pauline Arendt, Joan Thompson, Lois Fawcett, Merlyn Sheehan, John White, Marie Ford, Carol Bacevic, and John and June Greenwood.

And, finally, the FBI, CIA, NSA, DIA, State Department, Air Force, and many other federal agencies for providing valuable documentation, without which this book could not have been possible.

Contents

Foreword

The oft-repeated pronouncements of our government that UFOs are nonexistent and that the great many existing reports of them are merely the result of misidentifications and hoaxes has not been met in some quarters with trusting and total acceptance. In the absence, however, of incontrovertible proof of such suspected governmental duplicity—despite the many indications thereof (such as I have personally encountered)—no one of integrity could proclaim that the government, and in particular the military, have been hoodwinking the public and are guilty of a Watergate-type cover-up in the matter of UFOs.

Lacking such final proof, my standard response in the past years to frequent questions about government cover-up had been to approach the question from the opposite direction. I would respond that, to me, it was inconceivable that any responsible government, let alone ours, would *not* take serious cognizance of any matter which had elicited as much public interest and even concern as UFOs have, and which had been the subject of such wide media coverage for several decades. The literature on UFOs is extensive; as evidence, one needs only to note the bibliography on UFOs in the Library of Congress. Surely, in our country, it would seem quite inconceivable that the FBI, CIA, and NSA, which regularly pry into virtually every facet of American life that might affect the public weal or national security, would for some strange reason scrupulously avoid the subject of UFOs. It does not seem logical—but then, violation of logic does not constitute proof.

Experienced UFO investigators have, over the years, been the recipients of many tales and undocumented statements, generally from former military pilots and crew members about having their aircraft "scrambled" (launched in immediate response to an alarm) to pursue a UFO, of UFOs encroaching on high-sensitivity areas on military bases, of malfunctions of defense equipment in the presence of UFOs, of planes lost while pursuing UFOs, and, yes, even tales of crashed saucers and of alien beings kept in the deep freeze. Serious and responsible investigators, however, have not accepted such accounts at face value in the absence of the documentation necessary to establish such tales unequivocally.

Now, however, documentation which puts the UFO—U.S. government controversy in quite a new light has become available. The authors have made revealing use of documents released through the mechanism of the Freedom of Information Act and other data which have been made available to them, often through private sources, which show that the CIA and NSA protestations of innocence and lack of interest in UFOs are nothing short of prevarication. The implication of these documents (and of those whose existence has been established in court but whose release was forbidden by those courts on grounds that national security might be jeopardized) are indeed far-reaching.

The reader must judge for himself or herself just how far these implications extend, but certainly no one can deny any longer that various intelligence agencies of our government were long cognizant of UFOs and the global extent of this phenomenon. Official dispatches from our embassies and air bases in other countries to these agencies, to the State Department, and even, on occasion, to the White House, bear incontrovertible witness to this.

Not all existing UFO-related documents in the possession of these intelligence agencies have, however, been released through the Freedom of Information Act. Of special interest would be those documents held by the National Security Agency (NSA) whose release the courts denied, and which denial was the subject of the case the Supreme Court refused to hear. This upheld, in effect, the claim of the lower courts that the release of said documents would jeopardize national security. If this is true, then, of course, any loyal citizen would agree that such documents should and must remain undisclosed. But, if this is so, then this very fact loudly proclaims that UFOs are not figments of the imagination but are, instead, quite real and of vital interest.

For the government to continue to maintain that UFOs are nonexistent in the face of the documents already released and of other cogent evidence presented in this book is puerile and in a sense an insult to the American people. For, as one national newspaper proclaimed in a front-page headline, "If There Are No UFOs, Why All the Secrecy?"

J. Allen Hynek
Center for UFO Studies
1983 Evanston, Illinois

Preface

In the 3,000 pages of previously classified documents on UFOs released during the past four years by the Departments of State, the Army, Navy, and Air Force, the Federal Bureau of Investigation (FBI), the Central Intelligence Agency (CIA), the National Security Agency (NSA), and the Defense Intelligence Agency (DIA), we find the expert testimony of scientists, military and intelligence personnel, law enforcement officers, and other responsible people on the subject of UFOs. Nearly two-thirds of these documents have come to light through the efforts of UFO researchers such as Larry W. Bryant, Charles Huffer, Bruce Maccabee, Brad Sparks, Robert Todd, W. Todd Zechel, and ourselves, who have filed requests for UFO material through the Freedom of Information Act. Approximately one-third of the documents were released as a result of lawsuits that were handled by attorney Peter Gersten on behalf of an Arizona UFO organization, Ground Saucer Watch. Other suits for the release of UFO documents have been filed against the Defense Intelligence Agency, the National Security Agency, and various other federal organizations.

The official documents, which will be referred to throughout this book, allow us to draw certain conclusions as to the reality and nature of the UFO phenomena. They also attest to intense governmental interest in UFOs when the phenomena pose a threat to the national security of the United States. We find it most surprising that although UFOs have affected national security many times in the past, the government continues to perceive these reports on a case-by-case basis, referring to them as "isolated incidents."

Let's go back for a moment and take a brief look at a few past examples of national security being threatened by unconventional aerial objects. From the start, UFOs were a top-secret matter; of this, there is no doubt. The following excerpt from a formerly classified FBI document dated January 31, 1949, and sent to then FBI Director J. Edgar Hoover states:

> At a recent weekly Intelligence Conference of G2, ONI, OSI and FBI in the Fourth Army area, officers of G2, Fourth Army have discussed the matter of "unidentified aircraft" or "unidentified aerial phenomena," otherwise known as "flying discs," "flying saucers," and "balls of fire." *This matter is considered top secret by intelligence officers of both the Army and the Air Force* [emphasis in original].

This classification stemmed from the high number of sightings that were being reported in the vicinity of sensitive military and government installations, such as Los Alamos, New Mexico.

Another previously classified Air Force document that was sent to Brigadier General Joseph F. Carroll, Director of Special Investigations, USAF, on May 25, 1950, stated that the observations of these phenomena over Los Alamos were made by "scientists, special agents of the Office of Special Investigations IG, USAF, airline pilots, military pilots, Los Alamos Security Inspectors, military personnel, and many other persons of various occupations." Once again, we see that the reliability of the observers is not in question. The Air Force was given real cause for concern by the continued appearance of unexplained aerial phenomena in the vicinity of sensitive installations.

The Assistant Director of Scientific Intelligence for the CIA sent an interesting memo in December 1952 to then CIA Director Walter B. Smith. The concern over UFOs is once more apparent. The memo says: "Sightings of unidentified objects at great altitudes and traveling at high speeds in the vicinity of major U.S. defense installations are of such nature that they are not attributable to natural phenomena or known types of aerial vehicles." Attached to the CIA memo was a National Security Council memo and directive "establishing this matter as a priority project throughout the intelligence and the defense research and development communities." The memo to the Executive Secretary of the National Security Council also states: "It is my view that this situation has possible implications for our national security." What had been "cause for concern" two years before now had "implications for our national security." Furthermore, the directive calls for the CIA to "direct, formulate, and carry out a program of intelligence and research activities as required to solve the problem of instant, positive identification of unidentified flying objects."

Knowledge of the government's serious, top-level interest in UFOs even spread outside the United States. In a Canadian Department of Transport memo dated November 21, 1950, Wilbert B. Smith, senior radio engineer, forwarded a proposal to the controller of telecommunications suggesting a formal study of, among other things, using the Earth's magnetic field as a possible energy source. The subject of flying saucers happened to come up in the memo as follows:

> I made discreet enquiries through the Canadian Embassy staff in Washington who were able to obtain for me the following information:
>
> a. The matter is the most highly classified subject in the United States Government, rating higher even than the H-bomb.
> b. Flying saucers exist.
> c. Their modus operandi is unknown but concentrated effort is being made by a small group headed by Doctor Vannevar Bush.
> d. The entire matter is considered by the United States authorities to be of tremendous significance.

The Smith memo itself was classified "Top Secret."

These documents clearly show that during the early years of the UFO phenomena, the government expressed considerable concern over the potential threat that UFOs might pose to our national security.

In recent years, the situation has not changed. This excerpt from an October 20, 1969, Air Force document, which had suggested that the Air Force's UFO investigation Project Blue Book be terminated, revealed that Blue Book never received those reports that affected national security: "Reports of unidentified flying objects which could affect national security are made in accordance with JANAP 146 or Air Force Manual 55–11, *and are not part of the Blue Book system*" [emphasis added]. Quoting the same document again, "As already stated, reports of UFOs which could affect national security should continue to be handled through the *standard Air Force procedure* [emphasis added] designed for this purpose." The document was signed by Brigadier General C. H. Bolender, the Air Force's Deputy Director of Development. Sixteen attachments, that once accompanied the document, are no longer in Air Force files.

A NORAD document dated November 11, 1975, is probably one of the most significant modern examples of suspicious unknown air activity possibly affecting national security. It states that in October and early November of 1975, reliable military personnel at Loring AFB, Maine, Wurtsmith AFB, Michigan, Malmstrom AFB, Montana, Minot AFB, North Dakota, and the Canadian Air Force Station at Falconbridge, Ontario, had visually sighted suspicious objects. Once again, the reliability of the observers is established from the start and, once again, the UFOs are reported in sensitive military areas. These are missile control facilities, aircraft alert areas, and nuclear weapons storage areas where security is generally tight. In reporting on one incident, a Loring AFB teletype stated that an unidentified object "demonstrated a clear intent in the weapons storage area." The Air Force never explained what the "clear intent was, though it seems that, in this instance, it was a non-violent intent.

In the lawsuit of *Citizens Against UFO Secrecy (CAUS)* vs. *National Security Agency,* a U.S. District Court reviewed a top-secret, twenty-one page affidavit concerning the National Security Agency's UFO documents. The affidavit was partially declassified and released to us on May 18, 1982. Although virtually all reports of UFOs have been censored out of the affidavit, with the singular exception of a brief reference to a "1973 report," a few interesting comments are left to ponder. For example, UFOs are placed into a class of information that the NSA refers to as "surprise material" and another reference is made to a document which describes the NSA's ability to deal with "unusual phenomena." These terms hardly describe a trivial, unimportant subject.

A total of 239 UFO documents were discovered by the NSA in their files, with 79 originating from other government agencies. These agencies, unnamed, also refused to allow their documents to be released. The NSA documents primarily took the form of either "communications intelligence" reports (COMINT) or "signal intelligence" reports (SIGINT). The period covered by the documents spans twenty-one years, 1958 to 1979.

After reviewing the arguments, the court declared in its memorandum and order that release of the documents "could seriously jeopardize the work of the agency and the security of the United States." In balancing the public interest in the issue of UFOs against the agency's need for secrecy, the court further determined that "public interest in disclosure is far outweighed by the *sensitive nature of the materials* [emphasis added] and the obvious effect on national security their release may well entail." This reinforces both the continuous ties of UFOs to our national security and the fact that there is constant secrecy surrounding UFO documents. We are now certain that the government, after more than thirty years of secrecy, still manages to keep UFO-related information from the public.

We, the authors of *Clear Intent,* object to this policy of UFO secrecy. We feel that the public has a right to know, and we intend to serve it. By utilizing previously classified documents and news stories, we put together the series of events that took place during October and November of 1975 along the northern tier of continental United States SAC bases and explore the implication that UFOs pose a serious threat to our national security. We will also examine other extraordinary UFO events of the mid-1970s which have been made available to researchers through the use of the Freedom of Information Act.

The UFO phenomena warrant a worldwide scientific study with all governments working together to solve this mystery. Our survival may be at stake.

L. F.
B. J. G.
Stoneham, Massachusetts

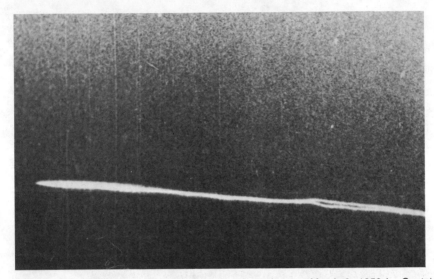

Frame from an Air Force 16mm gun camera film taken on March 3, 1953 by Captain Roderick Thompson. Thompson led a flight of three F-84s on a simulated bombing run about 130 miles west of Luke Air Force Base in Arizona when at 13:25 MST he spotted a peculiar object. He estimated that the UFO was 300-500 feet long with a long, thin vapor trail. The trail forked off about 1000 feet behind the object before re-joining again. 30 feet of film was shot before Thompson broke off the chase. This is the only publicly available Air Force gun camera film showing a distinct UFO. *Credit: National Archives*

UFO photographed on October 8, 1978 north of Tehran, Iran by Franklin Abrahim-Youri. It moved from north to south and during it's flight Yuri managed to take one snapshot before it disappeared beyond the roofline of his home. Duration: one minute. The UFO is virtually identical to an object photographed in Shiraz, Iran. (See Chapter 6.) *Credit: Franklin Youri and the Center For UFO Studies.*

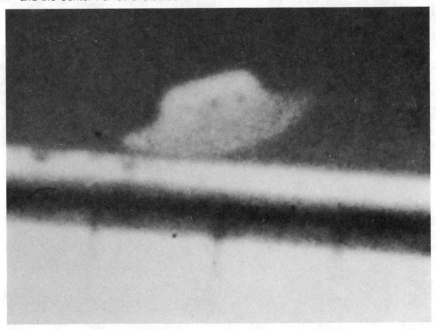

Entrance to Rendlesham Forest near Bentwaters Air Force Base in England. A sign erected soon after a UFO landing incident in 1980 warns that intruders may be prosecuted under the British "Official Secrets Act" for entering the area without authorization, despite the fact that the forest was previously a public picnic ground. (See Chapter 14.)

Photos of a cattle mutilation incident, April 1980 at Mesa County, Colorado. The injuries shown are common features of mutilations reported in 1975. (See Chapters 3 & 7.) *Credit: Tom Adams*

Note the unusual bore holes in the animal's underside. *Credit: Tom Adams*

CHAPTER ONE

The Freedom of
Information Act and UFOs

Since 1947, the beginning of the modern UFO era, one of the most frequent questions asked by the public has been: "What does the U.S. government know about UFOs?" Unfortunately, this question invariably has gone unanswered. Public inquiries have either been ignored or have been met with an array of fact sheets stating why the UFO phenomenon does not offer cause for concern. A typical form letter to a citizen has been as follows:

On December 17, 1969, the Secretary of the Air Force announced the termination of Project Blue Book, the Air Force program for the investigation of UFOs.

The decision to discontinue UFO investigations was based on an evaluation of a report prepared by the University of Colorado entitled "Scientific Study of Unidentified Flying Objects"; a review of the University of Colorado's report by the National Academy of Sciences; past UFO studies; and Air Force experience investigating UFO reports during the past two decades.

As a result of these investigations and studies, and experience gained from investigating UFO reports since 1948, the conclusions of Project Blue Book are: (1) no UFO reported, investigated, and evaluated by the Air Force has ever given any indication of threat to our national security; (2) there has been no evidence submitted to or discovered by the Air Force that sightings categorized as "unidentified" represent technological developments or principles beyond the range of present day scientific knowledge; and (3) there has been no evidence indicating that sightings categorized as "unidentified" are extraterrestrial vehicles.

With the termination of Project Blue Book, the Air Force regulation establishing and controlling the program for investigating and analyzing UFOs has been rescinded, and file copies of Project Blue Book records have been transferred to the Albert F. Simpson Historical Research Center, Maxwell Air Force Base, Alabama 36112, where they are available to the public for review. Although the Center does not have the reproduction capability to provide duplicate copies of Project Blue Book reports (some 26 standard file drawers of material), the complete University of Colorado report is available in paperback form at a nominal cost by Bantam Book Company.

Attached for your information is the Project Blue Book sighting summary for the period 1947–1969. Also included is a listing of UFO-related materials currently available through publication outlets of the federal government.

Since the termination of Project Blue Book, no evidence has been presented to indicate that further investigation of UFOs by the Air Force is warranted. In view of the considerable Air Force commitment of resources in the past and the extreme pressure on Air Force funds at this time, there is no likelihood of renewed Air Force involvement in this area.

There are a number of universities and professional scientific organizations such as the American Association for the Advancement of Science, which have considered UFO phenomena during periodic meetings and seminars. Such timely review of the situation by private groups insures that sound evidence will not be overlooked by the scientific community.

Your interest in the United States Air Force is appreciated.

In fact, every government-funded UFO investigation informed the public that UFOs are no threat to national security and that nothing is to be gained by further investigation of the subject. Thousands of reports had been sent to the government despite the denials, and of 12,618 reports received by the Air Force, 701 remained unexplained. The unexplained reports contained highly detailed accounts by reliable witnesses, and many Air Force officials privately have expressed great concern over the sightings.

After the Air Force's Project Blue Book UFO Investigation ceased operation in 1969, there was no source within the United States government to which one could report a sighting of an unidentified flying object in our skies. A person attempting to report a UFO to the Air Force would be told by an Air Force spokesman to call the police or a nearby university. In either case, chances of a follow-up investigation were slim.

This would seem to remove responsibility for civilian UFO sightings from the military. However, what of UFO reports originating within military circles? Certainly, Air Force pilots, radar operators, and other personnel had not suddenly stopped sighting UFOs because Project Blue Book had been closed.

Barry Greenwood sent an inquiry to the Department of the Air Force in Washington, D.C., asking what exactly was done with UFO sighting reports by Air Force personnel. He received the usual standard Air Force fact sheet, which did not respond in any way to the question.

In an attempt to force an answer, Greenwood contacted Massachusetts Congressman Edward Markey and asked him to obtain the information on

Greenwood's behalf. The reply was sent by Lt. Col. John Farr for the Air Force's Congressional Inquiry Division on April 20, 1977. It stated:

> With regard to Mr. Greenwood's desire for reports of current UFO sightings, a Joint Army Navy Air Force Publication, (JANAP 146) requires radio reports of any sighting which the pilot feels could be a threat to national security. Guidance in this directive could result in reports of UFOs. However, if such reports were made, they would be transient in nature with no permanent record or file maintained.

JANAP 146 E (1977 edition) states that:

> a. Sightings within the scope of this chapter, as outlined in paragraphs 102b(1), (2), (6) and (7), are to be reported as follows:
>   (1) While airborne and from land based observers.
>   (a) Hostile or unidentified single aircraft or formations of aircraft which appear to be directed against the United States or Canada or their forces.
>   (b) Missiles.
>   (c) Unidentified flying objects.
>   (d) Hostile or unidentified submarines.
>   (e) Hostile or unidentified group or groups of military surface vessels.
>   (f) Individual surface vessels, submarines, or aircraft of unconventional design, or engaged in suspicious activity, or observed in a location or on a course which may be interpreted as constituting a threat to the United States, Canada, or their forces.
>   (g) Any unexplained or unusual activity which may indicate a possible attack against or through Canada or the United States, including the presence of any unidentified or other suspicious ground parties in the Polar Region or other remote or sparsely populated areas.

Note here that a distinction is drawn between "unidentified flying objects," and "missiles" and "unidentified single aircraft or formations of aircraft." Thus, UFOs do not seem to mean the same thing as missiles or aircraft.

An Air Force Intelligence Manual dated September 1953 represents UFOs in an illustration as large, disc-shaped craft with glass-like domes and portholes around the edges. And a Naval publication (OPNAV 94-P-3B), titled "MERINT Radiotelegraph Procedure," shows UFOs again as a separate class from missiles and aircraft with an illustration under the UFO heading showing two very exotic aircraft designs: One a Saturn-shaped disc, and the other, a Buck Rogers-type rocket.

Getting back to the Farr letter, several points should be stressed. First, we are told that regulation JANAP 146 is still in effect in connection with UFO sightings. Second, we are told that this regulation's provisions "could result in reports of UFOs." Finally, the reports are "transient in nature with no permanent record or file maintained."

This brief paragraph, which amounts to nothing more than a brush-off of the UFO phenomenon, is quite revealing. UFOs are probably sighted by military personnel and have probably been reported under regulations. The letter does not specifically deny that UFO reports have been filed under JANAP 146; it would have been easy to say, "No reports have been filed under the regulation."

If UFOs are no threat to national security, then why does JANAP 146 still specifically include UFOs as reportable? This leads to another contradiction of official policy. Obviously, UFO reports are *investigated;* otherwise, why report them? Project Blue Book was closed. Who, then, investigated UFOs? Where did the reports go?

The reference to permanent records not being kept could mean one of two things: (a) records are destroyed after a short period of time. (This would be astonishing. To destroy reports of an extraordinary phenomenon would be a crime against science. Of course, it couldn't be ruled out entirely.) Or, (b) the records are not kept, but passed along elsewhere.

A skeptic might say that a lot is being read into the letter from the Congressional Inquiry Division. Maybe the letter could have been worded better to more clearly explain the official position on the subject. It would have been easy to accept this, but lingering doubts about the letter could not be brushed away.

The only way to verify the suspicions aroused would be to locate UFO records. How could this be done? By identifying a military UFO incident and using the Freedom of Information and Privacy Act to request the desired information.

What is the Freedom of Information Act (FOIA), and how does it work? In 1966, Congress acted to increase public access to government records. It provided that any records, documents, memoranda, statements of policy, and other similar materials be made available to those persons who requested such data. Nine types of information are exempt from release (according to the U.S. Code 5 USC, Section 552). These cover matters that are:

(1) (A) specifically authorized under criteria established by an Executive order to be kept secret in the interests of national defense or foreign policy, and (B) are in fact properly classified pursuant to such Executive order;

(2) related solely to the internal personnel rules and practices of an agency;

(3) specifically exempted from disclosure by statute (other than section 552b of this title), provided that such statute (A) requires that the matters be withheld from the public in such a manner as to leave no discretion on the issue, or (B) establishes particular criteria for withholding or refers to particular types of matters to be withheld;

(4) trade secrets and commercial or financial information obtained from a person and privileged or confidential;

(5) interagency or intra-agency memoranda or letters which would not be

available by law to a party other than an agency in litigation with the agency;

(6) personnel and medical files and similar files the disclosure of which would constitute a clearly unwarranted invasion of personal privacy;

(7) investigatory records compiled for law enforcement purposes, but only to the extent that the production of such records would (A) interfere with enforcement proceedings, (B) deprive a person of a right to a fair trial or an impartial adjudication, (C) constitute an unwarranted invasion of personal privacy, (D) disclose the identity of a confidential source and, in the case of a record compiled by a criminal law enforcement authority in the course of a criminal investigation or by an agency conducting a lawful national security intelligence investigation, confidential information furnished only by the confidential source, (E) disclosure investigative techniques and procedures, or (F) endanger the life or physical safety of law enforcement personnel;

(8) contained in or related to examination, operating, or condition reports prepared by, on behalf of, or for the use of an agency responsible for the regulation or supervision of financial institutions; or

(9) geological and geophysical information and data, including maps, concerning wells.

In 1974, a number of amendments were attached to the Act. Only those relevant to UFOs follow.

1. Agencies were to release documents to someone requesting them with a *reasonable description* of said data. *Exact* information would not have to be given to gather information on a particular topic.
2. Time limits were placed on agencies in responding to requests. They were allowed ten working days to respond to the first request, twenty working days for responding to an appeal of a denial of documents, and a single ten-day extension in responding to allow for administrative difficulties. Also, a thirty-day limit was placed on an agency in responding to a court case.
3. Set fees were provided for search and reproduction costs. This is rated at a 10¢ per page photocopy charge, plus fees for hourly clerical and professional time applied in preparing a response to an FOIA request.
4. Courts could examine and render decisions on whether or not to release documents from agencies brought to court by those filing requests.
5. A full report on FOIA requests and their handling by each agency would be provided to Congress annually.

The Privacy Act of 1974 allowed a person to request his or her file from federal agencies, and also to add to or change the information contained therein. The agency would be required to acknowledge if such files exist in full. Exempt from this are law enforcement files and national security information.

With this knowledge in hand, all that was needed was a military UFO report.

An opportunity came with the publication of a *National Enquirer* article, dated December 13, 1977, entitled "UFOs Spotted at Nuclear Bases and

Missile Sites." Normally, the *Enquirer* would not be relied upon for accurate information, in view of its past record of reporting on the UFO subject. However, the article did provide places, dates, and some details which could be verified. We were also anxious to test the accuracy of the Air Force's April 20 letter. An FOIA request was filed on December 26 for case files from Loring AFB, Maine, October 27, 28, and 31, 1975; Wurtsmith AFB, Michigan, October 30, 1975; Malmstrom AFB, Montana, November 7 and 8, 1975.

A reply dated February 6, 1978 was received from the Office of the Assistant Secretary of Defense, notifying us that the Office of the Joint Chiefs of Staff had identified twenty-four documents which complied with the request. As we were to find out later, the twenty-four documents released by the Office of the Joint Chiefs of Staff were *new* documents and were being revealed for the first time, an unexpected lucky break. There was some difficulty at first in getting fifteen of the twenty-four documents released, since the government wanted to claim an exemption under the FOIA covering release of internal records with only preliminary, raw information. This would prevent the labeling of unevaluated documents as "official" by those persons requesting the documents. It was later determined by Thomas Ross, Assistant Secretary of Defense, that no useful purpose would be served by withholding the records, so they were released.

The information in these documents has been included in later chapters of this book, with two exceptions, which we will discuss here.

On the first point, a National Military Command Center (NMCC) Memorandum dated November 13, 1975, concerned "Requests for Temperature Inversion Analysis." A representative for Air Force Global Weather Central (AFGWC) paid a visit to the NMCC to discuss arrangements for the Chairman of the Joint Chiefs of Staff to obtain weather information. According to the memo:

> The West Hem Desk Officer will act as the control officer for temperature inversion analysis requests initiated by the NMCC. These requests will be made in conjunction with sightings of unusual phenomenon along the northern U.S. border.

Here is clear evidence that the Air Force was investigating reports of UFOs at military bases. Whenever a sighting occurred, the NMCC would phone the AFGWC and ask whether an atmospheric temperature inversion existed in the area. (A temperature inversion is a layer in the atmosphere in which temperature increases with altitude. An inversion layer is remarkably stable, although strong wind shears can occur across the inversion layer. Changes in concentration of particles and water vapor are evident in passing through inversion layers. The existence of such inversions can be responsible, under some circumstances, for radar and visual UFO reports.)

UFO researcher Robert Todd of Ardmore, Pennsylvania, filed an FOIA request for all records of temperature inversion analyses (TIAs) performed by the AFGWC for the NMCC. Hopefully, this would give a list of UFO incidents which were important enough for the military to investigate. The AFGWC furnished copies of TIAs which dated to May 1977. No real specifics were released about the nature of the reports, only that analyses were done on certain dates. Follow-up FOIA requests by Todd in 1981 revealed that the NMCC Operating Instructions had been changed, and that TIAs were no longer required. Why was this done? Attempts to obtain information on the change met with Department of Defense denials that they knew anything about it. Could it be that the TIAs were discovered to be of little use in explaining the UFO reports being investigated and, therefore, were dropped?

The second point involves the distribution lists on several of the twenty-four documents released by the Assistant Secretary of Defense. Among the agencies listed was the CIA, which had insisted for years that its only involvement with UFOs was the Robertson Panel of 1952 (see Chapter 8). Yet, here it was receiving regular advisories on UFO activity in 1975! Why did the CIA become involved in obtaining UFO information long after its "official" interest ended? More on this will be discussed later.

At this point, inquiries into the government's UFO interest were turning out to be an unqualified success in terms of showing that the public was not getting a complete story. The next target of our initial probing was the FBI.

Little was known about the FBI's data base on UFOs before 1977, so this seemed like a prime source from which to obtain the release of a significant collection of information. An FOIA request was filed on February 20, 1978.

While awaiting an answer on the request, we discovered that another individual, Dr. Bruce Maccabee, had filed for FBI data and had eventually received about 800 pages. He published a series of articles in several UFO journals summarizing the main points of the files. This prepared us for what to expect when action was taken on our request. And action *was* taken.

Over the next fifteen months, a series of releases to us netted a grand total of about 1,700 pages of documents. While the material released was not earthshaking in the sense of proving that UFOs were absolutely real, it does provide a large amount of information on sightings, how the FBI dealt with them, and how the FBI dealt with the public.

Regarding the handling of UFO inquiries from the public, some of the standard FBI responses were: "The information in the files of the Federal Bureau of Investigation is confidential and available for official use only," and "The investigation of unidentified flying objects is not within the jurisdiction of the Bureau." Of course, the FBI was entirely within its rights to withhold its files, since no Freedom of Information Act existed prior to the 1960s—the period covering most of the file material. Yet, such statements contributed to the overall suspicion of the public toward the government's pronouncements on UFOs. By saying that investigation of the subject "is not within the jurisdiction of the Bureau," it implied that: (1) the FBI never investigated UFO reports, which is clearly untrue as is evident from a cursory examination of the files, and (2) the FBI had no information on the subject.

A more complete survey of the FBI files is contained in Chapters 10 and 11.

Assorted rumors came to our attention periodically. While some of these stories did not lead to any tangible results, others were quite tantalizing. For an example, take the case of "Project Bluebolt."

In response to a request for information concerning Department of Defense support of research into antigravity propulsion, the U.S. Army Research and Development Group Commander Colonel Benedict Freund stated on March 18, 1975:

> The Army is not doing any research on this subject to the knowledge of any member of this office. The Air Force has done such research and, until about a year and a half ago, had an ambitious effect known as Project Bluebolt. Bluebolt was *primarily* a study to understand gravity and of necessity addressed antigravity. To the knowledge of personnel assigned to the Air Force office in London, no antigravity propulsion research is presently being supported by the Air Force.
>
> It is our consensus here that if the Dept. of Defense is supporting such research it is funded by ARPA (Advanced Research Projects Agency). ARPA's mission is to support those research efforts that are of high risk and appear beyond the purview of any one service. I consider this unlikely and suspect that such research is more probably the responsibility of either ERLA, NASA, or NSF.

The authors filed an FOIA request with the Department of the Air Force in an effort to track down Project Bluebolt. The Air Force denied the existence of such a project in a letter dated October 29, 1979.

Another request was filed with the Air Force Office of Scientific Research. Included was a copy of Freund's letter. On April 28, 1980, Captain John Lindstrom, Chief of Administration, said, "I can be of little assistance. The letter from Col. Freund was helpful but I feel he may have misidentified Project Bluebook as Bluebolt."

A search of the National Technical Information Service and the Defense Technical Information Center was also conducted, with no results. Captain Lindstrom included an extract from the Air Force's copy of the *Code Names Directory* which contained an entry for a "Project Blue Bolt." It is defined as a "peacetime military exercise." Nothing more is said about it.

Lindstrom's opinion that "Bluebolt" was confused with "Bluebook" seems unlikely. Project Blue Book had nothing to do with antigravity propulsion research. Also, Blue Book had been closed down since 1970, a full five years before Freund's letter.

Again, we tried to pin down Project Bluebolt by contacting the U.S.

Army's Research and Standardization Group in Europe—Freund's former command with a new name.

According to Warren Grabau, Chief of Environmental Sciences for the group, in a letter dated April 24, 1980,

> Unfortunately, I regret to say that no one in this office has any information whatever on research on antigravity sponsored by the Department of Defense in general or by the U.S. Army or Air Force in particular. I fear that we can add nothing to the letter from Col. Freund, a copy of which you enclosed. In fact, it appears that he knew more than any of us."

This leaves us with a big question—one of a great many in this book. What was Project Bluebolt? What was once an antigravity research project had disappeared into oblivion. The Departments of the Army and Air Force claim to never have heard of Bluebolt. Every inquiry hit a dead end, except for a reference to Blue Bolt in the military *Code Names Dictionary*. And this simply describes a "peacetime military exercise," which covers a lot of ground. It may or may not be a coincidence that Blue Book and Bluebolt have one thing in common—the word "blue."

UFO researchers have been given stories by military personnel of special investigations into UFOs bearing "Blue" as part of the title. One might speculate that the "Blue" refers to the sky, since many of the *Code Names Dictionary* entries with more conventional uses of the word refer to high altitude aircraft and rockets. It would certainly be appropriate for use in connection with UFOs.

The North American Aerospace Defense Command (NORAD) is charged with the responsibility for the protection of the North American continent from air attack. This is done through continuous monitoring of the skies with sophisticated radar systems designed to detect any foreign objects in or approaching our airspace. When an unidentified aircraft is sighted by radar, NORAD attempts to communicate with it for identification purposes. If this is not successful, it becomes necessary to "scramble" interceptors to identify the craft visually. According to NORAD, this happens about fifteen times per month. Usually the aircraft are identified.

Sometimes they are not identified. These reports would be classified as UFOs or, as NORAD terms them, "Uncorrelated Observations." Two types of uncorrelated observations have been noted in NORAD data. One type involves the *atmospheric* detection of unknown aerial objects, and the other involves the *space* detection of unknown orbiting objects.

Space observations are recorded by the NORAD Space Detection and Tracking System (SPADATS) and a Navy counterpart, the Naval Space Surveillance System (NAVSPASUR). These systems track and maintain element sets on approximately 5,000 man-made, catalogued objects in space. Approximately 25,000 observations are sent to the NORAD Space Defense Center each day from the sensor systems. Most of these observations are directly correlated to catalogued objects. The ones that are not correlated are not necessarily all genuine UFOs. A great majority are either satellites too small to track or debris from satellite break-ups.

Estimates vary, but several hundred uncatalogued objects are orbiting the earth at present. These objects and the continuous need to update the element sets of catalogued objects due to natural phenomena are the largest contributors of uncorrelated observations. A certain percentage are never correlated with known objects and can literally be called unidentified flying objects or, in this case, "unidentified orbiting objects."

According to NORAD, between SPADATS and NAVSPASUR approximately *ten million* uncorrelated observations have been collected over the last twenty years. If we were to take the usual estimates of the percentage of true unknowns from all UFO reports sent to various sources (ninety-five percent, give or take a few percent), we are left with roughly five percent being UFOs. This agrees well with the government's figures.

Taking the NORAD space observations of ten million as a separate group of sightings and changing the percentage of unknowns to a very small one-tenth of one percent, we are still left with a potential *ten thousand* uncorrelated observations that can qualify as legitimate UFOs over the last twenty years. This data cannot be acquired by us from NORAD files because of the extraordinary fee asked by NORAD (over $155,000). Therefore, verification of these figures is not possible at this time.

The atmospheric observations are usually manifest in the NORAD Command Director's Log or the regional Senior Director's Log, where a summary entry of an unknown event would be recorded and kept on file for a period of two years. If the event required an air defense intercept by jets, it would be on permanent file in the Operations Analysis office at NORAD. This information is classified and unreleasable to the public.

Sightings in the NORAD Command Director's Log will be discussed in later chapters and in Appendix B. Generally, the information in the logs was provided for a nominal fee. However, this situation changed in 1981 when NORAD sent the following memo to all NORAD regions in North America, dated October 1981:

1. Interim message change 80–1 to AFR 12–30 tells us to automatically waive search and duplication costs for a single FOIA request if those costs total less than $30.00. This change also permits FOIA managers to set aside the automatic waiver provision when, on the basis of good evidence, they can demonstrate that waiver of fees is not in the public interest.

2. Because of cumulative and recurring FOIA requests, we will no longer waive FOIA search and duplication fees, even though they may total less than $30.00, for Mr. Robert Todd and the "Citizens Against UFO Secrecy" (CAUS). Further, we believe it is in the public interest to have Mr. Todd and CAUS pay for all records searches even though no responsive records are located.

3. Accordingly, NORAD Headquarters and NORAD Regions will, upon receipt of a FOIA request for records from Mr. Robert Todd or the "Citizens Against UFO Secrecy," advise him or them of estimated search and copying fees and obtain agreement to pay before processing the request. Advise that search fees will be assessed even though no responsive records are located. If Mr. Todd or CAUS appeals fee assessment, forward the request to HQ NORAD/DADF for further processing.

The reason for the change of attitude is unknown. Apparently, a person is allowed to use the Freedom of Information Act only when it doesn't become too detailed. One cannot help but have the feeling that NORAD decided to tap the resources of Mr. Todd and Citizens Against UFO Secrecy, being well aware of the modest financial resources of both. This would, therefore, discourage any additional probing for UFO information in NORAD's files. It seems that, in NORAD's eyes, it is not in the public interest to release UFO sighting information.

Sometimes dealing with UFOs and the Freedom of Information Act can have pitfalls. Hoaxes are perpetrated using government documents and the careless researcher can look very bad endorsing such material.

Witness this example. The following memo was stamped "SECRET" and was sent to a reporter by an anonymous source, but bearing the letterhead of Bolling Air Force Base, Washington, D.C., dated December 14, 1977:

In retrospect this is an open letter of apology to anyone, be he civilian or military, who has been involved with *UFOS* and subsequently was harassed because of his experience. Furthermore by writing this letter "hopefully" the Air Force and the U.S. Government can regain its believability in stating the truth, because what is stated here are the facts as they should've been presented long ago. Fortunately not everyone in the government has a closed mind or what has been termed the "military mentality" when it comes to using his intelligence to benefit humanity; even though there *does* exist a yet higher form of intelligence than the person(s) writing this letter. Therefore let us proceed by asking the following questions about two USAF Regulations concerning UFOS:

Question #1.　　　For what plausible reason was this regulation
AFR-200-2　　　classified *SECRET* in *1971, 2 years* after its
(JANAP-146, 146E)　effectiveness was supposedly no longer needed?

Question #2.　　　Why is this regulation entitled *PROJECT NICAP?*
AFR-200-23　　　What could possibly be *so secret* that its description is not even listed in the Official AFR Manual of USAF Regulations? And is it a mere coincidence that its name is identical to a civilian UFO organization called NICAP?

Likewise it is no coincidence that the date of this letter corresponds to the release of a new movie entitled "CLOSE ENCOUNTERS OF THE THIRD

KIND." Perhaps Hollywood glamourized it somewhat for effect, but essentially the movie is based on fact not fiction. For credibility just ask a certain French Ministery of Defense or an Air Force General in Spain, to name only a few high-ranking officials who know otherwise. Also numerous embassies and important people have received documents relating to UFOS in their own countries. For confirmation please contact those mentioned in Addenda A.

Over the past few years there has been a gradual release of information about UFOS, leading up to the final statement and conclusion that is undoubtedly inevitable: "WE ARE NOT ALONE IN THE UNIVERSE. UFOS *ARE* A REALITY." Never before has any government been willing to state this fact publickly, but the time is now appropriate, due to the overwhelming amount of evidence available. No matter how many denials are, or have been made, these words will stand the test of time.

If anyone should want to prosecute us(me) for releasing this information, then they will have to chastise many hundreds of thousands of persons who, like us(me), would love to make these same statements, but felt no one would take them seriously. However one looks at the situation though, it proves that there is and was a Cosmic Watergate; because to suppress or deny the existence of this letter and other pertinent information like it proves there is a cover-up. On the other hand to make public this letter shows that someone somewhere knows more than heretofore was known outside of the Pentagon. Either way the whole truth has to be eventually told; whether by us(me), or many other highly qualified people who seek an answer to perhaps the most baffling phenomenon of all time.

We(I) realize that to say such seemingly radical things can be dangerous for one's health, and especially hazardous because they were made by government officials, namely the military.

Therefore, in conclusion, we(I) hope that this letter will serve as a catalyst to probe and better understand the existence of other worlds and their inhabitants.

Unfortunately, due to the obvious repercussions, we(I) are unable to autograph this document at the present time. Later, however, after this knowledge has been recognized publickly, then we(I) would be deeply honored to sign this impressive, perhaps historic, statement establishing the *existence of UFOS*. Thank you.

The memo included a distribution list to various personalities in the UFO subject area and was sent in an official envelope.

Such a memo, uninvestigated, can generate much rumor and speculation in an unsuspecting public. An FOIA request was filed with the Air Force and the reply was received on November 18, 1981. It read as follows:

The following comments apply to the anonymous letter purportedly from Bolling Air Force Base.

a. It is not an official Air Force document.

b. The letterhead is incomplete since the MAC organization is not identified.

c. It contains the following administrative errors: date is wrongly written and placed; the "Secret" stamping is incomplete; and the overall construction does not conform to AFR 10–1, "Preparing and Processing Correspondence."

d. A determination was made by the Air Force Office of Special Investigation that an investigation would not be conducted.

Your request for AFR 200–23 is exempt from disclosure under Public Law 90–23, 5 U.S.C. 552 (b)(1) and Air Force Regulation 12–30, paragraph 10a. It is not releasable because it is classified and contains information relating to Air Force policy on visits proposed under the East-West Exchange Program. Denial authority in this instance is John B. Marks, Major General, USAF, Assistant Chief of Staff, Intelligence.

The organization NICAP, or the National Investigations Committee on Aerial Phenomena, was formed in 1956 to study unidentified flying objects. The committee was composed of private citizens and had no affiliation with USAF. We were unable to locate any records on Project NICAP.

The attachment to your letter asks why the regulation in entitled Project NICAP. The subject of AFR 200–23 does not concern UFOs.

So the document is a complete fraud. The only question left is who wrote it and why? It probably should not have even this much attention drawn to it, but it serves as a lesson to exercise extreme caution and to not take sensational documents at face value.

The hoax material amounts to nothing more than a nuisance to serious investigators. The real danger in such antics is that they greatly mislead the public. With media sources such as the press, radio, and television frequently more interested in entertaining than informing, unsubstantiated stories are played up far beyond what reason calls for. The average person cannot help but form a false impression of what the UFO subject is about.

One crucial event, occurring just before widespread use of the Freedom of Information Act by UFO researchers, was the case of the Air Force Academy textbook. This proved to be a pivotal discovery in exposing the serious interest that the government had in UFOs in the early post-Blue Book period.

In October 1969, a copy of a chapter from a textbook in use at the U.S. Air Force Academy was acquired by the National Investigations Committee on Aerial Phenomenon (NICAP). The book was titled *Introductory Space Science* and was provided for the Academy's Department of Physics course "Physics 370." It consisted of two volumes, with a total of thirty-three chapters. The last chapter was titled "Unidentified Flying Objects," and it took a very uncharacteristic objective approach to the subject for an Air Force-sanctioned publication.

After summarizing a number of impressive sighting reports, running through the various theories that have been used to explain UFOs, and pointing out the problems in dealing with data that has "excessive variety," "vagueness," and a "very high level of noise," the textbook concluded:

From available information, the UFO phenomenon appears to have been global in nature for almost 50,000 years. The majority of known witnesses

have been reliable people who have seen easily-explained natural phenomena, and there appears to be no overall positive correlation with population
density. The entire phenomenon could be psychological in nature but that
is quite doubtful. However, psychological factors probably do enter the
data picture as "noise." The phenomenon could also be entirely due to
known and unknown natural phenomena (with some psychological "noise"
added in) but that too is questionable in view of some of the available
data.

This leaves us with the unpleasant possibility of alien visitors to our planet,
or at least of alien controlled UFO's. However, the data are not well correlated, and what questionable data there are suggest the existence of at
least three and maybe four different groups of aliens (possibly at different
stages of development). This too is difficult to accept. It implies the existence
of intelligent life on a majority of the planets in our solar system, or a
surprisingly strong interest in Earth by members of other solar systems.

It is also stated that we should "keep an open and skeptical mind" about
UFOs and not to take a position on the issue that is either too pro or too
con.

The whole section came as something of a jolt to outsiders. Here was
a very clear admission that UFOs were a difficult problem and warranted
extensive scientific study. And this was being taught to Air Force cadets!
It made the entire Blue Book effort seem rather hollow and unsubstantial.
As it was, when the Air Force Academy saw the reaction to the chapter
by the public, a decision was made by officials at the Academy to discontinue
use of the textbook and issue a new edition of the book. The UFO chapter
was shortened from fourteen pages to seven pages and, while the first version
offered actual case descriptions, the second included no cases. The conclusion
section followed the official policy line more closely. After summarizing the
negative results of the Air Force's Condon Committee, the new version said:

Criticisms of the Condon report include the contention that the conclusions
reached are not supported by the bulk of the evidence in the report itself
and that the firing of two staff members for "incompetence" before the
completion of the final report raises questions concerning the objectivity
and completeness of the study. While some of the criticisms may possibly
be justified, it is unlikely that any new official scientific studies will be forthcoming, primarily because the conclusions of the Condon report have been
so widely accepted.

The UFO problem must now compete on its scientific merit with all the
other pressing scientific problems facing mankind. To receive attention from
scientists and the requisite economic support, the potential rewards from
UFO research must be shown to be commensurate with the resources
expended. Although the Condon committee cautioned that nothing worth-
while was likely to result from such research, it suggested that all of the
agencies of the federal government and private foundations should be willing to consider UFO research proposals along with the others submitted
to them on an open-minded, unprejudiced basis.

So, we might speculate that had the public not learned of the original textbook,
its use may have continued. While it is not suggested that the book served

as a training course on UFO study, it certainly did implant a positive attitude toward the subject which, judging from the poor effort put forth by Project Blue Book, would have helped military officials deal more effectively with the phenomenon. As it developed, in later years the same public relations mistakes were made. The UFOs did *not* go away as the military had hoped and as we shall see, they caused quite a few anxious moments.

The 1975 incidents mentioned earlier became the principal focus for the FOIA requests being filed, as there was every indication that much paper traffic had flowed as a result of the activity. A number of eyewitnesses had stepped forward, unsolicited, giving testimony as to what they recalled happened at their respective military bases. They felt it was important to get the story out to the people, that it was much too important to be hushed up.

The Freedom of Information Act has shown the way to breaking open a wealth of evidence that the UFO phenomenon is a sleeping giant in the world of scientific mysteries.

CHAPER TWO
Intrusions at Loring

On October 27, 1975, security personnel assigned to the 42nd Security Police Squadron, Loring Air Force Base, Maine, were on duty in the munitions storage area, positioned on the northern perimeter of the flight line. Nuclear weapons were stored there in igloo-type huts covered with dirt to camouflage them from aircraft flying in the air corridors above. The dump is more than a half mile long and is surrounded by a twelve-foot-high chain-link fence with barbed wire on top. The area in and around the dump is patrolled day and night by the 42nd Police with K-9 patrols and manned vehicles. It is a highly restricted location, both on the ground and in the air.

At 7:45 P.M., Staff Sgt. Danny K. Lewis of the 42nd Police was on duty at the dump when he spotted what he thought was an aircraft flying at low altitude along the northern perimeter of Loring. Lewis watched as the unknown aircraft penetrated the perimeter at an altitude of approximately 300 feet. From his location, Lewis could see a red navigation light and a white strobe light on the craft.

At about the same time, Staff Sgt. James P. Sampley of the 2192nd Communications Squadron, who was on duty in the control tower, observed the unknown aircraft on the tower radar screen. Its position was approximately ten to thirteen miles east-northeast of the base. Numerous attempts were made to radio the aircraft for identification and to advise it that it was entering a restricted area over the base. All communication bands, military and civilian, were used in an attempt to contact the unknown aircraft, but without results. The unknown aircraft began to circle, and at one point it came to within 300 yards of the nuclear storage area at an altitude of 150 feet.

At the storage area, Lewis notified the Command Post of the 42nd Bomb Wing that an unknown aircraft had penetrated the base and was within 300 yards of the weapons area. The commander of the 42nd Bomb Wing implemented a Security Option 3 alert, which brought the base up to major alert status. The Command Post called the tower and requested a radar tract on the unknown. At 8:45 P.M., Sgt. Grover K. Eggleston of the 2192nd Communications Squadron was on duty at the tower when the call from the Command Post came. He began observing the unknown aircraft. Six minutes later, while watching the radar screen, Eggleston noted that the unknown craft appeared to be circling approximately ten miles east-northeast of the base. This action lasted for forty minutes when, suddenly, it disappeared from the screen. Either the object had landed, or it had dropped below the radar coverage.

The Wing Commander arrived at the weapons storage area seven minutes after the initial sighting was made. Immediately, other units of the 42nd Police began pouring into the area. Security vehicles with blue flashing lights were converging from all over the base. Through the Loring Command Post, the Wing Commander requested fighter coverage from the 21st NORAD Region at Hancock Field, New York, and the 22nd NORAD Region at North Bay, Ontario, Canada. However, fighter support was denied by both regions. The Wing Commander then increased local security posture and requested assistance from the Maine State Police in trying to identify the unknown craft, which they presumed was a helicopter. A call was made to local flight services for possible identification, without results.

The 42nd Security Police conducted a sweep of the weapons storage perimeter inside and out. An additional sweep was made of the areas that the craft had flown over. All actions produced no results. The craft broke the circling pattern and began flying toward Grand Falls, New Brunswick, Canada. Radar contact was lost in the vicinity of Grand Falls bearing 065 degrees, twelve miles from Loring. Canadian authorities were not notified.

No further unusual events occurred throughout that night. Priority messages were sent to the National Military Command Center in Washington, D.C., the Chief of Staff of the U.S. Air Force, the USAF Forward Operations Division at Fort Ritchie, Maryland, and Strategic Air Command headquarters at the 8th Air Force and the 45th Division informing them of what had taken place. The base remained on a high state of alert for the rest of the night and into the early morning hours of October 28.

Could the unknown have been an aircraft that had strayed off course? Then why, when it was challenged by the tower, was there no response? Most pilots carry charts that show the restricted areas they cannot fly over. Why did the unknown circle at low altitude over the weapons storage area? Was this a one-time incident? Would it happen again? Probably all these questions were pondered while teletypes were sent, briefings were held, and phone calls were made.

The unknown craft was thought to be a helicopter because of its flight characteristics. It hovered at times and dropped straight down below radar sweeps, and its size was similar to that of a helicopter. Little did the baffled observers know that this was only the beginning of a series of events that would take place over the next few nights, not only at Loring, but at other SAC installations along the northern tier bases and surrounding area.

On October 28, 1975, at 7:45 P.M., Sgt. Clifton W. Blakeslee and Staff Sgt. William J. Long, both assigned to the 42nd Security Police Squadron, were on duty at the munitions storage area. Along with Sgt. Danny Lewis, both Sgts. Blakeslee and Long spotted what appeared to be the running lights of an aircraft approaching Loring Air Force Base from the north at 3,000 feet. The aircraft did not come closer to Loring than about three miles at this time, and it was observed intermittently for the next hour. On first spotting the craft, Sgt. Lewis called the Command Post and advised it that the unknown craft had returned to Loring. Lewis reported that he could see a white flashing light and an amber or orange light. Once again, the Commander, 42nd Bomb Wing responded. Rushing to the area of the storage dump, he observed the unknown craft. He reported seeing a flashing white light and an amber-colored light on the object also. The speed and movement in the air suggested that the craft was a helicopter. From 7:45 P.M. to 8:20 P.M., it was under constant observation, both visually by the personnel in the storage area and electronically by the control tower radar, which showed the craft at a position three miles north of the Loring perimeter.

The unknown craft would appear and disappear from view, and, at one point, appeared over the end of the runway at an altitude of 150 feet. The object subsequently shut off its lights and reappeared over the weapons storage area, maintaining an altitude of 150 feet.

At this time, Sgt. Steven Eichner, a crew chief on a B-52 bomber, was working out of a launch truck along with Sgt. R. Jones and other members of the crew. Jones spotted a red and orange object over the flight line. It seemed to be on the other side of the flight line from where the weapons storage area was located. To Eichner and Jones, the object looked like a stretched-out football. It hovered in midair as everyone in the crew stared in awe. As they watched, the object put out its lights and disappeared, but it soon reappeared again over the north end of the runway, moving in jerky motions. It stopped and hovered. Eichner and the rest of the crew jumped into the truck and started to drive toward the object. Proceeding down Oklahoma Avenue (which borders the runway), they turned left onto the road that led to the weapons storage area. As they made the turn, they spotted the object about 300 feet in front of them. It seemed to be about five feet in the air and hovered without movement or noise. Exhibiting a reddish-orange color, the object was about four car lengths long. Eichner described what he saw next:

> The object looked like all the colors were blending together, as if you were looking at a desert scene. You see waves of heat rising off the desert floor. This is what I saw. There were these waves in front of the object and all the colors were blending together. The object was solid and we could not hear any noise coming from it.

They could not see any doors or windows on the object nor any propellers or engines which would keep the object in the air. Suddenly, the base came alive. Sirens began screaming. Eichner could see numerous blue lights on police vehicles coming down the flight line and runway toward the weapons storage area at high speed. Jones turned and said to the crew, "We better get out of here!" They immediately did. The Security Police did not try to stop them. Their interest was in the object over the storage dump, not in the truck which was in a restricted area. The crew drove the truck back to its original location and watched from there. The scene at the weapons storage area was chaotic, with blue lights rotating around, and the vehicles' searchlight beams shining in all directions.

The men in the crew decided not to report what they had seen, because they had entered a restricted area and could have been arrested for the violation.

The object shut off its lights and disappeared, not to be seen again that night. The 42nd Police conducted a security sweep of the weapons storage area inside and out, with no results. Radar had once again briefly tracked the object heading for Grand Falls, New Brunswick, finally losing the unknown at Grand Falls itself.

Priority messages were sent to the National Military Command Center in Washington, the Chief of Staff of the Air Force, the Air Force Forward Operations Division at Fort Ritchie, Maryland, SAC Headquarters, and the 9th Air Force, 45th Division, advising them that an unknown object had penetrated the base and had been in the nuclear storage area.

Because of the activity of the previous two days, Col. Richard E. Chapman, Commander of the 42nd Bomb Wing, had requested air support in the form of a National Guard helicopter and crew that was currently located at Loring. He wanted to be ready in case the intruder returned on the night of the twenty-ninth. This request was sent through military channels and was approved with the following constraints: The helicopter was to be used for tracking and identification only; apprehension by U.S. personnel was not authorized. There was to be no crossing of international borders, and only U.S. personnel, preferably military, but including the FBI, FAA, and Border Patrol representatives, if necessary, could be on board the National Guard helicopter.

Orders were given to place the helicopter and crew on "Full Time Training Duty." This, in essence, federalized the National Guard helicopter.

Brig. Gen. C. D. Roberts, USMC, Deputy Director for Operations, National Military Command Center, established a conference call with Major General Burkhart at SAC and Chapman, informing them of their approval to use the helicopter. With the constraints, Chapman stated that there was no point in using the helicopter if it couldn't cross the border. Brig. Gen. Roberts notified Major General Sniffin, Director of Operations, DCSOPS (Deputy Chief of Staff for Operations and Plans) of the border-crossing issue. Permission to cross was requested of Canadian officials and subsequently was granted.

Sniffin called Roberts to inform him that permission had been granted to cross the border. This, in turn, was relayed to Col. Chapman at Loring. At 7:00 A.M., Col. Al White of the 112th Army National Guard Medical Company (Air Ambulance) in Bangor, Maine, ordered one UH 1 (Huey helicopter) to Loring with Chief Warrant Officer Bernard Poulin and Chief Warrant Officer Eugene E. Herrin aboard. After being told that their mission was secret, they were ordered to report to Col. Chapman.

On August 27, 1982, Bernard Poulin was interviewed by Larry Fawcett. His recollection of his mission was as follows:

> Upon our arrival at Loring AFB, we were briefed by the Wing Commander, Col. Richard Chapman. We were informed that all the sightings of this craft or whatever you want to call it had been late night or early morning. We launched the next morning. Aboard my helicopter were one member of the Canadian Royal Mounted Police, one member of the Maine State Police, and several Air Security police officers. The Air Police had a radio in the back of the helicopter and when the reports of the intruder started to come in, they would direct me to the location in which the object was seen. The reason the Maine State Police and the Canadian Police were aboard was that there had been a lot of drug operations going on in the area, and the powers to be thought that this is what was occurring at the base, but this never panned out, to the best of my recollection.
>
> Well, we were launched on the first search mission after ground personnel started to see or hear the, quote, if you will, "UFO" go by. So, we would launch, and I believe that we were in the air for around 40 minutes looking for this thing, with the idea that it was a rotary-type craft we were searching for. We were vectored in by ground personnel to different spots on the base where the ground personnel were seeing or hearing it. All this time we were being tracked by base radar [traffic control radar which is designed to pick up aircraft], and radar was not painting the object that was being reported. Ground personnel would call and say the object is at this location, but radar would not pick it up.
>
> Well, anyway, we hunted around, and we didn't see anything. Again they would call and say they could hear it at a location, and we would go there, but could not see it. We would then shut down and wait for the next call. And that went on for a couple of nights. This, again, was early evening or early in the morning. I can recall on the second night of the mission radar picked up a return, but it turned out to be a KC-135 tanker returning from overseas.

Poulin was asked: "According to some of the documents, personnel on the ground were reporting that at times you would bring your craft within 100 feet of the intruder, yet you could not see it?" He answered:

Yes, well, we could go real low to where they said it was and would turn on our search light and sweep the area with the light, but we never saw the craft. After it was over, we discussed our mission. The powers to be were quite concerned about what was going on and if we were able to see anything. They maintained all along up there, you know, those are pretty sensitive places and they have to know what the hell was going on.

When they arrived at the base, the security lid was on so tightly that both pilots were permitted to call their wives only once to say that they were on a mission. In a meeting with Chapman, Poulin recalled the Commander saying, "We've got to keep the lid on the fact that someone has been able to penetrate in and around the bomb dump, and we don't know what's going on. We've got to find out what is going on and prevent it from happening again."

At Loring, additional manpower was armed and ready for deployment. The Security Police Battle Staff was to be manned at Central Security Control. An additional two-man mobile patrol was assigned to the weapons storage area during the hours of darkness, while a ten-man reserve force was standing by, ready for deployment. A two-man patrol would be positioned at key vantage points about one mile north of the base for added surveillance. An SAC/SP message informed northern tier bases of the situation and recommended a "Security Option Three" alert all along the U.S.–Canadian border.

The message went to Pease AFB in New Hampshire, Plattsburgh AFB in New York, Wurtsmith AFB in Michigan, Kinchloe AFB in Michigan, Sawyer AFB in Michigan, Grand Forks AFB in North Dakota, Minot AFB in North Dakota, Malmstrom AFB in Montana, Fairchild AFB in Washington, and Barksdale AFB in Lousisiana. The subject-identifying line of the message was "Defense Against Helicopter Assault," and it read:

> The past two evenings at one of our northern tier bases, an unidentified helicopter has been observed hovering over and in the near vicinity of the weapons storage area. Attempts to identify this aircraft have so far met with negative results. In the interest of nuclear weapons security, the action addresses will assume Security Option 3 during hours of darkness until further notice. Actions also should be taken to re-establish liaison with local law enforcement agencies that could assist your base in the event of a similar incident. Bases should thoroughly review and insure all personnel are familiar with actions to take in association with the helicopter denial portion of your 207-xx plan.

On October 30, the Maine National Guard helicopter was replaced by a USAF helicopter and crew from Plattsburgh Air Force Base.

The following evening there were several reports of unknown objects suspected to be helicopters, at distances varying from directly over the base to 10 nautical miles northeast of the base. Some reports were confirmed on RAPCON radar with altitudes between 300 and 5,000 feet.

Additional, sporadic reports of helicopters continued well into December, though many of these were subsequently identified as normal helicopter traffic. In these reports, however, a distinction was drawn between the October sightings and later reports: Robert Fauk, Deputy Chief Patrol Agent with the U.S. Border Patrol, said he felt that an alleged helicopter report of November 18 was not the "Midnight Skulker of Loring." He added, "This craft was too slow and too small to be the craft they had problems with at Loring."

Two days before, Caribou police received telephone calls at 1:30 A.M. and 2:00 A.M. from an unnamed woman reporting bright, glowing lights that changed colors. Before long, reports came in from, among others, four Caribou police officers, one state Civil Defense officer, three Aroostook County deputy sheriffs, on-duty personnel at Loring, and several police officers from the communities of Limestone and Fort Fairchild. Descriptions were vague, but involved mainly blinking green and red lights and, in at least one instance, an exhaust or smoke emission.

After the woman's 2:00 A.M. call had come in, Officer Paul B. Michaud was on duty at the Caribou police station desk. He said, "When she first called, I thought she was seeing things or looking at the moon, but when I went out and looked, it was there."

"There was a real bright light. It hovered for a long time," Michaud said. He monitored the object for some time after. Referring to the original woman caller, Michaud said, "She called back about a half hour later and wanted to know what we were doing about it. She called back again. She probably stayed up all night."

Michaud was quite emphatic about his opinion of the object. "I'm twenty-eight years old, and I never saw anything like it. I don't believe in flying saucers or anything like that, but I don't know what that was."

An interesting addendum to this report is the fact that an airman at Loring told Caribou police that an unidentified object had briefly appeared on a radar screen and was located about fifteen miles across the border into Canada. Yet several days later, Lt. Robert Barca, Loring's Assistant Information Officer, said that his office was not too sure where the information came from, but a recheck showed Loring's radar screen did not track "the thing," according to reporter Christopher Spruce of the *Bangor Daily News.*

On October 12, 1982, Larry Fawcett interviewed Dean Rhodes, who, at the time of the overflights at Loring, was the reporter for the *Bangor Daily News* covering the story. During his investigation of the overflights, Rhodes traveled into Canada to check the possibility that the objects seen had originated from the Canadian side of the border.

He went to the airport in Grand Falls, New Brunswick, and spoke to pilots who were familiar with helicopters. No one there could shed any light on who or what had flown over Loring. A friend of Rhodes in the town of Van Buren, Maine, near the border, seemed convinced that this "helicopter" had come from a construction site located in the St. Johns Valley. Rhodes questioned people at that site, including workers who would have known about the usage of a helicopter. They stated that no helicopter flights went into Maine at any time and no one knew of anyone owning such a vehicle in the area.

When Rhodes checked with the FBI in Boston, he was told that the aerial intrusions over Loring remained under investigation and that they had no idea as to who was responsible. A later Freedom of Information request was filed by the authors with the Boston FBI office, asking for documents concerning the identity of the object. The FBI completely denied any knowledge of the craft or who may have been responsible for the flights.

The Royal Canadian Mounted Police (RCMP) also responded similarly to inquiries about the object.

Rhodes checked with the U.S. Customs office at the Limestone border station and learned that a Customs officer, John J. Stedman, saw a light to the east around 1:30 A.M. Its maneuvering caused Stedman to tentatively identify it as an aircraft, probably a helicopter. Stedman saw what appeared to be a single white landing light and noted "vertical and horizontal movement." He estimated the altitude at about 5,000 feet. Rhodes learned that an RCMP officer who viewed the object from Stedman's border point said he didn't think the object was moving. "It was more than a mile and a half inside Canada, because from the TransCanada Highway, it still was quite a distance away. The TransCanada Highway lies more than a mile and a half inside the border. The officer said he had thought the object was more like a heavenly body than an aircraft."

According to confidential RCMP reports, the object was spotted over Grand Falls, New Brunswick, each time it was seen at Loring. When asked how the object was detected, RCMP Superintendent G. E. Reid said he would just "like to leave it as it is." An RCMP investigation of the Grand Falls incident was conducted, but no details were ever released.

On October 31, 1977, *The National Enquirer* sent a series of questions to the Secretary of the Air Force about the Loring incident, among other events. The questions, with the Air Force's answers are as follows.

Reference mystery helicopters flying over Loring, Wurtsmith, Minot, October 27, 29, and 31, and November 7, 8, 9, and 19, 1975. Some over the weapons storage areas:

1. Were they identified or traced?
A. No, the overflights were not identified as helicopters. Unsuccessful attempts were made to trace the sighted craft.
2. Was it ever definitely established that they were helicopters, or was this an assumption made based on sound, light, etc?
A. No. The helicopter assumption was based on the sound and light perceptions of the eyewitnesses.
3. Were there any markings on any of the aircraft?
A. No markings were identified.

4. Did they appear to be any known type of helicopter?

A. Type of aircraft could not be identified due to limited visibility.

5. How is it possible that any unidentified craft can get inside an AFB without being detected?

A. On the dates in question the unidentified aircraft entered the airspace of each base at night and were detected.

6. Is there any explanation why OSI agents and others aboard could not see the intruding copter when people on the ground could see both the chase copter and the intruder?

A. No explanation of this occurrence has been postulated.

7. Why was no attempt made to contact the copter by radio?

A. Unknown.

Note the comments here. While the former public stance had been "helicopters," (as was also stated to Loring base personnel), suddenly the objects "were not identified as helicopters." No markings were identified nor could the type of aircraft be identified. And the objects could not be tracked with any certainty. Then, what was seen? Answer: Unknown!

According to an Air Force Office of Special Investigations (OSI) teletype dated October 29, 1975, Loring had been through this experience before. The teletype says briefly, "This incident closely parallels a similar helicopter sighting earlier this year." However, in a letter dated April 21, 1977, titled "Overflight of USAF Installations by Unidentified Aircraft," OSI states: "AFOSI files revealed no record of the overflight of Loring AFB, ME (LAFB) in Jan. 1975 as reported in referenced letter." The referenced letter is one written on March 31, 1977, by Col. Richard Chapman, Commander of the 42nd Bomb Wing at Loring, certainly one source who would know about the earlier incident. What was so sensitive about the January 1975 overflight that OSI denied any knowledge of it, even in the face of the Loring Commander's statement? The authors have been unable to obtain further details about this affair, but it adds one more piece to a puzzle of mystery.

Yet more evidence of the strange nature of the Loring intruder followed. A paralegal aide in Washington, D.C., Robert Kinn, responded to a story about the Loring sightings in the *Washington Post* of January 18, 1979. Kinn said that he and another student attended Bowdoin College during 1975. One night in October, when all the activity occurred at Loring, Kinn and his friend were near the Brunswick, Maine, Naval Air Station. According to Kinn, "It came in very low, at treetop level from the ocean. It was like a helicopter, but different. More than twice the size of a normal helicopter. It had red lights and a white light. It would make ninety-degree turns and fly very fast."

"The base lighted up like a Christmas tree. There were trucks going every which way. It stayed over the base for five or ten minutes and then scooted over the Atlantic."

"We thought it might have been a vertical takeoff plane. We could tell it was not a normal helicopter," Kinn said. He added, "Both of us associated the sighting with a UFO activity; the excitement on the base was way out of the usual."

Could the Brunswick Naval Air Station UFO be the same object as that which was seen at Loring? According to a spokesman for the station, there had been no UFO sightings at the base for eight years. A vertical takeoff plane was stationed at Brunswick at the time, but there was no evidence linking it to the UFO sighting.

Occurring on the same day as the first Loring report (October 27) was the experience of David Stephens. We present this case, with little comment, as *possibly* having some relation to the other sightings. We find no evidence that the witnesses knew anything about the intense activity in Maine at the time. Indeed, the story was reported in the *Lewiston Daily Sun* on October 28, only a day after the first Loring report and fully two days before the first Loring press notices.

During the morning of October 27, Stephens, twenty-one years old, and a roommate, Glen Gray, eighteen, were listening to records in their trailer in Norway, Maine. Suddenly, a loud bang was heard. Both men went out to see what happened, but found nothing.

Later, Stephens and Gray decided to go for a ride in their 1968 Plymouth to kill time. They headed south on Route 26 toward Lake Thompson in Oxford, Maine. After traveling a quarter of a mile, they claimed that an "unknown force" wrenched the wheel of the car away from them. According to Stephens, "The car automatically turned. From then on, we couldn't control it."

As it developed, the car traveled well over a hundred miles per hour, over a distance of eleven miles to a field at Poland, Maine. It was here that they noticed two bright lights. They thought that these were the lights on a truck, but shortly after they saw them, the lights began to rise, giving the impression of a helicopter.

Whatever it was, it rose above the trees adjoining the field and swerved silently in front of their car. The object was cigar-shaped, with red, green, and blue lights on the side, and about the size of a football field. The men, very frightened, drove away. After going a quarter of a mile, they noticed that the two bright lights on the object went out and another very bright light suddenly struck their car, causing Stephens and Gray to black out. They woke up after what they supposed was five minutes. It turned out that hours had apparently passed.

They started driving, only to lose control again and unwillingly drive to Tripp Pond. The huge UFO was there waiting. Two other domed, saucer-shaped objects were seen cavorting in the sky above the pond. The two saucers then skimmed low over the pond and released a gray smoke which surrounded the car. The men saw the large UFO high in the air through the smoke. Suddenly, all of the objects and the smoke disappeared. Dawn broke shortly after.

Both men drove home and discovered a variety of physiological effects. Their hands and feet were swollen. Teeth were loose. Red rings had appeared around their necks, and they had severe chills. The next night they phoned the sheriff, who turned out to be very skeptical of the report when he came out to visit the men. Who could blame him!

Later, during December and January, Stephens met with Dr. Herbert Hopkins of Old Orchard Beach, Maine, who put him through eight sessions of hypnotic regression to discover details of the missing time. An even more unusual story came out.

Stephens recalled his car moving sideways, and the next thing he knew, he was inside the large UFO, standing in a dome-shaped room. A humanoid creature entered the room. According to Stephens, "He was four and a half feet tall, dressed in a dark robe. His head was shaped like a big light bulb. He had slanted eyes, no hair, and no mouth." Stephens was told he wouldn't be harmed.

He entered another room with five other entities standing around a long table. They asked Stephens to get up on the table and prepare for an examination. Stephens resisted and struck one of the creatures, without effect.

Stephens next found himself on the table being examined with a small, square machine with an extension arm and a probe on the end. The machine had many dials and lights on it. With it, the entities took skin and nail samples, hair and blood, and a button off Stephens' jacket. He was injected with a brown fluid which acted like a sedative. They said it wouldn't hurt him.

Stephens woke up after an undetermined time in his car next to Gray. The car was facing an oak tree. At might be expected, no one believed Stephens' extraordinary story, but he was fully convinced, along with Glen Gray, that it did happen.

We should add that while no solid evidence exists to substantiate the story by itself, several curious factors appear. First, the account coincided with the first outburst of sightings at Loring. Second, the Stephens' sighting location was less than forty miles from the Brunswick Naval Air Station, scene of the Kinn report. Third, Stephens and Gray described their UFO at first as looking like a helicopter, again like the Loring and Brunswick reports.

This string of events in Maine turned out to be merely the tip of the iceberg in a nationwide UFO blitz which received remarkably little media attention at the time.

CHAPTER THREE

"Faded Giant"?

There are more than 2,000 missile sites spread across the United States. At Malmstrom Air Force Base in Montana, there are twenty Launch Control Facilities (LCF) housing Minuteman missiles underground. The Minuteman sites are alphabetically coded, such as "L-1," "K-1," "E-1," and the like, and are distributed over a wide area. One of these sites, K-7, which is located in the Judith Gap region just south of Lewiston, Montana, was the scene of an event which caused a major stir for the U.S. Air Force.

On November 7, 1975, remote electronic sensors triggered an alarm indicating that something was violating site security. Underground, in the launch control area, two officers noted the signal, but there was no television surveillance topside. The normal procedure for detecting what had violated security was to call for a missile security helicopter to check the area. At the same time, Sabotage Alert Teams (SAT), consisting of four to six men, were also alerted to the fact that a violation was taking place and were ordered to proceed to the site.

On this occasion, an SAT team drove down the highway and onto a dirt road which led to the K-7 area. About a mile away, the team could see an orange, glowing object over the area. As they closed to within half a mile, they could now see that the object was tremendous in size. They radioed to the Launch Control Facility that, from their location, they were viewing a brightly glowing, orange, football field-sized disc that illuminated the missile site. The SAT team was ordered by the launch control people to proceed into the K-7 site. However, they responded that they refused to go any farther, clearly fearful of the intimidating appearance of the object. It began to rise, and at about 1,000 feet, NORAD picked up the UFO on radar.

Two F-106 jet interceptors were launched from Great Falls, Montana, and headed toward the K-7 area. The UFO continued to rise. At about 200,000 feet, it disappeared from NORAD's radar. The F-106s were never able to get a visual sighting of the UFO.

All members of the SAT team were directed to the base hospital, where they were psychologically tested. It was determined that no one could identify the object that was seen, but that the members of the SAT team obviously had been through a traumatic experience.

Meanwhile, targeting teams, along with computer specialists, were brought to the missile site to check out the missile, and specifically, the computer in the warhead that targets the missile. Amazingly, when the computer was checked, they found that *the tape had mysteriously changed target numbers!* The re-entry vehicle was then taken from the silo and brought back to the base. Eventually, the entire missile was changed.

The Malmstrom K-7 story is excerpted from "A Strange Harvest: Thoughts Beyond the Scenes" by Linda Moulton Howe, *Denver Magazine,* September 1980, an article with background information about the development of "A Strange Harvest," a seventy-five minute TV documentary about the animal mutilation mystery which has haunted the United States, Canada, parts of Western Europe, Central and South America, and the Canary Islands since 1967. Linda Moulton Howe, Director of Special Projects for the Denver CBS affiliate KMGH-TV, produced, wrote, directed, and edited the film which was originally broadcast May 25, 1981, and drew the largest recorded audience for a locally produced program in Denver television history. Ms. Howe has received several state and national awards for her documentary work, including a 1981 Regional Emmy for Audio Achievement in "A Strange Harvest."

An additional bit of information surfaced later. In a National Military Command Center "Memorandum for Record" dated November 8, 1975, 6 A.M. EST, the following statement appeared in reference to Malmstrom:

At 405 EST, SAC Site L-5 observed one object accelerate, and climb rapidly to a point in altitude where it became indistinguishable from the stars. NORAD will carry this incident as a FADE remaining UNKNOWN at 320 EST since after that time only visual sightings occurred.

The reference to FADE is interesting. This would presumably refer to a target on a radar scope "fading" and disappearing from the screen. Yet both radar and visual sightings are described in the above extract.

Coincidentally, there is an Air Force term used to describe an incident in which a nuclear device is tampered with. This term is "Faded Giant," a phrase which very appropriately describes the K-7 report.

Could this mean that Malmstrom sites K-7 and L-5 both experienced missile-tampering activity in connection with the UFO sightings? No additional information has been forthcoming from the Air Force.

This was not the first time that such an incident had occurred at Malmstrom. In his book *Casebook of a UFO Investigator* (Prentice-Hall, Inc., 1981), author Raymond Fowler describes two earlier instances of "Faded Giants."

In the early spring of 1966, two officers had relieved an earlier shift in the underground launch control area for the evening. As they ran through the routine of monitoring the missile facility's instruments, alarms began to go off. It seems that all of the ten missiles at their location had *simultaneously* developed a problem. A quick check with each launching site indicated that none of the missiles could be launched, if indeed, due to a fault in all of their guidance and control systems. This is an unusual problem, because the guidance system is the most protected portion of a Minuteman missile. Personnel above ground had indicated that at the same time the problem developed, UFOs were seen in the area.

Another similar event, during the week of March 20, 1967, disturbed officials at Malmstrom. Again, a flight of ten missiles developed problems. A UFO was in the area and was confirmed on radar. Jet fighters were sent after the UFO, but the results of the pursuit are not known. Later inquiries to obtain additional information met with silence.

Other sightings were received at Malmstrom during November 1975. The following information is taken from the 24th NORAD Region Senior Director's log:

MALMSTROM AFB, MONTANA: Nov. 7, 1975 (1035Z) Received a call from the 341st Strategic Air Command Post (SAC CP) saying that the following missile locations reported seeing a large red to orange to yellow object: M-1, L-3, LIMA, and L-6. The general object location would be 10 miles south of Moore, Montana, and 20 miles east of Buffalo, Montana. Commander Deputer [*sic*] for Operations (DO) informed.

Nov. 7, 1975 (1203Z) SAC advised that the LCF at Harlow, Montana, observed an object which emitted a light which illuminated the site driveway.

Nov. 7, 1975 (1319Z) SAC advised K-1 saw a very bright object to their east is now southeast of them and they are looking at it with 10 × 50 binoculars. Object seems to have lights (several) on it, but no distinct pattern. The orange/gold object overhead also has small lights on it. SAC also advises female civilian reports having seen an object bearing south from her position 6 miles west of Lewiston.

Nov. 7, 1975 (1327Z) L-1 reports that the object to their northeast seems to be issuing a black object from it, tubular in shape. In all this time, surveillance has not been able to detect any sort of track except for known traffic.

Nov. 7, 1975 (1355Z) K-1 and L-1 report that as the sun rises, so do the objects they have visual.

Nov. 7, 1975 (1429Z) From SAC CP: As the sun rose, the UFOs disappeared. Commander and DO notified.

Then, yet another sighting was reported. An off-duty missile launch officer and his deputy had just retired for crew rest in the Soft Support Building (SSB). The deputy went to the window and observed the silhouette of a large aircraft hovering about ten to fifteen feet above the ground and about twenty-five feet outside the Launch Control Facility. He described two red and white lights at the front of the aircraft, a white light on the bottom, and white light on the rear. The craft hovered motionless in this position for about one minute and then departed. The missile launch officer did not personally observe the aircraft, but from its sound, he speculated that it was a helicopter. The deputy also felt that the sounds he heard were those of a helicopter. The deputy's observations were limited by the darkness of the night, which prevented any good description of the craft or its shape.

On November 7, 1975, Captain Roscoe E. Moulthrop advised the Air Force Office of Special Investigations (AFOSI) that during the evening hours of November 6 and 7, two adjacent Launch Control Facilities approximately fifty miles south of Lewiston reported moving lights as UFOs.

On November 8, the 24th NORAD Region picked up one to seven unknowns heading south-southwest at about 1,200 feet. Two F-106s were scrambled out of Great Falls at 7:45 P.M. Simultaneously, SAC reported visual sightings from SAT teams at K-1, K-3, L-1, and L-6. This time the teams were hearing jet sounds and seeing lights. At 8:35 P.M., SAT teams at sites K-3 and L-4 were reporting that they had visual sightings on the objects, with K-3 reporting targets at an altitude of 300 feet. As the F-106s arrived at the location, SAT teams reported that the UFOs turned their lights off. The F-106s, in searching for the unknowns, never gained a visual or radar contact at any time because of the low altitude of the UFOs. However, when they left the area, the UFOs would turn their lights back on! At 9:15 P.M., four different locations were reporting that they had the UFOs and fighters in sight. The UFOs seemed to be playing a cat-and-mouse game.

At 9:53 P.M., the team at L-5 reported to the Command Post that the unknowns had increased in speed, climbed rapidly, and, at that point, could not be distinguished from the stars. A while later, the team at site E-1 reported at 11:05 P.M. that a bright white light was seen approximately sixty nautical miles north of Lewiston.

On November 8, at 6 A.M., the National Military Command Center in Washington, D.C., distributed a "Memorandum for the Record." The subject was "Unidentified Sightings." It read as follows (excluding the L-5 report already mentioned earlier):

1) From NORAD Command Director: At 0253 EST 8 Nov, Malmstrom AFB, Montana received seven radar cuts on the height-finder radar at altitudes between 9,500 and 15,500 feet. Simultaneous ground witnesses observed lights in the sky and the sound of jet engines similar to jet fighters.

Cross-tell with FAA revealed no jet aircraft within 100 NM of the sighting. Radar tracked the objects over Lewiston, Montana, at a speed of 7 knots. Two F-106 interceptors from the 24th NORAD Region were scrambled at 0254 EST, and became airborne at 0257 EST. At the time of the initial voice report, personnel at Malmstrom AFB and SAC sites K-1, K-3, L-3, and L-6 were reporting lights in the sky accompanied by jet engine noise.

2) 0344 EST From NORAD Command Director. Objects could not be intercepted. Fighters had to maintain a minimum of 12,000 feet because of mountainous terrain. Sightings had turned west, increased speed to 150 knots. Two tracks were apparent on height-finder radars 10–12 NM apart. SAC site K-3 reported sightings between 300 feet and 1,000 feet, while site L-4 reported sightings 5 NM from their position. Sightings disappeared from radar at position 4650 N/10920 W at a tracked speed of three (3) knots.

3) At 0440 EST, NMCC initiated contact with the NORAD Command Director who reported the following: At 0405 EST, Malmstrom receiving intermittent tracks on both search and height-finder radars. SAC site C-1, 10NM SE of Stanford, Montana, reported visual sightings of unknown objects. 0420 EST: Personnel at 4 SAC sites reported observing intercepting F-106s arrive in area; sighted objects turned off their lights upon arrival of interceptors, and back on upon their departure. 0440 EST: SAC site C-1 still had a visual sighting on objects.

4) NORAD stated that Northern Lights will sometimes cause phenomena such as this on height-finder radars, but their check with weather services revealed no possibility of Northern Lights.

5) NMCC notified Washington FAA at 0445 EST of the incidents described above. They had not received any information prior to this time.

The Memorandum was signed by Brigadier General William D. Barnes, U.S. Deputy Director for Operations, NMCC.

On November 9, at 3:05 A.M., SAC crews at sites L-1, L-6, and M-1 observed a UFO. They described it as being a yellowish, bright, round light twenty miles north of Harlowton at an altitude of 2,000 to 4,000 feet. At 3:20 A.M., the SAC Command Post reported the UFO twenty miles southeast of Lewiston. The color of the object was reported as orange-white, and its appearance was round or disc-shaped.

The only response that the Air Force would give to public inquiries was: "All documentation at Malmstrom AFB has been destroyed in accordance with Air Force directives for the dates of the UFO sightings mentioned . . ."

Since when are all records of a serious incident or series of incidents of this magnitude destroyed? We must conclude that either there is gross incompetence in the military's handling of such situations, or that the UFOs, in these instances, presented so considerable a threat to the national security of the United States that the Air Force felt compelled to deliberately misinform the public, and, as a result, violated the Freedom of Information Act by stating that existing records had been destroyed.

Not only was the Air Force having trouble with UFOs and mystery helicopters over the missile silos, but also events began to happen in the air and on the ground in Cascade, Montana. The Cascade County sheriff's office was being flooded with reports of low-flying UFOs and peculiar, unmarked helicopters. They were also burdened with the task of trying to unravel another mystery: cattle mutilations.

Around 1974, strange reports had started to surface in the Western states about hundreds of beef cattle found dead across a section of the country running through Minnesota, Wisconsin, Kansas, Nebraska, Iowa, South Dakota, Colorado, Texas, Arizona, and California. By 1975, this activity had spread into Montana. Newspapers across the country carried stories of cattle mutilations and their possible connection with UFOs, which, in some cases, had been observed in close proximity to the time and place of the mutilation incidents.

Some of the cattle bore strange mutilations which could not be accounted for in the usual ways. Ears were carefully removed, tongues were cut out, udders and sex organs were gone, anuses sliced out, all with apparent surgical skill. Also, in such cases, involving mostly Black Angus and black, white-faced cattle, the carcasses were devoid of blood as if drained with a needle. No blood or footprints or vehicular tracks could be found on the ground. It almost seemed as if the bodies were mutilated elsewhere and dropped to the ground from the air.

Here are a few examples of what the Cascade County sheriff's office handled during the time of the overflights of missile silos at Malmstrom:

> "A mutilated cow is found in a plowed field, but there are no tracks in the soft earth."
>
> "The carcass of a mutilated animal is completely void of blood."
>
> "The cut area of a mutilated cow bears a neatly serrated edge, as though cut by a giant cookie cutter."
>
> "A farmer and his son watch four small UFOs darting about a larger one, described as being 'as big as a two-story building.'"
>
> "Strange, unidentified helicopters, some of them black, are seen but not heard—or heard but not seen."
>
> "An ordinarily aggressive watchdog becomes strangely quiet and refuses to bark as a strange light flooded his owner's home."

On October 16, 1975, at 10:25 A.M., a rancher stopped at the sheriff's department to report that one of his cows might have been mutilated. A deputy was sent to the ranch, located southeast of Great Falls. The cow was found in a securely locked pasture. The deputy could not find any visible tracks in the area, a feature which has been reported time and time again in cattle mutilation incidents, even when the ground is covered with snow. The deputy found that the cow's left jaw had been skinned. Its tongue had been cut out, and its right eye removed, not from its socket, but through the bone directly above the eye. The cow had been last seen alive at 5 P.M. on October 15, 1975.

During the morning of October 18, John Struble of Columbia Falls, Montana, was driving his truck in the area of Flesher Pass, about twenty-five miles northwest of Helena. At about 12:30 A.M., he noticed a large object, fifty feet in diameter and twenty-five to thirty feet in the air, pass over his truck from the rear and then hover and stop about one hundred yards ahead of him. As the object did this, it directed a very bright light at him, causing the truck's lights and engine to go out. The UFO stayed there for about five minutes before moving away. According to Struble, the object made a noise like a big jet, then rocketed straight up into the sky and moved away to the east at an incredible speed. When the UFO disappeared, the truck's lights and engine came back on. Struble also noticed that his *nonelectric* watch had stopped for five minutes, the duration of the UFO's appearance.

Another sighting occurred at 4:30 A.M. on the eighteenth. John Giacomino, the vice principal of Flathead Valley High School, was preparing to go hunting when he noticed out his window a "big, bright object" near the top of Columbia Mountain to the north. He observed the object for about half an hour, reporting that it "lit up the whole mountain before dimming and turning a red color." The object moved up over the mountain and disappeared to the north.

The reports were logged by the Flathead County sheriff's office. Later, a spokesman for the Air Force 716th Radar Squadron near Kalispell said that they "officially" had seen nothing out of the ordinary.

The next day, the publisher of the Shelby, Montana, *Times,* Lloyd Stinebaugh, was contacted by the local police department at 5:15 A.M. The officer on duty said that he had a flying object in view, and he wondered if Stinebaugh could take photographs of it.

The object was very clear in the east. Pictures were taken from the newspaper office. Then Stinebaugh drove to a ridge near town for more photos. The object was seen through field glasses and appeared as an upside-down cross or a cigar shape with a cross or wings at the bottom. It hovered for nearly an hour before disappearing. The photos were developed, and most did not come out. Some did, and they showed an egg-shaped, bright object.

Malmstrom Base Operations received reports of UFOs on the night of October 18 between 9 P.M. and 7:45 A.M. Nine of the sightings came from the Cascade Eden areas south of Great Falls. At about the same time, law enforcement officers were getting reports north of Great Falls as far as Shelby. At 4:20 A.M., the Shelby sheriff's office reported that officers had sighted a UFO, and it was moving from one place to another at a high rate of speed. Its altitude was estimated to be around 2,000 feet. Malmstrom was notified by the sheriff's office, and NORAD tracked the object on radar.

Both Malmstrom and NORAD confirmed that the object was not a conventional aircraft. The Shelby officer described the object as having a white light, with a red flame behind, and a green light on top; there were red lights on both sides. About fifteen minutes later, the object started to climb and headed west.

At 6:04 A.M. another report came in from the Power area northwest of Great Falls. An officer reported that he could see a UFO changing colors from red to white over Conrad.

On October 20, at about 4:30 P.M., a couple living on a ranch near Priest Butte, Montana, reported that they had seen a UFO about half a mile from their home, on the east slope of Priest Butte. Using binoculars, they described it as being egg-shaped, with the large end of the craft on the ground. It had one yellowish-gold light which at first gave off a dull glow and then became brighter. It had two arm-like appendages which came out of the craft, one on each side. The arms made a continual motion similar to a breaststroke. The craft remained stationary for five minutes. Then the appendages retracted into the craft, and it went straight up and out of sight.

Three men were hunting in the Ford Creek area in Augusta, Montana, on October 30. The men had gone to sleep in a horse trailer after tying the two horses to the back of the trailer. At about midnight, the men were awakened by the sound of the horses pulling back on the ropes and pawing the ground. The men looked up and noticed an object which they described as a solid, white light, shaped like a football. The object was five times as large as a star and was moving horizontally across the sky, heading north. They watched the object for only a few seconds, as it was moving at a very fast speed. After it had disappeared, the men checked the horses and found that one was missing. As they listened, they could hear it running down the road. They called out and it returned, but it was very nervous—something very unusual for this horse. After a while, both horses simmered down and there was no further trouble from them for the rest of the night.

Larry Fawcett interviewed Captain Keith Wolverton of the Cascade County Sheriff's Department. Wolverton was able to give a firsthand account as to what was occurring in Cascade County during October and November 1975. He stated, "During that period of time people were calling the Sheriff's Department from all areas of the county, reporting that strange aerial objects were flying low over the land and ranches." Wolverton and other officers responded to these complaints in an attempt to identify the objects, but all investigations conducted during the two-month period proved futile.

Wolverton told of a personal encounter with one of the flying objects on the night of November 11, 1975. He and a deputy were returning to Great Falls from Missoula. The evening sky was clear as the cruiser traveled over the highway at about 50 mph. Suddenly, out of the northern sky, a very large orange light descended, lighting up both sides of the road. This object was traveling at an incredible speed and passed directly over the cruiser at about 200 feet. Wolverton attempted to stop the cruiser to get a better view of the light, but it was traveling so fast that "It went from horizon to horizon in four seconds. It was impossible for us to determine its size or shape in the brief time we saw it!" There was no time to use the several thousand dollars' worth of photographic equipment in the cruiser. Both officers could not hear any sound from the light as it passed over the cruiser. Wolverton reported the incident to Malmstrom AFB, but they could not help him in identifying the light.

Wolverton told of another incident which occurred the same day. Occasionally, the Air Force would practice bomb runs over the missile sites by flying low over the silos and opening the bomb bay doors. As a B-52 bomber was flying over Freeze Out Lake, a Montana Fish and Game Department employee saw a light flying directly behind the bomber. Using his rifle scope to get a better look, he noted that the strange object seemed to be pacing the aircraft. It then briefly *attached itself to the bomber, detached itself, and climbed out of sight.* Wolverton said that this sighting was reported to Sheriff Pete Howard of Choteau County. Howard conducted follow-up interviews with military personnel and learned that as the object attached itself to the B-52, *the plane's radar equipment went out!* The Air Force has denied any knowledge of this report.

The authors would like to thank Captain Wolverton for his prompt attention and assistance in making the following information available. These police file entries document some of the aerial activities in and around Malmstrom AFB at the time of the overflights.

On October 7, 1975, the sheriff's department received a report that a neighboring county police department to the east had been working on two cows that had died and were cut up. The deputy who worked on that also ascertained that on or about October 1, two choppers were seen running together between 9:15 P.M. and 12:20 A.M.

On October 8, a report was filed by a Montana Highway Patrolman. On September 27, 1975, he was off-duty and camping in the mountains south of Great Falls, when he saw a helicopter fly over his camper. The canyon is a fairly narrow area. The helicopter was low enough to vibrate his mobile home. The time was about midnight. Also, on the eighth, the sheriff's department received a report that two ranchers south of Great Falls heard a chopper in their area during the night. The chopper stayed in one area for one half hour. This happened the third week in September.

On October 11, 1975, a black helicopter with a tinted bubble windshield and no markings was spotted flying east to west. This was reported by an unidentified caller. On November 2, a Choteau County police officer in a cruiser spotted a UFO south of Fort Benton. He watched it for thirty minutes. It was a very bright light flying in irregular patterns. RAPCON (Radar Approach Control) was called at 3:24 A.M. They told the sheriff's department that they did not have anything on the radar scope.

On November 8, the sheriff's department received a call from Lieutenant Peisher of Malmstrom AFB, who was in charge of the helicopter division. He told the sheriff's department that two nights prior, people around Lewiston saw a helicopter hovering and that last night two F-106s were scrambled to pursue a light in the sky. There was negative contact. Lt. Peisher also told Wolverton that two of Malmstrom's choppers would be on standby with armed guards and that they would notify the sheriff's department prior to launch.

On December 2, Malmstrom reported that missile crews reported a low-flying helicopter in the area of Juliet (Missile site), near the town of Brady, about twenty-five miles northwest of Malmstrom. This was first reported at 8:47 P.M. At 9:31 P.M., Malmstrom notified the sheriff's department that there were two craft being reported from different missile sites. On October 10, 1975, a man, his wife, and two boys observed a helicopter hover over their cattle at 8:30 P.M. It was one-quarter of a mile away. The craft was noiseless and had red and blue lights. This was in the county north of Wolverton's county and was handled by Sheriff Pete Howard. Also, on October 10, a local veterinarian observed a white light in the sky, with a red light on the side. It would disappear and then reappear. His observation was that the cattle in the area started howling louder than he had ever heard them howl. This lasted for about five minutes.

On October 16 and 17, a rancher south of Great Falls experienced a helicopter hovering over his ranch for fifteen to thirty minutes on both days. On October 17, 1975, a deputy observed a bright light southeast of Malmstrom AFB. It was hovering and reminded him of a landing light. On October 19, at 4:20 A.M., Shelby sheriff's office (Toole County) reported a UFO moving at a high speed at the altitude of 2,000 to 5,000 feet. NORAD at Malmstrom was notified. They indicated that it was not a conventional aircraft and that they would like more information. There were nine different sightings that night around Great Falls. On October 20, a black and white helicopter was reported flying one hundred feet off the ground, fourteen miles southeast of Great Falls. On October 25, 1975, an object was spotted ten miles southwest of Chester; it had green and blue lights. At 3:20 A.M., RAPCON was called. Nothing was sighted on radar. On October 26, Fort Benton reported a helicopter twenty miles east. At 12:06 A.M., Malmstrom reported no helicopter from base. On November 5, at 4:10 A.M., a man reported seeing several UFOs east of Great Falls. There were six objects together; one dropped down nearly to the level of his truck. On November 7, at 3:38 A.M., two girls traveling on the highway west of Great Falls reported being followed by a bright light, grayish in color with intermittent blue lights. On November 7, at 4:20 A.M., Malmstrom reported that SAC people around Lewiston had two UFOs in sight (Malmstrom scrambled two jets). On November 7, a man called, stating that he observed a bright light on November 2 around 9:30 P.M. around Belt; it was visible for fifteen seconds. On November 12, at 4:04 A.M., there was a UFO sighting east of Fairfield; RAPCON was called; negative on (radar) scope. On November 16, at 4:00 A.M., Teton County sheriff's office personnel spotted and observed an object which moved rapidly and changed colors. RAPCON was called. They stated negative on the (radar) scope.

On October 25, Captain Wolverton talked to a woman who lived fifteen miles east of Malmstrom AFB. She stated that on October 17, around 10:30 P.M., she observed a large craft fly from east to west over her house. She said it was about the size of a DC-10, but it had no wings and no noise could be heard emanating from it. It had a ring of lights around the middle and was visible for about thirty seconds. While speaking to a neighboring rancher, Wolverton was told that a member of the family also observed a green light, described as large with a white light behind it, fly between their house and the above-mentioned house between 7:30 P.M. and 8:30 P.M. It came down by a haystack and then flew away.

During a Tuesday night and Wednesday morning in mid-November, Cascade, Teton, Pondera, and Chouteau counties were reporting unidentified helicopters over a wide area, including overflights of missile installations. Some objects seen were reported as helicopters, and others simply as nocturnal lights. On November 19, 1975, Cascade, Teton, Pondera, and Chouteau counties, as on the previous nights, again experienced a helicopter/UFO wave. At least two helicopters were reported at once over a missile site. Malmstrom AFB verified that unidentified helicopters were in the area. On November 28, in Cascade County on the southeast edge of Great Falls, a law officer observed an unidentified helicopter which lifted up off the ground and flew away.

Between August 1975 and May 1976 in Cascade and surrounding counties, approximately 130 reports of unidentified helicopters and/or UFOs were logged. It should be noted that this Montana flap occurred at about the same time as similar phenomena which occurred over military bases in Michigan and Maine. The Cascade sheriff's office was swamped with so many calls on the aerial activity taking place over the county that the sheriff requested help from Malmstrom AFB. This help was granted in the form of security helicopters placed on twenty-four hour alert. The pilots would remain in the helicopter, even to sleep, in case a call came in from the sheriff's office.

We spoke to one of the pilots. He told us of an incident after a call for assistance had come in from the sheriff:

People were reporting a craft at low level that they thought was a helicopter. They were reporting that the craft had strobe lights on it, like disco lights. Well, the weather was so bad when the report came in that it would have been impossible to fly a helicopter, with the icing and so forth. This made it kind of strange. We could not fly due to very bad weather conditions, but this craft had no trouble flying in this weather.

Then, again, there was the Malmstrom activity. On November 7, 1975, at 3:45 A.M., reports were made from K, L, and M Launch Control Facilities regarding bright objects in the sky overhead. At the same time, teams at K-8 and L-6 were reporting objects with bright streamers, which appeared to hover and then descend. There were other simultaneous sightings from different locations in an area approximately 120 miles southeast of the base on a 120 radial. Two F-106s were launched from Great Falls. The lights dimmed and disappeared. All radar contact was lost. The temperature was 35°F, and visibility was 45 miles.

Sightings in Montana continued into 1976 and thereafter. Wolverton and Sheriff Pete Howard went to Fairfield on January 29, 1976, to investigate a report of a UFO sighting. They interviewed Bill Link (pseudonym) regarding an object he observed on January 21, 1976. Link stated that he, his wife, a brother, and his two sons had observed an object in a field near their house (about twelve miles west of Fairfield). It was 9:00 P.M., and they watched the object from their house until they observed red lights on the highway. Thinking the red lights were either that of a highway patrolman or the sheriff, Bill Link and his two sons, ages fifteen and thirteen, got into his truck and went toward the red lights on the highway. As they got closer, the lights ascended from the road and flew toward the larger object. Bill stopped his truck 500 yards from the large object and used his field glasses.

The following is a statement given by Bill Link on January 28, 1976, in the presence of Wolverton, Howard, and a deputy from Cascade County:

> *BILL LINK:* We first spotted them from the house. My boy saw them first just as we turned in to go into the house. My mother was visiting, and he said, "Dad, there's a funny light down in the field." So we all turned to look at it, and I went on into the house. It didn't look strange to me. My wife, boy, and little girl stayed out, and pretty soon she said, "Come out, Bill. Look at these. They're really funny!" So I went out there, and by this time there is a row of trees down the road about three-quarters of a mile. Well, by this time, these lights were coming back and forth out from behind this row of trees. And they appeared at that time to be landing in the field and taking off and landing in the field and so forth. So we watched them for quite a while, probably twenty minutes, there with the field glasses on. About this time we saw two red blinkers down on the highway and I said, "Well, somebody has reported it to the sheriff or somebody is out there now with a patrol car watching them, so we'll go down, too?" So I took the two boys and jumped in the pickup and as we turned the corner off our approach on the main highway, why, these red things that we thought were patrol cars, they then floated off the highway over this field, still blinking or they were then. So we drove

on down there and then as we approached the field where they had went, why we saw this structure that looked like a hotel. A two-story hotel sitting out there in the field and the other lights were grouped around it. About four sets of lights grouped around it."

SHERIFF HOWARD: The big one looked like it was sitting right on the ground?

BILL LINK: It looked like it. That's what the appearance indicated.

HOWARD: About how far away was it?

BILL LINK: Like I said before, I would judge it to be 500 yards.

HOWARD: Is that as close as you got to it?

BILL LINK: That was as close as we got, maybe it was three, maybe it was five, maybe it was seven, but I would say, knowing where that field is, it wouldn't have been over five hundred yards.

HOWARD: What did the machine look like? Angular? Cigar-shaped?

BILL LINK: The one that looked like a hotel? Why, it had a rectangular shape, you could see the outline of it. You couldn't see the outline till you put the field glasses on. Then you could see the dark outline."

HOWARD: Did it have cabin lights or whatever you want to call it?

BILL LINK: Ya! Ya! There were, there were lights, windows, I'd say about . . . there were two rows of those and they appeared to be probably, oh, five to six feet high, and maybe two, three feet wide. With no . . . that is standing on end like this.

WOLVERTON: Single pane windows?

BILL LINK: Single pane windows. No divisions at all in them.

WOLVERTON: Could you tell if there were windows all the way around it?

BILL LINK: Well, no, it looked like it was just . . .

WOLVERTON: One side?

BILL LINK: Face of one side of it.

HOWARD: But they were the full length of the machine?

BILL LINK: Ya, they were the full length of the machine. Well, they come about . . . they were . . . there was none in the exact corner of it. They started in a ways from each end of it. In the meantime, these other lights seemed to be kind of affiliated with it, cause they grouped around it. They would come up close to it and then they would leave, hover about it, and rapidly change places, and then they would appear to set down right in the stubble and then they would . . . some of them would die down to a very dim light and then we would watch them for a while and they would flare right back up very brilliant . . .

This is only a small excerpt of a much longer statement on this case. It does demonstrate, however, the high degree of strangeness characterizing the reported sightings.

Certainly what happened in Montana during this span of time must be regarded as one of the most concentrated series of bizarre encounters in the history of the UFO phenomenon. Perhaps even more interesting than what we've discussed here is the story we *haven't* been told by the authorities.

CHAPTER FOUR
Wurtsmith and Others

October 30, 1975. At the same time that plans were being prepared at Loring for the return of the intruder, things started to break open at Wurtsmith Air Force Base, Michigan, another of the northern tier bases that were put on a security option three alert.

Wurtsmith is a Strategic Air Command base located three miles northwest of Oscoda, Michigan. It serves as the home base for the 40th Air Division and the 379th Bomb Wing.

At approximately 10:10 P.M., personnel in the vicinity of the family housing area located in the southeastern portion of Wurtsmith reported seeing what appeared to be running lights of a low-flying craft which was thought to be a helicopter. The craft hovered and moved up and down in an erratic manner.

Airman Martin E. Tackabury, assigned to the Capehart housing area gate, said that he saw the object for about five seconds near the perimeter of Wurtsmith, due south of his location. Tackabury reported that the object had one white light pointing directly downward and two red lights near the rear. The object seemed to be heading in a west-southwest direction. Tackabury could not hear any sound coming from the aerial craft because a B-52 was in the air nearby to the north.

Near the main gate at Wurtsmith, Airman Michael J. Myers, assigned to Police Unit Seven, was on duty at the Wurtsmith motor pool. As Myers looked toward the west, he could see several lights near the western edge of the base. The lights turned north and appeared to lose altitude. He did not hear any sound.

Sergeant Robert J. Anderson, also at the motor pool, reported that he observed an airborne KC-135 tanker and another craft with a steady red light. The craft appeared to be flying slower, ahead and below the KC-135. Anderson believed he heard a sound similar to a helicopter. After thirty to thirty-five seconds, the object passed out of view.

Airman Roger Skipper, at the Wurtsmith main gate, said that when he responded to the activity at the motor pool, he heard sounds that diminished quickly.

At 1014, 1020, and 1025 P.M., at the back gate of Wurtsmith, security police reported to the command post that an unidentified helicopter with no lights came up over the back gate and hovered over the weapons storage area at a low altitude. Security police of the 379th security police squadron in the weapons storage area could not make out the type of craft. The craft started to move towards the northern perimeter where its lights were again turned on.

Sergeant James A. Miller of the Wurtsmith security police reported his observations of the unknown craft while on duty in the weapons storage area. He stated that he heard the sound of a possible helicopter coming from an area off the base toward the north. He thought he had heard the sound of a flying helicopter fifteen minutes earlier, but he didn't report it.

As he listened, the noise became drowned out by a military jet, and when the jet passed out of range, the original noise had stopped. No other similar sounds were heard.

The local police were notified; however, no evidence was found to corroborate a landing. Wurtsmith Control Tower personnel did not make visual contact with the craft, and no efforts were made to challenge the craft by radio.

Security police at the weapon storage area notified Colonel John J. Doran, Vice Commander, 379th Bomb Wing, that the guard posted at the back gate had reported what he thought was a helicopter overhead. The command post notified Col. Boardman (wing commander) and Col. Doran, and they proceeded to the flight line. It was at this time that Radar Approach Control (RAPCON) reported low-flying objects on their radar scope. They tracked the craft for approximately thirty-five miles on a southeastern bearing from Wurtsmith. Simultaneously, a KC-135 tanker was returning from a refueling mission. It entered Wurtsmith's traffic pattern and received permission to fly transition approaches. Col. Boardman ordered the KC-135 to attempt to identify the object. Wurtsmith air traffic control vectored the tanker in the object's direction.

Aboard the KC-135 was Major Frederick Pappas, the plane's commander; Captain K. E. May, co-pilot; Captain Rick Meier, the navigator; Captain Myron Taylor, instructor navigator; Captain Randy Higginbotham, instructor pilot; and Sergeant Steve Smith. The following statement on the KC-135 encounter with the UFO was given to the 379th Bomb Wing Historian, Staff Sergeant Paul J. Cahill, by Captain Taylor in a "Memo for the Record" dated January 18, 1979.

> We were returning from a refueling mission and during our first approach into the traffic pattern, RAPCON vectored us to check out a reported UFO in the area of the Wurtsmith Weapons Storage Area. As I recall, this activity occurred between 10:30 and 11:00 in the evening around the 1st of November. I remember seeing lights similar to strobe lights which were flashing irregularly. We followed the lights north out over Lake Huron and then the UFO swung south still over the lake toward the Saginaw Bay area of Michigan. At first it was difficult to determine whether there were two different objects because of the irregular flashing of the lights. But, after observing the lights we determined that there were in fact two objects and the irregular flashing appeared to be some sort of signal being passed from one to the other in an effort to maintain the same position. We were able to maintain visual contact most of the time and I was only able to paint an object on the radar scope for about 10 seconds. I would estimate that our altitude was about 2,000 feet and our speed approximately 200 knots. Shortly after turning south in pursuit of the UFO, we called Approach Control and received blanket clearance to follow the UFO at all altitudes and at all vectors. Occasionally, RAPCON would pick-up the UFO and help us by giving us vectors to the UFO's position. I would guess that we stayed close to the UFO most of the time, approximately one mile away, and each time we attempted to close on the object it would speed away from us. We followed the UFO down to Saginaw Bay and started across the Bay when we lost it because of all the fishing boat lights. At first we thought it had landed on one of the large oil tankers but later decided that we had been wrong. We continued to search the Bay area but didn't see it so we changed our heading for Wurtsmith. On the way back, we picked the UFO up again at our eight o'clock position. We turned away, and it proceeded to follow us. Finally, we turned back in the direction of the UFO and it really took off back in the direction of the Bay area. I know this might sound crazy, but I would estimate that the UFO sped away from us doing approximately 1,000 knots. We continued in the direction of the Bay until RAPCON called us again and said they were painting a UFO four to five miles over the coast traveling in a westerly direction. They vectored us to the position of the UFO and we proceeded but at that point we were low on fuel and were forced to return to Wurtsmith. I remember that while on final approach we saw the lights again near the Weapons Storage Area. Following the mission we discussed the incident and about a week later, Captain Higginbotham was questioned by the OSI and cautioned not to discuss the incident.

The historian obviously did his homework on the Wurtsmith sightings as this January 17, 1979, "Research Record of Events" will demonstrate.

> The following actions and research requests have been accomplished regarding the UFO incident experienced by the 379BMW in November 1975:
>
> 1. 15 Jan—0900L—Received a call from SAC/HO Mr. Caywood requesting that I provide him with any documents relating to subject incident.
> 2. Following that request, I checked the Oct–Dec 75 Wing History and found no references to the incident.

3. 15 Jan—1430L—Met with Colonel Doran, 379BMW/CC and asked him about the incident. He recalled the incident and described what he remembered. At that time, Colonel Doran was Vice Commander.

4. 16 Jan—0930L—Called Mr. Caywood, SAC/HO, and informed him of my findings. He requested that I prepare a "Memo for the Record" based on my discussion with Colonel Doran and send it to him as soon as possible.

5. 16 Jan—1000L—After talking to several crew members assigned to the 920AREFS who were at Wurtsmith at the time of the incident, I was able to obtain the names of three crew members aboard the KC-135 which tracked the UFO. All have separated from the USAF. One individual, Mr. Myron Taylor, was described as a good source. Mr. Taylor, formerly Capt. Taylor, had been aboard the flight as an instructor navigator. I requested that Mr. Taylor contact this office.

6. 16 Jan—1445L—received a collect call from Mr. Taylor, however, had to decline but instructed the operator to tell Mr. Taylor that I would attempt to call him. The operator gave me his number. Called the Command Section and informed Colonel Doran of my findings and requested permission to call Mr. Taylor. He agreed, however, instructed me to contact OI and prior to forwarding a "Memo for the Record" coordinate it with him.

7. 16 Jan—1500L—Call Mr. Taylor. He described in detail an account of the mission and further informed me that approximately one week after the mission, the aircraft commander, Capt. Higginbotham had been contacted by the OSI.

8. 16 Jan—1520L—Received a call from Mr. Caywood, SAC/HO. He requested that I send the "Memo for the Record" to Mr. Schoem, Administrative Officer for the Air Force Office of History. He also requested that the information be prepared as soon as possible since the information had been requested by Congressman Stratton and was the subject of a Congressional inquiry. Mr. Caywood stated that Mr. Schoem had a suspense date of 26 January.

9. 17 Jan—1600L—Delivered draft copy of "Memo for the Record" to Wing Commander's Office for coordination.

10. 18 Jan—1000L—Met with Col. Doran. He returned the draft Memo and explained some changes he had made. He also asked if I had contacted OI. Said no, had wanted to wait until coordination had been completed.

11. 18 Jan—1015L—Returned to Office and prepared "Memo for the Record" in final copy. Also called Office of Information and set up an appointment with Capt. Peck (10) for 1100L.

12. 19 Jan 1100L—Capt. Peck and Lt. Owens came to the office and we discussed the Memo. All agreed that the Memo should at the very least be marked For Official Use Only. Called Colonel Doran and he agreed.

13. 18 Jan—1345L—Sent "Memo for the Record" to USAF/CYAU (S), Bolling AFB, D.C. (Attn: Mr. Schoem). Send info copies to SAC/HO and BAF/HO. Also sent three copies to Capt. Peck (01).

Cahill's "Memo for the Record" also alludes to the other incidents at Loring and Plattsburgh AFB, New York, during the same period of time.

Plattsburgh?

This was the first time that Plattsburgh had been mentioned in connection with the other reports. Unfortunately, no other bits of information could be unearthed detailing anything about UFO activity at Plattsburgh. Is it possible that the report is spurious and nothing happened? Plattsburgh received notices of the activity at other bases, and it is mentioned frequently on the reference list of released documents. Could the historian have mistakenly listed Plattsburgh as a sighting location after glossing over a teletype?

It is difficult to believe that a mistake was made in including Plattsburgh as a sighting locale. Many other northern tier Air Force bases, besides Loring and Malmstrom, experienced the inundation of UFOs, as we shall soon see. It would seem strange that Plattsburgh was left out of all the action. The thoroughness of Cahill's research would seem to argue in favor of it being a real event.

So, what actually happened? Was Plattsburgh involved in what Loring, Malmstrom, and Wurtsmith went through? Is information on possible intrusions at Plattsburgh being withheld? At this point, the questions remain unanswered.

In any case, Wurtsmith had its hands full with explaining its own UFOs. Were the objects merely helicopters? No positive visual identification was ever given by any of the personnel involved in the Wurtsmith sightings. Only lights and sounds were reported.

To summarize briefly, radar picked up the craft over the weapons storage area and followed it to the southeast, where the task of identification was handed over to the KC-135 commander. The KC-135 crew picked it up visually and on radar. Taylor, in his statement to Cahill, never once called the craft a helicopter, but called it "a UFO" and an "object." He said that their speed was about 200 knots, and in each attempt to close with the object, "it would speed away from us." Taylor added that when they were heading back to Wurtsmith, "we turned back in the direction of the UFO, and it really took off . . . doing approximately 1,000 knots."

One thousand knots! Certainly no helicopter ever built could do such a thing!

A NORAD Senior Director's log entry dated October 31 was located with a brief reference to Wurtsmith (NCOC is the NORAD Combat Operations Center):

> Alerted by NCOC of a helicopter sighted over Wurtsmith AFB Wpns storage area, a tanker sighted same and pursued it 35 SE over Lake Huron. Upon request of NCOC—Gen Wainwright and concurrence of Gen Taylor—contacted 379BW CP and offered assistance. Also advised ML, LH & JL alert of possibility of a scramble.

The Joint Chiefs of Staff files in the Pentagon contained an "Operational Report" dated October 30, 1975, which offered this comment:

> Upon information that the Dept. of Natural Resources sends out aircraft searching for hunters spotting deer, the Dept. of Natural Resources was

contacted; however, they maintain none of their aircraft were in the area at the time.

The FBI field office in Saginaw, Michigan, was contacted by the Air Force and advised of the activity at Wurtsmith. The special agent in charge said that his office was "unaware of hostile threats against Wurtsmith Air Force Base."

There were efforts by the Air Force to confirm the route and arrival time of an Army helicopter from Wurtsmith to Selfridge Air National Guard Base, Michigan, and to identify any other Army craft in the area but this, too, did not explain the intruder.

Whatever buzzed Wurtsmith got away without a scratch.

On February 21, 1976, UFO researcher Robert Todd filed a request under the Freedom of Information Act for NORAD Command Director's logs. The logs were released to Todd on March 26, 1976, and confirmed that Canada was also having problems with UFOs. Taken from the logs are incidents related to UFO activity in the area of the Falconbridge Air Force Station, a radar site near North Bay, Ontario, Canada (times listed are Greenwich Zulu, 5 hours ahead of EST).

12 November 1975 0715 23rd NORAD Region. UFO Reported from Radar site at Falconbridge Ontario, Canada (Sudbury). Reported by Mr. Julian Prince of Sudbury thru Ontario Provincial Police (also observed by 2 OPP constables ZADOW & BRETT) 2 objects seen appeared to be artificial light fading on and off with jerky motion. Broken cloud layer with no estimated base. No radar contact made and no request for fighter scramble initiated.

15 November 1975 0742 UFO 23rd NORAD REGION. From Falconbridge Radar Site a civilian, Oliver Kizioja, Sudbury, Ontario, at 0615 was standing in back yard facing south. Observed one bright yellow object moving up and back, leaving a tail. It was very high but did not change position in regard to other stars. He watched for 15 minutes, then called radar site. Not observed on radar.

15 November 1975 1229 23rd NORAD REGION. From Falconbridge. At 1130, Lyman Paqutte, married student, residence Laurentian Univ., Sudbury, Ontario. Reported he had been looking due east, sky partly cloudy, saw one bright white object about 70° elevation, high out of range of binoculars. It climbed high out of range of binoculars. Observed for 20 minutes and witnessed by his wife, brother-in-law and sister-in-law. Negative radar contact.

17 November 1975 1705 24 NORAD Region UFO at 132345z Large orange ball with 2 red lights stationary; Azimuth 045° from River Court, Ontario. No radar contact. Called in to 24th NORAD at 16-1700z.

17 November 1975 1705 23rd NORAD region; UFO reported 0230z from a Mr. John Dunlops, address: Manitoulin Island, Ontario, Canada. Two objects, oval shaped with two yellow flashing lights, moving north to south, then became stationary, observed for 10 minutes, one above the other, sky was cloudy—no radar contact. Toronto AMIS advised no known traffic in area.

More entries appeared in the NORAD regional Senior Director's Log.

1205z 11 November 1975 Received unusual sighting report from Falcon-bridge AFS, Ontario, Canada. Info passed to NORAD Command Director, Intelligence and Weather.

1840z 11 November 1975 Actions pertaining to scramble of JL08 and 09 due to unusual object sighting. With Director of Operations approval. Scram-bled JL08/09 at 1745z, airborne at 1750z. NORAD Combat Operations Center notified of Falconbridge AFS incident. Aircraft over Falconbridge flying over incident, point no sighting, 1831 aircraft still in area, no ra-dar aircraft or visual contact. Falconbridge AFS still reporting object at 26,000 ft.

2235z 12 November 1975 Transmitted unknown report to NCOC Surveil-lance on incident at Falconbridge AFS which occurred on 11 Nov. 1975.

0533z 15 November 1975 UFO report from Falconbridge, occurrence time 0202z. Report sent to NCOC Surveillance, referred to Assistant Command Director Space Defense Center, and Intelligence. These 3 individuals con-sidered the report a UFO report and not an unknown track report.

On November 13, 1975, NORAD issued a press release to the media in Sudbury, Ontario. It stated:

"At 4:05 A.M. Nov. 11, the Canadian Forces radar site at Falconbridge, Ontario, reported a radar track of an unidentified object about 25–30 nautical miles south of the site, ranging in altitude from 25,000 to 72,000 feet. Persons at the site also saw the object and said it appeared as a bright star but much closer. Two F-106 aircraft of the US Air Force Air National Guard's 171st Fighter Interceptor squadron at Selfridge ANGB, Michigan, were scrambled; but the pilots reported no contact with the object." The release was approved by NORAD's commander in charge.

The Falconbridge reports spilled over into 1976 and spread to other areas in Canada.

An aircrew observed an object with green and white lights traveling from right to left across its front on June 23, 1976. The crew was sixteen miles from North Bay Ontario on a 158° heading. The UFO was at an altitude of 20,000 feet and flew at the speed of sound.

A number of objects were observed at Penticton Tower, 140 miles east of Vancouver, British Columbia, on August 10, 1976. The objects had steady, flashing green and red lights and were seen by civilians and members of the Royal Canadian Mounted Police.

On October 8, 1976, Falconbridge relayed a report from a woman of Gorson, Ontario, saying she heard a beeping sound and saw one object, which had flashing red and yellow lights. She observed the object for a minute, then it vanished.

Falconbridge again reported on October 18 that the October 8 report by the woman was confirmed by a police officer. He said the UFO was oblong, with blue, white, and green flashing lights.

Meanwhile, back in 1975, NORAD logged a sighting from Minot Air Force Base, North Dakota. Minot AFB, located thirteen miles north of Minot, North Dakota, is a SAC base. Units stationed here are the 57th Air Division, the 91st Strategic Missile Wing, the 5th Bomb Wing, and the 5th Fighter Interceptor Squadron of the Tactical Air Command. Around Minot AFB, 19,324 acres of land are reserved for missile sites.

On November 10, 1975, a brief report was received that Minot was buzzed by a bright object. The object was about the size of a car and flew at an altitude of 1,000 to 2,000 feet, completely noiseless. According to NORAD, no further information was received. Requests were filed to locate additional information on the Minot AFB report, but precious little was available.

A long entry from the 24th NORAD Region Senior Director's Log said:

> UFO sighting reported by Minot Air Force Station, a bright star-like object in the west, moving east, about the size of a car. First seen approximately 1015. Approximately 1120, the object passed over the radar station, 1000–2000 feet high, no noise heard. Three people from the site on local area saw the object. National Command Operations Center notified.

While UFO sightings in abundance took place at other Air Force bases, a different sort of activity was reported from Grand Forks AFB, North Dakota.

Located about sixteen miles west of Grand Forks, North Dakota, the base is the home of the 319th Bomb Wing and the 321st Strategic Missile Wing. On November 4, 1975, the following message was dispatched from the base at 3:01 A.M., Event/Incident:

> Command post identified at 04/0130z Nov 75 that there were possibly some shots fired from on base toward hard alert aircraft on the Sac alert ramp. Security Police have responded. Reportedly one alert tanker and bomber were hit. No damage to any aircraft was discovered after thorough inspection by maintenance and aircrews using artificial light. Inspection will be resumed during daylight hours. No injuries reported. Further reports to follow.

This report was followed by another, more detailed message on November 5, at 11:05 A.M.:

> Sources provided information concerning shots allegedly fired at aircraft at the Grand Forks AFB (GFAFB) ND alert facility. Inspection of the concerned aircraft yielded no evidence of damage. B. (1) on 3 Nov 75, source advised that four security policemen heard what they believed to be shots and possible hits on two aircraft. CNE 4 B-52 NO. 004, and one A KC-135, No. 7397. On 4 Nov 75, source, located in the vicinity of aircraft 7997, advised that he had heard five shots in groups of three and two with a space of approximately two seconds between the groups. Approxi-

mately three seconds later we heard two separate "thuds" on aircraft 7997.

On 4 Nov 75, source advised that he heard two shots and then three seconds later he heard eight or nine more shots evenly spaced. He believed the shots to be from a rifle probably more high-powered than a .22 caliber rifle. The shots came from a southeasterly direction, which is from the direction of the golf course. He was stationed at the alert facility gate.

On 4 Nov 75, source located in the vicinity of aircraft 004. Advised that he heard four or five shots in rapid succession from the direction of the golf course and then one hit which sounded like a large rock against aircraft 004. The shots were loud and clear and sounded as if they came from a small caliber rifle. Possibly a .22.

On 4 Nov 75, source. Located in the vicinity of aircraft 7997. Advised that he heard four or five shots in rapid succession. Possibly from a semi-automatic rifle. Probably a small caliber rifle. The shots came from a southeasterly direction from the golf course. Approximately two seconds later he heard what he believed to be two hits on the rear of aircraft 7997.

On 4 Nov 75. Source stated he reported to the southwest corner of the golf course. Approximately 150 yards from the south perimeter fence. "Omar" picked up a scent and scouted to the perimeter fence. Across the fence and south to N.D. Highway 2. Across Highway 2 and across the debris (broken concrete). The track turned east nearly parallel to the highway and "Omar" tracked approximately 100–150 yards to a small trailer court (20 trailers) then turned south along a tree line and then southeast toward a trailer. The track was lost at a picket fence adjoining the trailer. No lights were on in the trailer and no one was located in the vicinity. Source was accompanied by Capt Klawon: 321 Security Police Squadron, GFAFB, and by Luther Edmonds: Civilian, EMEPADC, ND, Police Department. Inspection of aircrafts numbers 004 and 7997 by the crew chiefs and maintenance personnel assigned to the 319 bomb wing revealed no evidence of damage to the aircrafts. The area surrounding the aircraft and that from which shots were believed to be fired were inspected. No spent cartridges or bullets were located.

The alert facility is located on the southwest portion of GFAFB. It is bounded on the south by ND highway 2 and on the east by the GFAFB golf course. No blast deflectors are located on the alert facility. The alert facility and surrounding area is flat and open territory. Aside from those structures in the alert facility, there are no buildings in the vicinity of the facility.

Press coverage included local television news coverage (WXJB) and newspaper coverage—*Grand Forks Herald*, Vol 37, Number 130: Section Two, Page 3, coverage reported that several shots were heard near the base perimeter and that inspection revealed no aircraft had been damaged.

The following individuals at GFAFB were notified of the transmission of this document: Dale E. Eppineer, Col. Commander, 321 CSE; Donald D. Johnson, CO, Commander, 319 Bomb Wing; William A. Cockayne, Col. Commander, 321 Security Police Group. This represents the first incident of this nature at GFAFB within the preceding 18 months.

It is difficult to correlate the Grand Forks events with what occurred elsewhere. There were no aerial craft involved. The shooting incidents all seemed rather pointless since no damage was done. Yet, this did take place in the midst of a wave of UFO reports at other bases.

At the risk of sounding like we are trying to rule out a potential explanation for at least some of what happened at bases along the U.S./Canada border, we feel that while the Grand Forks sniper firings are curious, and still unexplained, they probably weren't related to the UFO activity. To coin a phrase used by the Air Force, we regard them as "isolated incidents." We mention it here, because the government released data on the Grand Forks attacks concurrently with data on the other bases. It may have been, in some manner, an attempt to downgrade concern over the intrusions. The public, seeing that a base was attacked with hand weapons, would conclude that the other areas were experiencing attacks by protesters or terrorists and, thus, not push too hard for information on UFOs.

The aerial objects seen at Loring, Malmstrom, and Wurtsmith were something very much out of the ordinary. The vehicles showed such advanced aeronautical qualities that no possibility exists for terrorists being responsible. In essence, the Grand Forks activity served as a convenient "straw man" for the Air Force to use in diverting attention from the real problem.

The Commander-In-Charge of NORAD (CINCNORAD) sent this message to NORAD units in North America, dated November 11, 1975:

Part I. Since 28 Oct 75 numerous reports of suspicious objects have been received at the NORAD CU; reliable military personnel at Loring AFB, Maine, Wurtsmith AFB, Michigan, Malmstrom AFB, Mt, Minot AFB, ND, and Canadian Forces Station, Falconbridge, Ontario, Canada, have visually sighted suspicious objects.

Part II. Objects at Loring and Wurtsmith were characterized to be helicopters. Missile Site Personnel, Security Alert Teams, and Air Defense Personnel at Malmstrom Montana report an object which sounded like a jet aircraft. FAA advised there were no jet aircraft in the vicinity. Malmstrom search and height finder radars carried the object between 9,500 ft. and 15,600 ft. at a speed of seven knots. There was intermittent radar contact with the object from 0807532 thru 09002 Nov. 75. F-106s scrambled from Malmstrom could not make contact due to darkness and low altitude. Site personnel reported the object as low as 200 ft and said that as the interceptors approached the lights went out. After the interceptors had passed the lights came on again, one hour after they returned to base. Missile site personnel reported the object increased to a high speed, raised in altitude and could not be discerned from the stars.

Part III. Minot AFB on 10 Nov reported that the base was buzzed by a bright object the size of a car at an altitude of 1000 to 2000 ft. There was no noise emitted by the vehicle.

Part IV. This morning, 11 Nov 75, CFS Falconbridge reported search and height finder radar paints on an object up to 30 nautical miles south of the site ranging in altitude from 26,000 ft. to 72,000 ft. The site commander and other personnel say the object appeared as a bright star but much closer. With binoculars the object appeared as a 100 ft. diameter sphere and appeared to have craters around the outside.

Part V. Be assured that this command is doing everything possible to identify and provide solid factual information on these sightings. I have also expressed my concern to SAFOI that we come up soonest with a proposed answer to queries from the press to prevent overreaction by the public to reports by the media that may be blown out of proportion. To date efforts by Air Guard helicopters, SAC helicopters and Norad F-106s have failed to produce positive ID.

Note that the Falconbridge report mentioned here contains a few more details than had been available. The November 11 UFO appeared as a "100 foot diameter sphere" and was pockmarked with "craters" on the outside. Hardly a conventional aircraft!

There is also concern in the message that the press would overreact to the stories and that steps should be taken to prevent this. The media hardly reacted to the incidents at the time, and when they did, it usually was in the local press where very limited public reaction could be expected. The "prevent" tactic worked, and the magnitude of the UFO intrusions was recognized only well after the objects have come and gone.

The Air Force was lucky. Had full-blown media coverage been applied to the stories in the same general time frame when they happened, a Pandora's Box of criticism would surely have resulted over the Air Force's inability to deal effectively with the aerial invaders.

More information continued to flow. Two log entries from the Air Force Intelligence Service's Alert Officer's Log were released in 1977. The first one is dated October 31, 1975:

Per Ltc. Redican's direction. Contacted DIA OPS center and informed them of unidentified flight activity over two SAC bases near Canadian border. CIA indicated appreciation and requested they be informed of any follow-up activity.

Numerous requests to the CIA for information have met with denial after denial. However, here's clear evidence that they had received reports on the sightings from the Air Force. Another log entry, dated November 3, 1975, says:

Received call from AAC/IN (Alaskan Air Command/Intelligence). They had sent message 012224, Subject: Unidentified Foreign Object to INYSA and wanted to know if INYSA had received it. They wanted guidance from INYSA.

A UFO from the Alaskan Air Command now! We requested a copy of this report. The reply from the Air Force dated February 8, 1978, was very unsatisfying:

The Alaskan Air Command message 012224 referred to on 3 November 1975 of the attached INZA Alert Officer Log extract is not available. Information received on this subject is considered raw intelligence material and maintained for only the briefest period of time.

Whatever happened must have been interesting!

U.S. sightings, as those in Canada, carried well into 1976. The National Military Command Center held a number of reports of sightings which were released after considerable correspondence. A "Memorandum for the Record" dated January 21, 1976, tells of a sighting at Cannon AFB, New Mexico:

> The following information was received from the Air Force Operations Center at 0555 EST:
>
> Two UFOs are reported near the flight line at Cannon AFB, New Mexico. Security Police observing them reported the UFOs to be 25 yards in diameter, gold or silver in color with blue light on top, hole in the middle and red light on bottom. Air Force is checking with radar. Additionally, checking weather inversion data.

A very striking object to be sure. Twenty-five yards in diameter, gold or silver in color with a blue light on top, a hole in the middle, and a red light on the bottom. It's not something you see flying around every day!

A "Memorandum for the Record" dated January 31, 1976, told of activity at Eglin AFB, Florida:

> 1. At 310805 received phoncon from AFOC: MG Lane, CG, Armament and Development Test Center, Eglin AFB, Florida, called and reported a UFO sighting from 0430 EST to 0600 EST. Security policemen spotted lights from what they called a UFO near an Eglin radar site.
>
> 2. Photographs of the lights were taken. The Eglin Office of Information has made a press release on the UFO.
>
> 3. The temperature inversion analysis indicated no significant temperature inversion at Eglin AFB at that time. The only inversion present was due to radiation from the surface to 2500 feet. The Eglin surface conditions were clear skies, visibility 10–14 miles, calm winds, shallow ground fog on the runway, and a surface temperature of 44 degrees F.

Additional information on the Eglin report appeared in the NORAD Command Director's Log for January 31:

> The Command Post received a UFO report from Eglin, FL, that Duke Field personnel saw a row of lights with a central white light at 1043. The lights were about 2° above the horizon at a zenith of 350°, range unknown. A later report (1245) states that further investigation in daylight indicated that the lights were probably on a building.

The "Memorandum for the Record" is dated several hours *after* the 1245 report received by NORAD of the lights being part of a building, yet it makes no mention of this discovery. It's strange that no one saw the building lights before that time, and suddenly, one day, they became so sensational that official reports were filed with the National Military Command Center of a UFO. The memo refers to photos but all attempts to get them released, or to simply get an admission that they exist, were fruitless.

Another NMCC Memorandum dated July 30, 1976, from Fort Ritchie, Maryland, relates this information:

1. At approximately 0345 EDT, the ANMCC called to indicate they had received several reports of UFOs in the vicinity of Fort Ritchie. The following events summarize the reports (times are approximate).
   a. 0130—Civilians reported a UFO sighting near Mt. Airy, Md. This information was obtained via a call from the National Aeronautics Board (?) to the Fort Ritchie Military Police.
   b. 0255—Two separate patrols from Site R reported sighting 3 oblong objects with a reddish tint, moving east to west. Personnel were located at separate locations on top of the mountain at Site R.
   c. 0300—Desk Sgt. at Site R went to the top of the Site R mountain and observed a UFO over the ammo storage area at 100–200 yards altitude.
   d. 0345—An Army Police Sgt. on the way to work at Site R reported sighting a UFO in the vicinity of Site R.
2. ANMCC was requested to have each individual write a statement on the sightings. One individual stated the object was about the size of a 2½ ton truck.
3. Based on a JCS memorandum, subject: Temperature Inversion Analysis, dated 13 November 1975, the NMCC contacted the Air Force Global Weather Central. The Duty Officer, LTC OVERBY, reported that the Dulles International Airport observations showed two temperature inversions existed at the time of the alleged sightings. The first extended from the surface to 1,000 feet absolute and the second existed between 27,000 and 30,000 feet, absolute. He also said the atmosphere between 12,000 and 20,000 feet was heavily saturated with moisture. A hard copy message will follow.

Shades of Loring. One UFO was the size of a 2½ ton truck. Several other UFOs were "oblong with a reddish tint." And they were seen over weapons storage areas!

Temperature inversions were indeed reported over the area at the time. This would have been significant had the sightings been reported on radar. But they weren't. Temperature inversions do not come down to 100 to 200 yards in altitude and hover over ammo storage areas. Neither do they present such a vivid visual appearance as described by the security police and civilians in the area.

The "hard copy message" mentioned in the last sentence of the memo is currently unavailable.

Serious military concern is reflected throughout the documents discussing the concentrated UFO sightings over these bases between October 1975 and July 1976. What was the reaction to all this by our Senators and Congressmen, the ones who control the purse strings of the military and who should be most disturbed by the lack of control of the armed forces over these events?

They, in fact, had almost no reaction because they weren't informed about the sightings at any time. It was only in 1978, three years after the initial outburst of sightings, that Congressman Samuel S. Stratton (D—N.Y.) became the first legislator to voice his concern.

On December 10, 1978, the weekly *Parade* magazine carried a story titled "UFO's vs. USAF, Amazing (But True) Encounters" by Michael Satchell. Basing its information on government documents released through the Freedom of Information Act, *Parade* summarized the events at Loring, Malmstrom, Wurtsmith, and other bases, as well as some foreign incidents acquired through U.S. government sources (see Chapter 6).

The *Parade* article had a significant impact on public interest in the 1975 reports. A copy of the article was sent to Congressman Stratton, who was, at the time, the Chairman of the Armed Services Investigations Subcommittee. Stratton sent a letter, dated December 20, 1978, to Major General Charles C. Blanton, Director, Legislative Liaison for the Office of the Secretary of the Air Force. In the letter, Stratton says:

> The attached item from *Parade* magazine of December 10 reports that unidentified aircraft penetrated the airspace at several Strategic Air Command bases in the United States and Canada on several occasions during the period October 27—November 19, 1975. The article proceeds to quote from Air Force documents to the effect that the intruding aircraft had "a clear intent in the weapons storage area" at Loring Air Force Base. Those same documents reportedly refer to unsuccessful efforts of Air Force aircrafts to intercept and identify the intruder aircraft.
>
> This Subcommittee is concerned by the alleged ability of unknown aircraft to penetrate airspace and hover over SAC bases, their weapons storage areas, missile sites, and launch control facilities, and the inability of Air Force equipment and personnel to intercept and identify such aircraft. Accordingly, it is requested that all Air Force reports relating to each of the incidents described in this article be furnished to the Subcommittee. It is further requested that all reports of any similar incidents, either before or since the October–November 1975 events, be furnished to the Subcommittee.

The letter was handled in the usual manner for a Congressional inquiry and was staffed to various internal Air Force groups. Amazingly, many replied that they had little or nothing to provide as information in response to the request and, in one case, the Air Force's Directorate of Operations and Readiness stated in a January 8, 1979, memo:

> We have been unable to find any official information regarding the incidents described in the *Parade* magazine article. Contact with individuals assigned to operational units where the incidents were alleged to have occurred indicate some of these incidents *may not have happened at all* [emphasis added].

The Air Force, mindful of the inadequacy of such a response to Stratton, had to provide something since more than enough evidence was available showing that the events did occur.

A formal response to Congressman Stratton was sent on February 9, 1979, by Joseph J. F. Clark, Associate Director, Legislative Liaison for the Air Force:

> This is in response to your recent letter concerning an item from the *Parade* magazine of December 10, 1978 regarding unidentified aircraft penetrating the airspace at several Strategic Air Command bases in the United States and Canada on several occasions during the period October 27 through November 19, 1975.
>
> Attached is a partial compilation of available materials obtained in response to your request for Air Force reports pertaining and similar to the incidents described in the *Parade* magazine article. We have requested such reports from numerous Air Force organizations, some of which are outside of this Headquarters. Not all of this material has been received, and it will be forwarded when it becomes available to us.
>
> Please note that the attached material rarely includes formal reports as such; rather, it mainly consists of copies of documents such as messages, memoranda, and duty officer log entries. This is because unidentified flying object reports are of transitory interest to the Air Force and permanent files are not maintained. In addition, please note that much of the enclosed material has been released to various people and organizations under the Freedom of Information Act.
>
> We trust the information attached will be helpful and hope to get additional information to you as soon as possible.

Attachments to the letter included memos, messages, and log entries relating to the sightings at Loring, Wurtsmith, Malmstrom, Falconbridge, and miscellaneous other reports. Clark was careful to emphasize that UFO records were of "transitory interest" and that "permanent files are not maintained"; that is, UFOs are not important and are no cause for concern. This is almost the precise wording of the Air Force's response to Barry Greenwood in 1977 in which UFOs were described as "transient in nature" with "no permanent record or file maintained" (see Chapter 1). Apparently, even when you think you are getting a direct, personal reply, you still receive a canned response.

The letter also stresses the fact that the material had been released to various people and organizations under the Freedom of Information Act. If it were not for the relentless digging by researchers to unearth the information, much of which required lawsuits to obtain, what might the Air Force response have been?

There probably would have been no reason for a response. Congressman Stratton could never have read the *Parade* article, since *Parade* would have had nothing to write about. No documents would have been available.

Any hopes that a Congressional hearing might have been convened were dashed because Stratton did not pursue the matter after receiving the Clark letter and attachments. Why?

He pressed for various measures to close off the flow of information from the military to the public and even urged substantial penalties for those who might print more than what the Pentagon would allow them to print.

Under these circumstances, it's obvious why Stratton said nothing more of the 1975 incidents. He avoided all attempts by investigators to contact him in his office, and no statements were given. His interest in 1975 is quite understandable, as any heavily pro-military person would be concerned over the Air Force's difficulty in dealing with the UFOs.

The fact that some individuals managed to locate specifics about the sightings was a necessary evil that the Air Force had to live with. The hope was that the small number of people who had this information would not have enough of a voice to draw attention. This worked until *Parade* picked up the baton.

Fortunately for the Air Force, Stratton was the only Congressman who asked weighted questions. He was friendly to the military and would not make waves. Politics did not enter into the 1975 picture in a serious way hereafter. The ball was definitely back in the court of the UFO researchers.

As strange as the 1975 activity seems, it was only a microcosm of UFO activity over the years. It has been estimated that for each UFO sighting reported, ten others go unreported. We might apply the same figures to military-oriented UFO sightings. Perhaps the differential between reported and unreported sightings is even larger in this case due to the more restricted atmosphere within the military for revealing UFO information.

If the reports proved one thing, they showed that for a "transient" phenomenon, UFOs were pretty persistent.

CHAPTER FIVE

Echoes from the Past

It was probably inevitable that as we researched the reports on the 1975 military base sightings, other UFO reports from military sources would surface. To be frank, we were convinced that such reports would come to light with only a nominal amount of probing. The stories of government secrecy over the years contained too much substance to be exaggerations or outright hoaxes. With the Freedom of Information Act as the spearhead, the assault on the paper curtain of bureaucracy would be much easier.

These reports, like the 1975 reports, came out in two ways. Direct FOIA requests to agencies produced documents, mainly after 1970, which contained sightings from scattered areas around the U.S. Sometimes we had sought the information in question; sometimes it was released unsolicited, completely to our surprise.

Also, eyewitnesses came forward to report their recollections of experiences, first-, second- and thirdhand, involving UFOs seen at military facilities and UFOs seen by military personnel outside of these facilities. Unfortunately, their stories were usually unaccompanied by documentation, but we were not about to look a gift horse in the mouth. There was always a chance that the narrative report would match up with information we already had in our files.

In this chapter, we take a look at the more interesting and provocative stories collected during the last eight years since the official release of long-suppressed government UFO documents became a reality. We hope that publication of some of these accounts may help to verify the details given here in that additional eyewitnesses might come forward.

The first account comes from the current police chief of Hampton, New Hampshire, Robert Mark, who, in 1965, had a rather remarkable sighting when he was in the Air Force. He was assigned to the 509th Security Police Squadron and held the rank of Sergeant at Pease AFB near Portsmouth, New Hampshire. His recollection of the sighting was enhanced by the fact that it occurred on the same night as the now-famous "Incident At Exeter," September 3, 1965.

For those who are not familiar with the Exeter sighting and especially for those who confuse it with the so-called "Interrupted Journey" experience of Barney and Betty Hill (both the Exeter and Hill reports were the subjects of full-length books by John Fuller), here is a brief summary. On the night of September 3, Norman Muscarello was hitchhiking on Route 150, in Kensington, New Hampshire. At about 2 A.M., he noticed a huge, reddish-colored UFO come out of the sky toward him. Muscarello dove into a ditch out of sheer panic. When the UFO moved off, Muscarello flagged down a car and had the driver take him to the Exeter police station.

Later, Officer Eugene Bertrand drove Muscarello back to the sighting area where both saw the UFO return from behind a grove of trees. It was a huge, red object with sequentially flashing lights. The UFO hovered, then moved in a "falling leaf" motion. Another police officer, David Hunt, managed to see the UFO as it moved away.

Back to our police chief. His story, given to us on December 3, 1982, is as follows:

It was about 12 A.M. when I and two other airmen were at the Main gate to Pease. One of the airmen yelled, "Look at that!" I turned around to see an object drop out of the star-filled sky. It was coming straight towards the guard shack at an altitude of about 300 to 400 feet. The lights were approaching at a very fast rate of speed. What I saw as the object was coming straight on, was what looked like two headlights that were very bright.

As the object passed over the lighted areas of the base, the lights would go out as if someone were breaking the bulbs as they went by. It passed directly over the guard shack, but the men could not hear a sound, only the wind. When I first saw the two bright headlights drop out of the sky and come towards the shack, I thought it was a B-52 approaching, but this was dismissed when there was no sound whatsoever.

One of the airmen ran for the shack and grabbed the red hotline phone, which is a direct to CSC (Central Security Control). He began crying and yelling into the phone about what he was seeing. Then he dropped to his knees and lost all control of himself. I had to grab the phone away from him and shake the airman, telling him to control himself, that the thing was not going to kill him. As this was going on, the object headed towards the north end of Pease. When it flew over, the lights there went

out also. They remained out for about thirty to forty seconds, then came
back on. The whole area was black when the object passed over.

Mark recalled the object as being elongated, but due to the blinding headlights
as it approached, he could not make out much detail. There were other
lights on the object, but he did not remember just where they were.

Mark recalled running up into the base radar tower just in time to
see two fighters take off to chase the object. He could hear the pilot saying
"I can't get them; they're too fast! I'm at max." As the fighters were chasing
the object, the chief saw that they would gain some ground on the object
only to see it pull away and outdistance them. He remembers seeing the
rear of the object as the two planes were chasing it: "It looked like the
object had lights in the rear, like you see behind a jet where the flame
comes out."

Here we have direct confirmation by a reliable eyewitness that what
was probably the same UFO as that seen by Muscarello, Bertrand, and Hunt,
appeared over Pease AFB about two hours earlier. Pease vehemently denied
knowledge of any base reports during the entire Exeter controversy, though
stories circulated that the base frequently scrambled fighter jets after UFOs.
New Hampshire was a hotbed of UFO activity in the mid-1960s, and there
is no doubt that Pease was alerted many times to the appearance of UFOs
in the area.

During the fall of 1966, a helicopter from Ellsworth AFB, South Dakota,
carrying a crew of five members of the 821st APs, was on route to the
Launch Control Facility at site E, located sixty miles west of Wall, South
Dakota. The time was midmorning. About three-quarters of the way into
the flight, an object appeared to the right of the helicopter. It seemed to
hover about 300 yards away from the helicopter. Everybody aboard could
see the object, which was described to us by then Airman 1st Class William
Papanos as being fifty to sixty feet long. It was circular and looked as if it
had a cupped upper structure. The color of the UFO was a very light grey
and very bright. Papanos heard the pilot call the LCF and advise them
that they had a UFO in sight. The object suddenly moved its position from
the right side of the helicopter to the front with a burst of speed, remaining
the same distance from the helicopter. It hovered there for a few seconds
and then traveled back to the right side where it hovered again. It moved
back in front with blinding speed and then disappeared from view. The helicopter continued on to the LCF and landed.

The base advised all crew members not to talk with anyone at the
LCF about the incident and that someone would be out to the site to take
statements. Later that afternoon, a helicopter brought a Major to the LCF,
and all crew members were ordered to fill out a report on the incident and
to sign a document stating that they would not reveal the incident to anyone.

Consistently, in many of the reports relayed by current and ex-military personnel, they were ordered to sign documents swearing secrecy. Under what regulation this was done is unclear. JANAP 146 still requires reporting UFO sightings and the regulation carries a penalty of a $5,000 fine, 10 years in jail, or both for revealing information reported under the regulation. There is a question as to whether many of these sightings were reported within the requirements of JANAP 146. No particular procedure is spelled out in JANAP 146 for filling out secrecy oaths.

The next report came from a friend of a witness involved in a tragic UFO chase incident. Unfortunately, the witness died in Vietnam during the war, so little more information can be obtained:

> The incident happened sometime around 1969. He was a radar tracking airman located someplace in North Carolina and the situation involved a series of UFO reports over the Atomic Energy Commission research facility down at Oak Ridge. On the final date of the incidents which I . . . obviously, it was so long ago, I can only give you approximate times—it was sometime in October.
>
> The Air Force scrambled two Phantom F-4s, one with wing cameras and one equipped with air-to-air missiles. Obviously, one was supposed to have been a camera plane while the other was an attack plane.
>
> What he saw on the radar scope was two objects fairly stationary for about one half hour before the F-4s arrived on the radar screen. The F-4s got to within about five miles when the two unidentified objects took off at a fairly high rate of speed and outdistanced them by about sixty miles in less than about ten seconds.
>
> They stopped a second time. The F-4s continued their chase. They went to afterburners because there was a burst of speed on the radar scope. The next thing that happened was one of the blips from the F-4s completely vanished off the screen. About ten seconds later, the second F-4 vanished off the screen. At the time, they were within about three miles of the two UFOs when they finally disappeared.
>
> Okay, now he was told directly not to give out any information about this incident. The base he was stationed at had a paramilitary hospital, and they did find wreckage because he had to give them coordinates approximately where the F-4s went off the screen. A lot of material, like the titanium, had been crystallized. Some of the plastic had been shattered. The plane's parts were scattered over a distance of about eight to nine miles. Their approximate height when the first one went off the screen was about 25,000 feet, and at afterburners, if they exploded or whatever the situation was, they would have spread debris all over the place. And this was fairly consistent with what they found.
>
> They found both the captain of the aircraft and the ordnance officer who is the copilot. They found the captain and ordnance officer of the second one. As far as I know, they are still someplace in a military mental institution. They have little or no faculties.
>
> Now, he violated the trust in telling a few of his friends and, subsequently, sometime in 1971, he was sent to Vietnam. The last thing I had heard was that he had been killed in action someplace near Da Nang near one

of the perimeters, which didn't make any sense to me at the time because he was a trained radar intercept operator, and there would have been no reason for him to be going into a combat situation.

He was part of a special unit in 1969. I'm trying to remember what it was. He had been trained by the NSA, but the group that he was working with specifically had their own special radar set-up. It was probably sponsored by the NSA, but it was a military operation, it was all Air Force personnel except that the only strange thing about it was they didn't have a colonel in charge of their group. It was somebody from the NSA.

Naturally, without more specific information and in particular a more accurate date, the story is difficult to verify. We have been unable to locate any mention of the crash of two jets under the circumstances described. If such a thing happened in an isolated area, it is very possible to keep the story from the public.

UFO/jet chases and crashes are not new. A number of incidents have occurred over the years, and by using the Freedom of Information Act, crashed jet reports involving UFOs have been made public. Military-oriented aircraft accident reports are on file in the Air Force Inspection and Safety Center at Norton Air Force Base in California. Release of information is subject to the guidelines and restrictions of the FOIA so that only portions of the reports can be made available. Perhaps the most important part of these accident reports is the Board of Investigation Proceedings. This gives the full details of the circumstances surrounding the cause of a crash. In probing the crash files, we have not received *one* Proceedings of any crash report to date; the reason being that the FOIA allows an agency to protect internal decision-making procedures and, in the case of crash reports, to protect the methods used in investigation.

This is most convenient for the Air Force and most inconvenient for us in trying to obtain the facts behind UFO/jet incidents. Some revealing things have surfaced though.

One report, which is well-known among UFO researchers, is the story of the Walesville, New York, crash. The Air Force's accident report on this, released to us in 1980, contains a brief summary sheet in lieu of the full transcript of the investigation:

On 2 July 1954 at 1105 Eastern Standard Time (EST), an F-94C departed Griffiss Air Force Base (AFB) on an operation training mission. The aircraft was only a few miles out when the Griffiss control tower operator called the pilot and advised that he was being diverted to an active air defense mission. The aircraft was given a vector of 60 degrees and 10,000 feet altitude to intercept an unidentified aircraft. Some difficulty was experienced in finding this aircraft, so the controller then vectored the aircraft to a second unidentified aircraft in the area. This aircraft was identified as an Air Force C-47. The ground controller then gave the F-94 pilot a heading of 240 degrees as a vector back to the first unidentified aircraft. At this time, the F-94 was flying above the broken clouds at 8,000 feet. The unidentified aircraft was not found above the clouds, so the aircraft started to descend below the clouds. During the descent, a fire warning light came on. The engine was immediately shut down; also due to the low altitude, the crew members ejected and were recovered without injury. The aircraft continued for about 4 miles while on a heading of 199 degrees and crashed in an area known as Walesville intersection at 1127 EST. The aircraft struck a dwelling, killing a housewife and injuring her daughter, then struck an auto at tho intersection, killing all three occupants.

Without the full details of the crash, it is impossible to determine what caused the jet to malfunction. According to the "Unsatisfactory Report" form included in the file, the pilot, Lt. William E. Atkins, felt a sudden rise in cockpit temperature and noticed the forward fire warning light was on. He alerted the radar operator, Lt. Henry Condon, placed the throttle in the idle position, waited four seconds, then stop-cocked the throttle. After waiting another four seconds, Atkins and Condon successfully bailed out.

In the *Encyclopedia of UFOs,* edited by Ron Story (Doubleday Dolphin, 1980), an entry by Kevin Randle attempts to explain away the Walesville crash as nothing more than an engine fire which poured heat into the cockpit. His "documented evidence" is a news clipping from the *New York Times.* If the author of the entry had truly been interested in documented evidence other than a newspaper clipping, he would have noticed that the accident report on Walesville contained the following conclusions: *"Investigation of the wreckage disclosed no in-flight fire. The cause of the malfunction in the fire warning system could not be determined."* Who do we believe in this matter: a newspaper clipping or the Air Force's own accident investigation report?

So, while we have no specific evidence that the aircraft was attacked by a UFO, the cause of the crash remains unknown to this day. Is it merely coincidence that the jet developed a fault during a UFO chase or . . . ?

Other jet crashes during UFO encounters were released to us along with the Walesville report. This report details the experience of Lt. Col. Lee Merkel on January 31, 1956:

1. History of Flight: The pilot took off from Standford Field, Louisville, Kentucky at 1450 CST, 31 January 1956, on a local TPR clearance to perform a maintenance test flight for a carburetor and propellor change. The flight was proposed for one hour duration with two hours and thirty minutes fuel aboard. Climb to 20,000 feet was made and contact was established with the Oak Hill Air Defense Command Radar Station. A course was set for Terre Haute, Indiana, and the pilot informed "Oak Hill" he was at 20,000 feet at 1501 CST. The flight was continued and several minutes later "Oak Hill" informed the pilot his "blip" was fading on the scope. The pilot replied he had Terre Haute in sight. "Alley Cat," a nearby Direction Center was busy and could not take control. This was 1509 CST. At 1524 "Oak Hill" received another call from ANG 75091 (this error, i.e., ANG 75091 instead of ANG 73091

is believed to be an error of the pilot or of the radar operator at "Oak Hill"), and the pilot stated he was returning to Louisville, heading 1350 at 34,000 feet climbing to 35,000. The pilot was informed of an aircraft approaching from the right. The pilot stated he did not have the aircraft in sight and the "blip" faded from the radar scope. Communication between "Oak Hill" and ANG 73091 was lost at 1535 CST. The pilot's last communication was given in a normal voice. The next information was a telephone call by an unidentified civilian to an Air Defense Command Aircraft Control and Warning Station north of Terre Haute, Indiana, stating that an Air Force aircraft had crashed and the approximate location. The Control and Warning Station immediately notified the Bakalar Air Force Base Provost Marshal at approximately 1625 CST. It was determined that the aircraft ANG 73091M crashed at approximately 1535 CST, 31 January 1956.

Again, not enough information was released to draw any conclusions except that some sort of unknown aircraft was seen.

By pure chance, the son of Lt. Col. Merkel was located in Worcester, Massachusetts. As a writer for a Worcester newspaper, Lee Merkel, Jr., wrote a story on UFOs for the *Sunday Worcester Telegram* on February 6, 1977. A member of the Massachusetts chapter of the Mutual UFO Network advised the authors that he knew Mr. Merkel and would contact him.

Merkel kindly provided what he knew about his father's fateful flight, though he was only seven years old at the time. Initially, Lt. Col. Merkel's wife was told by the Air Force that the crash was caused by a failure of Merkel's oxygen equipment. Years later, Lee saw a reference to his father's death in a publication of the National Investigations Committee on Aerial Phenomena (NICAP). He asked NICAP for a copy of the material they had, which was later sent.

The file principally concerned an interview with an Indiana reporter who did a story on the crash. The reporter said he learned that a UFO was detected on radar and interceptors were scrambled after it. The object went much too high for the interceptors, and they broke off the chase. The radar controllers then contacted Lt. Col. Merkel who was oxygen-equipped in his P-51. They vectored Merkel to the UFO, and he climbed after it. Shortly after, the P-51 came down and Merkel was killed.

Another jet chase after a UFO ended in tragedy, and again no solid explanation could be offered as to what occurred.

One of the most famous jet chase incidents involved an F-89 sent after a UFO over Lake Superior on November 23, 1953, the so-called "Kinross case." According to the crash report summary:

F-89C, Serial No. 51–5853A, assigned to the 433rd Fighter-Interceptor Squadron, Truax Field, Wisconsin, was reported missing over Lake Superior at approximately 2000 Eastern Standard Time (EST) on 23 November 1953. The aircraft was scrambled from Kinross Air Force Base, Michigan, to participate in an Active Air Defense Mission. The aircraft and aircrew had not been located as of 1 January 1954.

On 23 November 1953, F-89C, Serial No. 51–5853A, was scrambled by "Naples" GCI (Ground Control Intercept) to intercept and identify an unknown aircraft flying over Lake Superior. The interceptor became airborne from Kinross Air Force Base, Michigan, at 1822 EST. Original radar control of the aircraft was maintained by "Naples" GCI and at 1841 EST control was transferred to "Pillow" GCI. The aircraft was flying at 30,000 feet at this time. At 1847 EST, at the request of "Pillow," the aircraft descended to 7,000 feet to begin the interception. Location of the aircraft was then approximately 150 miles northeast from Kinross AFB and over northern Lake Superior. At 1851 EST, the interceptor pilot was requested to turn to a heading of 20 degrees to the cut-off vector. After the turn was completed, the pilot was advised the unidentified aircraft was at 11 o'clock, 10 miles distant. Radar returns from both aircraft were then seen to merge on "Pillow's" radar scope. The radar return from the other aircraft indicated it was continuing on its original flight path, while the return from the F-89 disappeared from the GCI station's radar scope.

The unknown aircraft being intercepted was a Royal Canadian Air Force Dakota (C-47), Serial No. VC-912, flying from Winnipeg to Sudberry, Canada. At the time of interception, it was crossing Northern Lake Superior from west to east at 7,000 feet.

The pilot and radar observer were assigned to the 433rd Fighter-Interceptor Squadron, Truax AFB, Wisconsin. They were on temporary duty at Kinross AFB, Michigan, while the base's regularly assigned personnel were firing gunnery at Yuma, Arizona. The pilot had a total of 811:00 hours of which 121:40 hours were in F-89 type aircraft. He had 101:00 instrument hours and 91:50 hours night time. The radar observer had a total of 206:45 hours of which 11:30 hours were at night.

Search for the missing aircraft was conducted by both USAF and RCAF aircraft without success. Although 80 percent area coverage was reported, heavy snows precluded effective land search. All civilian reports of seeing or hearing the aircraft were investigated with negative results.

In fact, while this summary report states that the UFO was identified as a Royal Canadian Air Force C-47, such was not the case. According to Donald Keyhoe in *Aliens From Space* (Doubleday, 1973), he contacted the RCAF about this explanation, and they informed him that *no such flight had taken place.*

No wreckage or bodies were ever found and the incident remains unexplained, despite the Air Force's insistence upon clinging to the Canadian aircraft explanation.

Air Force officers, desiring complete confidence, have stated to the authors that many other pilot deaths have occurred as a result of jets being scrambled after UFOs. The officers feared that if the information were traced back to them, some form of retaliation would take place so their accounts provided only bare details. We had a little more than nothing but not much beyond that.

Jumping ahead to 1973, a number of startling reports came to our attention. This was a year of great UFO activity in the media. Beginning in the last week of August, sightings began streaming in from the southern states, and by mid-November the entire United States and a good portion of the world was "UFO-conscious." Thousands of reports hit the press, radio, and television with stories ranging from distant lights in the sky to landed UFOs and entity encounters. What is not known about the 1973 wave of reports is that a flurry of military UFO encounters seems to have occurred shortly before the outbreak during the fall.

One witness, coming to us as a result of a UFO adult education course by a researcher, bore the remarkable story that follows. A background check of the witness verified his former duty status in the Navy. Currently, he works for a technical firm in Connecticut. He expressed concern that he would experience problems with the Navy if his identity were revealed so we will honor his request for anonymity.

In 1973, Ed Sims (pseudonym) was a member of the United States Navy and was assigned to the nuclear submarine USS Abraham Lincoln. According to Sims, the ship was about one day out of the Panama Canal. It was night time. There were four men, including Sims, on the conning tower, filming night lights and algae in the water. The ship's photographer was using a 35mm still camera and 16mm movie camera. Suddenly, a crimson-colored, one-hundred foot, circular disc dropped out of the sky and made a wide sweeping arc around the ship at an altitude of about ten feet. At this point, all navigation and sonar were lost on the ship, and the ship was dead in the water. The photographer filmed the whole event with both cameras. After the object circled the ship two or three times, it took off at a high speed and, in a matter of seconds, was gone. As soon as the object disappeared, sonar and navigation came back on.

All four individuals went down and reported to the executive officer what had taken place topside. The photographer was ordered to develop all films immediately and to present them to the commander. The executive officer warned them not to talk to anybody else aboard the ship about the incident. Sims stated that the photographer later told him that everything they saw came out on the film. Sims claimed that he did not hear anything else about the incident until the ship docked in California.

After they docked, Sims was about to go on liberty when he and the other witnesses were summoned to the skipper's room. Once inside, they were greeted by two civilians and one Navy officer and were questioned for about one hour about the UFO incident. They were informed that their liberty was cancelled, and all four were taken off the ship by military police to some unknown location on the base. Once there, the men were put into an eight foot by ten foot room with only a desk and a chair in it. They were left alone for about one hour, with no one coming in or out. One of the civilians belonging to either the FBI, CIA, or OSI or Navy Intelligence, along with a naval officer, came into the room and interrogations began.

They tried to convince Sims that he didn't see anything on the day in question. When he tried to explain to them that even the ship's photographer took photos of the objects, they began telling him that he was lying and that the four men made up the story. Sims stated that this type of interrogation went on for hours. When they could not break Sims' story, they left him in the room, telling him that they would "see him tomorrow." After about forty-five minutes, he was taken under guard to a location on the base where they billeted him for the night, telling him that they would pick him up in the morning. The next day, two military policemen took him to the same eight foot by ten foot room, and he was interrogated for a full eight hours, this time by different civilian and Navy personnel. Again, the whole interrogation was structured around telling Sims that he did not see anything and that he and the other witnesses were lying.

He was put through the same process the next day, but this time, three civilians entered the room with an attaché case. The individuals told Sims that they believed his story and were going to show him photos of types of UFOs and wanted him to identify the one that he had seen. Sims stated that all photographs shown to him were eight-by-ten glossies showing different saucer-like objects. Some were cigar-shaped, some were elongated football-shaped, some looked like ice cream cones. Others looked like two headlights on a car. He was able to find one photograph that resembled the object that he saw on the night in question. He was then told to sign a secrecy document which said that if he revealed anything about the sighting or the photos he was shown, that he would be court-martialed, fined, and placed into solitary confinement for a long period of time. Sims signed. He was told to report back to the USS Abraham Lincoln, escorted by military police. Once aboard the ship, he was told to report to the commanding officer who informed him that he was being transferred. He was to pack all his belongings and report back when he was ready to leave. When this was done, Sims was again asked to sign a secrecy document and was again warned of the consequences if he told anyone about the incident. He was taken off the ship, placed on an airplane, and flown to his next duty station in Hawaii. Sims heard through aquaintances that the other three individuals were taken off the ship and assigned to other duty stations around the world—never seeing or hearing from the other men again. Sims showed no evidence of lying and desired no publicity about his experience. One reliable military source within the Air Force has confirmed the portion of the story in which the UFO appeared near the submarine.

Another 1973 story, given to us by a former member of Naval Intelligence, discusses the recovery of a "crashed" UFO in the Pacific:

It basically started when I entered the military services (Navy). I was trained as a gunners mate, and instead of being sent to school, as normal recruits would be, I was kept at the Great Lakes Naval Base at a place called the "Big Green House," which is their gunners school. This is located at the Great Lakes Naval Base in Chicago. The reason that they kept me there was that my aptitude tests showed me as being somebody reasonably good and intelligent. I had a very high ranking score on the intelligence test and the mechanical aptitude test. They wanted to keep me around as an instructor. The theory was that a recruit who was also an instructor could help other recruits become better gunners mates. While I was there, I went through boot camp for three months. I had to hold over for about two weeks in boot camp due to my eyes. I had to wait for a special medical commission to go on through, which I received. Three months after I went in the Navy, I was out of boot camp and I started taking courses in the Green House.

Six months later, which puts me in the service nine months, Naval Intelligence approached me to go to work for them as a normal gunners mate but to be aware of the things that go on around me and to report any sort of questionable activity that I had seen. I was given a triple A security clearance at that time and was told that if I kept my nose clean for a period of one and a half years that I would be sent overseas and given a triple five A class security clearance.

Now, I was sequestered one night for guard duty on a quonset hut at the northwestern end of the base. We were told that there was highly top-secret material in the quonset hut. We were not supposed to go inside and not to look in any windows. We were to guard the place and let no one in or out that didn't have the proper identification. We were not supposed to let anyone near the place, up to a one hundred foot perimeter around it. The quonset hut was near the lake, and it was in officer's territory. It was the older part of the base where they had used a lot of the dorms for officers who had their families there. There were warehouses in and around that area.

This one night I was Officer of the Guard. I was given a letter by a messenger that I was supposed to give to the OD (Officer on Duty). It was for his eyes only and it was a sealed envelope. I was to get a signed receipt from him. The receipt was on the front of the envelope; to do this, I had to go inside. I had to call and tell them what I was doing and the officer was busy at that time, so it was decided that I was to be allowed inside the building to his office, have him sign the receipt, then turn around and walk out. Now this was highly unusual; normally they would come to the door and sign the receipt and I would get inside, but that night, the OD was busy.

They let me in through this sliding door, a nice large metal door. I walked inside and was stopped to sign in. I was escorted down the hallway about twenty feet by three burly SPs. I took a turn to the right for about five feet, went down another hallway about eight feet, took a turn to the left for about another five feet, walked out into a warehousing area where I saw a strange craft off to my left. I was told to walk on, get my signed receipt, turn around, and leave. I was told not to pay any attention to what was going on around me.

As I went to the doorway, where the OD was, I saw a very highly unusual craft over to my left. The craft was possibly thirty to thirty-five feet long, about twelve to fifteen feet at its thickest part, then it tapered off in the front to a teardrop shape. I only caught it at an angular view. It looked like it did not have any seams to it. It had a bluish tint but that was only if you looked at it for a few seconds. If you looked at it and turned your eyes away real quick, all you saw were white lights, but as long as you stared at it, it took on a bluish appearance, a light bluish appearance. It was sitting on a pedestal or frame made out of four by four wooden blocks. It was held up by crossbeams underneath it and was sitting about a foot or two off the floor.

At that time, I had turned and walked into the office where the OD was sitting. There were several people in there, nobody was talking, nobody was doing anything; everybody was watching me. They seemed nervous. I laid the envelope on the desk, did a quarter of a turn to my left, so I could not see what was in the envelope. I was scared that I might see something that I wasn't supposed to.

At this time I had a very good view about halfway from the craft to the tail section. The whole craft tapered back to a very high edge. It looked as if it had a razor edge, a razor sharp edge. The bottom went about three quarters the length of the craft and then angled sharply upward.

I was then ordered by the Officer on Duty to take the receipt, which meant I had to turn back around and face him. The envelope had disappeared, and I don't know where it went. I was told to take my receipt and leave and not to say anything to anyone about what I had seen. I turned around to my left. As I did, I got a full scan of what the craft was, and then I did a very quick about-face and was escorted out.

I finished my shift as outside duty officer, and that's all. I turned the receipt in to the officer of the deck in the morning. I then slept until about four o'clock in the afternoon, and that was it.

About two months later, I went to San Diego to put some missiles in a sub and I was talking to one of the guys who was on a destroyer and it seemed as though they had tangled with some unidentified craft. He didn't know what it was. They brought it down in the Pacific in about 350 feet of water. The reason that nobody could tell if it was a craft or not is that it didn't look like anything that he had seen before. He sketched it for me. I was in a bar with him at the time and we had a few beers, so I took the story with a grain of salt, until I saw the sketch of what the craft looked like. It was an exact copy of the same craft I had seen in Chicago. This happened right around the time I was getting out of boot camp, which would have put it around June of 1973 that the craft was shot down. It as brought from San Diego by rail to Chicago, where it was worked on. I think one of the reasons that they had to get it out of that area was due to the large amount of publicity that it got. A destroyer does not shoot on an aircraft without drawing some publicity. They shot it down with a surface-to-air missile, according to what the sailor said. They hit the craft, but didn't destroy it. According to him, they didn't even dent it, but it sent up a concussion through the craft and whatever was inside of it was destroyed or hurt or whatever. I don't know, he didn't say. He did say that they were able to pull some sort of life form from out of it. That's all I heard from him. He did tell me that Glomar Explorer was used to extract the craft from 350 feet of water. And that the ship was a naval destroyer escort; destination of the vessel was Hawaii at the time of the incident.

FOIA inquiries were filed to locate any information on the story, but they proved to be fruitless. The Navy claimed to know nothing about it.

One would think that a story like this would be difficult to keep secret.

The source stands by his account, however, and he has repeated it to UFO researcher and authority on crashed UFO cases, Leonard Stringfield, for inclusion in his third Status Report on UFO crash/retrievals (UFO Crash/ Retrievals: Amassing the Evidence, Status Report 3, June 1982).

Is the story true? Or was it merely a test of the witness's reliability in keeping a sensitive matter secret since he was being primed for a position in intelligence? We include accounts like this in the hope that others will come forward to either confirm or deny that the events took place.

On June 17, 1974, the Hobart (Australia) *Mercury* carried the following news item:

> HUNTSVILLE, Alabama—Experts at an Army missile base say they are puzzled about strange "ghost ships" picked up by powerful radar scanners in the Pacific during a tracking exercise last summer.
>
> There has been little official comment on what the scientists found during the exercise but Major Dallas Van Hoose, an Army spokesman, confirmed recently that "some unexplained aerial phenomena" were observed during the exercise last August.
>
> Scientists, many of whom are reluctant to be named in interviews because of general public skepticism over unidentified flying objects, say privately they have been unable to find any explanation for the "ghost ships."
>
> "We have never seen anything precisely like this before," said one ballistic missile defense expert who works for an Army agency here and who is familiar with the advanced radar used to test missiles and warheads.
>
> Huntsville houses the Army's ballistic missile defense systems command which tests in the Kwajalein Atoll region of the Marshall Island Trust Territory held by the U.S.
>
> Last August, the Air Force launched a Minuteman intercontinental ballistic missile from Vandenberg Air Force base aimed for the Kwalaicin missile range which is used by the Army, Air Force, and Navy.
>
> The radar experts in the Pacific found they were also tracking an unidentified flying object next to the ICBM's nose cone.
>
> Radar picked up an inverted saucer-shaped object to the right and above the descending nose cone and watched it cross the warhead's trajectory to a point which was below and to the left of it before the phantom ship disappeared.
>
> The ghost ship was described as being 10 feet high and 40 feet long.
>
> Two separate radar systems saw it at the same time which may eliminate the probability that there was a malfunction in one of the radar systems.
>
> It was also reported that three other identical objects were seen in the vicinity—the same size, shape, and dimensions.
>
> One scientist said the data indicated that the phantom ship "flew under its own power," but could not explain what sort of power was involved.
>
> So far, none of the experts here believe the ghost ship was a natural phenomenon caused by freak weather conditions or echoes commonly seen on radar screens.

When FOIA inquiries were filed with the Army, they denied having any records concerning the sighting. We were referred to Vandenberg AFB, California. Vandenberg responded that "In accordance with Air Force Manual 12–50 which implements the Federal Records Act, the launch operations records for August 1973 have been destroyed."

Note that it is not stated that the UFO tracking record was destroyed, only a very general statement is given that "launch operations records" were destroyed. That such a mysterious event as this would not be kept somewhere for possible future use is incomprehensible. Yet, this excuse is offered time and time again to deny access to records.

The most publicized report of the 1973 wave was undoubtedly the Pascagoula, Mississippi, "abduction" of Charles Hickson and Calvin Parker on October 11. The two men were fishing off a pier on the west bank of the Pascagoula River when they saw a strange airborne object approaching them. The UFO was fish-shaped and emitted a bluish, hazy light. It came to within a few feet of the ground and hovered. One end of the UFO opened and three robot-like entities disembarked, took hold of the two men, and brought them inside the craft where they were put through what seemed like a physical examination. They were released and, soon after, they became the subject of intense media interest.

An incident occurring in Pascagoula on November 6 received much less publicity but was of considerable interest to the Navy. Two teletypes were sent, one on November 7 and the other on November 8, 1973, describing the event:

(November 7)

UNIDENTIFIED SUBMERGED ILLUMINATING OBJECT

1. 2130S Two local fishermen reported in person to this unit that they were fishing in approx. position 88–36W, when they located a strange illuminating object which was in approx. 4–6 ft of water and moving at approx. 4–6 kts. Subj fishermen tried to determine what object was but could not. They tried to hit it with paddles and object would go out and move to another position. Subj fishermen appeared sober and extremely concerned about the object.

2. 2140S This unit dispatched CG 1635 19 with BM2 nations and BM3 crews aboard to investigate. Station personnel did in fact locate object, which had an amber beam approx. 4–6 ft in diameter and attached to some bright metal object moving at 4–6 kts. Object did in fact cease illuminating, changed to a different course, and re-illuminate itself. Subj object traveled several courses while illuminated. Station personnel could not identify object and has never seen anything like it. 2230S CG 1635 19 moored station and stated fishermen will return to station at a later time. This unit will obtain their names and addresses.

(November 8)

1. The following statement has been released to news media this date concerning subject sighting: Quote at 0930 PM local time 6 Nov 73 two

local fisherman rptd in person to CG Sta Pascagoula that they were fishing in a position between the west bank of Pascagoula ship channel and round island, when they noticed an illuminating object beneath the water. The fishermen stated they attempted to determine what the object was but could not. The fishermen appeared extremely concerned. CG Sta Pascagoula dispatched its small boat with two station members on board to investigate. The object was relocated by unit members and appeared to be 4–6 ft in diameter and showing an amber color. The glow eventually became extinguished and could not be relocated. A daylight investigation on the morning of 7 Nov. proved negative unquote.

2. The following persons were on scene and saw the reported glow:

   Raymond Ryan, age 42, 1403 Larson St. Pas.

   Earl Ryan, age 16

   Edward Rice, age 48

   Freddy Rice, age 35

   Velma Rice, age 37

   Eddie Rice, age 15

3. Further inquiries from media relating to subj will be directed to your office.

These messages were followed by a more detailed account on November 12 by two Coast Guardsmen, E. A. Wilbanks and Lt. Commander C. E. Dorman, sent to investigate the sighting from their base at the Naval Ship Research and Development Laboratory in Panama City, Florida:

1. In response to verbal orders from Executive Officer, we departed Panama City at 0905, 9 Nov 73, on board NA 473. Purpose of trip was to informally investigate nature of UFO sighted night of 6 Nov 73, in order to obtain background data for comparison with possible future sightings. Upon arrival Mobile, Alabama, we were met by LTJG M. J. DONOHOE, Coast Guard Group Mobile Port Security Officer (and Public Information Officer). LTJG DONOHOE drove us to the CG Station Pascagoula, outlining the general train of events along the way. Arrived Pascagoula approximately 1140. Four civilian personnel and two CG enlisted who had seen the object were at the station, and we commenced to interview them. Three additional civilian personnel who had sighted the object arrived approximately one hour later and were also interviewed. The majority of the interview, conducted informally in the CG Station mess hall, is in Enclosure (1). Enclosures (2) through (4) are newspaper articles and official releases concerning the event. Enclosure (5) is a photograph of participants. Upon completion of the interview, a short release to Mobile, Alabama Channel 10 news personnel (Rennie BRADNER and one cameraman) was made. LTJG DONOHOE drove us back to Mobile, and we returned to Panama City on board NA 32.

2. Principals:

   NATIONS, Lawrence A., BM2, USCG

   CREWS, Charles, BM3, USCG

   RYAN, Rayme, Fisherman, age 42; 2115 Briggs, Pascagoula

RYAN, Larry, son of Rayme Ryan; age approximately 17

RYAN, Raymond, Fisherman, age 42 (twin brother of Rayme), 1403 Lawson Ave, Pascagoula

RYAN, Earl, son of Raymond Ryan, age approximately 16

RICE, Fred N. Jr., Fisherman, 2202 Briggs, Pascagoula, age 35

RICE, Edward, age 48, Fisherman, 255 Dupoint St, Lewis Trailer Park, Pascagoula

RICE, Velma, sister of Fred N. Rice, age 37 (Also mentioned in Enclosure (4) as witness to sighting, but not present at interview, was Eddie Rice, age 15)

3. General Sequence of Events: On the evening of 6 Nov 73, the RYAN's and RICE's, and 4 skiffs (and associated "kicker" boats) were mullet fishing in the mud/oyster bed flat area to the SW of Pascagoula, Miss. (approximately 88–36W, 30–20N and surrounding 4 sq mile area). Sky was clear, little moon, slick calm with intermittent breeze from N; high tide (+1 approx 2200). First person to spot object was Rayme RYAN: object was stationary, in the water, near his anchored skiff. Water depth in area approx 4–6'. RYAN attempted to strike object with an oar; object dimmed, and would reilluminate when left alone. He summoned his brother and later the RICE's to the scene. When disturbed, object would dim, move, and reilluminate. After approximately 30 minutes, Rayme RYAN struck at object with intent to "kill" or "destroy" it. Object disappeared. All boats resumed fishing, after attempts to relocate object were unsuccessful. This first sighting occurred approximately 2000; no fish had been caught by any boat up to that time. Approximately 30–40 minutes later, Rayme RYAN had set and was retrieving his net approx ½ mile to the SW of the initial sighting. As he came back to his buoy, he again noticed the object, stationary, near his buoy. He again summoned the others (RYAN caught approx 400# of mullet in this net; those were the only fish caught during the night). They decided not to disturb it, and summoned the Coast Guard. NATIONS and CREWS arrived in a 16' BW at approx 2140. They essentially repeated the earlier attempts to deal with the object, namely striking at it with an oar. The object again dimmed and/or moved (at 4–6 knots), and after 10–15 minutes extinguished and could not be relocated. CG personnel returned to station, and fishermen resumed normal activity.

4. Characteristics of object and area:

1. Area of sighting is old oyster bed (mud/shell bottom). Land area to North is uninhabited marsh. Object travelled in SW direction, toward deeper water, and appeared to remain in or near a "gully" on the seafloor (not on chart, but known to fishermen to have fished area for over 30 years).

2. Typical fish catch in area is approximately one ton/boat/night (verified by buyers' tickets); catch on night of 6–7 Nov. was 400# for all four boats (about 2.5 hours of fishing time was lost due to object sighting).

3. Current during period of sightings was "negligible"; object moved in various directions, though primarily to SW in relatively straight course, and at speeds up to 4–6 knots. Object did not consistently move when disturbed or passed over in boats.

4. Light from object was directed toward surface; it appeared to come from a coherent source approximately 3″ diameter, with a surface intersection circular or elliptical in shape and approximately 10′ x 12′ in size. Color was generally described as yellowish-amber, or with a light red tint. Intensity varied from "almost too bright to look right at" to zero, depending on amount of disturbance (brightest when first approached). When seen from the side, it was described as looking like a parachute underwater.

5. Object felt metallic when struck, but could not be consistently struck. Portion of oar underwater was not visible from surface when in light beam from object. Object "turned off" when struck with beam from flashlight; when light removed, object reilluminated to previous intensity in about 1 minute.

6. None of the observers had ever seen "anything like" the object; reactions ranged from fear to curiosity. Descriptions of witnesses were generally consistent and did not appear rehearsed. Phenomena observed were not consistent with any known fish or other marine life, nor with flashlight, lantern, navaid, or other known light source.

7. There were no other boats in the area during this period.

8. In its generalized SW travel, object appeared to stop when it encountered an anchored boat (although it was not physically against the boat or appurtenances). It would then illuminate, and remain in area until disturbed for 15 to 30 minutes.

9. No attempt was made to capture object or to take sensory measurements of it and the environment, except for the visual observations and striking with the oar.

10. CREWS claims to have seen a "metallic" object with light source attached.

11. Draft of skiffs and motors was 1.5′ maximum; minimum water depth was 4–5′. Object was not struck when passed over.

5. Conclusions:
   a. At least nine persons witnessed an undetermined light source between the hours of 1930 and 2200 on the night of 6 November 1973, at two locations separated by approximately ½ mile, in the vicinity of 88–36W, 36–20N.
   b. The characteristics and actions of the light source are not consistent with those of known marine organisms or with an uncontrolled man-made object. The object can not be identified at this time.
   c. The presence of the object was associated with a significant variation in the fish catch in the area.

The Coast Guard, strangely enough, turned out to be a fruitful source of UFO information later. It seemed to be easier to obtain sighting reports of UFOs in the vicinity of bodies of water than it was to obtain other types of sightings. This could be attributed to a more liberal policy of releasing documents by the Coast Guard.

UFO activity in the area of the Great Lakes began to rise in 1976. Witness these reports taken from NORAD's 23rd Air Division Senior Director's Log for September 7, 1976. (Times given are Greenwich Zulu, or 5 hours greater than Eastern Standard Time):

> 0710z UFO sighting z-61 reported receiving a call from the Huron County Sheriff's Department. We had z-61 establish a patch and talked to the deputy sheriff that observed two objects showing white lights over Lake Huron. The objects moved vertically. We also talked to Carl Baily of Port Austin who initially reported the objects. He observed one object directly above the trees showing a flashing red and green light and a white floodlight. This object moved out over Lake and merged with another object showing the same lights. He later observed these lights hovering over the site at z-61. He also reported observing, "all kinds of them" moving across the Lake. He had been observing these objects almost continuously for approximately two and one-half hours and was still observing them when we talked to him. All information was forwarded to the NCOC (National Combat Operations Center).
>
> 0825z Huron County Sheriff's Department called to update information on the UFO sighting. Deputies Gary Krul and Greg Gordon, observed an object the shape of a paper cup that was apparently changing shape and showing a flashing white-green-white light. This object moved away from the lake in a southeasterly direction and the officers lost sight of the object at about 0827z. Information was forwarded to the NCOC.

Sporadic activity continued until 1978 when the Great Lakes area was suddenly deluged with reports.

On July 23, 1978 a spectacular UFO sighting took place around Lake Michigan. The witnesses to this event were personnel from four Coast Guard stations around Lake Michigan. The bases involved were Coast Guard Station St. Joseph, Michigan; Coast Guard Station Ludington, Michigan; Coast Guard Station Two Rivers, Wisconsin; and Coast Guard Station Sturgeon Bay, Wisconsin. All four Stations reported seeing an object described as being cigar-shaped with colored lights and traveling at speeds in excess of 1,200 mph. Between the hours of 3:53 and 7:30 A.M., both civilian and Coast Guard personnel were reporting the sightings. The following is a chronological sequence of the events obtained through a Freedom of information Act request filed with the Office of Assistant Secretary of Defense.

At 0353, the Coast Guard station (CGS) at Two Rivers received a call via VHF-FM from CGS Ludington, asking Two Rivers to look over Lake Michigan between Ranley Pt. and Big Sable for a UFO. At the time Ludington had a UFO in sight, the object was heading towards the CGS at Two Rivers. Observers at Ludington were describing the UFO as having red, white, orange, and green lights, flashing and moving across the sky at a high rate of speed, in a westerly direction. At 0359, the Two Rivers CGS called CGS Sturgeon Bay requesting Sturgeon Bay personnel to attempt a visual contact with the UFO, giving them the same description of the UFO as that from Ludington. It headed westerly towards Two Rivers until it disappeared from sight.

At 0359, CGS St. Joseph received a report from a Mr. and Mrs. Gruss of Benton Harbor, MI. They had sighted an object, described as being a long cylinder shape, silver in color, just above the Rocky Gap area which is located 4208N, 086-28W. The object was hovering at an altitude of 2,000 yards. The object was reported to have stayed stationary for 30 minutes, from 0020 to 0050 hrs, then began to move in a southwesterly direction. At 0400 hrs personnel at CGS Sturgeon Bay sighted the object south of the station. The approximate position of the object was reported to be angle 25 degrees. Distance from the station was unknown. At 0401 hrs CGS Ludington reported that personnel were observing the UFO heading in a westerly direction. The object had red lights and a very bright strobe-type light which flashed erratically. It was traveling at an extremely high rate of speed.

At this time the station at Two Rivers could not see the object, but at 0404, CGS Two Rivers saw the object approaching. It had red lights with extremely bright white lights flashing in irregular manner. The object was heading in a northerly direction towards Sturgeon Bay. At 0407, CGS Two Rivers reported the object was passing from view. At 0425, Green Bay Light House reported to CGS Two Rivers that they were observing the UFO heading in a westerly direction. It bore red and white lights and moved at a high rate of speed. The white light was very bright and flashed in a irregular manner. At 0445, CGS Two Rivers reported sighting a white light in the southern sky, moving in the direction of the station and blinking in a non-rhythmic beat. The light then took off northeast and went straight up and out of sight. The light was visible for approximately 3 to 5 minutes.

At 0455, CGS Ludington received a call from a Mr. Wagner who reported seeing a UFO that hovered over U.S. Rt. 31, then began to move in a westerly direction at a rapid speed. He described it as having flashing white lights like strobes. An occasional red flash was seen. FNMK Burden and SN Clark looked over the Lake and spotted the object. Personnel at CGS Two Rivers took approximately 10 35mm pictures of the object.

In response to an FOIA request for NORAD Command Directors Log for the month of July 1978, two entries were sent pertaining to the UFO sightings over Lake Michigan, as follows:

28 July 78 at 0423z Cleveland, Ohio, Coast Guard Station St. Joseph, MI, reported a UFO (long cylinder-shaped object) hovering at 6,000 ft. over Lake Michigan. After a short period of time, it departed northward at a high rate. St. Joseph called Coast Guard Station at Ludington, Michigan (approx. 200 miles) and while they were talking it came into view (a distance of 200 miles was covered in 3 minutes). Object turned west and came into view of Coast Guard Station Two Rivers, WI in a short period of time. It turned and disappeared traveling northward up Lake Michigan. Coast Guardsmen at St. Joseph took photos with a 35mm single lens reflex camera.

28 July 78, at 0650z, Coast Guard Station Cleveland, Ohio. At 0636z, Coast

Guard craft in vicinity of Apostle Island, Lake Superior 46 degrees 50N, 90 degrees 40N reported sighting large cylindrical object, pink in color with four lights, two on each end, white and red lights. Object very high saw it about five times for total duration of 5–6 minutes. Object directly overhead—no direction of travel.

FOIA researcher Robert Todd requested the St. Joseph photos in a letter dated February 1, 1980, to the United States Coast Guard. On February 27, Todd received this answer:

This office never received the negatives which were mailed from Ludington Coast Guard Station to this office on 5th Oct. 1978. When they failed to arrive within a reasonable amount of time, personnel from this office initiated a tracer or Mail Nondelivery Report with the Postal Service on the 16th of Oct. 1978. The post office informed this office that they were unsuccessful in their attempts to locate the negatives.

This matter became confused when we sent an inquiry to the Commander of the Ninth Coast Guard District at Cleveland, Ohio, in a separate attempt from Todd to obtain the photos. After first being advised on September 16, 1980, that "ten 35mm photographs" were lost in the mail between CGS Two Rivers and the District Office, as Todd was told, we were informed in a letter from the Ninth District dated October 24, 1980 that:

The film in question was sold to the *National Enquirer* by the individual taking the pictures at CGS Two Rivers, MN. Subsequently, the Ninth Coast Guard District requested and received two color prints from the *National Enquirer.*

We were also given the reason for the "lost in the mail" explanation:

Our letter dated 16 September 1980 was referring to another incident in late August 1978 involving one lost picture, with no connection to this case.

Several discrepancies turn up in these letters. Todd was told that the negatives were mailed from CGS Ludington while we were told that they were sent from CGS Two Rivers. Then, the mail loss was changed to a mix-up between *two different cases.* What was the "late August 1978" incident to which they refer? The Coast Guard never told us. Was it a fouled up administrative effort or was the Coast Guard suppressing information? Or was it both?

The Coast Guard can now be added to the many military-oriented agencies that have been completely baffled by the UFO influx during the 1970s. Not one of these agencies has been able to handle the subject adequately, which might partially explain their lack of candor. As a result, sightings continued to leak out.

In February 1977, a former Air Force officer, stationed at Pease AFB,

New Hampshire, signed an affidavit for us, stating that one night Pease had an "Operational Readiness Inspection." At approximately 10 P.M. a large round object penetrated the northern perimeter of the base, where the weapons storage area is located. The object hovered at low altitude for fifteen minutes at which time it shut off its lights and disappeared. It was never identified. An FOIA request to Pease met with a denial of any knowledge that the sighting occurred.

On March 23, 1977, seven airmen at March AFB, California, a SAC base, reported seeing two UFOs in the early morning, travelling at high speed from south to north at approximately 3,000 feet. The airmen described the objects as diamond-shaped, silver in color with a blue stream trailing behind them. Duration of the sighting was fifteen seconds.

Undoubtedly, many more accounts can be described, but it would take the better part of another book to do it. The Project Blue Book files stored at the National Archives in Washington, D.C., give a vast background of similar incidents to those reported in recent years. The intrusions into high security areas have become much more concentrated than the earlier sightings, though. Defense has been ineffective. Worry has been high. And foreign governments have not escaped the onslaught.

CHAPTER SIX

Foreign Intrigue

$\mathbf{U}$FO activity outside the United States was no less abundant during the 1970s. Whoever or whatever they were that caused such great disturbances at U.S. military facilities also found their way to other countries, creating an equal amount of concern on the part of officials in those respective nations. Publicly, the official reaction was very much the same as the official U.S. reaction to the Malmstrom and Loring sightings. There was not an excessive amount of press coverage of the reports, and the sightings that did receive prominent play were quickly dealt with in the usual manner: either downplay the mysterious nature of the reports, or do not follow up with additional information and the public would forget soon enough.

Privately, foreign government officials tried in every way to determine what was happening—without success. Occasionally they would contact the U.S. government for assistance in attempting to identify the aerial objects being seen. We have found that most of the UFO data sent in this way went through the Department of State via American embassies in the various countries.

It turned out to be an extremely difficult task to try to locate every UFO sighting in the Department of State's files. Many millions of pages of paper traffic make their way through the State Department every year, and blanket requests under the Freedom of Information Act for *all* UFO data from a particular nation would be very costly and time-consuming. However, some individual reports were located, and they paint an intriguing picture of the UFO activity overseas in the 1970s.

The first report we will present was sent to then Secretary of State, Henry Kissinger, from the American embassy in Algiers, in message number 071792, March 1975:

1. SECRETARY GENERAL OF MINISTRY DEFENSE, COL. ABDELHAMID LATRECHE, ASKED ME TO CALL AT MINISTRY MARCH 7. PURPOSE OF CALL WAS TO ASK ME IF WE COULD SHED ANY LIGHT ON STRANGE "MACHINES" WHICH HAD BEEN MANEUVERING OVER ALGERIAN AIRSPACE IN RECENT WEEKS.

2. HE SAID STORY STARTED LAST JANUARY WITH APPEARANCE OF THREE AMERICAN JOURNALISTS IN BECHAR WHO ANNOUNCED THEY WERE THERE TO COVER ARRIVAL OF BALLOON WHICH TAKING OFF FROM CALIFORNIA. I SAID THIS WAS PRESUMABLY REFERENCE TO JOURNALISTS WHO HAD COME TO COVER MALCOM FORBES' PROPOSED FLIGHT WHICH HAD BEEN ABORTED AT LAST MINUTE. HE SAID THAT MIGHT BE, BUT ALMOST IMMEDIATELY THEREAFTER, ALGERIANS BEGAN SEEING STRANGE OBJECTS IN SKY. THEY HAD BEEN SEEN NEAR MILITARY INSTALLATIONS BY RESPONSIBLE PEOPLE, AND ALGERIANS WERE ASKING US FIRST BECAUSE SIGHTINGS HAD OCCURRED SO SOON AFTER APPEARANCE AMERICAN JOURNALISTS.

3. HE SAID OBJECT HAD BEEN SEEN FIVE TIMES, USUALLY ABOUT 1900 OR 1930 AND ON ONE OCCASION IT HAD REMAINED VISIBLE FOR OVER TWO HOURS. HAD BEEN SEEN TWICE NEAR ORAN, ONCE IN CENTER OF COUNTRY, ONCE NEAR BECHAR AND, MOST RECENTLY, OFF THE COAST LAST NIGHT (MARCH 6). OBJECT HAS VERY BRIGHT LIGHT (HE KEPT COMPARING IT TO HEADLIGHT OF A CAR) WHICH OBSCURES ITS SHAPE. OBJECT MANEUVERS AND HAS BEEN SEEN TO LAND AND TAKE OFF. SIGHTING LAST NIGHT, AT ABOUT 1930, WAS FIRST BY RADAR AND SECONDLY VISUALLY. OBJECT WAS AT ABOUT 15,000 (SIC) METERS ALTITUDE. ON OTHER OCCASIONS IT HAS BEEN SIGHTED AT ESTIMATED ALTITUDE OF 2,000 METERS. LATRECHE EMPHASIZED THAT IT WAS ALWAYS SEEN BY MORE THAN ONE PERSON AND THAT IT WAS THEREFORE NOT HALLUCINATION. HE DID NOT SEEM PARTICULARLY WORRIED, BUT DID SEEM TO BE TAKING STORIES SERIOUSLY.

4. I REMARKED THAT ALGERIANS HAD PREVIOUSLY ASKED US ABOUT MYSTERIOUS BALLOON AND OUR QUERIES HAD ELICITED NO INFORMATION. LATRECHE SAID THAT CASE HAD BEEN CLOSED AND THIS WAS ANOTHER. HE SAID ALGERIANS WERE FOLLOWING DEPLOYMENT OF SIXTH FLEET BY RADAR AND AIRCRAFT SURVEILLANCE AND WONDERED WHETHER THESE NEW SIGHTINGS WERE RESULT OF SIXTH FLEET MANEUVERS OF SOME SORT. I SAID IT POSSIBLE THAT SOME PHENOMENON SEEN OFF COAST COULD BE PRODUCED BY FLEET BUT COULD ASSURE HIM CATEGORICALLY THERE WERE NO AIRCRAFT, MACHINES, BALLOONS, OR ANYTHING ELSE AMERICAN USING ALGERIAN AIRSPACE WITHOUT EXPLICIT PERMISSION OF ALGERIAN AUTHORITIES. NEVERTHELESS, I WOULD IMMEDIATELY SEND MESSAGE TO APPROPRIATE CIVILIAN AND MILITARY AUTHORITIES ASKING IF THEY HAD ANY RELEVANT INFORMATION.

5. COMMENT: OUR 2447 REPORTED THAT MYSTERIOUS BALLOON HAD BEEN SIGHTED BY ALGERIANS NEAR ORAN JANUARY 25. THIS WAS EVIDENTLY FIRST SIGHTING OF OBJECT REFERRED TO IN TO-DAY'S CONVERSATION. WE HAVE NO OTHER DATA ON TIMES BUT ASSUME ALGERIANS CAN PROVIDE IF WE INTERESTED. LATRECHE IS NOT AN EXCITABLE PERSON AND ALGERIAN MILITARY ARE IN GENERAL PRETTY MATTER-OF-FACT. WE ASSUME THEY HAVE IN-DEED SEEN SOMETHING, BUT ASSUME IT WAS A NATURAL PHENOM-ENON OF SOME SORT WHICH HAS ENGENDERED A MILD HYSTERIA AND REPORTS OF REPEATED SIGHTINGS. GIVEN LEVEL AT WHICH QUERY MADE, WE MUST TAKE IT SERIOUSLY, HOWEVER.

6. ACTION REQUESTED: CAN ANY OF ADDRESSES SHED ANY LIGHT ON MATTER, AND PARTICULARLY ON ALLEGED RADAR SIGHTING MARCH 6? WOULD BE USEFUL TO HAVE SERIOUS REPLY TO GIVE TO LATRECHE. HE HAS ALREADY REJECTED MY THEORY THAT OB-JECT IS SATELLITE OR THAT IN CASE OF SIGHTING OFF COAST IT WAS SEARCHLIGHT BOUNCING OFF CLOUDS. PARKER

The UFOs in this report were seen by multiple witnesses. The objects landed and took off. They were also spotted on radar and seen visually simultaneously. Algerian authorities, after running out of explanations, contacted American military officials with the U.S. Sixth Fleet in the Mediterranean Sea and asked if they were responsible for the objects. The Algerians were informed that the Sixth Fleet had no aircraft of any kind in Algerian airspace.

This message contained many curious aspects, but in view of the fact that no more information was released by the State Department, it is not possible to speculate as to what the objects might have been. We are left with, literally, *unidentified* flying objects.

A confidential teletype, labeled 0294, Aug. 76, relates information about sightings in Tunisia.

SUBJ: TUNISIAN UFOS

1. (C) A VERY CONCERNED CHIEF OF MILITARY SECURITY, GENERAL BALMA, CALLED DATT AND ALUSNA TO HIS OFFICE AT 1100 HRS, 9 AUG 76. BALMA PROVIDED DATT WITH COPY OF MEMO HE HAD PRE-PARED FOR THE MINISTER OF DEFENSE LISTING UFO SIGHTINGS THAT HAVE BEEN OCCURRING OVER TUNISIA SINCE FIRST RE-PORTED THE NIGHT OF 3 AUG 76. ENGLISH TRANSLATION OF MEMO PROVIDED FOR INFO, QUOTE "SUBJECT: FLYING MACHINES. THE AP-PEARANCE OF UNEXPLAINED FLYING OBJECTS HAVE TAKEN PLACE AS FOLLOWS: DURING THE NIGHT OF 3–4 AUG 76—AT 2325 HRS THE PILOT OF TUNIS AIR FLT TU8953, ENROUTE FROM MONASTIR TO TUNIS REPORTED SIGHTING FLYING OBJECT AT 1000 TO 1200 METERS, GOING NORTH TO SOUTH. AT 2327 HOURS FIVE FLYING OBJECTS SHOWING RED AND GREEN POSITION LIGHTS WERE VISU-ALLY SIGHTED OVER MONASTIR AND CONFIRMED BY RADAR—AT 0024 HRS TILL 0400 HRS, FIVE SEPARATE RADAR RETURNS WERE TRACKED AND VISUALLY CONFIRMED. DURING THE NIGHT OF 4–5 AUG 76, AN AIR FRANCE PILOT ENROUTE TO MONASTIR REPORTED

BEING FOLLOWED BY AN AIRCRAFT AS HE APPROACHED HIS DE-
SCENT POINT TO MONASTIR FROM 2243 HRS TO 2252 HRS (LOCAL).
DURING THE NIGHT OF 5–6 AUG 76, POLICE AT SOUKRA REPORTED
SEEING WHAT SEEMED TO BE FOUR LIGHTED HELOS AT 0020 HRS.
AT 0040, TWO REMAINED—AT 0115, ONE REMAINED FLYING VERY
SLOWLY. ALL OBJECTS WERE GONE BY 0145 HRS (LOCAL). THESE
OBSERVATIONS NOT CONFIRMED BY RADAR. DURING THE NIGHT
OF 7–8 AUG 76, AT 2348 THE CONTROL TOWER AT JERBA SIGHTED
UNKNOWN TRAFFIC 7KM NW OF AIRPORT, SIGHTING CONFIRMED
BY TUNIS AIR PILOT, FLT 8321, ENROUTE TO JERBA FM PARIS. PILOT
OF TUNIS AIR 717 APPROACHING JERBA AIRPORT REPORTED A FLY-
ING OBJECT SHOWING ONE LIGHT SEEMED TO TOUCH DOWN NEAR
AIRPORT THEN TURN SOUTH CLIMBING AS IT WENT, DISAPPEARING
AT 2412 HRS (LOCAL). DURING NIGHT OF 8–9 AUG 76—AT 1950 HRS
LOCAL RADAR TRACKED UNKNOWN TRAFFIC THAT OVER FLEW SIDI
AHMED AIRPORT AT BILERTE GOING EAST TO WEST THEN 37 KM
WEST OF THE BASE TURNED AND DISAPPEARED GOING SOUTH"
END QUOTE 2. (C) THE TUNISIAN GOVERNMENT IS VERY PUZZLED
BY THESE SIGHTINGS AND WANTS TO KNOW IF SIXTH FLT CAN SHED
ANY LIGHT ON WHO OR WHAT THEY MIGHT BE. BALMA SHOWED
RADAR PLOTS OF UFO TRACKS ON NIGHT OF 4 AUG 76 PLOTTED
ON CHART. TRACKS COME GENERALLY FM NE OVER GULF OF TUNIS
AND THEN PROCEED TO SOUTH OF CITY, TURNING TO EAST AND
WEST AND DISAPPEARING FROM RADAR SCREENS. BALMA AGREED
TO CALL ALUSNA AT HOME IF FURTHER SIGHTINGS WERE OB-
SERVED. NO REPORTED SIGHTINGS MADE NIGHTS OF 9–10 AUG 76.
3. (C) REQUEST ADVISE IF ANY UNUSUAL ACTIVITY HAS BEEN NOTED
IN VICINITY OF TUNISIAN COAST. BALMA REPORTS THAT VISUAL
SIGHTINGS OF RED AND GREEN POSITION LIGHTS AND RADAR
SIGHTINGS HAVE BEEN MADE AND ON SOME OCCASIONS CORRE-
SPOND WITH ONE ANOTHER. OBJECTS HAVE TRAVELLED AT HIGH
SPEEDS (350KTS), SLOW, AND SEEMINGLY HOVERED BUT HAVE
MADE NO AUDIBLE SOUND. PHENOMENA COMPLETELY UNEXPLAINA-
BLE FM THIS END. ANY ASSIST OR IDEAS WILL BE APPRECIATED.
AMB CONCURS.

Again, in this report, no follow-up data has been made available. However,
the similarity to the Algerian incidents is striking. We have radar-visual
reports from the air and from the ground. The UFOs traveled at speeds
from slow to 350 knots, hovering at times, and, in at least one instance, a
UFO landed near Jerba Airport and took off again. To Tunisian authorities,
the UFO sightings were "completely unexplainable."

Just one month later, in Iran, one of the most sensational UFO incidents
in recent years took place. The first public indications that something extraordinary happened on September 19, 1976, appeared in the English language
Kayhan International, published in Tehran, Iran. It stated in the September
25 edition:

And now . . . the REAL story about that "UFO." Unfortunately, it's not
quite as exciting as the tales we've been hearing over the last day or

two about the bright light "thing" that allegedly had the audacity to chase two jets of the Imperial Iranian Air Force across Tehran.

Nevertheless, the true facts as outlined by an official source this week still have the ring of science fiction about them.

The source said individuals telephoned Mehrabad Airport's control tower to report a bright light in the night sky. Two jets were scrambled to investigate and one of the pilots reported seeing an object with a light so bright it illuminated the ground below. But the apparition soon disappeared and . . . that's it.

The pilot did not report seeing red, blue, and green flashing lights as the newspaper reports said. And, most emphatically, said the source, it did not switch round and chase the jets.

The newspaper reports also said that when the object came to within five kilometers of the jets, all electrical appliances on the aircraft went out of action, they lost radio contact with the ground and could not fire on the objects as they intended.

"Not so," said the official. "The pilots made no attempt to open fire, and at no time did the aircrafts' electronic gear fail to function."

And, since everything on the plane from controls to fuel pump is electronically operated, it's a little puzzling to figure out how the plane could possibly have kept in the air anyway.

The official summed it all up by saying the reports, which first appeared in afternoon papers this week, were "exaggerated." A reported verbatim conversation between Pilot "J" and ground control, in which he reported the different lights and the chase, left the official "frankly puzzled."

But he agreed that there was no apparent explanation for what the pilot DID see.

Judging from the newspaper report, the sighting amounted to nothing more than a light in the sky. Rumors of jet chases and electrical failures were "exaggerated," according to officials. But the rumors originated from the Iranian Air Force! What were the facts behind this confusion?

As a result of this kind of publicity, UFO researchers sprang into action. One individual, Charles Huffer, a teacher at the Berlin American High School in Germany, attempted to locate information from the files of the Secretary of Defense relating to the Iranian report. They denied this request in a July 5, 1977, letter. Huffer appealed the decision and finally obtained the release of a three-page message about the report on August 31, 1977, via the Defense Intelligence Agency (DIA). The details are fascinating.

This report forwards information concerning the sighting of a UFO in Iran on 19 September 1976.

A. At about 1230 A.M. on 19 Sep. 76 the (deleted) received four telephone calls from citizens living in the Shemiran area of Tehran saying that they had seen strange objects in the sky. Some reported a kind of bird-like object while others reported a helicopter with a light on. There were no helicopters airborne at that time.

After he told the citizens it was only stars and had talked to Mehrabad Tower, he decided to look for himself. He noticed an object in the sky similar to a star bigger and brighter. He decided to scramble an F-4 from Shahrokhi AFB to investigate.

B. At 0130 hrs on the 19th the F-4 took off and proceeded to a point about 40 NM north of Tehran. Due to its brilliance, the object was easily visible from 70 miles away. As the F-4 approached a range of 25 NM, he lost all instrumentation and communications (UHF and intercom). He broke off the intercept and headed back to Shahrokhi. When the F-4 turned away from the object and apparently was no longer a threat to it, the aircraft regained all instrumentation and communications. At 0140 hrs a second F-4 was launched. The backseater acquired a radar lock on at 27 NM 12 o'clock high position with the VC (rate of closure) at 150 NMPH. As the range decreased to 25 NM the object moved away at a speed that was visible on the radar scope and stayed at 25 NM.

C. The size of the radar return was comparable to that of a 707 tanker. The visual size of the object was difficult to discern because of its intense brilliance. The light that it gave off was that of flashing strobe lights arranged in a rectangular pattern and alternating blue, green, red, and orange in color. The sequence of the lights was so fast that all the colors could be seen at once. The object and the pursuing F-4 continued on a course to the south of Tehran when another brightly lighted object, estimated to be one-half to one-third the apparent size of the moon, came out of the original object. This second object headed straight toward the F-4 at a very fast rate of speed. The pilot attempted to fire an AIM-9 missile at the object but at that instant his weapons control panel went off and he lost all communications (UHF and interphone). At this point the pilot initiated a turn and negative G dive to get away. As he turned the object fell in trail at what appeared to be about 3–4 NM. As he continued in his turn away from the primary object the second object went to the inside of his turn then returned to the primary object for a perfect rejoin.

D. Shortly after the second object joined up with the primary object another object appeared to come out of the other side of the primary object going straight down at a great rate of speed. The F-4 crew had regained communications and the weapons control panel and watched the object approach the ground anticipating a large explosion. This object appeared to come to rest gently on the earth and cast a very bright light over an area of about 2–3 kilometers. The crew descended from their altitude of 25,000 to 15,000 and continued to observe and mark the object's position. They had some difficulty in adjusting their night visibility for landing, so after orbiting Mehrabad a few times they went out for a straight in landing. There was a lot of interference on the UHF and each time they passed through a mag. bearing of 150 degrees from Mehrabad they lost their communications (UHF and interphone) and the INS fluctuated from 30 degrees to 50 degrees. The one civil airliner that was approaching Mehrabad during this same time experienced communications failure in the same vicinity (Kilo Zulu) but did not report seeing anything. While the F-4 was on a long final approach the crew noticed another cylinder-shaped object (about the size of a T-bird at 10M) with bright steady lights on each end and a flasher in the middle. When queried the tower stated there was no other known traffic in the area. During the time that the object passed over the F-4 the tower did not have a visual on it but picked it up after the pilot told them to look between the mountains and the refinery.

E. During daylight the F-4 crew was taken out to the area in a helicopter where the object apparently had landed. Nothing was noticed at the spot where they thought the object landed (a dry lake bed) but as they circled off to the west of the area they picked up a very noticeable beeper signal. At the point where the return was the loudest was a small house with a garden. They landed and asked the people within if they had noticed anything strange last night. The people talked about a loud noise and a very bright light like lightning. The aircraft and area where the object is believed to have landed are being checked for possible radiation.

More information will be forwarded when it becomes available.

Equally as fascinating as the report itself was a form attached to the basic information given in the message. Titled, "Defense Information Report Evaluation," it was an assessment of the quality of the Iran sighting details as determined by the Defense Intelligence Agency, a military version of the CIA which deals with foreign military intelligence. The form indicated in checked boxes that the reliability of information was "Confirmed by other sources," that the value of information was "High (Unique, Timely, and of Major Significance)," and that the utility of information was "Potentially Useful." The form added in the "Remarks" section:

> An outstanding report. This case is a classic which meets all the criteria necessary for a valid study of the UFO phenomenon:
> a) The object was seen by multiple witnesses from different locations (i.e., Shamiran, Mehrabad, and the dry lake bed) and viewpoints (both airborne and from the ground).
> b) The credibility of many of the witnesses was high (an Air Force general, qualified aircrews, and experienced tower operators).
> c) Visual sightings were confirmed by radar.
> d) Similar electromagnetic effects (EME) were reported by three separate aircraft.
> e) There were physiological effects on some crew members (i.e., loss of night vision due to the brightness of the object).
> f) An inordinate amount of maneuverability was displayed by the UFOs.

Judging from the comments by the DIA, the Iranian UFO chase was undoubtedly one of the premier UFO encounters in the history of the subject. A highly advanced vehicle, performing well beyond our present-day capabilities, created fits for the American-equipped Iranian Air Force. That the blackouts of the missile firing control panel, just before the pilot was about to launch his air-to-air missile, could be attributed to a mechanical fault seems beyond what sheer odds would allow. That an instrumentation blackout should occur on *two separate F-4 aircraft* as they were chasing a UFO is even more unlikely. The incidents described are such that to merely dismiss the report as unsupportive of UFO reality, which we anticipate will happen from some quarters, borders on the absurd.

Unfortunately, as in many other sightings we've discussed, while it has been stated in the Iranian message that "more information will be forwarded when it becomes available," such information has not been made available to the public. Reliable sources within the government have told us that the Iranian case file was about one and a half inches thick, yet absolutely no admission to having this file has come from any government agency with a possible connection to the case.

Two more interesting details came to light. In the October 1, 1976, issue of the *Iran Times* from Washington, D.C., an apparent firsthand account from one of the pilots involved in the chase was published (based on a tape of the actual pursuit). It says:

> The tape of Imperial Air Force Lt. Jafari's reports to the control tower at Mehrabad airport was made available.
>
> The 23-year-old pilot told controllers that the UFO had doubled back on its pursuers, and he was in danger of being forced down.
>
> Jafari was piloting the first of two jet fighters which took off from Shahrokhi Air Base in Hamadan to investigate the object.
>
> The aircraft flew toward Tehran at over the speed of sound, and the pilot contacted Mehrabad control after he had made contact with the UFO. He said on seeing him coming, the UFO increased its speed.
>
> "It was half the size of the moon as seen from earth," he said. "It was radiating violet, orange, and white light about three times as strong as moonlight."
>
> Although the pilot was flying at maximum speed, he could not catch the UFO up.
>
> The control tower told the pilot to return to base if he was not able to get near. The pilot agreed to do so, but a moment later radioed, "Something is coming at me from behind. It is 15 miles away . . . now 10 miles . . . now 5 miles."
>
> "It is level now, I think it is going to crash into me. It has just passed by, missing me narrowly . . ."
>
> The disturbed voice of the pilot was clear on the tape. He then asked to be guided back to base.
>
> It was at this time that a second plane was ordered to take off. Flying over Shahre Rey, the pilot reported having seen the UFO and told the control tower that it had reduced speed.
>
> The pilot said the plane was working well and he was preparing to fire missiles at the UFO. After a moment's silence he said he had seen a "bright round object, with a circumference of about 4.5 meters, leave the UFO." A few seconds later the bright object joined the mother craft and it flew away at many times the speed of sound.
>
> The authenticity of the object, however, already confirmed by several control tower officials at Mehrabad and the two pilots, was further backed up Sunday night by eyewitness reports from the area. People in the vicinity reported having seen a "bright body" flit across the sky while others claimed to have seen "some bright thing" falling from the sky.

It was only in 1981 that the Air Force revealed another bit of information regarding the Iranian case. Requests for information on the sighting, directed to the National Security Agency (N.S.A.), revealed that an article written by a Captain Henry Shields was published in a periodical called the *MIJI Quarterly*. Published four times a year, the *MIJI Quarterly* contains narrative summaries of all "meaconing," "intrusion," and "jamming incidents" (therefore, MIJI) and is published by the Headquarters Electronic Security Command at San Antonio, Texas.

In case one may wonder, "meaconing" is a classified Air Force term and we cannot provide a definition for it.

Captain Shields' article, titled "Now You See It, Now You Don't," was included in the third quarter 1978 issue (then classified "Secret") and detailed the Iranian case in a three-page summary. The lead-in to the article is particularly interesting:

> Sometime in his career, each pilot can expect to encounter strange, unusual happenings which will never be adequately or entirely explained by logic or subsequent investigation. The following article recounts just such an episode as reported by two F-4 Phantom crews of the Imperial Iranian Air Force during late 1976. No additional information or explanation of the strange events has been forthcoming: the story will be filed away and probably forgotten, but it makes interesting, and possibly disturbing, reading.

The article basically recounted the details given in the message to the DIA.

Here we have an important endorsement for the anomalous nature of the sighting. It is very likely that a significant portion of what happened in the aftermath of the pilots' experiences has been highly classified, so high that even the author of the *MIJI Quarterly* article could not obtain further data regarding the landing.

The sighting in Iran was not all that occurred on the night of September 18 & 19. The American embassy in Rabat, Morocco, forwarded message 250801Z Sep. 76 to the State Department as follows:

Subject: Request for Info. Unidentified Flying Objects.

1. Yesterday, the 23rd of September . . . requested to see me at 1000 hours the same day. When he arrived . . . had sent him to discuss the sightings of unidentified flying objects (UFOs) over Morocco on the night of 18–19 September. According to . . . the Gendarmerie had received calls from Frog Agadir, the Marrakech Area, Casablanca, Rabat, Kenitra, and other areas reporting the sighting of UFOs between the hours of 0100 and 0130, the night of 18–19 September. Reports from these widely separate locations were remarkably similar, i.e., that the object was on a generally southwest to northeast course, it was a silvery luminous circular shape and gave off intermittent trails of bright sparks and fragments. And made no noise. He promised to provide further details today, the 24th of September, and asked that we furnish any information that we might have on these sightings.

I promised that we would do what we could.

2. Today, the 24th. A . . . met with Datt and gave him a summary of the sightings. . . . also permitted Datt to look at drawings of the UFO prepared by various individuals, including himself, who had sighted the UFO.

3. The times of the sightings varied from 0100 to 0200 hours on the morning of 19 September. With the majority of them occurring between 0100 and 0130 hours. Sightings were reported from Agadir Kalaa-Sraghna, Essaouira, Casablanca, Rabat, Kenitra, Mfknes, and the Fex region. There was general agreement that the UFO was proceeding on an approximately south to north course. Generally parallel to the Moroccan Atlantic Coast, at an estimated altitude of 1,000 meters, and that there was absolutely no sound from the UFO.

4. Descriptions of the UFO fell into two general categories, i.e., a type of silver-colored luminous flattened (illegible) disc-shaped, or a large luminous tube-shaped object. Observers reported that the object intermittently emitted bright sparks from the rear.

5. . . . said he was sent to brief Datt on the subject because he had himself sighted the UFO while returning from the city of Kenitra at about 0115 in the morning. He described the UFO as flying parallel to the coast at a relative slow speed as if it were an aircraft preparing to land. It first appeared to him as a disc-shaped object, but as it came closer he saw it as a luminous tubular-shaped object.

6. I frankly do not know what to make of these sightings, although I find intriguing the similarity of descriptions reported from widely dispersed locations. In any event, I wish to be able to respond promptly to . . . request for information. And would appreciate anything you can do to assist me in this. Anderson.

After a delay in responding to the embassy's request for information, Secretary of State Henry Kissinger provided the following in message 052041Z Oct. 76:

1. IT IS DIFFICULT TO OFFER ANY DEFINITIVE EXPLANATION AS TO THE CAUSE OR ORIGIN OF THE UFOS SIGHTED IN THE MOROCCAN AREA BETWEEN 0100 AND 0130 LOCAL TIME 19 SEPTEMBER 1976.

2. AN EXTENSIVE INVESTIGATION OF THIS SUBJECT WAS MADE IN THE US IN 1969: *SCIENTIFIC STUDY OF UNIDENTIFIED FLYING OBJECTS,* E. U. CONDON. PUBLISHED BY BANTAM BOOKS. NEW YORK. THIS STUDY INDICATES THAT DETAILED SIGHTINGS OF UFOS BY RELIABLE WITNESSES CAN BE EXPLAINED IN MANY WAYS, E.G.: IN TERMS OF LOCAL BALLOON, AIRCRAFT, OR SATELLITE ACTIVITY; BY METEOROLOGICAL AND ATMOSPHERIC CONDITIONS, INCLUDING METEOR EVENTS; AND BY ASTRONOMICAL OBJECTS.

3. THE USG IS UNAWARE OF ANY US AIRCRAFT OR SATELLITE ACTIVITY, EITHER MILITARY OR CIVILIAN, IN THE MOROCCAN AREA WHICH MIGHT HAVE BEEN MISTAKEN FOR SUCH SIGHTINGS ON THE 19 SEPTEMBER 1976. THIS DOES NOT PRECLUDE AIRCRAFT FLIGHTS OF OTHER COUNTRIES OR UNUSUAL ATMOSPHERIC CONDITIONS OR EVENTS AS A POSSIBLE CAUSE.

4. THE WHOLE SUBJECT OF UFOS HAS BEEN ONE OF MUCH CON-TROVERSY. AT PRESENT, THERE IS NO USG AGENCY STUDYING THIS MATTER, THE VIEW BEING THAT SUCH SIGHTINGS, WHERE SUFFI-CIENTLY DETAILED AND RELIABLE DATA ARE AVAILABLE, CAN BE ATTRIBUTED TO NATURAL CAUSES AND THAT FURTHER STUDY IS NOT WARRANTED.

5. ALTHOUGH THERE IS NO MAJOR METEOR SHOWER IN SEPTEM-BER, THE SPORADIC METEOR RATE IN THE NORTHERN HEMISPHERE IS AT A MAXIMUM IN THE EARLY MORNING AND IN THE AUTUMN MONTHS. BUT, METEORS ARE USUALLY VISIBLE AT AN ALTITUDE AROUND 100 KM, NOT 1 KM. HOWEVER, SUBJECTIVE ESTIMATES OF THE HEIGHT OF SUCH SIGHTINGS ARE USUALLY TOO LOW. THE FLAT TRAJECTORY SW TO NE COULD CONCEIVABLY BE COMPATIBLE WITH A METEOR, OR DECAYING SATELLITE. TANGENTIAL TRAJECTO-RIES ARE NOT THE MOST LIKELY FOR METEORS, BUT ARE NOT IM-POSSIBLE. IT IS UNLIKELY FROM THE DESCRIPTION THAT THE EVENT COULD HAVE BEEN A REFLECTION FROM A POLAR ORBITING SATEL-LITE.

6. WE ARE CHECKING FURTHER WHETHER OR NOT THIS PHENOME-NON WAS SIGHTED BY THE SMITHSONIAN ASTROPHYSICAL OBSER-VATORY'S GROUND STATION IN SOUTHERN SPAIN. THE CONTACT AT THE SAO, CAMBRIDGE, MASS. IS JAMES CORNELL, PHONE 617-495-7461.

7. IF THIS EVENT WERE A METEOR, A COMPARABLE SIGHTING IN THE US WOULD BE THE ALBERTA FIREBALL OF AUGUST 1972 WHICH TRAVELED S TO N FROM LAS VEGAS, NEVADA, USA TO EDMONTON, ALBERTA, CANADA AND WAS ROUGHLY TANGENTIAL TO THE EARTH'S SURFACE, ITS LOWEST POINT IN ALTITUDE BEING ABOUT 40 KM. THIS WAS A VERY STRIKING OCCURRENCE AND ONE IN WHICH THE METEOR SEEMS TO HAVE ENTERED AND THEN LEFT THE ATMO-SPHERE.

8. IN ORDER TO ANALYZE THE MOROCCAN EVENT THOROUGHLY, FURTHER DESCRIPTIONS OR PHOTOGRAPHS FROM THE LOCAL AREA WOULD BE NEEDED. IN THE MEANTIME, ONE WOULD TEND TO BELIEVE THAT THE EVENT WAS A METEOR, AND PROBABLY A SPECTACULAR ONE, OR ON ACCOUNT OF THE DESCRIPTION OF SLOW VELOCITY, NO NOISE, AND BURNING FRAMENTS, A DECAYING SATELLITE PART, OF WHICH THERE IS NO PRECISE RE-ENTRY RECORD. KISSINGER.

Kissinger's response followed the official U.S. policy line on UFOs. It's likely that the reason for the delay in Kissinger's reply to the embassy was due to the fact that he probably required a briefing on the UFO subject. This briefing would have come from the Air Force, which almost certainly had supplied the information on the Condon Report and its negative conclusions on UFOs.

Is it impossible for a bright meteor to have been responsible for the sightings? Not really, if one examines the information very generally. A silvery, luminous object giving off a bright trail and sparks is not unlike a description of a meteor. However, the sightings were reported over a span of about an hour. The UFO, according to some witnesses, traveled at a slow speed, like an aircraft about to land. And the southwest to northeast course of the UFO would have brought it in the general direction of Iran, where other UFO activity was ongoing. Coincidence?

An outburst of reports from 1978 dominated the State Department's information on UFOs that has been released.

Back in Iran, a July 1978 message from the U.S. Defense Attaché's Office in Tehran said:

1. Details: The following information is quoted from the 10 July '78 edition of the *Tehran Journal* newspaper:

"UFO SPOTTED OVER NORTH OF TEHRAN"

Tehran—An unidentified flying object was seen by a number of people in the Northern part of the city on Sunday night. Officials from the control tower at Mehrabad Airport and a Lufthansa Aircrew also reported unusual readings on their instruments. Residents in northern Tehran were the first to spot the strange glowing object floating towards Daveh. They had been sleeping on the terraces of their houses, and immediately informed the control tower at Mehrabad Airport and the National Radio Network. The control tower confirmed the existence of the object but would give no further details. Soon afterwards, the Lufthansa plane sent in its report.

Similar flying object was seen last April by local airline pilot, who claimed that he had photographed the object, but could not release the photographs until the security division of the civil aviation authorities gave their permission. He claimed that while flying between Ahvaz and Tehran at (illegible) feet, he and his co-pilot had sighted a glittering object and had managed to photograph it.

Mehrabad radar control official said that on that occasion they had detected an object some 20 times the size of a jumbo jet on their screens.

Civil aviation organization chief Haj Moniti called for an investigation, but the results of this inquiry have not yet been made public. An eyewitness said yesterday that he was alone on his balcony on Sunday night when suddenly he saw the object emerge in the sky and hover directly above him.

"I was so upset that I wanted to scream, but could not do so," he said. He added that he felt better once he realized that his neighbors had also seen it.

This current report is the third UFO sighting in Iran in less than a year.

This message referred to another incident involving a photograph of a UFO. A newspaper report from the *Kayhan International* for June 28, 1978, stated that sixteen-year-old Jamshid Saiadispour photographed a disc-shaped UFO with three portholes in the Shiraz area of Iran. The youth claimed it was the second time that he had seen UFOs in a one-month period. Again, the intelligence report containing the news story promised additional information which is not currently available.

The government of Kuwait was thrust into the UFO picture with an incident from one of its oil fields. Message 290606Z, Jan. '79, from the American embassy in Kuwait City to the State Department discusses the events.

SUBJECT: UFO SIGHTINGS CAUSE SECURITY CONCERN IN KUWAIT

1. A series of UFO sightings on November 9 caused the GOK to appoint an investigatory committee of experts from the Kuwait Institute for Scientific Research (KISR). The committee's report which was released January 20 described eight sightings from November to December 14. A number of the early sightings took place near a Kuwait oil company gathering center north of Kuwait City. Release of the committee's report was something of a media event as it coincided with Jan. 21 front page stories of yet another UFO sighting over Kuwait City, which included photographs in local newspapers.

2. The KISR committee rejected the notion that the UFOs were espionage devices but remained equivocal about whether they were of extraterrestrial origin. The KISR committee representative, Ratib Abu Id, told Emboff that the scientists did not know enough about the phenomena to say with certainty that they weren't spaceships. The report went on to recommend that the government take all possible measures to protect Kuwait's airspace and territory as well as the country's oil resources.

3. Some local wags have made light of the first UFO sightings which came near the end of the long and traditionally exuberant holiday celebrations of Id Al Adha. However, we have learned recently of an event coincident with one of the UFO sightings which has confounded some of our most level-headed Kuwaiti friends and may have been what persuaded the GOK to make a serious investigation of the matter. A senior Kuwait Oil Company (KOC) official told us the UFO which first appeared over the northern oil fields seemingly did strange things to KOC's automatic pumping equipment. This equipment is designed to shut itself down when there is some failure which may seriously damage the petroleum gathering and transmission system, and it can only be restarted manually. At the time of the UFO's appearance, the pumping system automatically shut itself down and when the UFO vanished, the system started itself up again. This event was not addressed by the KISR committee report.

4. Even those who are not inclined to believe in visitors from outer space do tend to think something strange has been going on in Kuwaiti airspace. There has been speculation, for example, about helicopters or hovercraft bringing refugees or money out of beleaguered Iran. At the least, the phenomena have stimulated a new degree of interest among top Kuwaiti officials in the country's air defense system which did not react in any way to the "events" in the KOC north field because it was closed down. Maestrone.

Though it didn't seem likely that the KISR Committee Report mentioned in the message would be available, several requests were filed by UFO researchers with the Kuwait Institute for Scientific Research for copies of the report. As expected, the KISR denied all such requests, stating that the report was "confidential" and, if this status changed, the report would be released. It hasn't been, to date.

When we filed for a copy of the Kuwait message, we asked for any subsequent information relevant to the case. While no follow-up data on the 1978 reports appeared, a completely new incident was forwarded to us. This sighting, in message 080805Z July '80, states:

> According to . . . is investigating report by Senior Kuwait Airways pilot of an unusual "light phenomenon" on June 22, 1980. The pilot operations director H. Shamlan said that during descent through approximately 15,000 ft and before reaching Wafra Vor, while operating flight number KU542 from Cairo to Kuwait, "The crew and I sighted a huge ball of bright light shaped like a hemisphere (half a moon shape) estimated diameter to be around ten miles, with the flat base of the sphere approximately the same level as the aircraft, i.e., 15,000 ft.
>
> "Its position was northwest of the city of Kuwait and steadily moving eastbound at a slightly lesser speed than my aircraft which was 320 knots at that state.
>
> "When I turned north at Wafra the phenomenon was still clearly visible and remained so until we descended below the haze layer and started approach to the runway.
>
> "The crew of flight KU 708 who were 20 miles away from Kuwait reported sighting the same phenomenon. My sighting and the KU 705 sighting were reported to Kuwait Centre who could not pick up any trace of it on their radar. Neither could we pick it up on our weather radar.
>
> Though a time for the sighting was not given, it must have been close to 2100 hours local time, assuming both flights were on time. KU542 was scheduled to have arrived at Kuwait International Airport from Cairo at 2112 hours, while KU708 was due in from Khartoum at 2055 hours.
>
> "Above report is reminiscent of Reftel's report of January, 1979 and November, 1978 on UFO sightings in Kuwait's skies. According to senior KOC official, UFO which appeared over northern oil fields in November 1978 did strange things to KOC's pumping system. Some wags are blaming current Kuwait electric power failures (see Kuwait 3220) on UFOs.
>
> Adom, who knows operations director Shamlan, assesses him as levelheaded competent individual, who almost certainly reported accurately upon what he observed this past June. . . . Interviews with inhabitants of Wafra Area (also an oil collection center) have not yet produced anyone who admits seeing the phenomenon. Dickman.

Ten miles in diameter! Even for a UFO, it's unbelievable! Yet no other information is offered as an explanation for this sighting. The huge object traveled at a slightly lesser speed than the jet, was regularly shaped and brightly lit. The only possible thing that could remotely approach this size would be a cloud layer, but it is difficult to imagine a cloud appearing and performing the way this object did.

Another interesting pilot report came from the Italian government.

Italy's military, in response to UFO researchers' requests, released small amounts of information in the late 1970s, perhaps to allay public concern over several bursts of UFO activity. This transcript of a conversation between Flight IH662 and "Minimum Two Control" in Milan involves a sighting on March 9, 1978:

7:41 P.M./z
PLANE: As a point of reference, we're the IH662, at an altitude of 2,600 feet, and on our right we have, that is, it has appeared here like a . . .
MILAN: UFO.
PLANE: No UFO. No, let's say a green rocket but for purposes of signaling, it's a little bit high or low depending on your point of view.
MILAN: Received 622, and what is your distance from Florence?
PLANE: We're 75 miles from Florence at 2,600 feet.
MILAN: 75 miles from Florence?
PLANE: I beg your pardon, 75 miles inbound to Vicenza.
MILAN: Received.
PLANE: However, this happened about a mile on our right and the phenomenon was intense enough.
MILAN: Received but you don't see anything now?
PLANE: Ah! Have they disappointed you?
MILAN: 662 from Milan, the phenomenon is finished?
PLANE: Could you repeat that?
MILAN: The phenomenon you saw about a minute ago, is it finished?
PLANE: It's finished, it's finished, yes.
MILAN: Then if you can, give a fast report on it on frequency 133.7.
7:43 P.M./z
MILAN: IH662 Milan.
PLANE: Excuse the error.
MILAN: 662, are you there?
PLANE: Yes, affirmative.
MILAN: Very good, then if you have a minute, you can talk with landing control on the other set about the sighting so we can write it down.
PLANE: All right, but I bet you'll be biting your tongue, after a minute. At 2,600 ft., 75 miles inbound to Vicenza, there appeared on our right something lit up like a green rocket, similar to the type the tower sends up to tell us we have to land, but very luminous and a mile off. That's it.
MILAN: Perfect, IH662, we copied you perfectly, and we can confirm, in any case, that at your position and altitude there was no plane within 40 miles of you and therefore, you were really alone from the point of view of the AT.
PLANE: Now we can tell you, there was a thought that it could have been a back burner (as of a jet) because it had the same kind of intensity but there being no airplanes in flight, we don't know what it could have been. It might be a meteorite or anything else, but I doubt it would make a flare of that kind at 2,600 feet; in other words, it was very bright.
MILAN: Perfect and the news is encouraging to us because we can corroborate by official channels that there is no other plane.

PLANE: Wonderful, I don't know what to say. Wonderful. We thank you and good night.

MILAN: Attention, attention, we have some more news for you. There's a Malta Airways plane on Ancona that just saw it.

PLANE: A Malta Airways that has seen it, then . . .

MILAN: It's something strange that is moving now in the direction we were talking about . . . also, a third, a fourth plane are seeing now in the Ancona zone, in the Ancona zone the same thing you saw.

PLANE: In that case, make sure we verify it for you because I have the impression that they just made a pass over us and then made a counter thrust. I didn't say anything before because I didn't want anyone to think I was crazy.

MILAN: No, no, the news is corroborated now. Other planes in the Ancona zone are reporting a green flash, some beneath them, others report it 15 miles away from them.

PLANE: Ours was very close, a little too close.

MILAN: Excellent, we thank you, we're making a note and would appreciate your doing the same, thanks.

PLANE: O.K., as a point of information, my name is Luciano Ascione, if anyone is interested. 662IH. Good night.

One of the more well-publicized reports outside the U.S. was the tragic encounter between Frederick Valentich, a twenty-year-old pilot, and a UFO on October 21, 1978. The story has been extensively covered in newspapers and periodicals since that time, but, for our purposes, we will discuss what the Australian government said, on an *official* basis, about the sighting.

In 1982, the Commonwealth of Australia's Department of Transport issued an "Aircraft Accident Investigation Summary Report" as its statement on the affair. In its statement of relevant events, the report, dated April 27, 1982, says:

The pilot obtained a Class Four instrument rating on 11 May 1978 and he was therefore authorized to operate at night in visual meteorological conditions (VMC). On the afternoon of 21 October, 1978 he attended the Moorabbin Briefing Office, obtained a meteorological briefing and, at 1723 hours, submitted a flight plan for a night VMC flight from Moorabbin to King Island and return. The cruising altitude nominated in the flight plan was below 5000 feet, with estimated time intervals of 41 minutes to Cape Otway and 28 minutes from Cape Otway to King Island. The total fuel endurance was shown as 300 minutes. The pilot made no arrangements for aerodrome lighting to be illuminated for his arrival at King Island. He advised the briefing officer and the operator's representative that he was uplifting friends at King Island and took four life jackets in the aircraft with him.

The aircraft was refueled to capacity at 1810 hours and departed Moorabbin at 1819 hours. After departure the pilot established two-way radio communications with Melbourne Flight Service Unit (FSU).

The pilot reported Cape Otway at 1900 hours and the next transmission received from the aircraft was at 1906:14 hours. The following communications between the aircraft and Melbourne FSU were recorded from this

time. (Note: The word/words in parentheses are open to other interpretations).

TIME	*FROM*	*TEXT*
1906:14	VH DSJ	MELBOURNE this is DELTA SIERRA JULIET is there any known traffic below five thousand
:23	FSU	DELTA SIERRA JULIET no known traffic
:26	VH-DSJ	DELTA SIERRA JULIET I am seems (to) be a large aircraft below five thousand
:46	FSU	DELTA SIERRA JULIET what type of aircraft is it
:50	VH-DSJ	DELTA SIERRA JULIET I cannot affirm it is four bright it seems to me like landing lights
1907:04	FSU	DELTA SIERRA JULIET
:32	VH-DSJ	MELBOURNE this (is) DELTA SIERRA JULIET the aircraft has just passed over me at least a thousand feet above
:43	FSU	DELTA SIERRA JULIET roger and it, it is a large aircraft confirm
:47	VH-DSJ	er unknown due to the speed it's traveling is there any airforce aircraft in the vicinity
:57	FSU	DELTA SIERRA JULIET no known aircraft in the vicinity
1908:18	VH-DSJ	MELBOURNE it's approaching now from due east towards me
:25	FSU	DELTA SIERRA JULIET
:42		// open microphone for two seconds//
:49	VH-DSJ	DELTA SIERRA JULIET it seems to me that he's playing some sort of game he's flying over me two three times at speeds I could not identify
1909:02	FSU	DELTA SIERRA JULIET, roger what is your actual level
:06	VH-DSJ	my level is four and a half thousand four five zero zero
:11	FSU	DELTA SIERRA JULIET and confirm you cannot identify the aircraft
:14	VH-DSJ	affirmative
:18	FSU	DELTA SIERRA JULIET roger standby
:28	VH-DSJ	MELBOURNE DELTA SIERRA JULIET it's not an aircraft it is//open microphone for two seconds//
:46	FSU	DELTA SIERRA JULIET MELBOURNE can you describe the er aircraft
1909:52	VH-DSJ	DELTA SIERRA JULIET as it's flying past it's a long shape // open microphone for three seconds// (cannot) identify more than (that it has such speed) // open microphone for 3 seconds// before me right now Melbourne
1910:07	FSU	DELTA SIERRA JULIET roger and how large would the er object be
:20	VH-DSJ	DELTA SIERRA JULIET MELBOURNE it seems like it's stationary what I'm doing right now is orbiting and the thing

TIME	FROM	TEXT
		is just orbiting on top of me also it's got a green light and sort of metallic (like) it's all shiny (on) the outside
:43	FSU	DELTA SIERRA JULIET
:48	VH-DSJ	DELTA SIERRA JULIET// open microphone for 5 seconds //it's just vanished
:57	FSU	DELTA SIERRA JULIET
1911:03	VH-DSJ	MELBOURNE would you know what kind of aircraft I've got is it (a type) military aircraft
:09	FSU	DELTA SIERRA JULIET confirm the er aircraft just vanished
:14	VH-DSJ	SAY AGAIN
:17	FSU	DELTA SIERRA JULIET is the aircraft still with you
:23	VH-DSJ	DELTA SIERRA JULIET (it's ah nor)//open microphone for 2 seconds// (now) approaching from the southwest
:37	FSU	DELTA SIERRA JULIET
:52	VH-DSJ	DELTA SIERRA JULIET the engine is is rough idling I've got it set at twenty three twenty four and the thing is (coughing)
1912:04	FSU	DELTA SIERRA JULIET roger what are your intentions
:09	VH-DSJ	my intentions are ah to go to King Island ah Melbourne that strange aircraft is hovering on top of me again // two seconds open microphone// it is hovering and it's not an aircraft
:22	FSU	DELTA SIERRA JULIET
:28	VH-DSJ	DELTA SIERRA JULIET MELBOURNE // 17 seconds open microphone//
:49	FSU	DELTA SIERRA JULIET MELBOURNE

There is no record of any further transmissions from the aircraft.

The weather in the Cape Otway area was clear with a trace of stratocumulus cloud at 5,000 to 7,000 feet, scattered cirrus cloud at 30,000 feet, excellent visibility, and light winds. The end of daylight at Cape Otway was at 1918 hours.

The Alert Phase of SAR procedures was declared at 1912 hours and, at 1933 hours when the aircraft did not arrive at King Island, the Distress Phase was declared and search action was commenced. An intensive air, sea, and land search was continued until 25 October 1978, but no trace of the aircraft was found.

OPINION AS TO CAUSE

The reason for the disappearance of the aircraft has not been determined.

So, no reason for the disappearance could be determined. The plane and pilot were never found. The circumstances are reminiscent of the jet crash incidents discussed in Chapter 5, but in this case, the involvement of the UFO is much more clearly defined. The pilot had a good look at it and described it in a recorded conversation. While we can't say for certain that the UFO caused the plane's disappearance by either abducting the pilot or shooting him down, it obviously upset the pilot to such a degree that, at the very least, we can say the UFO played a major role in the events that led to his apparent death.

Isn't this a compelling argument for serious, unbiased, government-funded investigations of UFOs? Or maybe the "powers that be" just don't care. We would like to think that the latter is not the case and that such investigations do go on away from the public eye.

Just over our own border, in Canada, a most unusual phenomenon literally burst upon residents of Bell Island, Newfoundland, on April 2, 1978. Bell Island is one of the Grey Islands group located due east within sight of the coastal town of Englee.

According to press reports and as subsequently reported in several issues of the *Res Bureau Bulletin,* a now defunct newsletter on unusual phenomena, the island was suddenly and mysteriously rocked by a tremendous explosion. One resident, Jim Bickford, stated, "My son, I can't tell you what happened. I heard a racket, that's all I can call it, a racket. This thing broke over the house. I've worked in mines and we shot 300 plugs of powder at one time, and there was never a racket like that." Bickford's television was destroyed and his telephone was blown off the wall by what must have been a massive surge of electrical power. Yet there was no evidence of a lightning strike or burn marks anywhere.

Other residents reported varying degrees of damage. Several chickens were killed, smoke was rising from the woods nearby, and one resident said her oven "sparked." Electrical outlets were blown off the walls in some homes. A report was received of not one, but three, explosions followed by earth tremors.

Witnesses outside at the time of the event said they saw balls of fire in the sky descending over the island along with "streaks of super bright silvery-white light." One resident found three circular holes arranged in triangular formation pressed into the snow about a foot and a half deep.

Immediately, officials attempted to explain what had happened. The causes ranged from the Concorde SST to lightning hitting an island transformer to ball lighting. However, when the weather bureau was contacted, they stated that there was no unusual atmospheric activity at the time of the explosion. Interestingly, the Bell Island blast occurred just after a period of intense, open air acoustic activity along the east coasts of the U.S. and Canada. According to a publication released by the Naval Research Laboratory in Washington titled *NRL Investigations of East Coast Acoustic Events, 2 December, 1977–15 February, 1978,* nearly 200 aerial explosions were noted between November 28, 1977, and January 16, 1978, from the records of the Western (Mass.) Observatory alone! Many of the events could be attributed to sonic booms by aircraft, but many others were not identified. The Bell Island flash was certainly one of the most dramatic events of this type.

The story does not end here, though. According to the Center for

Defense Information in Washington, D.C., the event was picked up by an American Vela satellite. The Vela satellite system is designed to detect nuclear explosions as a means of monitoring whether current restrictions on atmospheric nuclear tests are being obeyed. It also allows the U.S. to keep track of testing by nations not covered in the 1963 Nuclear Test Ban Treaty. The Bell Island flash was of such intensity that the event registered as a "potential nuclear blast" on the satellite's detection system.

Additionally, the April 10 *St. John's Evening Telegram* (Newfoundland) reported that within a day after the blast, two military attaches from a defense facility in Los Alamos, California (it was probably Los Alamitos, since Los Alamos is in New Mexico), arrived in St. John's on their way to Bell Island. They inspected the damage and left without attracting attention. The paper, two days later, identified the men as simply "Freyman and Warren" and stated that they were there at Bell Island in the hope of developing a death-ray-type weapon. A rather curious reason, to be sure, but in the United States, research and development is in progress to perfect laser satellite weapons and particle beam generators as a defense against nuclear attack. Could the two defense attaches have been at Bell Island to inspect the results of an experiment gone crazy? Or could they have gone to get new ideas from a truly mysterious event?

We attempted to get answers through the Freedom of Information Act. Requests were initiated for listings of anomalous events detected by Vela satellites, including the Bell Island event. The requests went through a number of Air Force groups, with each group thinking that the other had the information requested. On June 10, 1980, Barry Greenwood received a call from a Lt. Col. Philiber in Washington, D.C., requesting specific times on the events. The Bell Island report we had available did not contain the exact moment of the event so this could not be provided. Philiber, after hearing specifics about Bell Island, suggested that it was a "superbolt" of lightning and nothing more.

What about superbolts of lightning? Such phenomena have been reported by scientists studying the planet Jupiter via the Voyager space probe. Intensely bright lightning strobes were photographed from thousands of miles out in space on the dark side of Jupiter. Clearly, there is a precedent for lightning superbolts. Why couldn't this explain what happened at Bell Island?

Several things come to mind. The weather bureau reported nothing unusual about the weather patterns over Bell Island at the time of the incident. The atmosphere of Jupiter is turbulent and extremely dynamic, the type of conditions under which one might expect active electrical discharges in the open air. Also, in previous suspected cases of superbolts, no damage occurred; only loud booms and light flashes were reported. The report of a triangular formation of marks in the snow on Bell Island is reminiscent of UFO landings, though we do not know whether there was an object sighted in that particular area.

After a few more weeks, the final answer to the FOIA letter was given by Major General John Marks, Air Force Assistant Chief of Staff, Intelligence on July 28, 1980. The only event answerable to the request for Vela records was a flash detected off South Africa on September 22, 1979. The data existed *only* for this event, not Bell Island or any of the others, even though the source of several of the events was the Naval Research Laboratory's acoustic event report previously cited. And it was stated that the events were Vela events!

The South African flash, itself, is still quite controversial. An *Ad Hoc Panel Report on the September 22 Event* was issued by the White House in July 1980 discussing the Vela detection of the South African flash. The panel did not say specifically what the event was, but it did say that it was not a nuclear blast. Other military sources disagreed with this assessment and opinion today is still divided.

Besides this, the report referred to the fact that the light sensors on the Vela satellite systems "have been triggered several hundred times by signals of *unknown* origin, *zoo events* [emphasis added]!"

Zoo events? We now have another synonym for UFO. In this case, the UFO is an "unidentified *flashing* object," bright enough to be seen from space. How many UFO sightings might have been picked up by the Vela light sensors that we don't know about? It would certainly explain the government's reluctance to release listings of "zoo events" like Bell Island. The dates and places could be correlated with actual sighting reports by surface observers, and we would then have *scientific confirmation* from *government sources* that a true UFO incident took place. It would be very difficult to explain away.

Therefore, it seems unlikely that much more will be heard about Bell Island and the other "zoo events." But it does provide one more nail in the coffin of official secrecy on the UFO phenomenon.

CHAPTER SEVEN
Mystery Helicopters

In previous chapters, we have seen many examples of eyewitness reports that describe UFOs as sounding like helicopters and exhibiting lighting patterns that resemble a helicopter's lighting arrangement. The objects hovered or landed within the confines of military bases, yet none of the aircraft were ever positively identified. We believe that a strong case has been made that, in a *majority* of the more detailed reports we have covered, the objects were not helicopters.

It would be foolish to rule out a helicopter in *all* situations, however; some of the sightings are best explained as probable helicopters. Yet, we are still left with a problem. Where do they come from? Who is in them?

The military base sightings obviously involve a combination of UFOs and what we can only call "mystery helicopters." Not only do they play an important part in the military base reports, but they figure prominently in cattle mutilation incidents which have already been discussed in Chapter 3.

The connection between helicopters, UFOs, and mutilations is becoming more distinct, but what is the ultimate purpose behind this seemingly incongruous association?

To explore the mystery helicopter story, we will take a few steps back and look to an expert on the helicopter/mutilation story for an explanation of this offshoot of the UFO phenomenon.

Tom Adams, head of Project Stigma (P.O. Box 1094, Paris, Texas 75460), has spent the better part of the last decade trying to fathom the disturbing cattle mutilation occurrences. In his group's periodical, *Stigmata,* Adams presents reports and analyses of mutilations and other mysterious events which could shed light on the cause for this relatively new and growing trend.

While reports of UFOs and animal mutilations occurred sporadically over the years, it wasn't until 1975 that the events increased dramatically to epidemic proportions. Adams observed the situation closely and found that large numbers of helicopters were being seen by ranchers, police officers, and others. The following accounts are taken from *The Choppers and the Choppers: Mystery Helicopters and Animal Mutilations* (privately published by Tom Adams).

OCTOBER 1975

On Oct 2, 1975, Thursday, beginning at 8:00 P.M., Colorado, Baca County—An unidentified helicopter was observed as it flew around in an area near Campo for 1½ hours.

Oct. 3rd, Friday, at 11:00 A.M., Colorado, Baca County—Two choppers fly over grazing lands.

Oct. 4th, Saturday, at 9:00 P.M., Colorado, Baca County—Two helicopters fly over Laverne Jenkins' property, where a mutilated cow has been found this date (dead perhaps 3–5 days).

Oct. 5th, Sunday, 3:00 A.M., Colorado, Alamosa County—A helicopter with a bright searchlight was seen and chased NE of Alamosa by Under-sheriff Barney Bauer and Deputy Bill Lobato. A similar helicopter was seen SE of Alamosa, moving east with a bright light shining off and on.

Oct. 6th, Monday, 8:00 P.M., Colorado, Costilla County—A helicopter with red and green blinking lights was seen landing on a mountain SE of San Luis. A mutilated cow was discovered in the same area on 10/7/75.

Oct. 7th, Tuesday, Colorado, El Paso County—A UH-1 "Huey helicopter" crashed in a remote area of the Fort Carson Military Reservation, killing five men and injuring five. Speculation was that high winds in the area may have caused the crash, but public information officer, Major Arne Anderson, refused to speculate on the cause or to release any information on the investigation. However, Lt. Col. S. K. Fisk told the *Denver Post* that the cause of the crash was considered to be "unknown."

Oct. 7th, Tuesday, P.M., Colorado, Baca County—Two reports of helicopters flying low over ranches were called in to sheriff's office.

Oct. 8th, Wednesday, early A.M., Colorado, Baca County—Gloria Claunch saw, through binoculars, a helicopter shining a light on the ground, illuminating what she thought were two men.

Oct. 8th, Wednesday, 7:00 P.M., Colorado, Costilla Country— A low-flying helicopter with a bright red light was seen by several witnesses.

Oct. 9th, Thursday night, Colorado, Costilla County—Deputies watched a helicopter land and remain on the ground three minutes before taking off. Two "fresh" mutilations were discovered in the area this date.

Week of October 5th through 9th, Colorado (Alamosa County)—Under-Sheriff Barnery Bauer reported that unidentified helicopters were seen all over the county between 10:30 P.M. and 3:00 A.M. each night. Some high-flying craft with regulation lights were seen, as well as others flying low without lights. Helicopters were sometimes reported with bright searchlights here and in adjoining Costilla County. This light was frequently described by witnesses as "very, very powerful."

October, first half, Wyoming (Uinta County)—Late one afternoon during this period, at the height of the mutilation furor in Uinta County, a reserve lawman engaged in a shootout with an aggressive mystery helicopter.

October 11th, Saturday, (daylight), Montana (Cascade County)—A woman reported seeing a black helicopter without markings flying from east to west. The bubble on the front was tinted dark and the witness could not see inside.

Oct. 13th or 14th (Monday or Tuesday), Colorado (Weld County)—A "fairly small blue and white helicopter" circled low over cattle on ranches in northwestern Weld County.

October 13th through 17th, (Monday through Friday), Colorado (Alamosa County)—On each of these dates an "Army green" helicopter, apparently unmarked, flew west over Mosca Pass near the Great Sand Dunes National Monument during the day and returned by the same route in the evenings. It sounded just like an airplane, but we could see the top revolving propeller.

October 20th, Monday, 3:10 A.M., Montana (Cascade County)—A woman reported a black and white helicopter without markings flying at an altitude of about 100 feet over her property.

October 20th, Monday afternoon, Oklahoma (Cimarron County)—Three unidentified helicopters were seen near Wheeless, near the New Mexico border (a harbinger of things to come in the northeastern New Mexico area).

October 20th, Monday, 8:00 P.M., New Mexico, (Union County)—Three observers reported a low-flying helicopter without lights over the Bill Watters ranch, north of Clayton.

October 21st, Tuesday, Colorado (Las Animas County)—Several unidentified helicopter sightings were reported this date: One mutilation occurred in the county this week. Fort Carson Military Reservation near Colorado Springs announced that a group of military helicopters had moved through this area on the 21st, en route to Fort Hood, Texas.

October 21st, Tuesday, early morning, Oklahoma (Cimarron County)—A family reported seeing seven helicopters flying low over their home near Felt. Five dead cattle had been found in this area at about this time—unconfirmed as mutilations.

October 21st, Tuesday, 10:00 A.M., New Mexico (Union County)—In this county, which borders Cimarron County on the west, five helicopters buzzed a herd of cattle on the Kennann Ranch near Seneca.

October, third week, Colorado (Baca County)—In this county, adjoining Cimarron County, Oklahoma, and Union County, New Mexico, on the north and northeast, there were scattered accounts of mystery choppers. In the early morning on the 20th, a blue copter circled "real low" near Midway, and a dark green, "almost black" small helicopter was seen headed into Oklahoma.

October 27th, Monday evening, New Mexico (Union County)—Five helicopters "milled around" over the Heinmann ranch, flying close together, but not in formation. Three helicopters were reported in another sighting and, during a four-hour period, single choppers were seen in the area.

October 28th, Tuesday, New Mexico (Union, Quay Counties)—There were several sightings of unidentified helicopters this date in eastern Union and northeastern Quay Counties.

October 29th, Wednesday, New Mexico (Union County)—Observers reported several separate sightings of unidentified helicopters in the area east of Nara Visa.

Mid to late October, Colorado (Routt County)—Around the time that a five-year-old cow was mutilated near Hayden, an unidentified blue-green helicopter was seen in the area.

November 1975

November 2nd, Sunday night, New Mexico (Quay County)—A helicopter flew over two ranches, flashing red, white, and blue lights, with beams of white light shooting intermittently.

November 2nd, Sunday night, Colorado (Baca County)—A helicopter flew low over a house south of Springfield. Perhaps 12 mutilations occurred in Baca County in September through November, along with scattered accounts of unidentified helicopters.

Early November, New Mexico (Valencia County)—A rancher who saw low-flying helicopters over his property during this period, found that four of his cattle had disappeared.

November, first week, Wyoming (Johnson County)—Hunters and ranchers reported sightings of a low-flying helicopter with a "pontoon-type" landing gear in the Buffalo vicinity. Four calves were mutilated in the Buffalo area during this period.

November 3rd, Monday night (approximate date), New Mexico (Union County)—Three unidentified helicopters flew over the Howard Robinson property, and on another night during the week, two helicopters flew over the house.

November 6th, Thursday night, New Mexico (Union County)—The Clayton Police Dept. reported that an unidentified helicopter landed just east of town. Other airborne lights were observed Northeast of Clayton and were thought to be helicopters.

Between October 30th and November 13th, New Mexico (Union and Quay Counties)—At least 30 unidentified helicopters and/or UFO sightings occurred during this period, while at least four cattle mutilations were reported. Though since denied, the FAA announced an investigation into the sightings of unknown aircraft.

Late 1975 through early 1976, Maine, Massachusetts, and New Hampshire—Though cattle mutilations have occurred in New England, none were known during this period. However, there were disappearances of smaller animals and the mutilation of fowl, such as geese (and not for the first time). Geese had been mutilated in Colorado in 1975. Some of the animal-owners had seen low-flying, suspiciously behaving unmarked helicopters.

November 7th and 8th, Friday and Saturday nights, Montana (Fergus and Wheatland Counties)—UFOs were reported over missile installations. In a reply to press queries, the Strategic Air Command stated that "The craft were suspected to have been helicopters, due to hovering ability of the craft, witness interpretations of the sound produced, and placement of lights on the craft. Positive identification of the UFOs as helicopters was precluded due to darkness."

Mid-November, Texas (Guadalupe County)—A mutilated calf was found on the 10th. There were unconfirmed reports of "silent helicopters" in the area at about this time.

December 1975

December 2nd, Tuesday night, and December 3rd, Wednesday morning, Montana, (Cascade, Teton, Pondera, and Chouteau Counties)—Unidentified helicopters were seen over a wide area. Included were overflights over missile installations. Some objects seen were reported as helicopters, others simply, nocturnal lights. At least two helicopters were involved as there were simultaneous sightings in widely separated areas.

December 3rd, Wednesday night, Montana (Cascade, Teton, Pondera, and Chouteau Counties)—The previous night's helicopters/UFO wave was repeated. At least two helicopters were reported at once over a missile site. Malmstrom AFB verified that unidentified helicopters were in the area.

December 4th, Thursday night, Montana (Cascade County)—On the southeast edge of Great Falls, a law officer observed an unidentified helicopter which lifted off the ground and flew off.

Between August 1975 and May 1976, Montana (Cascade and surrounding counties)—Approximately 130 reports of unidentified helicopters and/or UFOs were logged during this period.

This listing amounts to only a *portion* of the activity occurring in the West and Midwest during this time. What is clear in these sightings is that where there was once relatively quiet airspace, a sudden rash of helicopters appear for no obvious reason. The residents were startled and concerned, and, most of all, they wanted answers.

In late 1975, following several weeks of mutilations and mystery helicopter and UFO reports in northeastern New Mexico, the Tucumcari, New Mexico, *News,* November 7, 1975, announced that James Gordon, Federal Aviation Administration Area Coordinator, announced late Wednesday, November 5, that the FAA has officially entered into the investigation of the sightings of the aircraft over northeastern New Mexico. At the time, the FAA investigators in the field were taking depositions from individuals who had actually seen these aircraft.

In response to Freedom of Information Act requests in 1978 and 1979 to FAA offices in Albuquerque and Tucumcari, to Southwest region office in Fort Worth, and to the Rocky Mountain region office in Denver, the FAA denied having any information about the northeastern New Mexico mystery helicopters and UFOs or any investigation thereof. If there was such an investigation, what did it find out? The FAA isn't saying.

Another official attempt to address the problem of mutilations, UFOs, and unmarked helicopters appeared in 1980. Supported by a grant from the Department of Justice, Kenneth M. Rommel, Jr., of the District Attorney's office for the First Judicial District, served as Project Director of what was known as "Operational Animal Mutilation" (OAM).

As a result of a deluge of inquiries and complaints to the FBI's field offices in New Mexico, FBI headquarters financed a "full investigation" into the helicopter/UFO/mutilations to ease public concern. This would not be an easy job, for in scanning the report's introduction, the events were widespread and very bizarre:

> According to some estimates, by 1979, 10,000 head of cattle had been mysteriously mutilated. Of the states that have been affected by this phenomenon, New Mexico has been unusually "hard hit." Since 1975, over 100 cases have been reported. The New Mexico reports, like those from other parts of the country, describe the mutilations as being characterized by the precise surgical removal of certain parts of the animal, particularly the sexual organs and rectum. Predators, it is claimed, avoid the carcass, which is said to be devoid of blood. Mutilation accounts are often accompanied by sightings of *strange helicopters or UFOs* [emphasis added].
>
> The link between UFOs and the New Mexico incidents is further supported by the alleged discoveries of carcasses with broken legs and visible clamp marks, indicating to some investigators that the animals are being *airlifted to another place* [emphasis added] where they are mutilated, and then returned to the spot where they are found. This belief is further supported by two additional reports—one of a case in which the cow's horn was sticking in the ground as if the animal had been dropped there; the other of a steer *found in a tree five feet above the ground* [emphasis added].

Aside from the summary of the general tenor of events as described in the OAM report, investigator Rommel concluded that most mutilations were attributed to "scavengers" and "predators" and that the helicopter/UFO reports "invariably" had "a simple, practical answer."

Certainly, as with most reports of UFOs, a majority of the mutilations were explainable in a number of nonsensational ways. Others aren't so easily dismissed, especially when unusual aircraft are involved. And the OAM report did not bother to concern itself with mystery helicopters of UFOs to any great extent, as an examination of the report will show.

While the Project's Director conducted a thorough investigation of the cases he studied, it should be noted that the OAM project was limited to New Mexico, after much of the important activity had passed. The investigation covered a one-year period, but only fifteen cases were studied personally by the Director, out of hundreds of reports nationwide. If we allow that, say, ninety percent of all reports were explainable, then, statistically, the Director should have found perhaps one baffling case in his small sample. He didn't. This is probably because the Director conducted no detailed investigations of already existing unusual incidents, but essentially waited for new reports to come in. The chances of such a strange event occurring for the

OAM Project are comparable to one standing on a street corner waiting for an accident and the likelihood of seeing one occur.

The mystery helicopters were responsible for a number of upsetting experiences in Vietnam. The July 1, 1968, issue of *Newsweek* described incidents in South Vietnam when virtually every night Americans stationed at radar outposts just south of the Demilitarized Zone separating then North and South Vietnam reported picking up dozens of unidentified aircraft moving across the border.

The South Vietnamese government issued statements which explained that the unknown objects were merely "Communist helicopters" and that twelve of them had already been shot down. Such was not the case, though. A *Newsweek* reporter, Robert Stokes, had been present when some of the first radar reports had come in.

Stokes reported on an incident one evening at 11 P.M. in which Army Captain William Bates was stationed at the regimental headquarters at Dong Ha in front of his radio set. A Marine observer had radioed that he observed through his electronic telescope "thirteen sets of yellowish-white lights" which moved towards the west at an altitude of between 500 and 1,000 feet over the Ben Hai River. A check with authorities at Dong Ha revealed no known aircraft in the area. Another check with radar unit Alpha 2, the northernmost outpost of the 1 Corps, was positive. The tracker said that he was surrounded by blips on his scope!

Air Force and Marine jets were in the air by 1:00 A.M. About forty-five minutes later, a Marine jet pilot reported that he had shot down a helicopter. An Air Force reconnaissance aircraft overflew the area with infra-red detectors to pinpoint the burning wreckage, but found none! All they reported was a burned spot and nothing more.

As a result of this activity, the U.S. reinforced its DMZ outposts, expecting an assault from enemy helicopters for the first time in the war. No such assault occurred. In fact, about a week after the reports, the South Vietnamese government suggested that the "whole thing had probably been a mistake." They also suggested that the jets sent after the phantom helicopters may have been responsible for the sinking of a U.S. Navy Swift boat in the South China Sea.

Unexpected confirmation of this mystery helicopter blitz at the DMZ came from Air Force Chief of Staff General George S. Brown to reporters on October 16, 1973. In response to a question about the Air Force's position on UFOs, General Brown said:

I don't know whether this story has ever been told or not. They weren't called UFOs. They were called enemy helicopters. And they were only seen at night and they were only seen in certain places. They were seen up around the DMZ in the early summer of '68. And this resulted in quite a little battle. And in the course of this, an Australian destroyer took a hit and we never found an enemy. We only found ourselves when this had all been sorted out. This caused some shooting there and there was no enemy at all involved, but we always reacted. Always after dark. The same thing happened up at Pleiku at the Highlands in '69.

Of course, there is a tendency for us to say, "Well, that was war time. There's all kinds of aircraft flying around under such conditions." While this dismissal may make sense in general terms, it is simplistic and ignores some basic facts. Allied Forces acknowledged that no known air traffic was in the area and the North Vietnamese Air Force was hardly an equal to the U.S./South Vietnamese forces. All unknown helicopters managed to elude *jets,* except one which was "shot down" according to one pilot's story. Yet, when a reconnaissance aircraft, equipped with devices specifically designed to detect burning wreckage, was dispatched to the scene, only a "burned spot" was found. No aircraft was identified. This is reminiscent of many UFO landing reports where burned areas were the only traces left of whatever touched down.

One of the most remarkable mystery helicopter/UFO sightings occurred on December 29, 1980. at 9 o'clock in the evening, Betty Cash, fifty-one, Vickie Landrum, fifty-seven, and Colby Landrum, seven (Vickie's grandson), were driving on the Cleveland–Huffman Road north of Lake Houston, Texas, on the way to Dayton, Texas, where they lived. The road was lined with trees on both sides and was very quiet with hardly any traffic.

Down the road a few miles, a very bright light was visible above the trees, but it quickly disappeared from view. As the witnesses drove along, they were suddenly stunned to see a large, diamond-shaped object hovering straight over the road a short distance away. The object gave off an extreme brightness that hurt their eyes, and it lit up the surrounding landscape. On occasion, the UFO would shoot a blast of flame from underneath, much like a rocket exhaust.

Betty Cash stopped the car in the middle of the road, fully expecting that, if they passed under the UFO, it would roast them alive. At first, all three of them left the car to observe the object, but Colby quickly became frightened and had his grandmother, Vickie, get back into the car with him. Betty stood by the door on the driver's side and then walked in front of the car. Vickie asked Betty to get back into the car, which she did, and as Betty grabbed the door handle to get into the car, she found it painfully hot to the touch. She wrapped a leather coat around her hand and managed to open the door.

As the three sat in the car watching the spectacle, they noticed an increase in temperature, which soon forced them to put the air conditioner on (on December 29!). The object bobbed up and down in direct relation to the blasts of flame underneath and an audible beeping could be heard by all the witnesses. The UFO soon rose to the southwest and disappeared.

However, a number of helicopters were seen in the area a distance from the object.

Betty started the car and left the scene, but five minutes later, on FM2100, the UFO and a large number of helicopters were seen. The helicopters made a tremendous racket and caused the witnesses to fear that there were so many of them in the sky that some might collide. More than twenty helicopters were counted by the women.

Betty kept driving, turned into the Huffman–Eastgate Road, then road FM1960. The UFO was still in view as a fading light climbing into the sky. Betty took Vickie and Colby to their home and returned to her own home at approximately 9:50 P.M.

All witnesses immediately began to notice physical problems. Vickie complained of a headache. Betty did also, along with nausea, swelling of the neck, and an outburst of red blotches on her face and head. Days later, Betty's condition worsened. Her eyes swelled shut. She had nausea and diarrhea and the red blotches had turned into blisters. Vickie took Betty to a hospital emergency room where Betty was treated as a burn victim. She spent twelve days in the hospital, during which time patches of skin came off her face and much of her hair fell out.

Betty left the hospital briefly, but soon had to return for another fifteen days for further treatment. Although Vickie's and Colby's symptoms were somewhat less severe, they still experienced considerable discomfort. Vickie suffered painful, swollen eyes, stomach pains, diarrhea, some hair loss, anorexia, sores on her arms, reddened skin, hair loss, and diminished vision along with other symptoms. Colby suffered stomach pains, diarrhea, anorexia, swollen eyes, reddened skin, and weight loss. Colby also had nightmares for weeks after the incident and became fearful of helicopters and bright lights in the night sky.

What were these symptoms related to? After an extensive investigation of this report by John Schuessler, a Project Manager for Space Shuttle Flight Operations for the McDonnell Douglas Corporation and Deputy Director for Administration for the Mutual UFO Network in Seguin, Texas, it seems that the witnesses may have suffered some form of radiation sickness, although the precise type of radiant energy is unknown. The symptoms are well-known to those of us who remember the Civil Defense educational programs of the 1950s and 1960s.

To this day, the witnesses still suffer varying degrees of discomfort. Betty Cash spent time in the intensive care unit repeatedly, after recurrences of her problems. Vickie Landrum suffers outbreaks of sores, infections, swellings, and fatigue.

What about the helicopters? Where did they come from? Schuessler determined that two types of helicopters were seen. One type was a double rotor Boeing CH47 Chinook and the other type was similar to a Bell Huey, although there is uncertainty about this on the witnesses's part.

Attempts to locate a large number of these helicopters at airports or airbases proved fruitless. All denied having this number of aircraft in the air in the vicinity of Betty's car that night. Later investigations were equally negative, but a new twist was added to the controversy. Someone else had seen the helicopters that night!

Dayton, Texas, Police Officer L. L. Walker reported to Schuessler that several hours after the Cash/Landrum encounter, he observed helicopters in groups of three with their searchlights on. The helicopters behaved as if they were searching for something in the area. Walker identified these as Chinooks. The helicopters were in view for only a short time, because Walker was driving home with his wife, and he assumed that maneuvers were being conducted by the National Guard or another military group.

Many questions remain unanswered in this story. There is no doubt that the incident occurred; the witnesses's injuries attest to that. Why were the helicopters following the UFO? Was the UFO an unearthly vehicle in trouble and in the process of being trapped by the military? Or, was it a U.S. government project gone awry?

Betty Cash and Vickie Landrum don't have an explanation yet, but they are holding the U.S. government responsible for the affair. Both will sue for damages to compensate for medical expenses.

Betty Andreasson Luca has become a well-known name in the UFO field. This is mainly due to two books by Raymond Fowler (*The Andreasson Affair,* Prentice-Hall, 1979; and *Andreasson Affair: Phase Two,* Prentice-Hall, 1982), which describe Betty's claims of numerous contacts with extraterrestrial beings over many years.

During the early part of 1980, when Larry Fawcett was working on the *Andreasson Affair: Phase Two* as the chief investigator for author Raymond Fowler, mystery helicopter events plagued both Betty and her husband Bob. They reported that their home was overflown numerous times by black, unmarked helicopters of the Huey UH-1H type and that these helicopters would fly over their home at altitudes as low as 100 feet. The Luca's described these helicopters as being black in color, with no identifiable markings on them. They noticed that the windows were tinted black also, so that no one could see inside. During many of the overflights, Bob was able to take close to 200 photos of the helicopters. These overflights were witnessed not only by Fawcett, but by the Luca's neighbors as well.

Why the Luca's should be subjected to these intrusions is unknown. If they lived under a normal air route, this should have been easily determined. But there was no reason for helicopters to be overflying the Luca's house. Even in the face of photographic evidence, all agencies and airports contacted denied any knowledge of such flights, despite our using the Freedom of Information Act to locate additional information.

One letter that Bob Luca sent to the Army's Office of the Adjutant General, dated May 8, 1982, was the culmination of complaints for the previous several years of overflights. After getting negative answers from all agencies contacted, Luca demanded a final answer on why the helicopters continuously intruded upon his property. He included a comment by an FAA spokesman who had listened to Luca's description of the flights. The spokesman suggested that the helicopters might belong to the CIA! The CIA later denied that this was possible, but the FAA spokesman's comment was certainly suggestive.

The Army's Adjutant General, Major General John F. Gore, stated, "It is difficult to determine what particular aircraft is involved or the owning unit." That was as far as the Luca's could get in their efforts to solve the mystery.

Later, the Luca's discovered another case of mystery helicopters. They were at the Goodspeed Airport in Connecticut one day. Bob was taking flying lessons there. Bob flew in a light plane while Betty sat in the car. Suddenly, six black, unmarked helicopters flew over the airport at a low altitude. Betty had been told previously by both Fowler and Larry Fawcett to try to get an additional witness if the black helicopters were seen again. Betty saw a man sitting in his car at the airport, so she went over and asked him if he could see the helicopters flying over the field. He said, "Yes." Betty then remarked that the craft had no markings on them, to which the man remarked, "Yes, it is funny that the craft have no markings on them and that's a violation of FAA regulations." The man turned out to be a pilot, and after Betty told him of the problems of the black helicopter overflights over her house, he told her of an incident that had happened to a friend of his on Long Island involving a black helicopter landing on the beach. Betty was able to get the man's name from the witness, and she passed this information on to Larry Fawcett. Fawcett tried to contact the man on numerous occasions by phone and letter, but all attempts failed due to the witness's constant cross-country business trips. It wasn't until 1982 that Bob Luca was able to make contact with the witness at his home on Long Island.

We will call the witness Bill Smith to honor his desire for anonymity. Luca called Fawcett and said that Smith had told him that during 1974 a black, unmarked helicopter had landed by his home in Long Island and that armed guards had gotten out and had spoken with him. Bob gave the man's name and phone number to Fawcett, and on November 21, 1982, Fawcett conducted an interview with Smith. Here is Smith's story.

It was in 1974. It was early in the morning when a Chinook helicopter came down across the way from my home. As the helicopter landed on the beach, men began to jump out of the craft, which was charcoal black in color with no markings. These men were dressed in black pajama-type uniforms and carried M-16 rifles. The area where the helicopter came down is called the "Sore Thumb" and is about 500 feet from my home in an open area on the beach. The men in the black uniforms began to set up a perimeter on the beach. I walked down towards one of the guards who came to within about 200 yards of my house. I tried to talk to him, but he did not answer me, he was all business. I could see that he had no patches on his uniform and there was a microphone attached to his shirt. He was wearing a black, baseball-type hat and had black jump boots on.

A police car from the Suffolk County police department came into the area and a police officer went over to the guard and asked some questions. The officer asked, "Who are you and what is going on?" The guard didn't answer. The officer then said, "Look, you're standing here carrying a weapon and you're in an unidentified uniform. I'd like some identification." Again, the guard didn't answer. The policeman stated, "If you don't answer me pretty soon, you're going to end up on the ground in handcuffs." The guard in the black uniform said, "I don't think so; look around." Apparently all these guys could talk to or hear one another over the microphones.

As the police officer turned around, the other men in the black uniforms were all pointing their guns at the officer. The officer went to his cruiser and called his superior and told him what had happened. He was told to get out of the area. The officer left in his car. I could see other helicopters out over the ocean. These were smaller craft but they were black in color and had no markings.

As if by signal, all the men suddenly returned to the large helicopter and lifted off and disappeared. We later learned that the Air Force had been removing warheads from missiles on Long Island and was flying them to a holding area in New Jersey when one of the helicopters developed engine trouble and made a forced landing three miles down the beach in parking lot 9. The helicopter that landed in front of my home was a security group to protect the downed craft.

What are some of the prominent speculative explanations which might provide answers to the mutilation/helicopter/UFO link? Let's suggest several:

1) The helicopters are UFOs disguised to appear as terrestrial craft.
2) The helicopters are government vehicles directly involved in conducting animal mutilations.
3) The helicopters are government vehicles not directly involved in the mutilations, but engaged in investigating and monitoring the activities of the real mutilators.
4) The helicopters belong to a "para-government," a group operating as a government within a government much like the rumored "54–12" group that supposedly began during the Eisenhower administration.

Or, could the answer lie in a combination of the above? The first explanation might be considered possible in the same sense that travel through black holes is possible (i.e., there is no real evidence to disprove the theory). But this surely is the weakest explanation. Besides the fact that there is no evidence to support this, even a sympathetic observer to the UFO scene would cast a skeptical eye toward someone looking up into the sky and upon seeing a helicopter, saying, "That's a UFO in disguise!"

Similarly, the idea of the government performing the mutilations using helicopters as the means of transportation, suffers from lack of any real evidence and a seeming lack of motive for such a wide-scale operation. No eyewitness reports have been filed describing government operatives ever getting caught doing the things that have been done to the mutilated animals.

We cannot rule out a "para-government" operation, although we would like to be more specific about possibilities in this area. If a "54–12" group exists, we feel that the idea of helicopters being used by the government, or para-government, to monitor UFO and mutilation activity seems to be the most attractive hypothesis. We've seen convincing evidence that the government is quite baffled by these reports. To handle a problem like this, it would make sense to organize a "quick response unit," much like the "rapid deployment force" used by the military to react to volatile political situations around the world. This quick response unit could be sent to areas of high UFO and mutilation activity to assess each case or possibly to surprise the perpetrators. This unit would come under the highest security classification since to admit that (1) these incidents are real and (2) they are unexplainable would not be in the government's best interest.

For years, there have been rumors of a very elite group within the Air Force that was highly mobile and was used for retrieval of crashed UFOs and for other emergency situations.

Long-time UFO researcher Leonard H. Stringfield, who has been working in the area of "Retrievals of the Third Kind," had come across similar information about this elite group from military sources. This is well-documented in his work "A Case Study of Alleged UFOs and Occupants in Military Custody," which was presented at the MUFON Symposium held at Dayton, Ohio, on July 29, 1978.

We know this may sound unnecessarily evasive to the detractors of the UFO/mutilation link, but at least one highly placed source within the military, who has asked to remain anonymous, has told us that *some* of the mutilations were UFO-related. However, he could not discuss the details of the cases because the information is classified. We wish we could be more detailed about the source's reliability, but we will honor his request that we not identify him. We can say, however, that we have documented evidence, through the FOIA, of his standing within the government.

It may take some time before the pieces fall together, but ultimately, we believe that the government will have to admit to deep involvement in this aspect of the UFO mystery.

CHAPTER EIGHT
CIA Involvement: 1949–1953

The possible involvement of the CIA in UFO research has long been a hot topic of controversy. Up until the mid-1970s, the CIA's response to inquiries about UFOs would be either not to answer or to forward the correspondence to the Air Force for attention. This was not very satisfying to individuals who had heard rumors, or had even experienced firsthand, stories of the CIA collecting and analyzing information on UFO sightings from around the world. There was little that could be done to gain more information. No legal means existed to force the CIA to answer any questions, let alone release documents.

When the Freedom of Information Act became law, this means was finally made available to UFO researchers. Initial attempts were not without frustration, however. One of the first organizations to pursue the CIA for UFO documents was Ground Saucer Watch (GSW) of Phoenix, Arizona. Headed by William Spaulding, GSW was at the forefront of document research and made great strides in allowing public access to government UFO activities.

A request was filed on July 14, 1975, by GSW, stating,

> There exist within the CIA files hundreds of data points on various UFO witnesses (possibly the CIA has relinquished this information to the AFOSI or another intelligence organization). I have encountered numerous witnesses to a UFO incident, since the conception of our group in 1957, that have told of "silencing" pressures through their employments, film (photographic) confiscation, and even the "plowing" of the ground where a UFO has temporarily landed.

The letter asked for copies of all UFO case investigation/evaluations by the CIA. After a long delay, the CIA responded on March 26, 1976:

> In order that you may be aware of the true facts concerning the involvement of the CIA in the investigation of UFO phenomena, let me give you the following brief history. Late in 1952, the National Security Council levied upon the CIA the requirement to determine if the existence of UFOs would create a danger to the national security of the United States. The Office of Scientific Intelligence established the Intelligence Advisory Committee to study the matter. That committee made the recommendations found at the bottom of page 1 and the top four lines of page 2 of the Robertson Panel Report. At no time prior to the formation of the Robertson Panel and subsequent to the issuance of the panel's report, has the CIA engaged in the study of the UFO phenomenon. The Robertson Panel Report is summation of the Agency's interest and involvement in this matter.

This, then, was the CIA's only involvement in UFOs, according to the CIA. A much protracted legal battle ensued and resulted in the ultimate release of nearly 900 pages of UFO-related documents. More will be said on the court case in Chapter 13.

In the meantime, let's take a look at the information that has been released. The documents may be classified in several ways.

1) Information reports. Reporting and translation of UFO sightings from other countries.
2) Documents discussing UFOs as "psychological warfare devices."
3) Documents relating to the "Robertson Panel," the CIA's official investigation of UFOs.
4) Memoranda on miscellaneous sightings and internal policy.

Some of the documents are difficult to read. In the 1950s, the Thermofax copy machine was the standard office copier of the day. Unfortunately, copies made on this system gradually deteriorated due to passage of time and irregular temperature control. When the Thermofax copies were recopied, the result was a semi-readable document. This only affected a small number of pages, however.

The first memo, written on March 15, 1949 by a Dr. Stone of the CIA's Office of Scientific Investigation (OSI) states:

1. A rapid perusal of your documents leaves one confused and inclined to supineness.
2. The following considerations seem not to have been included in the survey:
   a. No suggestion is noted that there is a possibility that many of the objects may be "free" meteorological sounding balloons.
   b. If a tame "flying saucer" is to be involved, it is extremely unlikely that they be found over the U.S. because:

(1) U.S. developments would be closely coordinated with USAF or commercial designers.

(2) Foreign aircraft development would hardly be tested at such a range from home areas, *even if* fuel could be supplied.

(3) Guided aircraft at a range of several thousand miles are beyond any known capabilities, including ours.

c. What is the psychological probability that *any* object seen briefly against "zero" background will be circular, or oval, in appearance?

d. Has any one commented on the curious time distribution of the observations? Note chart below.

The documents referred to in section 1 were not included with the memo. The chart mentioned shows a graph of numbers of sightings per month between December 1946 and January 1948, with a peak indicated during the summer of 1947.

The memo exhibits initial curiosity and puzzlement over the phenomena. Notice the dismissal of the possibility of flying saucers being "secret weapons" at this stage.

No other documents are available for the rest of 1947 and all of 1948. A report on an April 24, 1949, sighting appears as follows:

On 24 April 1949, at 3 miles north of Arrey, New Mexico (107° 19½' W 32° 52½'N), 4 Navy enlisted men from White Sands Proving Ground (Chief Akers, Davidson, Fitzsimmons, and Moorman) and I saw a rapidly moving object while making a pibal wind run. We had released a 350 gram balloon at about 1020 MST and were following it with a standard ML-47 (David White) Theodolite. After the 1030 reading, Davidson took over the theodolite, and Akers and I looked up to find the balloon with naked eye. We thought we had the balloon when we saw a whitish spherical object right along the direction the theodolite (45° elevation and 210° azimuth) was pointing. The object was drifting east rapidly (5°/sec. as estimated by stopwatch and width of fingers) but we had thought to encounter similar winds on the balloon. When the difference in angle between the theodolite and supposed balloon became apparent, I took over the theodolite and found the true balloon still there, whereupon I abandoned it and picked up the object after it came out of the sun. (The computed bearing of sun was 127° azimuth and elevation 60°.) The object was moving too fast to crank the theodolite around, therefore one of the men pointed the theodolite and I looked.

The object was an ellipsoid about 2½:1 slenderness ratio, length about .02° subtended angle, and white in color, except for a light yellow of one side as though it were in shadow. I could not get a hard focus on the object due to the speed at which the angles changes. Therefore I saw no good detail at all.

The Azimuth angle continued to decrease as the object continued on a north heading, growing smaller in size. At around 20°–25° Azimuth the Azimuth held constant and the elevation angle began increasing from the 25° minimum to about 29°. The object then apparently disappeared due to distance after a total time of observation of about 60 seconds.

The object was not a balloon and was some distance away. Assuming escape velocity, a track was figured which put the elevation about the station of about 300,000 feet over the observed period. If this is true, the flight would have probably gone over the White Sands Proving Ground, Holloman Air Force Base and Los Alamos.

We made another pibal wind run 15 minutes later. This balloon burst after an 88 minute flight of 93,000 feet only 13 miles due south of us. Therefore, this object could not have been a free balloon moving at such angular speed below 90,000 feet.

Information is desired if this was some new or experimental aircraft or for any explanation whatsoever.

The report included no comment by the CIA.

The next "Information Report" dated August 4, 1950, details an unusual sighting in the North Atlantic:

SOURCE [two lines deleted] reported the following observations at 10:00 AM EDT on 4 Aug 50 at 39°35' North, 72°24½' West.

[2 lines deleted]
1. "On 4 Aug 50 at 10 AM my ship, while on a heading of 245° true, with a smooth sea and clear weather, visibility 14 miles, barometer reading 30.03, was underway from Walton, Nova Scotia, to an East Coast US port. I was in the chart room just aft the bridge when Third Mate, who was at mid-bridge checking the compass, shouted that there was a flying object off the starboard bow. I immediately ascended the conning tower and by this time the object was on our starboard beam. It was traveling on a reciprocal course to ours about 50 or 100 feet above the water at an estimated speed of over 25 mph. From the conning tower I observed it with my binoculars for a period of approximately a minute and a half when it disappeared into the horizon in a north-easterly direction. I would estimate that the closest it approached my ship was one thousand feet and it was an ovular, cylindrical shaped object the like of which I have never seen before. The object was quite small and I would judge that its diameter was approximately 10 feet. It had depth but to what extent I was unable to observe. The object made no noise, and as it passed abeam our ship, it appeared to pick up considerable speed. It was not flying smoothly but impressed me as having a churning or rotary motion. It had a shiny aluminum color and sparkled in the sunlight."

[lines deleted]
2. "I was on the main deck, port side, just forward of the bridge when the Third Mate shouted there was an object on our starboard bow. I looked off to the starboard and saw an object of elliptic shape looking like half an egg cut lengthwise traveling at a great rate of speed on a course reciprocal to our own. I immediately ran to the stern, port side, and with my glasses was able to observe the object disappearing into the horizon. From the time I was first alerted to its presence until it disappeared from sight, 15 seconds elapsed. I believe that it was traveling at a tremendous rate of speed, possibly faster than 500 mph. During the time I saw it, it was approximately 70 feet off the water and I judge it was approximately 10 miles away. I clearly saw its shadow on the

water. I last observed it off the starboard quarter and it seemed to be increasing its speed and ascending. It had an elliptic shape and I could clearly see that it had three dimensions. It wobbled in the air, made no noise, and was a metallic white in color. The length was approximately six times the breadth and its belly had a depth of possibly 5'."

3. "At 10:00 AM on 4 Aug 50 as I was checking the compass at mid-bridge through a bridge port hole, I observed a flying object off the starboard bow. I immediately shouted to the Captain, who was in the chart room, and the Chief Mate, who was below on the port deck, of my observation and went out on the flying bridge myself. The object was approximately 70' above the horizon at a distance of 12 miles. It came toward us, then ran on a course reciprocal to ours and turned off into the horizon in the northeast. I clearly saw its shadow on the water. My impression of the object was that it was elliptical, not unlike a Japanese diamond box kite in shape. I have no idea of its size but the length was about six times the breadth and it had a depth of from two to five feet. It made no noise and was traveling at a tremendous rate of speed. As it traveled through the air, it made a spinning or wobbly motion. After it disappeared in the horizon, I saw it reappear several seconds later, ascending at an even faster speed than when I first observed it. I have no idea what this object was, I never saw anything comparable to it before, and it was one of the most frightening experiences I have ever had. I roughly estimate that the object traveled 28 miles during the 15 seconds I had it under observation."

Collector's Note: The Chief and Third Mates were interviewed on 8 August by two Intelligence Officers. The Captain, who was absent at that time, was interviewed on 9 August by only one of the two Intelligence Officers. In describing the occurrence, the Chief and Third Mates reenacted their behaviour at the time of sighting, and the period from the time the Chief Mate saw the object abeam until he reached the after deck and saw it disappear off the starboard quarter was timed at 15 seconds. In laying the angles of observation out on a chart and assuming the object was ten miles distant and taking the time into account, it is evident it was certainly traveling at a very high rate of speed, which approximated 400 to 500 miles per hour. It will be noted that there is a tremendous discrepancy between the Captain's estimate of the speed and the estimate of the two officers which could not be explained as they were very careful in making their statements and asserted that their observations had been correct. All three men were quite evidently very much upset by the sighting. Aside from the discrepancies, it was quite evident to the Intelligence Officers who interviewed these men that they had certainly seen some very unusual object which they could not identify but was just as certainly not any conventional type of aircraft. . . .

The following reports were collected by the CIA from various radio broadcasts, press reports, and "foreign documents." They reflect the worldwide nature of the sightings and certainly contributed to the increased interest by the CIA in UFOs during 1952.

Flying Saucers Over Belgian Congo Uranium Mines
Recently, two fiery disks were sighted over the uranium mines located in the southern part of the Belgian Congo in the Elizabethville district, east

of the Luapula River which connects the Meru and Bangweolo lakes. The disks glided in elegant curves and changed their position many times, so that from below they sometimes appeared as plates, ovals, and simply lines. Suddenly, both disks hovered in one spot and then took off in a unique zigzag flight to the northeast. A penetrating hissing and buzzing sound was audible to the onlookers below. The whole performance lasted from 10 to 12 minutes.

Commander Pierre of the small Elizabethville airfield immediately set out in pursuit with a fighter plane. On his first approach he came within about 120 meters of one of the disks. According to his estimates, the "saucer" had a diameter of from 12 to 15 meters and was discus-shaped. The inner core remained absolutely still, and a knob coming out from the center and several small openings could plainly be seen. The outer rim was completely veiled in fire and must have had an enormous speed of rotation. The color of the metal was similar to that of aluminum.

The disks traveled in a precise and light manner, both vertically and horizontally. Changes in elevation from 800 to 1,000 meters could be accomplished in a few seconds; the disks often shot down to within 20 meters of the tree tops. Pierre did not regard it possible that the disk could be manned, since the irregular speed as well as the heat would make it impossible for a person to stay inside the stable core. Pierre had to give up pursuit after 15 minutes since both disks, with a loud whistling sound which he heard despite the noise of his own plane, disappeared in a straight line toward Lake Tanganyika. He estimated their speed at about 1,500 kilometers per hour.

Pierre is regarded as a dependable officer and a zealous flyer. He gave a detailed report to his superiors which, strangely enough, in many respects agreed with various results of research.

"Flying Saucers" in East Germany
Berlin, July—Furnished with the sworn testimony of an eyewitness, Oscar Linke, a 48-year-old German and former mayor of Gleimershausen, West Berlin intelligence officers have begun investigating a most unusual "flying saucer" story. According to this story, an object "resembling a huge frying pan" and having a diameter of about 15 meters landed in a forest clearing in the Soviet Zone of Germany.

Linke recently escaped from the Soviet Zone along with his wife and six children.

Linke and his 11-year-old daughter, Gabriella, made the following sworn statement last week before a judge: "While I was returning to my home with Gabriella, a tire of my motorcycle blew out near the town of Hasselbach. While we were walking along toward Hasselbach, Gabriella pointed out something which lay at a distance of about 140 meters away from us. Since it was twilight, I thought that she was pointing at a young deer.

"I left my motorcycle near a tree and walked toward the spot which Gabriella had pointed out. When, however, I reached a spot about 55 meters from the object, I realized that my first impression had been wrong. What I had seen were two men who were now about 40 meters away from me. They seemed to be dressed in some shiny metallic clothing. They were stooped over and were looking at something lying on the ground.

"I approached until I was only about 10 meters from them. I looked over a small fence and then I noticed a large object whose diameter I estimated to be between 13 and 15 meters. It looked like a huge frying pan.

"There were two rows of holes on its periphery, about 30 centimeters in circumference. The space between the two rows was about 0.45 meters. On the top of this metal object was a black conical tower about 3 meters high.

"At that moment, my daughter who had remained a short distance behind me, called me. The two men must have heard my daughter's voice because they immediately jumped on the conical tower and disappeared inside.

"I had previously noted that one of the men had a lamp on the front part of his body which lit up at regular intervals.

"Now, the side of the object on which the holes had been opened began to glitter. Its color seemed green but later turned to red. At the same time, I began to hear a slight hum. While the brightness and hum increased, the conical tower began to slide down into the center of the object. The whole object then began to rise slowly from the ground and rotate like a top.

"It seemed to me as if it were supported by the cylindrical plant which had gone down from the top of the object, through the center, and had now appeared from its bottom on the ground.

"The object, surrounded by a ring of flames, was now a certain number of feet above the ground.

"I then noted that the whole object had risen slowly from the ground. The cylinder on which it was supported had now disappeared within its center and had reappeared on the top of the object.

"The rate of climb had now become greater. At the same time my daughter and I heard a whistling sound similar to that heard when a bomb falls.

"The object rose to a horizontal position, turned toward a neighboring town, and then, gaining altitude, it disappeared over the heights and forests in the direction of Stockheim."

Many other persons who live in the same area as Linke later related that they saw an object which they thought to be a comet. A shepherd stated that he thought that he was looking at a comet moving away at a low altitude from the height on which Linke stood.

After submitting his testimony to the judge, Linke made the following statement: "I would have thought that both my daughter and I were dreaming if it were not for the following element involved: When the object had disappeared, I went to the place where it had been. I found a circular opening in the ground and it was quite evident that it was freshly dug. It was exactly the same shape as the conical tower. I was then convinced that I was not dreaming.

Linke continued, "I had never heard of the term "flying saucer" before I escaped from the Soviet Zone into West Berlin. When I saw this object, I immediately thought that it was a new Soviet military machine.

"I confess that I was seized with fright because the Soviets do not want anyone to know about their work. Many persons have been restricted to their movements for many years in East Germany because they know too much."

Glowing Spheres Seen Over Almansa, Spain
Almansa, 21 April—At 0800 hours today, many persons saw a series of four glowing spheres crossing the sky along the Murcia–Valencia trajectory at high speed and at a great height. The spheres looked like locks of

wool of a vivid reddish color which changed to an intense yellow as they flew farther away. They gradually disappeared in the distance. No unusual sound was heard. The spectacle lasted hardly a minute.

Andujar Residents Report Saucer
The Cifra news agency reports that on the night of 30 July 1952, many residents of Andujar, Spain, saw what was presumed to be a so-called flying saucer. The object was red, round, and approximately the size of a dessert dish. It flew noiselessly, at great speed, and left behind a long trail of very bright greenish light.

FRENCH EQUATORIAL AFRICA

Luminous Object Seen Over Port Gentil
The master of a cargo ship anchored in front of the wharf of Port Gentil (in Gabon, French Equatorial Africa) reported that at 0240 hours on 1 June 1952 a mysterious object came up from the area behind Port Gentil, made a double loop, passed over the roadstead, and then dived toward the sea at great speed. He submitted the report to the local authorities and to the administrative offices of his company. The following is a summary of his story.

On 1 June 1952 at 0240 hours, the ship was riding at anchor in the roadstead of Port Gentil, heading 150 degrees. The northern sky was clear and starry; the southern, slightly cloudy. Visibility was excellent, a slight southwest breeze prevailed, and the sea was calm. There was a quarter moon.

The first mate was at his forward post ready to weigh anchor while the master was on the bridge with the officer on duty. With the exception of the mooring lights, the ship was in complete darkness, thus permitting excellent night visibility.

At 0240, the first mate telephoned the master informing him that he had just sighted an unknown luminous object in the sky which came from Port Gentil and passed directly over the ship. Training his binoculars (Zeiss 7 x 50, for night vision) skyward, the master was able to see quite clearly, on the port quarter, a very bright and phosphorescent orange light, circular in shape and moving at a great speed in a seemingly straight-line course. Standing on the wing of the bridge, and with the aid of the gyrocompass repeater, the master estimated its average direction to be about 10 degrees.

He followed the light quite easily in his binoculars for about 3 minutes and lost sight of it when it moved at great speed over the Prince buoy, about 7 miles from the ship. The master was unaware of any accompanying sound and admits that it was difficult to estimate the altitude of the object, yet he judged this to be 3,000–4,000 meters. Its diameter was that of a planet.

The first mate stated that before he telephoned the master, he saw that object come from the direction of Port Gentil, stop, make a right turn, and resume its initial course. As it passed directly over the ship, it repeated the same sort of gyration.

The master stated that his 20 years of sea duty enabled him to affirm that what he saw was neither a known celestial phenomenon, such as a falling star or meteor, nor a current type of aircraft.

Furthermore, it was confirmed that there were no planes in the air that night over Port Gentil.

Strange Objects Seen in Sky over Algeria
At 2300 hours on 15 July 1952, in the town of Boukanefis, two bakers clearly saw a plate-shaped flying object in the sky. It moved with unusual agility, giving off a greenish smoke and lighting up the sky. It seemingly did not alter its course as it increased its speed and disappeared toward the south.

Similarly, in Lamoriciere on 11 July 1952, one Thomas Martinez saw a sudden illumination above and at first took it to be a falling star. Actually, it seemed more like a meteor followed by two other bodies, all trailing a yellow cloud of smoke. Then, these disappeared and out of nowhere appeared an oval-shaped, longish ball of fire. Flying at a low altitude and clearly visible, it rapidly followed a rectilinear course.

At 1537 hours, Maurice Dubessay, who works for *L'Echo d'Oran,* saw what appeared to be a brilliant disk going in a southwest direction at a great speed and at medium altitude. It disappeared after 5 seconds. In a similar time interval, Atias and Karsenty, two grocers, also saw the unknown object before it disappeared behind a cloud.

Saucers Observed in Two Areas of Oran
On 26 July 1952, people in two areas of Oran reported seeing unusual flying objects, described as "saucers."

At about 2300 hours, three women in the Eckmuhl district of Oran noticed a large, orange-red, luminous patch in the sky, of the size of a duck's egg, but flatter. Traveling from east to west, it appeared to halt for a second then vanished.

Three trustworthy individuals living on the Tiaret plateaus saw an unusual flying object at 1045 hours. The local parish observed it for about 40 seconds and described it as a shining, cigar-shaped mass without a smoke trail. It disappeared toward the northwest. A teacher and his wife gave a similar description, adding that the object had a dark center, was in an oblique position, and moved at an altitude of about 3,000 meters. No one heard any sounds of a motor.

Cities Several Appearances
of Flying Saucers in Algeria
On the evening of 29 July 1952, two new flying saucers were sighted. The first, appearing at 2050 hours over Mostaganem, was visible only a few seconds. The second one appeared at 2300 hours at Ain Teledes. It flew above the city for about a minute, emitting a whitish trail of smoke. The manner in which it attained various altitudes revealed a surprising maneuverability. When it disappeared, it was headed south.

This is the fifth time in a matter of weeks that this phenomenon has been noted in the Department of Oran. A saucer appearing to be about the size of a teacup was observed by two policemen over Frenda (at the east end of Oran Department). It consisted of a dark nucleus within a luminous mass. Near Tlemcen, motorists noted a strange cigar-shaped object at a height of 600 meters. There was a luminous cloud in its wake. And finally, at Lamoriciere, about 40 kilometers from the Abdellys area, motorists saw a phosphorescent disk for a brief period of time.

Points to Frequency
of Flying Saucer Reports in Oran Department
(After it had received and published a series of flying saucer reports, the newspaper *L'Echo d'Oran* carried a review of the occurrences, as well as several late reports. The following is a summary of the article.)

Our correspondents have sent us word of saucers appearing everywhere in Oran Department during the past few days. This seems to be the saucer's favorite area, one which is no doubt salutary for their development. They have appeared here with greater frequency than in France or in the US. It is impossible, moreover, to doubt the veracity of the observers, since they include policemen, . . . a priest, and a cadi.

At 0400 hours today, Raymond Botella, a Public Works Department employee in Tlemcen, saw a flying object moving rapidly north and trailing a whitish smoke cloud. A half hour before, the mysterious saucer had been seen in Oued Taria, traveling at the same speed and, like the saucer observed yesterday, making abrupt turns and changes of direction.

On the night of 30 July, in Sainte Barbe du Tlelat, a police adjutant, two policemen, and a cadi observed a luminous flying object for about 30 seconds. The daily police reports will henceforth include all such observations by the police.

In the morning of 30 July, a resident of Algiers saw, for several seconds, a shining black disk on the horizon. It made a rapid vertical descent, then suddenly moved in a horizontal direction.

Two observations were made in Lodi. On 25 July, at about 2130 hours, a yellowish object flew at a dizzy speed in the sky, and on 28 July, at 2150 hours, a much larger object appeared for several seconds; it had the shape of an inverted cone.

Observe Unusual Flying Object for over a Minute
At 1130 hours on 31 July 1952, an Oran resident and his wife, while driving on the road between Saint Denis Du Sig and Le Tlelat, saw something flying in the sky about 1,000 meters up. They stopped the car and watched its course for 1½ minutes. It was spindle shaped and tapered at both ends. It differed from ordinary aircraft in that it showed no exhaust smoke, made no noise, and had a great speed.

Disks Appear over Marrakech
Marrakech (special correspondent)—At 2100 hours [presumably on 16 July 1952], many people saw a large, luminous disk flying horizontally, with a leaping and bounding motion. Then, there was a burst of light. A second disk of smaller dimensions appeared, going off horizontally toward the southwest. The whole appearance lasted about one minute.

From several points of the Marrakech region, luminous disks were seen traveling at a dizzy speed.

On 14 July, flying saucers had been seen over the Ifrance region, flying toward Meknes.

Luminous Disk or Ball Seen over Moulay Bousselham
On 2 August 1952, at about 2045 hours, a group of five trustworthy persons saw a luminous disk or ball in the sky over Moulay Bousselham, French Morocco. The object, red in the center and bluish around the edge, flew very rapidly from southeast to northwest, remaining visible for at least 20 seconds before it disappeared over the horizon.

Luminous Objects Seen over Algeria
In Ain Sefra, on the night of 12 August 1952, a railroad agent observed a ball of fire suddenly appearing against a background of clouds, racing

across the sky from east to west and leaving behind a luminous pink trail. Apparently increasing in volume, the object stopped suddenly, became bright red, and seemed to explode, but the observer did not hear any noise. . . .

At 2115 hours on 14 August 1952, two persons in the city of Constantine saw a luminous object flying at high speed toward Guelma. According to the witnesses, the apparatus, which had no resemblance to a flying saucer, emitted a very bright light. At the time this happened, the local weather bureau had not launched any weather balloons.

The same day, at 1920 hours, many people at the docks of Phillippeville saw in the sky an enormous red disk going from north to west, leaving behind a greenish trail.

Saucer-Like Craft Seen in Spain

According to the Cifra news agency, on the evening of 10 August 1952, a resident of Cuenca, Spain, while walking along the Cuenca–Madrid road, saw an object similar to the so-called flying saucers. It crossed the sky at high speed in a matter of seconds. The object was round and gave off two luminous trails.

Observe Two Strange Flying Objects in Spain

Several inhabitants of Puerto Real, 6 kilometers from San Fernando, recently saw two elongated oval objects in the sky approaching each other from opposite directions. When it seemed that they were about to collide, each object made a right turn, picked up speed, and then disappeared. The objects flew at a great height, seemed lead-gray in color, and appeared to be piloted.

Describe Unusual
Object Flying Along Algerian Coastline

On 6 October 1952, at 1830 hours, a luminous object was seen flying for several seconds along the western coastline of Algeria, above Sidi Ferruch and Sain Eugene. Numerous witnesses described it as cigar-shaped and enveloped in orange flames.

FRANCE

Many Witness
"Flying Saucer" Formation in Tarn, France

About 100 inhabitants of Gaillac (Department of Tarn, France) reported witnessing a "flying saucer" formation at about 1600 hours on 27 October 1952. The objects were said to have been 16 in number, ranged in twos, and disk-shaped, except for a swelling in the center. According to the report, they revolved giving off a bluish light at the sides.

The spectators said that they also saw a kind of elongated cylinder, a "flying cigar," traveling in the center of the saucer formation. All the objects were said to have discharged shining whitish particles, which looked like glass wool and accumulated on tree branches and telegraph wires. Many persons said that they had been able to gather clusters of such particles, but that these had quickly disintegrated, making it impossible to have them analyzed later in a laboratory.

The weather conditions were reported as ideal for observation. The mysterious objects, which had come from the southeast, reportedly remained in the area about 10 minutes and then continued on their way in a straight line.

Two important memos during 1952 defined the UFO problem and expressed serious concern over how the subject might affect the national security of the United States. The first memo, dated August 1, 1952, was sent by the Acting Chief of the CIA's Weapons & Equipment Division to the Deputy Assistant Director of Scientific Intelligence.

> 1. Pursuant to your request for overall evaluation of "flying saucers" and associated reports, the following is pertinent:
>
>   a. Of 1000 to 2000 such reports received by ATIC, a large percentage are clearly "phoney." An equally large percentage can be satisfactorily explained as known flights of currently operational U.S. equipment (aircraft, weather balloons, etc.) and many others are undoubtedly of natural phenomena (meteorites, clouds, aberration of light caused by thermal inversion or reflections, etc.).
>
>   b. Less than 100 reasonably credible reports remain "unexplainable" at this time; regarding these reports, there is no pattern of specific sizes, configurations, characteristics, performance, or location. The sources of these reports are generally no more or less credible than the sources of the other categories. It is probable that if complete information were available for presently "unexplainable" reports, they, too, could be evaluated into categories as indicated in "a" above.
>
> 2. Notwithstanding the foregoing tentative facts, so long as a series of reports remains "unexplainable" (interplanetary aspects and alien origin not being thoroughly excluded from consideration), caution requires that intelligence continue coverage of the subject.
>
> 3. It is recommended that CIA surveillance of subject matter, in coordination with proper authorities of primary operational concern at ATIC, be continued. It is strongly urged, however, that no indication of CIA interest or concern reach the press or public, in view of their probable alarmist tendencies to accept such interest as "confirmatory" of the soundness of "unpublished facts" in the hands of the U.S. Government.
>
> 4. The undersigned has arranged with the Commanding Officer of the Air Technical Intelligence Center at Wright-Patterson Air Force Base, Ohio, for a thorough and comprehensive briefing related to this subject on 8 August 1952. Subsequent to obtaining full details, a detailed analysis will be prepared and forwarded.

No possibilities were being ruled out, not even "interplanetary aspects and alien origin." The problem still had to be approached in an organized way, though.

On September 24, 1952, the Assistant Director for Scientific Intelligence, H. Marshall Chadwell, issued this memo to the CIA Director, Walter Smith.

> 1. Recently an inquiry was conducted by the Office of Scientific Intelligence to determine whether there are national security implications in the problem of "unidentified flying objects," i.e., flying saucers; whether adequate study

and research is currently being directed to this problem in its relation to such national security implications; and what further investigation and research should be instituted, by whom, and under what aegis.

2. It was found that the only unit of Government currently studying the problem is the Directorate of Intelligence, USAF, which has charged the Air Technical Intelligence Center (ATIC) with the responsibility for investigating the reports of sightings. At ATIC there is a group of three officers and two secretaries to which come, through official channels, all reports of sightings. This group conducts investigation of the reports, consulting as required with other Air Force and civilian technical personnel. A worldwide reporting system has been instituted and major Air Force bases have been ordered to make interceptions of unidentified flying objects. The research is being conducted on a case basis and is designed to provide a satisfactory explanation of each individual sighting. ATIC has concluded an arrangement with Battelle Memorial Institute for the latter to establish a machine indexing system for official reports of sightings.

3. Since 1947, ATIC has received approximately 1500 *official* reports of sightings plus an enormous volume of letters, phone calls, and press reports. During July 1952 alone, *official* reports totaled 250. Of the 1500 reports, Air Force carries 20 percent as *unexplained* and of those received from January through July 1952 it carries 28 percent *unexplained*.

4. In its inquiry into this problem, a team from CIA's Office of Scientific Intelligence consulted with a representative of Air Force Special Studies Group; discussed the problem with those in charge of the Air Force Project at Wright–Patterson Air Force Base; reviewed a considerable volume of intelligence reports; checked the Soviet press and broadcast indices; and conferred with three CIA consultants, who have broad knowledge of the technical areas concerned.

5. It was found that the ATIC study is probably valid if the purpose is limited to a case-by-case explanation. However, that study does not solve the more fundamental aspects of the problem. These aspects are to determine definitely the nature of the various phenomena which are causing these sightings, and to discover means by which these causes, and their visual or electronic effects, may be identified immediately. The CIA consultants stated that these solutions would probably be found on the margins or just beyond the frontiers of our present knowledge in the fields of atmospheric, ionospheric, and extraterrestrial phenomena, with the added possibility that the present dispersal of nuclear waste products might also be a factor. They recommended that a study group be formed to perform three functions:

a. analyze and systematize the factors which constitute the fundamental problem.

b. determine the fields of fundamental science which must be investigated in order to reach an understanding of the phenomena involved; and

c. make recommendations for the initiation of appropriate research.

Dr. Julius A. Stratton, Vice President of the Massachusetts Institute of Technology, has indicated to CIA that such a group could be constituted at that Institute. Similarly, Project Lincoln, the Air Force's air defense project at MIT, could be charged with some of these responsibilities.

6. The flying saucer situation contains two elements of danger which, in

a situation of international tension, have national security implications. These are:

a. *Psychological*—With world-wide sightings reported, it was found that, up to the time of the investigation, there had been in the Soviet press no report or comment, even satirical, on flying saucers, though Gromyko had made one humorous mention of the subject. With a State-controlled press, this could result only from an official policy decision. The question, therefore, arises as to whether or not these sightings:

    (1) could be controlled,

    (2) could be predicted, and

    (3) could be used from a psychological warfare point of view, either offensively or defensively.

The public concern with the phenomena, which is reflected both in the United States press and in the pressure of inquiry upon the Air Force, indicates that a fair proportion of our population is mentally conditioned to the acceptance of the incredible. In this fact lies the potential for the touching-off of mass hysteria and panic.

b. *Air Vulnerability*—The United States Air Warning System will undoubtedly always depend upon a combination of radar screening and visual observation. The U.S.S.R. is credited with the present capability of delivering an air attack against the United States, yet at any given moment now, there may be current a dozen *official* unidentified sightings plus many unofficial ones. At any moment of attack, we are now in a position where we cannot, on an instant basis, distinguish hardware from phantom, and as tension mounts we will run the increasing risk of false alerts and the even greater danger of falsely identifying the real as phantom.

7. Both of these problems are primarily operational in nature but each contains readily apparent intelligence factors.

8. From an operational point of view, three actions are required:

a. Immediate steps should be taken to improve identification of both visual and electronic phantoms so that, in the event of an attack, instant and positive identification of enemy planes or missiles can be made.

b. A study should be instituted to determine what, if any, utilization could be made of these phenomena by United States psychological warfare planners and what, if any, defenses should be planned in anticipation of Soviet attempts to utilize them.

c. In order to minimize risk of panic, a national policy should be established as to what should be told the public regarding the phenomena.

9. Other intelligence problems which require determination are:

a. The present level of Soviet knowledge regarding these phenomena.

b. Possible Soviet intentions and capabilities to utilize these phenomena to the detriment of the United States security interests.

c. The reasons for silence in the Soviet press regarding flying saucers.

10. Additional research, differing in character and emphasis from that presently being performed by Air Force, will be required to meet the specific needs of both operations and intelligence. Intelligence responsibilities in this field as regards both collection and analysis can be discharged with maximum effectiveness only after much more is known regarding the exact nature of these phenomena.

11. I consider this problem to be of such importance that it should be brought to the attention of the National Security Council in order that a community-wide coordinated effort towards its solution may be initiated.

The CIA's UFO panel was convened on January 14, 1953, at 9:45 A.M. The panel members consisted of: Dr. H. P. Robertson, Chairman of the panel, Director of the Weapons Systems Evaluation Group in the Office of the Secretary of Defense, and a CIA employee; Dr. Luis Alvarez, a high-energy physicist and winner of the Nobel Prize for physics fifteen years later; Dr. Samuel Goudsmit, physicist, Brookhaven National Laboratories; Dr. Thornton Page, former professor of astronomy at the University of Chicago and Deputy Director of the Johns Hopkins Operations Research Office; and Dr. Lloyd Berkner, physicist and one of the directors of the Brookhaven National Laboratories.

Other CIA employees and Air Force personnel participated to varying degrees. The UFO investigations were explained to the panel by the Air Force, and about twenty UFO reports were discussed, along with movie films of two UFO incidents.

After a grand total of twelve hours' work examining six years' worth of data, the panel adjourned on January 17. Its concluding statement was issued:

1. Pursuant to the request of the Assistant Director for Scientific Intelligence, the undersigned Panel of Scientific Consultants has met to evaluate any possible threat to national security posed by Unidentified Flying Objects ("Flying Saucers"), and to make recommendations thereon. The Panel has received the evidence as presented by cognizant intelligence agencies, primarily the Air Technical Intelligence Center, and has reviewed a selection of the best documented incidents.

2. As a result of its considerations, the Panel *concludes:*

    a. That the evidence presented on Unidentified Flying Objects shows no indication that these phenomena constitute a direct physical threat to national security.

We firmly believe that there is no residuum of cases which indicates phenomena which are attributable to foreign artifacts capable of hostile acts, and that there is no evidence that the phenomena indicate a need for the revision of current scientific concepts.

3. The Panel further *concludes:*

    a. That the continued emphasis on the reporting of these phenomena does, in these perilous times, result in a threat to the orderly functioning of the protective organs of the body politic.

We cite as examples the clogging of channels of communication by irrelevant reports, the danger of being led by continued false alarms to ignore real indications of hostile action, and the cultivation of a morbid national psychology in which skillful hostile propaganda could induce hysterical behavior and harmful distrust of duly constituted authority.

4. In order most effectively to strengthen the national facilities for the timely recognition and the appropriate handling of true indications of hostile action, and to minimize the concomitant dangers alluded to above, the Panel *recommends:*

a. That the national security agencies take immediate steps to strip the Unidentified Flying Objects of the special status they have been given and the aura of mystery they have unfortunately acquired;

b. That the national security agencies institute policies on intelligence, training, and public education designed to prepare the material defenses and the morale of the country to recognize most promptly and to react most effectively to true indications of hostile intent or action.

We suggest that these aims may be achieved by an integrated program designed to reassure the public of the total lack of evidence of inimical forces behind the phenomena, to train personnel to recognize and reject false indications quickly and effectively, and to strengthen regular channels for the evaluation of and prompt reaction to true indications of hostile measures.

The panel's conclusions set the tone for the remainder of the government's "official" involvement in UFOs. Since agencies had, up to this point, great difficulty in explaining some rather extraordinary reports, the conclusions could be interpreted in another manner.

Feeling that most reports were explainable and concerned that reports of UFO sightings from civilian sources clogged intelligence channels, the CIA decided that debunking the UFO subject would discourage public interest and inquiry and, therefore, reduce the likelihood that UFO "waves" would occur in the future. The truly strange reports received through military and intelligence sources (i.e., familiar sources) could then be dealt with in a secure manner, away from prying eyes. They might not be explained, but at least they would be secret.

The good reports, if not reported through government sources, would become known anyway to government authorities, and they could be dealt with according to the situation. Either way, the government would be on top of things and the public, barring leaks, would know little about what was happening.

To sum up, the Robertson Panel could be described not so much as a "scientific" panel as a "propaganda" panel. Its purpose was to justify the CIA's new policy of keeping the UFO subject out of the public domain as much as possible. Labeling a twelve-hour round table discussion of UFOs a "scientific study" is ludicrous, especially considering the fact that, in at least one instance, 1,000 hours was spent on one case (Tremonton, Utah, 1952) by Navy analysts and the conclusion was *unknown.*

Is it scientific to ignore information for which no logical answer is available after rigorous investigation? Any scientist who believes this is not worthy of the title bestowed upon him. Science stands for the investigation of the unexplained; not the explanation of the uninvestigated.

The CIA's panel did not stop the UFOs from appearing throughout 1953 as evidenced by the following reports:

Danish Defense Leaders
Take Serious View of Flying Saucers
[Comment: The information below is the full text of an article which appeared in the Stockholm daily, *Morgon-Tidningen,* on 13 July 1953. The leading Copenhagen dailies, *Berlingske Tidende, Social-Demokraten, Politiken,* and *Information,* during the period around the above date, did not carry the story.]

Copenhagen, 12 July—Danish defense authorities take a serious view of the problem of flying saucers. The military experts are of the opinion that although most of the observations (of flying saucers) have turned out to be astronomical phenomena, there remain the reports of trained observers which, among other things, would seem to indicate that the saucers are dispatched from Soviet bases in the Arctic Ocean.

The Danish Air Force Command has recently turned over to the Defense Staff a report on various phenomena in the air over Denmark and the waters adjacent to Denmark. The report is based on observations from Danish Air Force radar stations. These observations are compared with information regarding the remote-controlled projectiles which have been traced in the atmosphere over the northernmost part of Norway and Finland. On the basis of these observations, the members of the Defense Intelligence Service have come to the conclusion that the projectiles could have been dispatched from a Soviet base on Novaya Zemlya in the Arctic Ocean.

The report discusses the incident in which an officer and seven privates from Karup Airfield on Jutland, on 12 November 1952, sighted an object in the air which resembled an aircraft, but which moved more rapidly than any known type of aircraft. The (Danish) observations are compared with a number of Norwegian observations, among them one which occurred in October 1952 when, according to the Norwegian Defense Staff and the Norwegian Navy, an aircraft of hitherto unknown design flew over the naval base at Horten at the entrance to Oslofjord. Another incident which is pointed out occurred on a maneuver recently in northern Norway, when the crew of an anti-aircraft battery outside of Bodo observed a mysterious object at a great height. A jet plane was sent up, but it was not able to reach the object, which disappeared at a terrific speed.

The report of the Danish Air Force Command emphasizes that the "flying saucer traffic" over Scandinavia seems to be a fact of great aerotechnical interest.

FRENCH EQUATORIAL AFRICA

Delayed Report
on Four "Saucers" Seen in Ubangi-Shari
The Meteorological Service of French Equatorial Africa has authorized this newspaper to publish today the following account about four "flying saucers" seen on 22 November 1952 over Bocaranga, Ubangi-Shari.

At approximately 2200 hours, Father Carlos Maria (a Capuchin missionary),

Lasimone, his companion, and four other persons were driving on the road to Bocaranga, when they suddenly noticed a large disc traveling overhead in the same direction as they. Lasimone extinguished the car's lights, but the disc disappeared in the distance. A short while later, in the same spot, they saw four discs, motionless in the air. Father Maria's description follows:

"We could see them clearly. Two were above and two below, but all four had no point of contact. At that moment, they had a silvery color like that of the moon. I would say that their diameter was somewhere between 30 and 40 centimeters.

"They moved several times, but each time it seemed that only the two lower ones were rotating. Just before they (all four) began to move, they lit up brightly, like suns. Then it looked as though they arranged themselves to move in circular fashion so as to return to their starting point. On stopping, they lost their brilliant color and regained the silvery one. During their rotation, they seemed slightly oval. I cannot say whether it was due to a new shape they assumed while in flight or to the oblique position they had assumed while moving. Each time they turned, they had that shape and that profusion of light. We observed them for about 20 minutes. After their final turn, they remained motionless in their initial position for several moments. Then they disappeared, headed in the direction from which we had come. What I saw was no aerolite, shooting star, or anything of the kind. It could only have been a man-made machine."

Lasimone then gave an equally detailed version, as follows:

"At about 2200 hours, we observed four halos of silvery light grouped in a square formation and located above light clouds. The night was very clear.

"At one point, the four halos were on the horizon, ranged in a line in the direction of Bouzoum. Suddenly, one of them lit up in vivid red, causing its shape to be distinguished. It was like a cigar, thicker in the fore section. The center section constituted about one third of the total length, and appeared opaque in the light, with perfectly symmetrical lines. Flying above the clouds, this object headed in our direction at considerable speed, about equal to that of an average plane. About 5 or 6 kilometers away, it halted without changing its lights and then climbed again, vertically. The stop was abrupt and the glow became silvery again. The other three on the horizon then began to move in the same way as the first and joined it to form a square once again."

SYRIA

Report "Flying Saucers" Seen in Syria
The Damascus newspaper *Al Ahaya* reports that "flying saucers" were seen recently above the city of Homs, Syria, coming from the south.

IRAN

Luminous Object Seen in Sky over Abadan
This newspaper was informed by its correspondent in Abadan that at 1855 hours, on 18 May 1953, a luminous object was seen in the sky over Abadan. The object was reported to be as bright as the sun and to have the shape of a new moon (but several times larger than a new moon). It traveled

extremely fast and could be seen for 20 minutes. It was also reported that the same object was seen over all the oil areas in Khuzistan."

SOUTH AFRICA

Flying Saucer Follows Man
Heretofore, *Die Landstem* has not been able to publish the full story of the incident described below, which occurred on 26 May 1953. The incident was reported by the observer to the Department of Defense in Pretoria. The latter acknowledged receiving the report but did not make it public.

Dr. D. Beyers of Uppington, while driving in his automobile from Capetown to Uppington, had reached a point about 80 miles south of Brandvlei (between Kenhardt and Calvinia), when, at about 0510 hours, he suddenly saw a bright yellowish green light which illuminated the clouds from behind. Shortly thereafter it came out from behind the clouds. Beyers stated that it was ten times as bright as any star he had seen. It moved up and down and sometimes also forward. The emitted light had the appearance of burning hydrogen. Also, the object emitted three streaks of light which maintained a fixed position with respect to the main light. Beyers observed the phenomenon from 0510 until 0600. He added, "I was under the impression that the object was following me because each time I stopped the car to watch it, it increased its altitude."

DAHOMEY, FRENCH WEST AFRICA

Luminous Flying Body Sighted at Djogou
At about 2330 hours on 11 October 1953, many residents of Djogou in northwest Dahomey observed in the sky an oblong-shaped, luminous object flying at a high speed toward the north, at an altitude of about 1,500 meters and on a horizontal plane. This is the first reported sighting of a so-called flying saucer over Dahomey.

FRANCE

Celestial Disk Changes Form
At about 1545 hours on 9 December, Charles Huaut, a carpenter from Saint-Emilion, Gironde Department, observed a luminous, golden, round object poised motionless at a high altitude. After 10 minutes, it changed position noiselessly and assumed the form of several horseshoes, measuring about 100 meters in diameter, enveloped in smoke trails. Then the entire phenomenon disappeared. Several other persons reported having seen it at the time indicated above.

At approximately the same time as Huaut made his obervation, a man named Simonneau and his wife, from Surgeres, Charente-Maritime Department, saw a round object in the sky. It glowed with the colors of the rainbow and flew at a great speed from north to south.

Brilliant White Disk Sighted
Recently, Madet, a civil servant of Montlucon, Allier Department, sighted a brilliantly luminous white disk in the sky at approximately 2100 hours. It was visible for 2 minutes, then traveled off at a great speed and disappeared, without seeming to change its altitude, in the direction of the Auvergne Mountains. A short while later, Madet saw a red, crescent-shaped object

which appeared to be three times as large as the moon in its first quarter. The object disappeared at a great speed toward the southwest.

The effect of the Robertson Panel's conclusions was quite evident on U.S. reports of UFOs since a significant drop in sightings took place after the report's release. The report was classified secret, yet the "trickle down" of the CIA's UFO policy dictate made its way throughout the official reporting structure, including Project Blue Book. The policy would serve as the Air Force's model for the next sixteen years, whereby the public would essentially see the UFO world through the CIA's rose-colored glasses. The CIA still had to deal with the real world, however, and UFOs were an annoyingly persistent part of it going into 1954.

CHAPTER NINE
CIA Involvement: 1954–1977

A significant number of unusual sightings occurred in Europe during what has become known as the "Great Wave of 1954." Much of this wave has already been documented in UFO literature, but what was not known until the release of the CIA files is the fact that the CIA collected many of the sightings through normal intelligence channels, something which they had supposedly fought to block with the Robertson Panel inquiry.

The following reports have been excerpted from official CIA information sheets:

Unidentified Aircraft at Marignane Airfield France
Shortly after 2100 hours on January 4, 1954 a round luminous machine, coming from the South, landed at the Marignane airfield in Bouches-du-Rhone Department. There was only one witness present at the field. The machine disappeared while he was telephoning the control tower. Careful scrutiny of the runway in the morning turned up a few pieces of metallic debris. The witness story was confirmed by that of a Marseilles resident who driving from Arles to Marseilles saw a large, round, reddish fire ball in the sky, but placed the time at 2245 hours.

Round Flying Object Sighted at Luneville, France
Three residents of Luneville, Meurthe-et-Moselle Department claim to have seen a round object flying from North to South at about 0600 hours on January 9, 1954. The object flew more slowly than a jet plane and left a luminous yellow trail. It flew noiselessly, although appearing to be at a low altitude. Several students of the College de Luneville also saw the object.

Fiery Disk Seen at Arras, France
At approximately 0427 hours on January 7, 1954, a fiery disk, followed by a luminous trail, was sighted in Arras, Pas-de-Calais department. An observer stated that the disk remained motionless in the sky for an instant, after which it flew away and disappeared over the horizon.

"Flying Saucer" Over Montevideo
On March 1, 1954, numerous bathers at the beaches near Montevideo observed a "flying saucer," a sort of metallic disk emitting yellowish reflections. It remained stationary for 2 minutes at an altitude of several thousand meters.

Unidentified Object Over Saint Mexant
On April 15, 1954, two residents of Saint Mexant, Correge Department, observed an elongated, cone-shaped object with two red and green lights at the base, flying at a high altitude from the northwest toward the southwest.

Sight Unidentified Object Over Pyrenees
On April 28, 1954, a group of persons taking a walk near Sare in the region close to the Pyrenees border observed a cigar-shaped object traveling rapidly at an altitude of 2,000 meters in the direction of Spain.

Sightings Over Sweden, Northern Norway
On the morning of May 13, 1954, three persons in three different areas of Norrbotten Province, Sweden, observed a "brilliant, silver colored sphere with a tail." It was reported from Hammerfest, Norway, that on the same day three bright objects passed over Kautokeino (in northern Norway) at a great speed. They flew in a V-formation and disappeared towards the southwest. A deputy constable who had observed them with binoculars stated that they flew so high that he could not ascertain their shape but that they were not ordinary aircraft. He added that they seemed to be red on one side and white on the other and appeared to be rotating.

Flying Object Reported
Over Three Constantine Department Towns, Algeria
At 1330 hours on January 18, 1954, many persons in Saint Arnaud observed an object leaving a double trail of white smoke, describing an immense circle over the town. Several officers at La Remonte Military base nearby even heard a strange sound made by the object which seemed to have come from the north. (A similar observation had been made on January 16, 1954, when the object had come from the west). The meterorological station at Oued Hamimime airport (near Constantine) reported that it had observed a double trail of smoke at 1400 hours but concluded that the smoke came from a plane flying at great altitude. At 1430 hours, inhabitants of Setif saw an object arrive from the east, emitting bluish smoke trails and moving relatively slowly. After circling above the town for several seconds, it suddenly headed back in the direction of Saint Arnaud at great speed. Most of the spectators described it as it being cigar-shape and flying at high altitude.

Finally at 1645 hours on the same day, a large, luminous, rectangular-shape object was seen over Ouled Djellal (200 kilometers southwest of Setif) for over 30 minutes following a rectilinear course. The object came from the east and disappeared toward the west.

Unidentified Flying Object
over French Equatorial Africa
Monsignor Verhille, Apostolic Vicar of Fort Rousset, reported in the Brazza-ville newspaper *LaSemaine de L'akf* that he and others had sighted an unidentified flying object over Laketi in the Likuala Mossaka region of the middle Congo on 18 June 1954 at 1935 hours. A luminous globe, it came from the north towards the Laketi Mission. It suddenly stopped, rose and dropped, stoppod again, gyrated, and seemed to shake. A noise like that on an airplane engine, heard until that moment, also stopped. Seen through binoculars, the object had a dark mass in the center with light rays of unequal length coming out of it alternately. It went through its rising, falling, and stabilizing movements for 15 minutes, then shot back over the northern horizon.

Unidentified Objects over Southern Rhodesia
On July 25, 1954, J. H. Flanagan (a policeman) and some friends recently observed six unidentified objects in the sky over Enkeldoorn, South of Salis-bury. The objects, which were almost immobile, were visible for about 20 minutes, but disappeared when night fell.

Flying Saucers over Helsinki
Several people reported having seen a circular flying object over Helsinki on the night of September 14, 1954. The object, flying at an altitude of 800 meters, gave off an intense light and left a trail of reddish smoke about three times its diameter. It was visible for about 7 seconds.

Flying Disk Sighted in Aisne Department
At about 0030 hours on September 7, 1954 Robert Chovel and his wife and father-in-law were driving home from the theater in Hirson, Aisne De-partment when they saw a luminous, red-orange "disk" flying above the railroad tracks. The "disk" stopped suddenly across the road, 300–400 meters from the ground. It seemed to have on its upper side a small luminous tail, forming an integral part of the object. When the travelers reached the bridge at Buire, they saw what they believed to be a "flying saucer" increasing its altitude. As soon as the car lights beamed on it, the object started flying at great speed towards LaHerie 3–4 kilometers away and disappeared.

Flying Saucers over the Hague, Netherlands
Ten firemen and their chief observed the two flying saucers over the Hague on the night of August 4, 1954 between 2300 and 2400 hours. The objects were seen in the clear night air at a high altitude. They moved at incredible speed, at times remaining motionless for as long as 30 seconds. They were described as being flat ovals with whitish-gray light. All of the observers agreed that the objects could not have been aircraft or balloons.

The files for 1955 became somewhat sparse, probably reflecting a general lack of activity worldwide. It may have been the calm after the storm of the 1954 avalanche of UFOs. Nevertheless, a singular report, not identified by witness name or sighting location (but most likely the Soviet Union) appears in an October 4 "Information Report":

1. At 1630, 4 Oct 55, I boarded a train at . . . for . . . in the company of . . . , one of whom shared a wagon-lit compartment with me; the other

two occupied the adjoining compartment. The train ran very slowly, making every stop; I would estimate its overall speed at 20 mph. Exactly two hours and forty minutes out of . . . one of our group in the compartment next door entered my compartment and said, "Did you see that out there? I just saw a flying saucer." I and my compartment companion were about to laugh it off when the man from next door pointed out of the window again, and then we all saw the following sight.

2. On the lefthand side of the train, between the train . . . was a large airfield. The evening was dark but clear. A huge search . . . on the field itself, . . . on a triangular object on the ground which I would say was probably not more than two miles distant from the railroad. (*Collector's Comment:* Source first estimated that the airfield was about five miles away, but on further reflection, changed the distance to the object to two miles.) The size of the object was comparable to that of . . . jet fighter, with a squat shape and in the form of an equilateral triangle. There were three lights on the object, one on each point of the triangle, presumably two wing lights and a tail light. As we watched, it was ejected from its launching site, making not less than three and not more than seven fast spirals in the air, after which it climbed extremely fast at about a 45 degree angle. We watched it climb and saw it reach a high altitude; the search . . . followed it all the way.

3. I wish to emphasize that this was no ordinary takeoff but a launching procedure more like a missile ejection. Our companion from next door reported that this was the second launching in rapid succession.

4. I believe that the train at the time of the sighting was between 50 and 65 miles south of. . . . While the four of us were still watching the object ascending, the steward came in and pulled down the blinds. When I began to protest, the steward pointed toward the rear of the car and shook his head. . . .

The year 1956 was equally light in activity, but a policy statement did appear in a February 9, 1956, memo titled "Responsibility for Unidentified Flying Objects." As a result of a January 9 memo assigning the Applied Science Division (ASD) of the CIA's Office of Scientific Intelligence (OSI) the task of holding UFO reports, the ASD acknowledged that files would be held for incoming raw reports which in ASD's judgment might provide information on foreign weapons research and development. Reports not under this category would be forwarded to the "Fundamental Sciences Area" for review of information on *foreign science developments* for either retention or destruction. (This group could have been a clearinghouse for genuinely mysterious reports of UFOs which contained much detail but could not be linked to a foreign government. The question here is what does "foreign" mean?) Reports that did not fall under these categories would be destroyed.

Later in the memo it is clearly stated that the ASD tried to avoid collecting trivial UFO reports (i.e., reports of little hard data content) that could not be analyzed "in a manner useful to OSI in carrying out its mission." Recommendation was that raw intelligence and obsolete finished UFO reports filed with the previous holder of UFO files, the CIA's Electronics Division, be destroyed.

UFO skeptics have stated that this is evidence of the CIA's lack of interest in the subject. Why would they destroy sighting reports if they were unimportant? Yet, it is quite obvious that only UFO reports of *minor* interest were intended for destruction. Nowhere in the memo is it stated that *all* UFO reports were to be destroyed.

An April 1, 1957, document titled "UFOs Over Budapest" related an unusual account. Again the source is deleted.

> 1. During the early part of May 1956, I was told by several engineers, close associates whom I believe to be reliable, that the Ministry of Defense was alerted concerning the over-flight of a formation of unknown flying objects, flying in an easterly direction during that month.
>
> 2. My friends related that what appeared to be aircraft, flying in formation at an extremely high rate of speed at approximately twenty-five thousand meters, were observed by radar units of the . . . Air Defense Command. Nothing was done to disturb this flight, the probable reason being that the . . . Air Defense Command had no weapons at its disposal to reach these intruders.
>
> 3. During the same period, May and June 1956, many reports originating from all sections of Hungary cited the appearance of "flying saucers." For two or three weeks, reports appeared almost daily, describing these objects as fast-flying objects which could change direction of flight, acceleration, and deceleration with utmost ease. My friends told me of discussions at the War Technical Institute in which Hungary's leading mathematicians, engineers, and technicians took part concerning these objects. It was decided that they did not exist and that if anything, the reports were labeled US propaganda. An official announcement appeared in ". . ." declaring the entire "flying saucer" scare was a myth.
>
> 4. An interesting observation of . . . was "Even if they don't exist, I hope they are on their way to bomb Moscow."

Another striking memo, dated October 1, 1958, deals with "Reported Photographs of Unidentified Flying Objects" and stands in stark contrast to the impression of indifference the CIA was trying to demonstrate to the public on UFOs. The writer of the memo is unknown.

> 1. It has come to my attention that a civilian . . . has been experimenting with new kinds of film and emulsions which he has been exposing through a telescope set-up in his backyard here in Washington. During the course of his photographic experiments in the last three months, he managed, it is reported to me, to photograph on a number of occasions geometrically shaped flying objects as they passed between his telescope and the moon. I have not seen these photographs and have had no business to look for same but I have had them reported to me as a result of our investigation of . . . photographic process which reportedly delivers a very high degree of resolution. Incidental to the examination of some of these high resolution photographs at his home, one of my men . . . did notice the objects reported and in questioning of the man found that he had photographed different groups at several different times during the past three months.

2. . . . However, I would not like to overlook some evidence of an often reported phenomenon which might be of interest to . . . and to the intelligence community generally.

3. . . . reports to me that the photographs of these objects were remarkably clear and certainly indicated a phenomenon for which he had no ready explanation and for which in the past he found some considerable amounts of interest particularly in. . . . I do not wish to get involved with . . . if there is no interest in . . . in these reported materials, and I would therefore welcome your counsel and suggestion as to how we might get our hands on these materials to examine them firsthand and to make a more complete analysis of them. . . . is exceedingly cagey in his handling of these materials and would not permit anyone to borrow any of these materials. He explained that he was currently out of work and he had had a couple of recent contracts with the Air Technical Intelligence Center at Dayton. A contact with the Air Force reveals that he has no contracts which are in effect at the present time. . . . appears to feel that he has some real evidence of the existence of unidentified flying objects in his photography and I am sure he would consider delivering them to somebody only for a price, yet unspecified. By copy of this memorandum to . . . I would bring him up to date on this subject in case you would like to take it up unilaterally with him.

4. For background information, it is also reported to you that our original contact with . . . was set up through . . . and therefore there is some information on him already available in their files. You are also undoubtedly aware that the House committee investigating outer space and space phenomena has recently been addressing itself to the problem of the unidentified flying objects and has been seeking to review the evidence for certain House representatives to determine what validity this concept might have. According to the best information I have at the present moment, after several hearings on this subject this committee has suspended its investigation for several months after which time it intends to reopen them.

Significant here is the admission that the UFOs photographed were "remarkably clear" and indicated as phenomena for which there was "no ready explanation." And what was photographed? Geometrically-shaped flying objects passing across the face of the moon! The CIA expressed a desire to "get our hands on the material" for a more complete analysis. Whether this was done is unknown because no further file material on this affair has been released but it certainly belies claims by the CIA at the time of not being interested in UFOs.

Later in 1958, a teletype dated December 11 discussed a sighting on the USSR/India border.

On 6 December 1958 between 1838 and 1840 local time source observed, by telescope, an artificial object having a continuous brightness of magnitude 3 (same as the Belt of Orion) cross his position [field of vision] while source was observing Mars. The object traveled north to south. There was no sign of disintegration, smoke, flame, or noise. There was no sign of any fall. Source did not photograph the object, but he is sure that the object was identical with Sputnik III. Subsequent observations proved negative.

Headquarters Comment: A preliminary check showed that Sputnik III was not within source's area of visibility at the time indicated, nor is the direction cited in agreement with computed orbits. The carrier rocket for Sputnik III reentered the earth's atmosphere on 3 December 1958 according to a Soviet announcement.

Headquarters Comment: Evaluation requested of Air and OSI. Field Dissemination: None.

A case of mistaken identity in reverse! This time the object was, at first, explained away but after investigation it became an unknown.

The only reports of interest for 1959 came from Scandinavia. One dated January 20 described a sighting over Stigsjoe, Sweden, where an object, six to eight meters in diameter and surrounded by a two-meter-wide luminous ring, approached a group of observers from the south over Lake Laangsjoen. Duration was three minutes.

The other sighting involved a procession of bright bodies over Bergen, Norway on March 12. Several witnesses described sighting a bright object passing north to south and taking about two minutes to go from horizon to horizon. Several minutes later another appeared, following the same course. This was soon followed by objects three, four, and five, all traveling in the same manner.

A March 17, 1960, document told of a UFO at Norrtaelje, Sweden.

Two unidentified flying objects were observed and photographed on the morning of 6 March by photographer Esse Jansson of Norrtaelje. He states that he had gone out into a field early in the morning to photograph the unidentified satellite, 1960 Alpha, which was expected to pass the Stockholm latitude in a southerly direction about 0525 hours. Between 0515 and 0527 hours he observed two objects which came from the north and were moving in a southeasterly direction. Their movement was slow but otherwise initially was not entirely unlike that of the satellites he had seen before. Suddenly, however, the direction of movement changed, and the objects turned such that they were going back in the same direction they came from. On one of his plates he even caught a third luminous object of the same kind.

The photographs did not appear with the report. Here the unknown objects appeared as satellites would have travelled and the matter at this point would have been closed. However, the objects suddenly *reversed direction* in flight, an impossibility for a satellite.

May 1962 intelligence reports included this:

Unidentified Flying Objects—Buenos Aires—The appearance of unidentified flying objects over the city of Bahia Blanca, south of Buenos Aires, is causing the most varied comment among the people there. The most extraordinary occurrence was on 21 May when many people observed a strange luminous body suspended for several minutes over the city, and then saw it disappear quickly. A local photographer was able to take two pictures of the object, which looks like a luminous oval on the print. The Cordoba Astronomical Observatory is compiling data about this phenomenon which has been observed in other regions of Argentina, although not as clearly as in Bahia Blanca. The observatory has asked the public to submit their observations in order to determine whether the phenomenon was a cluster of meteorites, part of an artificial satellite, or due to other causes. (Lima AFP Spanish Latin America 0354 GMT 25 May 1962—W) A luminous object which was crossing the heavens above Bahia Blanca was photographed by a reporter of the local newspaper NUEVA PROVINCA, according to that newspaper. The reporter was walking along the street when he first noticed the object. Seeing that it was not leaving the city, he drove to the Maldonado Canal, and there took several photographs, one the very instant the mysterious body stopped and changed its course. This was when the object was closest to earth. (Lima AFP Spanish Latin America 1525 GMT 24 May 1962—W).

More photographs and still the CIA claims that no visuals are available in the files. One would think that if intelligence is being collected, a picture would be worth a thousand words. The CIA undoubtedly had the resources to obtain photographic information. Where is it all?

Moving onward to 1964, an undated "Narrative of Socorro, New Mexico Sighting, 24 April 1964" appears in the file, and since the document is rather lengthy, we will excerpt only the basic story from the first two pages of the document:

Shortly after 5:30 P.M. on Friday, 24 April 1964 Sgt. Lonnie Zamora of the Socorro Police Department was chasing a speeding auto North on US 85 in the line of duty. While in pursuit he heard a roar and saw flames in an area where a dynamite shack was known to be located. He abandoned chase of the auto and proceeded to where he thought an explosion had occurred. In order to reach this spot he had to travel a little-used road over several hills and gullies. After two or three efforts to drive his car up a gravel-covered incline he reached a crest where the object was visible. At this point, 800 ft from the object, he observed what he thought to be a car overturned and standing on its end. There were one or two objects described as coveralls which he assumed to be occupants of the vehicle. He radioed in to police headquarters that he was proceeding to investigate a 10–74 (auto accident). Proceeding up the road to a point about 15 ft from the gully where the object was, he stopped the car, got out, and headed toward the object. The object was on girderlike legs, white (not chrome) and egg shaped or oval. As he approached the object there were some noises and flame and smoke began to come from the bottom of the vehicle. The noise increased from low pitch to high pitch, was different from that of a jet or helo and not like anything Sgt. Zamora had ever heard. The flame was blue like a welders torch, turning to orange or yellow at the ends. Thinking that the object was going to explode he became frightened. The time was approximately 1745 (1½ hours before sunset), the sun was to his back, slightly to the right. He turned, ran back to get behind the police car, bumping his leg and losing his glasses on the way. He crouched down, shielding his eyes with his arm while the noise continued for another 10 seconds. At this time the noise stopped and he looked up. The object had risen to a point about 15–20 ft. above the ground and the flame and smoke had ceased to come from the object. The object had a red marking about 1 ft or maybe 18 inches in height, shaped like a crescent with a vertical arrow and horizontal line underneath. The object hovered in this spot for several seconds and then flew off in a SW direction following the center of the gully. It cleared the dynamite shack by not more than 3 ft. He watched the object disappear in the distance over a point on Highway 85 about 6 miles from where he was standing. The object took about 3 minutes to travel that far. Disappearance was by fading in the distance and at no time did he observe the object to rise more than 20 ft off the ground.

While proceeding to the location when the object was assumed to be an auto, Sgt. Zamora was in radio contact with police headquarters. The State Police use the same network and his call was monitored by Sgt. Chavez of the New Mexico State Police. Sgt. Zamora attempted to direct Sgt. Chavez to the location while he was driving toward the object. Sgt. Chavez took the wrong road and was, in fact, heading in the opposite direction for part of the time and would not have been in a position to see the object. He arrived at the point where Sgt. Zamora was parked about three minutes after the object had disappeared. Sgt. Zamora was pale and upset at what he had witnessed. Sgt. Chavez was skeptical of the situation and proceeded to where Zamora had observed the object. Here he found the marks and burns. Smoke appeared to be coming from a bush which was burned but no flames or coals were visible. Sgt. Chavez broke a limb from the bush and it was cold to the touch. The marks were fresh and no other marks were in the area. Diagonals of the four impressions intersect in a perpendicular and the major distance seems to be approximately 13 ft. Sgt. Chevez secured the area and contacted local military authorities. This resulted in the investigation of the sighting.

A surprising bit of information relating to the Socorro case was evident in another CIA file entry. An article titled "The Investigation of UFOs" by Hector Quintanella, Jr., appeared in a classified publication, *Studies in Intelligence,* Volume 10, Number 4, Fall 1966. Quintanella was, at the time, the head of Project Blue Book. After discussing UFO sightings in general and the Socorro case in particular, Quintanella stated in a paragraph headed "Diagnosis: Unsolved":

There is no doubt that Lonnie Zamora saw an object which left quite an impression on him. There is also no question about Zamora's reliability. He is a serious officer, a pillar of his church, and a man well versed in recognizing airborne vehicles in his area. He is puzzled by what he saw, and frankly, so are we. This is the best-documented case on record, and still we have been unable, in spite of thorough investigation, to find the vehicle or other stimulus that scared Zamora to the point of panic.

This is an Air Force statement in a classified intelligence publication! They are saying quite clearly that something happened to Zamora that is completely unexplainable. How can one take seriously the giggles and taunts of those who regard the UFO subject as abject nonsense when the head of Project Blue Book, the figurehead of Air Force skepticism, endorsed a UFO sighting in this way?

The next file entry concerns the visit of Dr. Edward Condon to the CIA's National Photographic Interpretation Center (NPIC). The February 23, 1967, memo discusses the Air Force's 1966 agreement with the University of Colorado to investigate UFOs, which was supervised by Dr. Condon, and then it enters into the interrelation that the NPIC would have with Condon's investigation (excerpt):

> 2. On 20 February 1967 at 0915 Dr. Condon and four members of his investigative team visited NPIC. With Dr. Condon were Dr. Richard Lowe, University of Colorado, Dr. David Saunders, University of Colorado, Dr. William Price, Executive Director of AFRST, and Dr. Rachford, USAF. The purpose of this visit was to familiarize Dr. Condon and members of his team with selected photogrammetric and photographic analysis capabilities of NPIC.
>
> 3. The clearance level for the meeting was SECRET.
>
> 4. Upon arrival at NPIC, 0915, . . . escorted the group to Mr. Lundahl's office. In the ensuing 10–15 minute discussion between Mr. Lundahl and Dr. Condon the following points were clearly established:
>
> > a. Any work performed by NPIC to assist Dr. Condon in his investigation will not be identified as work accomplished by the CIA. Dr. Condon was advised by Mr. Lundahl to make no reference to CIA in regard to this work effort. Dr. Condon stated that if he felt it necessary to obtain an official CIA comment he would make a separate distinct entry into CIA not related to contacts he has with NPIC.
> >
> > b. NPIC will not prepare any written comments, will not analyze information with the intent of drawing a conclusion, nor prepare written reports. NPIC personnel will be available to assist Dr. Condon by performing work of a photogrammetric nature, such as attempting to measure objects imaged on photographs that may be part of Dr. Condon's analysis. Work performed by NPIC will be strictly of a technical nature using services and equipment generally not available elsewhere.
>
> 5. Following this brief discussion in Mr. Lundahl's office the group adjourned to the . . . conference room where a series of briefings was presented to Dr. Condon and his group. Following a short introduction by . . . the following briefings were presented:
>
> > a. General discussion of photogrammetry, including definition, terminology *and, in general,* what photogrammetry is and what it can do. . . . presented this discussion.
> >
> > b. . . . followed with a presentation of the analysis he had been conducting on UFO photography furnished NPIC by Dr. Rachford. . . . discussion was of a general nature and outlined the problems he had encountered because of lack of basic information, such as camera focal length, make of camera, unspecified enlargements, etc.

The rest of the memo discussed various photoanalysis techniques and types of equipment used by NPIC. While NPIC's work for Condon was done quietly and without preparation of written reports, it is obvious that important photographic evidence of UFOs probably has gone to NPIC via normal CIA intelligence channels before and after that period. Condon was public figure and the CIA could not allow its unofficial interest to be disclosed through its contacts with Condon's people.

Despite the caution the CIA practiced in its dealings with the Condon Committee, many people suspected a much closer connection between the two. In a July 29, 1970, internal memo, it is reported that a citizen, identified only as Vartorella, expressed his opinion that the CIA used the Condon Committee as a "whitewash to cover a CIA-initiated program begun prior to January 1953." After running through a brief history of the Robertson Panel, the writer, signing himself as "Karl," suggested a response to Vartorella saying that "We're sorry, but we have had *no interest in the UFO matter for many years, have no files* or persons knowledgeable on the subject and hence are unable to respond to his charges and questions [emphasis added]."

Either the writer of the memo was incredibly ignorant of CIA involvement in the subject, which should have disqualified him as a spokesman, or he deliberately and boldly falsified information to an inquiring citizen. We accept the latter explanation since extensive files were already in the CIA's hands on UFOs, a fact that could not have been unknown to agency officials. As such, we must conclude that the CIA holds the public in little regard when it comes to answering serious, legitimate questions.

A January 26, 1976, document titled "International Congress of Space Medicine" deals with UFOs in brief, the information apparently gleaned from discussions at the International Congress during September 1975. Aside from the UFO comment, the document is entirely censored.

> U.S. scientists believe that low magnetic fields do not have a serious effect on astronauts, but high magnetic fields, oscillating magnetic fields, and electromagnetic fields can or do have considerable effect. There is a theory that such fields are closely associated with superconductivity at very low temperatures, such as in space. This in turn is related to the possible propulsion system of UFOs. There is a rumor that fragments of a possible UFO found in Brazil bore a relationship to superconductors and magnetohydrodynamics.

UFOs are hardly the stuff dreams are made of if they have electromagnetic propulsion systems! The comment that high magnetic fields, oscillating magnetic fields, and electromagnetic fields can have "considerable effect" on people lends credence to UFO sightings involving physiological and electromagnetic effects on individuals, vehicles, and other electrically-powered sources. The rumor of Brazilian UFO fragments probably refers to pieces of an exploded UFO over Ubatuba, Brazil, in 1957 which were later discovered to be fragments of magnesium of high purity.

It could be inferred that the next series of memos, cables, and the like may bear some relation to the information acquired on magnetic fields at the International Congress. We don't know if this is so because substantial deletions have been made, but the data is both cryptic and revealing.

SUBJECT: New DCD Case—UFO Research
REFERENCE: Form 610 Dated 9 April 1976 Transmitting UFO Study
1. We are attempting to provide some sort of analytical guidance on the reference. In the meantime, please forward by TWX the full name of the source of the reference as well as his affiliation. In addition, please advise whether the material was classified confidential at the request of the source.
2. In view of the unique quality of this information . . . we request that you provide this information asap.

April 14, 1976:
1. Source's full name is . . . He is employed as . . . .
2. Referent B material classified confidential at his request. Source seeks guidance from CIA UFO experts as to material in his report that should remain classified.

April 1976 undated:
The UFO study was turned over to Dr. . . . (Adds&T) who was also briefed on the developments to date. Dr. . . . said he would show the study to a few people to determine possible implications of the information and would be back to us soon on this matter.

April 26, 1976:
1. Per the request in reference (B), we attempted to obtain analytical guidance on the UFO . . . subject.
2. We contacted the Adds&T (Dr. . . . to see if he knew of any official UFO program and also to attempt to answer some of the questions posed by Dr. . . . exhibited interest in . . . which was handcarried to his office. After a short examination of its contents Dr. . . . advised us that he would personally look into the matter and get back to us. As we discussed in reference (A) Dr. . . . has since contacted us and relayed the following information.
3. It would appear to be best if you advised . . . that he should . . . .

It does not seem that the government has any formal program in progress for the identification/solution of the UFO phenomena. Dr. . . . feels that the efforts of independent researchers, . . . are vital for further progress in this area. At the present time, there are offices and personnel within the agency who are monitoring the UFO phenomena, but again, this is not currently on an official basis. Dr. . . . feels that the best approach would be to keep in touch with and in fact develop reporting channels in this area to keep the agency/community informed of any new developments. In particular, any information which might indicate a threat potential would be of interest, as would specific indications of foreign developments or applications of UFO related research.
4. Dr. . . . has advised us that he would evaluate any additional information

we might receive as well as disseminate significant developments through appropriate channels should it be warranted.

5. We wish to stress again, that there does not now appear to be any special program on UFOs within the intelligence community and this should be relayed to. . . .

May 27, 1976:
Dr. . . . : Regarding our recent discussion . . . some material in which you may be interested. In particular please note attachment A. Our sources obtained it . . .

Our source felt that . . . work might be of interest to the U.S. Government and that it should be evaluated by the Agency. The source also felt that it could be analyzed outside the context of its UFO connection if necessary to remove it from a controversial subject.

As before we are faced with the problem of having UFO related data which is deemed potentially important for the U.S. by our S&T sources . . . evaluated. As you are aware, at this time there is no channel or working group to which we can turn for this type of analysis and dissemination. Thus, if it is acceptable to you we will continue to periodically advise you or your designee of any new or potentially important FI developments which might arise from current independent scientific research on the UFO phenomena.

If you feel that . . . offers some potential we can obtain a more detailed report through our source.

1976 undated:
On 25 June 1976, . . . met with . . . of ORD . . . regarding possible interest by that office in the UFO case. . . . as provided copies of the . . . and the later memo, as well as the original. . . . These items were provided at his request.

. . . felt that there may be some ongoing ORD interest, depending on the evaluation by that office of the material provided. . . . asked that we obtain additional info on the . . . system which we agreed to do. (A TWX was sent to the . . . Office requesting additional information on 25 June 1976.)

. . . asked that the ORD interest be kept at a low profile until some evaluation could be made, but at the same time indicated that he would be in touch with me on a fairly regular basis.

July 14, 1976:
Mr. . . . : At a recent meeting to evaluate material from . . . mentioned a personal interest in the UFO phenomena. As you may recall, I mentioned my own interest in the subject as well as the fact that DCD had been receiving UFO related material from many of our S&T sources who are presently conducting related research. These scientists include some who have been associated with the Agency for years and whose credentials remove them from the "nut" variety.

The attached material came to my attention through these sources and it appears to have some legitimate FI or community interest potential.

The . . . work being carried out by Dr. . . . should, in the view of our S&T sources, be evaluated by the Agency or community.

In view of the expertise associated with your office, as well as your interest in the subject, I felt you might like to see the material.

(If you need additional information or if you feel there is some potential, I would be glad to do this with you. If not, please feel free to destroy the material.)

We haven't the foggiest idea what this research is about, but it certainly caught the imagination of CIA analysts!

According to the last memo, the CIA's Domestic Collections Division "has been receiving UFO related material." These materials came from "Science and Technology" sources and their credentials remove them from the "nut" variety.

The scientist, whoever he is, performed, and may still be performing, UFO-related research which should be "evaluated by the Agency [CIA] or community [intelligence]," in their words.

This is a lot of concern over nothing more than "swamp gas"!

Is the Robertson Panel the CIA's last word on UFOs, as they have told us many times in the past? We think not. There is an unambiguous pattern of continuing interest and monitoring of the UFO phenomenon by the CIA.

One more report rounds out the nearly 900 pages of CIA files. A *Tass* news release from the U.S.S.R. described a UFO seen over Petrozavodsk, the capital of the Soviet Republic of Karelia on September 20, 1977. The UFO appeared like a huge star which flared up in the sky and sent shafts of light to the ground. A later investigation by science writer, James Oberg, determined that the phenomenon was, in reality, a Cosmos rocket launch from the top secret Northern Cosmodrome near Plesetsk.

We think that the interest stems from the fact that the UFO phenomenon is extremely elusive and, therefore, troublesome as a *real* manifestation for U.S. intelligence agencies. The best that they can do at present is to observe and collect whatever hard data can be gleaned from these observations and hope for a breakthrough. There is also the hope that once a breakthrough is achieved, practical, hard science benefits will be available to us in the form of possible new energy sources, new engineering techniques, or a rewriting of our physics textbooks.

It should also be stressed that we have not been given the full story in the released material. By the CIA's own word, at least fifty-seven documents have been withheld from the public after extensive legal battles and by UFO researchers' estimates based on references in released documents, another two hundred plus documents exist.

Victor Marchetti, the former executive assistant to the Deputy Director of the CIA and co-author of *The CIA and the Cult of Intelligence,* wrote of the CIA's UFO interest for the now defunct magazine, *Second Look,* May 1979. In the article, Marchetti stated that during his time with the CIA UFOs were not a common topic of discussion within the Agency due to the fact that it fell into the area of "very sensitive activities." Some rumors which Marchetti had come across within "high levels" of the Agency involved the crash and recovery of UFOs and bodies of little men and many very good sightings by highly qualified observers. Marchetti had not seen conclusive evidence of UFO reality in his position with the CIA, but he concluded that CIA attempts to dismiss the UFO phenomenon as a nonsense problem had all the classic earmarks of a cover-up.

Whether the CIA releases any more UFO information is entirely up to them. Lawsuits have forced some documents out, but the best remains to be seen. We believe that the CIA, in conjunction with other federal agencies, may have the story of the century. The public, as a whole, must make its voice heard on this matter. Only through a concerted effort can the truth be known.

CHAPTER TEN

FBI Involvement: 1947–1949

Beginning in early 1978, we received the first of numerous shipments of FBI documents relating to UFOs, as requested through the Freedom of Information Act. In a letter dated February 10, 1978, then FBI Director Clarence Kelley said, "Investigation of UFO sightings does not fall within the investigative jurisdiction of the FBI; however, the FBI for a limited period of time did assist the Department of the Air Force in investigating alleged UFO sightings."

Over a two-year period, approximately 1,700 pages of UFO files were released by the FBI's Freedom of Information and Privacy Acts Branch. This is not the total amount of UFO data in the FBI's files, however. Many documents have been withheld to protect the personal privacy of eyewitnesses who had reported sightings, a legitimate exemption which we did not challenge. Another reason given for withholding information was the "b one" or "national security" exemption, although this was not used extensively by the FBI.

The "limited period of time" of the FBI's official interest in UFOs, as referred to by Director Kelley, covered a two-month span, from July 31 through October 1, 1947. During this time, FBI agents conducted extensive investigations of UFO sightings, usually at the request of the Air Force. Let's take a look at how this situation developed.

The first document of any consequence was filed July 10, 1947. It was written by an FBI official, E. G. Fitch, and is titled "Flying Discs":

At request of Brigadier General George F. Schulgen, Chief of the Requirements Intelligence Branch of Army Air Corps Intelligence, Special Agent

Reynolds discussed the above captioned matter with him on July 9, 1947. General Schulgen indicated to Reynolds that the Air Corps has taken the attitude that every effort must be undertaken in order to run down and ascertain whether or not the flying disks are a fact and, if so, to learn all about them. According to General Schulgen, the Air Corps Intelligence are utilizing all of their scientists in order to ascertain whether or not such a phenomenon could in fact occur. He stated that this research is being conducted with the thought that the flying objects might be a celestial phenomenon and with the view that they might be a foreign body mechanically devised and controlled.

General Schulgen also indicated to Reynolds that all Air Corps installations have been alerted to run out each reported sighting to obtain all possible data to assist in this research project. In passing, General Schulgen stated that an Air Corps pilot who believed that he saw one of these objects was thoroughly interrogated by General Schulgen and scientists, as well as a psychologist, and the pilot was adamant in his claim that he saw a flying disk.

General Schulgen advised Reynolds that the possibility exists that the first reported sightings of the so-called flying disks are fallacious and prompted by individuals seeking personal publicity, or were reported for political reasons. He stated that if this was so, subsequent sightings might be the result of a mass hysteria. He pointed out that the thought exists that the first reported sightings might have been by individuals of Communist sympathies with the view to causing hysteria and fear of a secret Russian weapon.

General Schulgen indicated to Reynolds that he is desirous of having all the angles covered in this matter. He stated that reports of his scientists and findings of the various Air Corps installations will be available in his office. He advised that to complete the picture he desired the assistance of the Federal Bureau of Investigation in locating and questioning the individuals who first sighted the so-called flying disks in order to ascertain whether or not they are sincere in their statements that they saw these disks, or whether their statements were prompted by personal desire for publicity or political reasons. General Schulgen assured Reynolds that there are no War Department or Navy Department research projects presently being conducted which could in any way be tied up with the flying disks. General Schulgen indicated to Reynolds that if the Bureau would cooperate with him in this matter, he would offer all the facilities of his office as to results obtained in the effort to identify and run down this matter.

Reynolds advised General Schulgen that his request would be made known to the Bureau and an answer made available to him as soon as possible.

Reynolds also discussed this matter with Colonel L. R. Forney of MID. Colonel Forney indicated that it was his attitude that in as much as it has been established that the flying disks are not the result of any Army or Navy experiments, the matter is of interest to the FBI. He stated that he was of the opinion that the Bureau, if at all possible, should accede to General Schulgen's request.

At the end of the memo the following comments appeared:

I would recommend that we advise the Army that the Bureau does not believe it should go into these investigations, it being noted that a great bulk of those alleged discs reported found have been pranks. It is not believed that the Bureau would accomplish anything by going into these investigations.

David M. Ladd (Assistant Director)

I think we should do this.

Clyde Tolson

I would do it but before agreeing to it we must insist upon full access to discs recovered. For instance in the La. case the Army grabbed it & would not let us have it for cursory examination.

J. Edgar Hoover

Hoover's statement would seem to support the idea that authentic crashed UFO incidents had occurred in the past and that the FBI was interested in examining objects recovered by the military. This was not the case, however. In the Project Blue Book files, a case dated July 7, 1947, from Shreveport, Louisiana (the "La." case), is listed. According to the report, a sixteen-inch aluminum disc allegedly landed with smoke coming out of it. Coils of wire were strung on the disc. When the Army was called in to see what the object was, they discovered the inscription "Made in USA" on the disc.

It was a crude attempt to hoax a landed UFO, but Hoover's comment has been taken out of context by various writers as evidence of alien beings coming to earth.

Another memo dated July 29, 1947, from E. G. Fitch on "Flying Discs" provides follow-up information to the July 10 memo:

Reference is made to my memorandum to you in the above captioned matter dated July 10, 1947, indicating that Brigadier General George F. Schulgen of the Army Air Corps Intelligence had requested that the Bureau cooperate with the Army Air Corps Intelligence in connection with the above captioned matter. The Director noted on the referenced memorandum, "I would do it but before agreeing to it we must insist upon full access to discs recovered. For instance in the La. case the Army grabbed it and would not let us have it for cursory examination."

This is to advise that Special Agent Reynolds has recontacted General Schulgen and advised him in connection with the Director's notation. General Schulgen indicated to Reynolds that he desired to assure Mr. Hoover of complete cooperation in this matter and stated that he would issue instructions to the field directing that all cooperation be furnished to the FBI and that all discs recovered be made available for the examination by the FBI Agents. General Schulgen pointed out to Reynolds that he will from time to time make the results of the studies of his scientists available to the Bureau for the assistance of the FBI Field Offices. General Schulgen indicated to Reynolds that there has been a decrease in the reported sightings of the discs which might be because of the fact that it has lost much of its publicity value. He indicated, however, that he believed it necessary to follow this matter through to determine as near as possible if discs were in fact seen and to determine their origin.

General Schulgen inquired of Reynolds the method by which the Bureau would make the information obtained from the Bureau's inquiries known to the Air Corps, in the Field as well as at the War Department level. Mr. Reynolds pointed out to General Schulgen that the best procedure appeared to be through the regular established channels. It was pointed out to General Schulgen that the Bureau Field Offices maintain close liaison with the Intelligence Divisions of the various Armies as well as close liaison with the Intelligence Division of the War Department. General Schulgen indicated that he would be satisfied to receive information through this means.

General Schulgen indicated to Reynolds that he believed that there was a possibility that this entire matter might have been started by subversive individuals for the purpose of creating a mass hysteria. He suggested that the Bureau keep this in mind in many interviews conducted regarding reported sightings. General Schulgen stated to Mr. Reynolds that he would make available to the Bureau all information in the possession of the Air Corps regarding the sightings which were first reported so that the Bureau could conduct some investigation regarding these individuals to ascertain their motives for reporting that they had observed flying discs. When General Schulgen makes the information available regarding these individuals, it will be promptly brought to your attention.

As a result of these discussions, the following FBI policy statement appeared, dated July 30, 1947:

FLYING DISCS—The Bureau, at the request of the Army Air Forces Intelligence, has agreed to cooperate in the investigation of flying discs. The Air Forces have confidentially advised that it is possible to release three or more discs in odd numbers, attached together by a wire, from an airplane in high altitudes and that these discs would obtain tremendous speed in their descent and would descend to the earth in an arc. The Army Air Forces Intelligence has also indicated some concern that the reported sightings might have been made by subversive individuals for the purpose of creating mass hysteria.

You should investigate each instance which is brought to your attention of a sighting of a flying disc in order to ascertain whether or not it is a bona fide sighting, an imaginary one, or a prank. You should also bear in mind that individuals might report seeing flying discs for various reasons. It is conceivable that an individual might be desirous of seeking personal publicity, causing hysteria, or playing a prank.

The Bureau should be notified immediately by teletype of all reported sightings and the results of your inquiries. In instances where the report appears to have merit, the teletype should be followed by a letter to the Bureau containing in detail the results of your inquiries. The Army Air Forces have assured the Bureau complete cooperation in the matters and in any instances where they fail to make information available to you ro make the recovered discs available for your examination, it should promptly be brought to the attention of the Bureau.

Any information you develop in connection with these discs should be promptly brought to the attention of the Army through your usual liason channels.

While hoaxed UFO models had taken up much of the FBI's valuable time up to this point, good quality UFO sightings began to pour into the files

after Bureau Bulletin No. 42 took effect. The following reports are taken
from Army Air Forces messages to the FBI:

FROM: A. M. LONDON
TO: FAFDEL
AIX 6328 Aug. 8th 1947
Your AIX 14 July 29th
During normal night flying practice at 2230 on 16th January, 1947, one
of our Mosquitos was vectored on to an unidentified aircraft at 22,000
feet. A long chase ensued commencing over the North Sea about 50 miles
from the Dutch coast and ending at 2300 hours over Norfolk. Two brief
AI contacts were made but faded quickly. The unidentified aircraft appeared
to take efficient controlled evasive action.

No explanation of this incident has been forthcoming nor has it been repeated.

The next report is a classic "flying saucer" report by an airline crew, dated
July 4, 1947:

Interview Report
SUBJECT: Interviews with . . ., United Air Lines pilots, who reported seeing
flying disks.
Smith was interviewed at 1500, 9 July 1947, concerning the "flying disks,"
and stated substantially as follows:
"We left Boise, Idaho, at 2304 Pacific Standard Time. At approximately
2315, the co-pilot, . . . called my attention to the first object seen. We
were then in the vicinity of Emmet, Idaho, our altitude was approximately
6500, and we were climbing to our proposed cruising altitude of 8,000
from there to Pendleton, Oregon. The heading of the plane at the time
was 300 degrees Magnetic North, and the object (one) was sighted at
approximately 290 degrees or ten degrees to our left. Then an additional
four objects appeared to the left of the main, or first, object. These four
objects appeared slightly smaller than the first object sighted, but all of
the objects appeared on the same plane. I estimated the altitude of the
objects to be about 8,500. They were within our sight for approximately
two minutes, then they disappeared.
"Shortly after the first group disappeared, probably one or two minutes
later, the second group appeared about 310 degrees, or to the right of
the plane. Their altitude was the same as the first group. Three of the
objects appeared to be on the same plane, and one object appeared slightly
higher and to the right of the others. The second group stayed within our
sight twelve to fifteen minutes, then disappeared. We had levelled off by
the time the second group disappeared.
"The objects were flat on the base, the top slightly rough in contour. The
dimensions appeared the same as a DC-8 approximately five miles from
us. In other words, it could have been ninety miles away if it would be
possible for an object as large as that would have to be to be flying, but
since we didn't know what we were looking at or how large it was, we
decided that if it were the size of a DC-8 wing span (90 feet), it was about
five miles distant. Actually, we have no idea just how large it was since

we could not determine its distance from us. When we first sighted the objects, we decided they were either going away from us or coming towards us. After a short while, however, we know they couldn't be coming towards us, because we never approached them. I don't believe they could have been going a great rate of speed and still stayed in sight for as long as they did. I would judge they might have been travelling about 300 miles per hour.

"My personal opinions regarding the objects are that their speed varied, was not constant. When first sighted, they were going slow and stayed within sight for quite some time. However, when we lost sight of them, they seemed to disappear practically immediately. I think they either put on a tremendous burst of speed and disappeared from sight, or else they dissipated. Also, it appeared that only one object, the large one, was controlled, and it in turn controlled the other objects, and I think they were ground controlled.

"In both instances, the co-pilot sighted the objects first and called my attention to them. The weather was clear and unlimited, with not a cloud in the sky. We checked the wind, and it was 230–10, or out of the Southwest at ten miles per hour. The air speed of the ship was about 135 MPH. The sun was below the horizon and the objects were silhouetted against the sky, hence we could distinguish no color or reflection.

. . . , co-pilot of the plane, was interviewed at 2130, 9 July 1947. . . . corroborated the remarks made by Smith concerning the flight of the plane, the time the objects were sighted, direction of the flight of the plane, etc. There were two discrepancies in their statements as to the size of the smaller objects and the altitude at which they were flying. . . . stated that there was a big difference in the size of the large objects and the smaller ones, and that it was hard to distinguish the shape of the smaller ones. . . . also stated that the objects were at the same altitude as their plane and seemed to be climbing with them. In addition to confirming Smith's statements concerning the flight, etc, . . . stated substantially as follows:

"I was flying the plane when I spotted the first object at 2012 on the 4th of July, eight minutes after departure from Boise, Idaho. I thought it was an oncoming aircraft similar to ours (DC-3) about five miles away, so turned on our landing lights, which is the usual signal to another plane to let it know you're in the vicinity. I mentioned this fact to Smith, and he watched the object also. While we were both watching, four more objects appeared at the same altitude as the first. They seemed to be at the same altitude as our plane, about 6000 feet. They were heading about 290 degrees Magnetic North, so I turned to follow them. We watched them for four or five minutes, then they all merged as one and disappeared. I don't know whether they merged in line of flight or not, nor do I know whether they went beyond our vision or whether they dissipated.

Two minutes later, the large object reappeared with three smaller ones on its left and one smaller one a great distance to the right. We had the second group in sight for about twelve minutes. The last time seen, they were still in that formation and disappeared into the sunset. Also, when we last saw them, they seemed to have continued climbing after we leveled off and were about nine or ten thousand feet.

"At the time we saw the objects, the sun was below the horizon, but there was quite a bright red glow above the horizon from the sunset. I couldn't really say what distance they were from us, not knowing what they were or how large they were. However, while we were watching them we radioed ahead to Ontario, Oregon, about thirty miles distant, to the weather station there, and told them what we were seeing and asked them to go outside and see if they could see them. They radioed back and said they could see nothing, so the objects could have been beyond Ontario, since we had told them that they were between our plane and Ontario. It should also be noted that the personnel at Ontario would be looking at a dark sky and may not be likely to be able to see them anyway.

"I can't say whether they are man-made disks or not, whether they are radio controlled or not, or anything about them. They did not maneuver much at all, except when the first group merged. All I can say is that they were going our direction and were climbing. I don't think they were clouds, as there hadn't been a cloud in the sky, and it would have been quite a phenomenon as it was like nothing I had ever seen before. There was a big difference in the size of the objects. The smaller ones were hard to distinguish as to shape; they were not shiny, nor did they "flip." I couldn't swear on a stand that they were not clouds, but I think it impossible. Had they been clouds, they wouldn't have appeared and disappeared so suddenly, and we would have approached them.

"As we were taxiing out to take off from Boise, the tower called us and asked us if we had seen any disks lately. As a consequence, we were and had been talking about the flying disks when we sighted them. I don't believe, however, that it was a figment of the imagination, as Smith and I were seeing the same things, even the object far off to the right in the second group. We also called the stewardess, who had not been in on the conversation, and without mentioning "disks" asked her what she saw. She stated that she saw the same things we did, which seemed to prove to us that it was not our imagination."

In addition to the above, . . . stated, off the record, that he was rather disappointed in Smith and all the publicity he was getting. He thought that Smith was probably "Grand-standing" some, and that as far as he, . . . , was concerned, he was not going to be interviewed by any reporters, or go on the radio, etc. He stated that he was glad to talk to a Navy representative about it, or to any other government official, and help in any way he could, but he certainly didn't want to be bothered with a lot of interviews with newspapers and radio stations. . . . seemed to the writer to be a very level-headed, sensible man, and not in favor of a lot of publicity, whereas Smith although a sensible man and all, seemed to be more in favor of all the publicity he was getting."

The next memo comments on the character of the pilot.

MEMORANDUM FOR THE OFFICER IN CHARGE:

On 12 July 1947, E. J. Smith, of the United Airlines, was interviewed at the Boise Municipal Airport, Boise, Idaho. Smith was passing through Boise on a schedule flight at the time and had a 20 minute stop-over. Smith reiterated the statements originally made by him to the press as to what he had seen in the late evening of July 4th, when 8 minutes out of Boise on the route to Seattle, Washington. It is the opinion of the interviewer that due to the position Smith occupies, that he, Smith, would have to be very strongly convinced that he actually saw flying disks before he would open himself for the ridicule attached to a report of this type.

Another sighting, dated May 19, 1947, involved a railroad crew. The memo bore a curious title which, somehow, never seems to have caught on as another nickname for flying saucers:

SUBJECT: Supersonic Platters   July 2, 1947
SUMMARY OF INFORMATION:
The following information was related to Counter Intelligence Corps Personnel at Headquarters Fifteenth Air Force, Colorado Springs, Colorado on 27 June 1947 by . . . , Colorado Springs, Colorado, Mr. P. J. Smith, 24 Fairview, Manitou Springs, Colorado and . . . Colorado Springs, Colorado. All three of the men are employees of the Pikes Peak Railway, Manitou Springs, Colorado.

On or about 19 May, 1947 during their lunch period 1215–1315, a member of a train crew called attention to a silver object in the sky approaching from the North East. It appeared to be travelling at a great speed. All three men stated that the altitude of the object was very difficult to determine because of its apparent smallness. They further stated that because of this it was difficult to view the object as being large and having high altitude or small and being at a relatively low altitude. They did say though that it appeared to be higher than the top of Manitou Mountain which is over 1000 feet higher than the shops which are situated at its base. No definite shape of the object could be determined and even with the aid of binoculars it still could not be brought into focus. The binoculars used were of about 4 to 6 power. The men stated that they were certain that the object did not have any of the physical characteristics of modern conventional aircraft.

The day was described as being clear and sunny with not a cloud in the sky and no ground wind.

On reaching the area just North of Manitou Mountain the object remained in the immediate area for several minutes during which time it was seen to execute maneuvers such as climbing, diving and reversal of direction of flight. This happened every few seconds. The distance and location between views prompted two of the men to think that there were more of the unidentified objects in the sky. At times the object seemed to hover in the air and then start on another path of flight. When last seen the silver object was climbing very fast towards the west almost directly into the wind.

This interview, dated July 10, 1947, relates the sighting of an object which was not only seen visually by multiple witnesses but also was photographed, showing the effects of the object's passage:

Interrogation of (Deleted), Harmon Field, Newfoundland, taken at 1430 AST, 16 July 1947, by Captain William K. Smith, AC, Intelligence Officer.

Q. Were you with . . . on the evening when they saw an object of flying disk passing over the sky on 10 July 1947?

A. Yes, I was.

Q. Were you or any members of the party drinking?

A. No, I had one can of beer, that was about half hour before that.

Q. Can you tell me the circumstances under which you saw the object or its trail?

A. Well, . . . saw it first and said he saw the thing travelling through the sky. We did not believe him at first but when he was so concerned about it we stopped the car and got out. I had my camera so took a picture of it. There was a bluish streak left in the sky which could not have been a cloud formation. It was a definite trail and caused the clouds to break open as it went through.

Q. Did it cut a path through the cloud?

A. Yes, it was very clear, and you could see the trail right through the cloud, it looked to be travelling in a big circle and it left sharp edges to the clouds.

Q. What was the trail like?

A. I would not say it was exhaust, it looked as if an object passed through similar to that of a pebble leaving a ring in the pond.

Q. Was there any difference in the color?

A. No, it looked as if the object broke the cloud and left this opening.

Q. Was the trail horizontal, going up, or coming down?

A. It looked horizontal.

Q. What was the altitude of the clouds?

A. I don't know, sir, they were pretty high though.

Q. What time was this?

A. I don't know exactly sir, but it was between three and five o'clock in the afternoon, we were coming back from fishing.

Q. Did you see the object?

A. No.

Q. How long do you think the trail was?

A. I don't know, sir, but the trail was very long, that is why I think something went through the sky because of the trail and blank space it left, you could easily see it.

Q. Was the trail on a straight course?

A. Well, as I said before, it looked to me from the ground, that it was travelling at a terrific rate of speed in a circle because of the area in the path.

Q. Have you ever seen a meteor?

A. No.

Q. Can you estimate the size of the cut in the clouds?

A. No.

Q. How long have you been working around planes, etc.?

A. Six (6) years.

Q. Were you in the Army during the war?

A. No.

Q. How many pictures did you take?

A. Two.

Q. What type camera did you have?

A. An Argus, F-2.

Q. Was the film black and white or Kodachrome?

A. It was Kodachrome.

Q. Where is the film now?

A. Well, I took three or four rolls and I am not sure which one the pictures are on.

Q. I understood from . . . that they are being developed.
A. I think it is out of the camera, sir, but I have not sent them out yet.
Q. Will you give us the four rolls of film so we can have them processed officially?
A. Yes, sir.
Q. Are you willing to give the Army a copy of the picture of the trail?
A. Yes.

The FBI and Army Air Forces cooperation began to deteriorate beginning with a September 3, 1947 letter from Air Defense Command Headquarters at Mitchel Field, New York:

SUBJECT: Cooperation of FBI with AAF on Investigations of "Flying Disc" Incidents.

TO: Command Generals, First, Second, Fourth, Tenth, Eleventh and Fourteenth Air Forces.

ATTENTION: Assistant Chief of Staff, A-2.

1. The Federal Bureau of Investigation has agreed to assist Air Force Intelligence personnel in the investigation of "flying disc" incidents in order to quickly and effectively rule out what are pranks and to concentrate on what appears to be a genuine incident.

2. It was the original intent of the AC/AS-2, Headquarters, Army Air Forces that whereas the ADC Air Forces would *interview* responsible observers whose names would be furnished by AAF, the FBI would *investigate* incidents of so-called "discs" being found on the ground. The services of the FBI were enlisted in order to relieve the numbered Air Forces of the task of tracking down all the many instances which turned out to be ash can covers, toilet seats, and whatnot.

3. It is requested that each A-2 informally coordinate and cooperate with the FBI, generally keeping the FBI informed of any proposed calls intelligence personnel will make on this subject. Very shortly, with the separation of the AAF from the War Department, a firm policy will be established to clarify the liaison arrangements between A-2's and FBI Special Agents. Presently, it is considered inadvisable to promulgate a formal interim policy—only to have it replaced in a month or so by another.

BY COMMAND OF LIEUTENANT GENERAL STRATEMEYER:
                                        /s/R. H. Smith
                                        R. H. Smith
                                        Colonel, GSC
                                        Asst. Chief of Staff–Intell.

An agent at the San Francisco FBI office took great exception to this letter as follows:

Attention: Assistant Director D. M. LADD   Sept. 19, 1947
RE: REPORTS OF FLYING DISCS
Dear Sir:
I am transmitting herewith copies of a "restricted" later dated September 3, 1947, which was furnished to me by Lieutenant Colonel Springer, A-2,

Army Air Forces, Hamilton Field, California, which letter is designated to certain Commanding Generals in the Army Air Forces from Colonel R. H. Smith, Assistant Chief of Staff–Intelligence, Headquarters Air Defense Command, Mitchel Field, New York, concerning "Cooperation of FBI with AAF on Investigations of 'Flying Disc' Incidents."

It is my understanding from recent Bureau instructions that we are to assist the Air Force Intelligence personnel in the investigation of flying disc incidents. However, it will be noted from the attached letter that it is the Army interpretation that it was their intent that the Bureau would investigate those incidents of the so-called "discs" being found on the ground and apparently not those which are observed only in flight. Further, the attention of the Bureau is respectfully called to·paragraph two of this letter and to the last sentence therein which states, "The services of the FBI were enlisted in order to relieve the numbered Air Forces of the task of tracking down all the many instances which turned out to be ash can covers, toilet seats, and whatnot."

In the first place, the instructions issued by the Army Air Forces in this letter appear to limit the type of investigations which the Bureau will be asked to handle and secondly it appears to me the wording of the last sentence in the second paragraph mentioned above is cloaked in entirely uncalled-for language tending to indicate the Bureau will be asked to conduct investigations only in those cases which are not important and which are almost, in fact, ridiculous.

The thought has occurred to me the Bureau might desire to discuss this matter further with the Army Air Forces both as to the type of investigations which we will conduct and also to object to the scurrilous wordage which, to say the least, is insulting to the Bureau in the last sentence of paragraph two.

In the event the Bureau decides to discuss the matter further with the Army Air Forces, it is recommended that no indication whatsoever be given indicating this letter was referred to me by Lieutenant Colonel Springer in as much as it would undoubtedly cause him serious embarrassment and would certainly cause the excellent personal relationship which exists between Lieutenant Colonel Springer and this office to be endangered.

> Very truly yours,
> (signed) Harry M. Kimball
> Harry M. Kimball
> Special Agent in Charge

After Assistant Director Ladd received the September 19 letter, he issued a memo dated September 26:

SUBJECT: FLYING DISCS

The Bureau was requested by the Air Forces Intelligence to assist the Air Forces in attempting to arrive at an explanation of the above phenomena. The Air Force indicated that the alleged sightings of flying discs might have been made by individuals of Communist sympathies for the purpose of causing mass hysteria in the United States over the fear of a secret Russian weapon. The Bureau agreed to assist in the investigation of the reported sightings, and the Field was advised in Bureau Bulletin No. 42, Series 1947, dated July 30, 1947, that they should investigate each instance which was brought to their attention of the sighting of a flying disc in order to ascertain whether or not it was a bona fide sighting, an imaginary one, or a prank. The results of the investigation conducted by the Bureau Field Offices in this matter have failed to reveal any indication of subversive individuals being involved in any of the reported sightings.

The Bureau has received a communication in the captioned matter from the Special Agent in Charge at San Francisco, dated September 19, 1947, which attached a "restricted" letter that was furnished confidentially to the SAC at San Francisco by Lieutenant Colonel Donald L. Springer, A-2, Army Air Forces, Hamilton Field, California, a copy of which is attached hereto. It is noted that the letter, which is dated September 3, 1947, is signed "By Command of Lieutenant General Stratemeyer" by Colonel R. H. Smith, Assistant Chief of Staff Intelligence, Headquarters, Air Defense Command, Mitchel Field, New York, and is addressed to the Commanding Generals of the various Air Forces. This letter is entitled "Cooperation of FBI with AAF on Investigations of 'Flying Disc' Incidents."

This letter states in substance that it was the original intent of the AC/ AS-2, Headquarters Army Air Forces that whereas the ADC Air Forces would interview responsible observers, the FBI would investigate incidents of so-called discs being found on the ground. Further, it indicates that the services of the FBI were enlisted in order to relieve the numbered Air Forces of the task of tracking all the many instances which turned out to be "ash can covers, toilet seats, and whatnot."

RECOMMENDATION:

It is recommended that the Bureau protest vigorously to the Assistant Chief of Air Staff–2. It is also recommended that the Bureau discontinue all activity in this field and that the Bureau Field Offices be advised to discontinue all investigations and to refer all complaints received to the Air Forces. A proposed Bulletin is attached for your approval.

On September 27, J. Edgar Hoover himself became embroiled in the controversy. Addressing his remarks to Major General George MacDonald, Assistant Chief, Air Staff, Hoover said:

Dear General McDonald:

The Federal Bureau of Investigation has been requested by your office to assist in the investigation of reported sightings of flying discs.

My attention has been called to instructions disseminated by the Air Forces relative to this matter. I have been advised that these instructions indicate that the Air Forces would interview responsible observers while the FBI would investigate incidents of discs found on the ground, thereby relieving the Air Force of running down incidents which in many cases turned out to be "ash can covers, toilet seats, and whatnot."

In view of the apparent understanding by the Air Forces of the position of the Federal Bureau of Investigation in this matter, I cannot permit the personnel and time of this organization to be dissipated in this manner.

I am advising the Field Divisions of the Federal Bureau of Investigation to discontinue all investigative activity regarding the reported sightings of flying discs, and am instructing them to refer all complaints received to the appropriate Air Force representative in their area.

Finally, on October 1, 1947, all FBI cooperation ended with the issuance of Bureau Bulletin 59:

> FLYING DISCS—Effective immediately, the Bureau has discontinued its investigative activities as outlined in Section B of Bureau Bulletin No. 42, Series 1947, dated July 30, 1947.
>
> All future reports connected with flying discs should be referred to the Air Forces and no investigative action should be taken by Bureau Agents.

This did not mean that the FBI had stopped receiving UFO information. While detailed investigations, in cooperation with the military, had ceased, many interesting incidents continued to be reported to FBI headquarters and field offices.

The FBI spent much of 1948 advising its field offices of Bureau Bulletin No. 57 and instructed them to forward any new UFO reports to the Air Force. A few reports had trickled in during the summer, including a July 24 report from Montgomery, Alabama, involving an Eastern Airlines plane piloted by Captain C. S. Chiles and John B. Whitted; a well-published incident in UFO literature. We will see some comment on this report in a significant 1949 memo next. In the meantime, the FBI took little action of 1948 reports other than simply filing them away for posterity.

The FBI file for 1949 shows considerably more interesting material than the previous year. Although the FBI's official responsibility for UFO reports was removed, this did not mean that they ignored information coming their way. The responsibility to investigate important information still belonged in the FBI's lap.

The first memo of significance was one dated January 31, 1949, titled "Protection of Vital Installations." It was sent to the Director of the FBI by the San Antonio, Texas, field office:

> At recent Weekly Intelligence Conferences of G-2, ONI, OSI, and FBI, in the Fourth Army Area, Officers of G-2, Fourth Army have discussed the matter of "Unidentified Aircraft" or "Unidentified Aerial Phenomena," otherwise known as "Flying Discs," "Flying Saucers," and "Balls of Fire." *This matter is considered top secret by Intelligence Officers of both the Army and the Air Forces* [emphasis in the original].
>
> It is well known that there have been during the past two years reports from the various parts of the country of the sighting of unidentified aerial objects which have been called in newspaper parlance "flying discs" and "flying saucers." The first such sightings were reported from Sweden, and it was thought that the objects, the nature of which was unknown, might have originated in Russia.
>
> In July 1948, an unidentified aircraft was "seen" by an Eastern Airlines Pilot and Co-pilot and one or more passengers of the Eastern Airlines plane over Montgomery, Alabama. This aircraft was reported to be of an unconventional type without wings and resembled generally a "rocket ship" of the type depicted in comic strips. It was reported to have had windows;

to have been larger than the Eastern Airlines plane, and to have been traveling at an estimated speed of 2700 miles an hour. It appeared out of a thunderhead ahead of the Eastern Airlines plane and immediately disappeared in another cloud narrowly missing a collision with the Eastern Airlines plane. No sound or air disturbance was noted in connection with this appearance.

During the past two months various sightings of unexplained phenonema have been reported In the vicinity of the A.E.C. Installation at Los Alamos, New Mexico, where these phenomena now appear to be concentrated. During December 1948 on the 5th, 6th, 7th, 8th, 11th, 13th, 14th, 20th, and 28th, sightings of unexplained phenomena were made near Los Alamos by Special Agents of the Office of Special Investigations; Airline Pilots; Military Pilots; Los Alamos Security Inspectors; and private citizens. On January 6, 1949, another similar object was sighted in the same area.

. . . , a Meteorologist of some note, has been generally in charge of the observations near Los Alamos, attempting to learn the characteristics of the unexplained phenomena.

Up to this time little concrete information has been obtained.

There have been day time sightings which are tentatively considered to possibly resemble the exhaust of some type of jet propelled object. Night-time sightings have taken the form of lights usually described as brilliant green, similar to a green traffic signal or green neon light. Some reports indicated that the light began and ended with a red or orange flash. Other reports have given the color as red, white, blue-white, and yellowish green. Trailing lights sometimes observed are said to be red. The spectrum analysis of one light indicates that it may be a copper compound of the type known to be used in rocket experiments and which completely disintegrates upon explosion, leaving no debris. It is noted that no debris has ever been known to be located anywhere resulting from the unexplained phenomena.

Recent observations have indicated that the unidentified phenomena travel at a rate of speed estimated at a minimum of three miles per second and a maximum of twelve miles a second, or 27,000 miles an hour. Their reported course indicates that they travel on an East–West line with probability that they approach from the Northern quadrant, which would be the last stage of the great circle route if they originated in Russia. When observed they seem to be in level flight at a height of six to ten miles and thus traveling on a tangent to the earth's surface. They occasionally dip at the end of the path and on two occasions a definite vertical change in the path was indicated. These phenomena have not been known to have been sighted, however, at any intermediate point between Russia and Los Alamos, but only at the end of the flight toward the apparent "target," namely, Los Alamos.

In every case but one the shape of the objects has been reported as round in a point of light with a definite area to the light's source. One report gives a diamond shape; another indicates that trailing lights are elongated. The size is usually compared to one-fourth the diameter of the full moon, and they have also been compared in size to a basketball with trailing lights the size of a baseball.

On no occasion has sound been associated directly with the phenomena, but unexplained sounds have been reported from Los Alamos. On two occasions reports have been received of the sightings of multiple units.

Some nine scientific reasons are stated to exist which indicated that the phenomena observed are not due to meteorites. The only conclusions reached thus far are that they are either hitherto unobserved natural phenomena or that they are man-made. No scientific experiments are known to exist in this country which could give rise to such phenomena.

So, while flying saucers were being dismissed publicly as misidentifications, hoaxes, and the product of Saturday night drinking parties, the Army and Air Force looked upon the matter as "Top Secret."

Paragraph 2 of the memo refers to the so-called "Ghost Rocket" phenomena over Scandinavia in the summer of 1946. Speeding objects, resembling meteors but behaving in unmeteor-like fashion, were seen by hundreds of people. Attempts were made to link the sightings with Russian rocket experiments and, in fact, American authorities paid a visit to Sweden to examine this possibility. There was never any concrete evidence supporting this theory and ultimately the sightings ceased without a hint as to their origin.

The memo also alludes to sightings of greenish UFOs in New Mexico, a rather important phase of the UFO phenomena which we will discuss later in the chapter.

A memo dated March 25, 1949, sent to a large number of FBI offices and officials, offers the following curious comment:

For your confidential information, a reliable and confidential source has advised the Bureau that flying discs are believed to be man-made missiles rather than natural phenomenon. It has also been determined that for approximately the past four years the USSR has been engaged in experimentation on an unknown type of flying disc.

The "reliable and confidential source" never produced information to back up the claims as cited in the memo. The FBI probably thought later that the claim was spurious as no other data relating to this can be found in the files. The same memo contained a restatement of policy on UFOs, whereby "no investigation should be conducted," yet provided for "securing data from persons who desire to voluntarily furnish information."

One of the small number of detailed UFO sightings for 1949 was contained in a memo dated May 13, 1949, from the Los Angeles field office titled "Flying Disc Report."

On May 5, 1949, . . . , a reporter from the *Sun-Star* newspaper, Merced, California, advised Special Agent . . . that his paper had been contacted by Lt. Colonel STANLEY JACOBS, Intelligence Officer, Castle Air Force Base, Merced, California, relative to any reports that the newspaper might have received concerning "flying disks" in the Merced vicinity.

. . . stated a close friend of his, one . . . Merced, had advised him that he had observed a strange object, and as he is in the Air Corps Reserve, he reported same to the Intelligence Officer at Castle Field.

On the same date, MR. GEORGE BREMER, Detachment Commander,

Office of Special Investigations, Castle Air Force Base, Merced, California, advised SA . . . that he had heard that an individual had reported seeing a "flying disk" to the Intelligence Office at the Base but that the Intelligence Officer had not furnished the information to him. . . . later on the same date contacted SA . . . and exhibited a letter written by STANLEY F. JACOBS, Lt. Col., USAF, Adjutant (Intelligence Officer) to Commanding General, Air Material Command, Wright-Patterson AFB, Wright Field, Ohio. This letter contained a statement given by Mr. . . . which read as follows: "I had occasion to step from my home, located approximately one mile west of the town of Merced, on the night of April 4, 1949, at approximately 2220. My attention was diverted to a clicking noise of considerable intensity. I stopped on the sidewalk about 20 feet from the front steps and recognized the source of this clicking to be in the sky in an area about 40 degrees from the surface of the earth in an easterly direction. The sky condition was 20,000 thin broken with 12 miles visibility and surface winds were reported as north nine M.P.H. at Castle Air Force weather station. My home is approximately seven miles south of Castle Air Force Base and in an area somewhat sheltered from surface winds, and no appreciable surface wind was apparent at the time the aural observation was made. After about ten seconds of looking into the area described previously as being the source of this sound, an object was observed blanking out stars in describing a flight path in a west or north-westerly direction. Only one object was apparent, its shape can be described as only a solid mass. Its size can be estimated as four or five feet in diameter in keeping with an estimated altitude of considerably less than 1000 (one thousand) feet. Color was shown by the reflection of ground lights on only two occasions, and appeared to be dull surfaced, light colored metal. The only ground lights of intensity were a row of street lights behind me one half block which leads me to believe the under surface of this object to be curved in shape.

This object, when first sighted, was moving very slowly in a west or northwesterly direction. I would estimate that I had it in my range of vision for 35 seconds, after having heard it about ten seconds before locating it. It passed on beyond the house and maneuvered through an arc of turn to the left of about ninety degrees. The clicking sound was continuous throughout this turn; however, it became louder as it returned on its new heading of south or southwest. On its return the clicking sound became louder, but I was unable to see it at this time. The clicking stopped when it was at its greatest intensity and appeared to come from a position directly over head. I was unable to see the object after the sound stopped.

This clicking sound retained the same pitch and speed throughout the entire course observed, but intensity varied. There was no whistle or roar, but only the clicking noise which might be compared to beaters of a home mixer that were not properly meshed. No lights or flame were observed during the entire course with exception of the previous described reflections twice. No exhaust trail was distinguishable.

My dog was with me and directed her attention in the general direction of this object's flight throughout its course. She had been romping with me on coming out of the house but without spoken word stopped and directed her attention onto the previously described area. The clicking sound might not have been unusual to the dog, but there is a possibility of sounds on wave lengths discernable only to the dog, being emitted."

It is to be noted that . . . is a member of the Active USAF Reserve with rank of Major. He attained rating of pilot in August 1941 and has approximately 2200 hours flying time. During his active duty period in WW2 he stated that he had considerable night flying experience in connection with his military assignment. The Intelligence Officer in the above mentioned letter made the following statement, "An attempt to locate other witnesses in the area or through the local newspaper proved unsuccessful."

. . . advised that he is planning to clear with his headquarters office and will probably conduct an investigation.

The following memo, dated June 2, 1949, from the New Orleans field office, discusses sightings over New Orleans on several dates:

The Bureau is advised that through the Office of Naval Intelligence, New Orleans, Louisiana, this office has been advised that within the past ten days three sightings of flying discs have been reported in the City of New Orleans. The information seems to be that the single discs were in straight flight and traveling in a general direction of North, in late afternoon, about the size of an observation plane, but the shape of a saucer. The Navy stated that two witnesses have advised that the object was traveling end over end; that weather conditions were good; that sightings were made outdoors by persons who did not wear glasses; that the dates were May 18, 19, and 23, 1949. The Navy states that it was possible these objects were weather balloons, but that these are used from only one airport, released over an hour before the times of sighting and would generally be out of sight in a few minutes.

The above is being furnished the Bureau for future reference since the Navy has informed that all three instances were investigated by the Army Intelligence.

Activity was on the upswing. Some of the more interesting reports in the FBI files were yet to be seen.

CHAPTER ELEVEN
FBI Involvement: 1950–1977

$\mathbf{A}$n abundance of good information appears in the FBI's files for 1950. The first item is a report from the old Office of Naval Investigation regarding UFO sightings on January 22 and 23, 1950, in the area of Kodiak, Alaska. The report lacks a number of enclosures which were once with the original but many details remain:

Date of Report: 10 Feb. 1950
Place: Kodiak, Alaska
Copies to: CIA (8), DI/USAF (5), FBI (2), STATE (5), ID.GS.USA (16)
Enclosures 1–8 went to OP322F2 along with summary
From: DIO/17ND
Source: Official U.S. Navy
Evaluation: A-2
Subject: Unidentified phenomena in vicinity of Kodiak, Alaska
Brief: A report of sighting of unidentified airborne objects, by various naval personnel, on 22 and 23 January 1950, in the vicinity of Kodiak, Alaska is contained herein.
1. Enclosures (1), (2), and (4) are completed forms suggested by Commander in Chief, Alaskan Command, Fort Richardson, Alaska for the reporting of sighting of unidentified objects. Enclosure (3) is a sketch of radar interference experienced in aircraft piloted by Lt. SMITH. Enclosure (5) is a track chart of aircraft in which Lt. BARCO was embarked when he sighted unidentified object. Enclosure (6) contains statements by MORGAN and CARVER relative to their sighting. Enclosure (7) is a copy of Lt. BARCO's

statement and enclosure (8) is a summary of weather and baloon release information.

2. A summary of the information contained in enclosures (1) through (8) follows:

a) at 220240W January Lt. SMITH, USN, patrol plane commander of P2V3 No. 4 of Patrol Squadron One reported an unidentified radar contact 20 miles north of the Naval Air Station, Kodiak, Alaska. When this contact was first made, Lt. SMITH was flying the Kodiak Security Patrol. At 0248W, 8 minutes later a radar contact was made on an object 10 miles southeast of NAS, Kodiak. Lt. SMITH checked with the control tower to determine known traffic in the area, and was informed that there was none. During this period the radar operator, GASKEY, ALC, USN reported intermittent radar interference of a type he had never before experienced (see enclosure (3)). Contact was lost at this time, but intermittent interference continued.

b) At some time between 0200 and 0300W, MORGAN was standing watch on board the USS Tillamock (ATA 192), which was anchored in the vicinity of buoy 19 in the main ship channel. MORGAN reported sighting a "very fast moving red glow light, which appeared to be of exhaust nature, seemed to come from the southeast, moved clockwise in a large circle in the direction of, and around Kodiak and returned but in a generally southeast direction." MORGAN called CARVER, also on watch, to observe this object, and they both witnessed the return flight. The object was in sight for an estimated 30 seconds. No odor or sound was detected, and the object was described to have the appearance of a ball of fire about one foot in diameter.

c) At 220440W, conducting routine Kodiak security patrol, Lt. SMITH reported a visual sighting of an unidentified airborne object at a radar range of 5 miles, on the starboard bow. This object showed indications of great speed on the radar scope. (The trailing edge of the blip gave a tail-like indication.) At this time Lt. SMITH called attention of all crew members to the object. An estimated ten seconds later, the object was directly overhead, indicating a speed of about 1800 MPH. Lt. SMITH climbed to intercept and attempted to circle to keep the object in sight. He was unable to do this, as the object was too highly maneuverable. Subsequently the object appeared to be opening the range, and SMITH attempted to close the range. The object was observed to open out somewhat, then to turn to the left and come up on SMITH's quarter. SMITH considered this to be a highly threatening gesture, and turned out all lights in the aircraft. Four minutes later the object disappeared from view in a southeasterly direction.

d) At 230435W, the day following Lt. SMITH's sighting, Lt. CAUSER and Lt. BARCO of Patrol Squadron One were conducting the Kodiak Security Patrol and sighted an unidentified object. At the time of the sighting the aircraft in which those officers were embarked was approximately 62 miles south of Kodiak. The object appeared to be on an ascending westerly course, and was in sight for ten minutes. During this period the object was observed by Lt. CAUSER and BARCO, and PAULSON, ADi, plane captain. At no time was radar contact made on the object. Lt. CAUSER was unable to close the object at 170 knots.

e) The objects sighted have been described as follows:

(1) To Lt. SMITH and crew it appeared as two orange lights rotating about a common center, "like two jet aircraft making slow rolls in tight formation." It had a wide speed range.

(2) To MORGAN and CARVER it appeared as a reddish orange ball of fire about one foot in diameter, travelling at a high rate of speed.

(3) To CAUSER, BARCO, and PAULSON it appeared to be a pulsating orange yellow projectile shaped flame, with a regular period of pulsation on 3 to 5 seconds, off 3 to 5 seconds. Later, as the object increased the range the pulsation appeared to increase to on 7 to 8 seconds and off 7 to 8 seconds.

3. A check with the Navy Weather Central, Kodiak, Alaska revealed that balloons were released at the following times:

22 January—0445W and 2200W (approximately)

23 January—0400W (approximately)

4. On 23 January winds aloft at 1000 feet were reported at 0400W as from 310°, at 36 knots, and at 2000 feet, from 240° at 37 knots, while the object was reported to be on an ascending-westerly course.

COMMENT: In view of the fact that no weather balloons were known to have been released within a reasonable time before the sightings, it appears that the object or objects were not balloons. If not balloons, the objects must be regarded as phenomena (possibly meteorites), the exact nature of which could not be determined by this office.

The opinion of OP322C2C:

"The *possibility* exists that incidents covered by para. 2.a,b&d might be jet aircraft; however, there is insufficient intelligence to definitely identify the unidentified objects as aircraft. Several reports of similar radar interference have been received from DIO/17ND. It is possible that this is interference from another radar in the vicinity, malfunctioning of components within the radar set, or both."

The opinion of F2:

"Many of the previous reports of radar interference tend to indicate local interference (generated within the aircraft). This looks more like external interference from sources outside the aircraft than previous reports, though it is far from conclusive. These reports are always of interest."

The above-mentioned "OP322V2C" and "F2" were apparently classified research groups. "D10/17ND" is the 17th Naval District's Intelligence group.

It is quite obvious that the Navy went to every effort to explain away the reports, although paragraph 2c bore the handwritten notation "?" indicating puzzlement as to how to explain this feature. Also, the "F2" opinion failed to take into account the visual nature of the sightings. With all things considered, the Kodiak reports are positive evidence that the UFO subject is well-deserving of scientific attention.

After reading reports like this, which seemed to contradict the official Air Force policy of UFOs being unimportant, J. Edgar Hoover asked the following in a March 1950 note, "Just what are the facts re "flying saucers"? A short memo as to whether or not it is true or just what Air Force, etc. think of them."

The Air Force produced the standard reply of "misidentifications," "weather balloons," etc. Whether this satisfied Hoover or simply exasperated him is unknown, but the UFOs continued to fly.

In August 1950, the following memo was received by FBI headquarters. Title: "Summary of Aerial Phenomena in New Mexico."

Purpose
To advise that: (1) OSI has expressed concern in connection with the continued appearance of unexplained phenomena described as green fireballs, discs and meteors in the vicinity of sensitive installations in New Mexico. (2) Dr. Lincoln LaPaz, meteor expert of the University of New Mexico, reported that the phenomena does not appear to be of meteoric origin. (3) OSI has contracted with Land-Air Inc, Alamogordo, New Mexico, to make scientific study of the unexplained phenomena.

Nature of Phenomena
Observations of aerial phenomena occurring within the vicinity of sensitive installations have been recorded by the Air Force since December, 1948. The phenomena have been classified into 3 general types which are identified as follows:
1. Green fireballs, objects moving at high speed in shapes resembling half moons, circles and discs emitting green light.
2. Discs round flat shaped objects or phenomena moving at fast velocity and emitting a brilliant white light or reflected light.
3. Meteors, aerial phenomena resembling meteoric material moving at high velocity and varying in color.

The above phenomena have been reported to vary in color from brilliant white to amber, red and green.
Since 1948, approximately 150 observations of aerial phenomena referred to above have been recorded in the vicinity of installations in New Mexico. A number of observations have been reported by different reliable individuals at approximately the same time.

Results of an Inquiry by Professor Lincoln LaPaz
Dr. Lincoln LaPaz, Institute of Meteoritics, University of New Mexico, submitted an analysis of the various observations on May 23, 1950. He concluded, as a result of his investigation, that approximately half of the phenomena recorded were of meteoric origin. The other phenomena commonly referred to as green fireballs or discs he believed to be U.S. guided missiles being tested in the neighborhood of the installations. LaPaz pointed out that if he were wrong in interpreting the phenomena as originating with U.S. guided missiles that a systematic investigation of the observations should be made immediately. LaPaz pointed out that missiles moving with the velocities of the order of those found for the green fireballs and discs could travel from the Ural region of the USSR to New Mexico in less than 15 minutes.

He suggested that the observations might be of guided missiles launched from bases in the Urals.

On the basis of the investigations made by LaPaz and the Air Force, it was concluded that the occurrence of the unexplained phenomena in the vicinity of sensitive installations was a cause for concern. The Air Force entered into a contract with Land-Air, Inc., Alamogordo, New Mexico, for the purpose of making scientific studies of the green fireballs and discs. It was pointed out in the summary furnished by DSI on July 19, 1950, that the unexplained green fireballs and discs are still observed in the vicinity of sensitive military and Government installations.

Results of Air Force Investigation
The Air Force together with Land-Air, Inc., have established a number of observation posts in the vicinity of Vaughn, New Mexico, for the purpose of photographing and determining the speed, height and nature of the unusual phenomena referred to as green fireballs and discs. On May 24, 1950, personnel of Land-Air, Inc., sighted 8 to 10 objects of aerial phenomena. A 24-hour day watch is being maintained and has been designated "Project Twinkle."

Conclusions
The Albuquerque Office, in a letter dated August 10, 1950, advised that there have been no new developments in connection with the efforts to ascertain the identity of the strange aerial phenomena referred to as green fireballs and discs. The Albuquerque Office advised that Dr. . . . Project Engineer, had been informed of the Bureau's jurisdiction relative to espionage and sabotage and arrangements have been made so that the Bureau will be promptly advised in the event additional information relative to this project indicates any jurisdiction on the part of the Bureau.

Here, again, the military is confronted with aerial objects that cannot be identified as conventional aircraft. And, still, the military's public stance is "no such thing." Note also the distinction drawn between the green fireball phenomena and "discs" or flying saucers. This distinction will be made even more apparent in the next memo dated May 25, 1950. This is a letter to Brigadier General Joseph Carroll, Director of Air Force Special Investigations from Lt. Col. Doyle Rees, Commander of the 17th District Office of Special Investigations. It surfaced in the FBI files along with other green fireball information periodically being sent to Washington. It is titled "Summary of Observations of Aerial Phenomena in The New Mexico Area December 1948–May 1950."

1. In a liaison meeting with other military and government intelligence and investigative agencies in December 1948, it was determined that the frequency of unexplained aerial phenomena in the New Mexico area was such that an organized plan of reporting these observations should be undertaken. The organization and physical location of units of this District were most suitable for collecting these data, therefore, since December 1948, this District has assumed the responsibility for collecting and reporting basic information with respect to aerial phenomena occurring in this general area. These reports have been distributed to the Air Material Command, USAF, in accordance with Air Intelligence Requirements No. 4, and to other interested military and government agencies.

2. There is attached, as a part of this summary, a compilation of aerial phenomena sightings that have occurred mostly in the New Mexico area and have been reported by this District Office subsequent to December 1948. This compilation of sightings is not a complete record of all reported observations, but includes only those in which sufficient information was available to justify their inclusion. The observers of these phenomena include scientists, Special Agents of the Office of Special Investigations (IC) USAF, airline pilots, military pilots, Los Alamos Security Inspectors, military personnel, and many other persons of various occupations whose reliability is not questioned. This compilation sets forth the most important characteristics with respect to each observation and evaluates each sighting into one of three classifications: (1) green fireball phenomenon, (2) disc or variation, and (3) probably meteoric.

3. There is also attached an analysis of the green fireball occurrences in this area made by Dr. Lincoln LaPaz. Dr. LaPaz is the Director of the Institute of Meteoritics and Head of the Department of Mathematics and Astronomy at the University of New Mexico. He was Research Mathematician at the New Mexico Proving Grounds under an OSRD appointment in 1943 and 1944, and Technical Director of the Operations Analysis Section, Headquarters, Second Air Force, 1944–45. Since 1948, Dr. LaPaz has served on a voluntary basis as consultant for this District in connection with the green fireball investigations.

4. On 17 February 1949 and again on 14 October 1949, conferences were held at Los Alamos, New Mexico, for the purpose of discussing the green fireball phenomena. Representatives of the following organizations were present at these meetings: Fourth Army, Armed Special Weapons Project, University of New Mexico, Federal Bureau of Investigation, U.S. Atomic Energy Commission, University of California, U.S. Air Force Scientific Advisory Board, Geophysical Research Division Air Material Command USAF, and the Office of Special Investigations (IG) USAF. A logical explanation was not proffered with respect to the origin of the green fireballs. It was, however, generally concluded that the phenomena existed and that they should be studied scientifically until these occurrences have been satisfactorily explained. Further, that the continued occurrence of unexplained phenomena of this nature in the vicinity of sensitive installations is cause for concern.

5. The Geophysical Research Division, Air Material Command, Cambridge, Massachusetts, has recently let a contract to Land-Air, Inc., Holloman AFB, Alamogordo, New Mexico, for a limited scientific study of green fireballs. The results of this scientific approach to the problem will undoubtedly be of great value in determining the origin of these phenomena.

6. This summary of observations of aerial phenomena has been prepared for the purpose of re-emphasizing and reiterating the fact that phenomena have continuously occurred in the New Mexico skies during the past 18 months and are continuing to occur, and, secondly, that these phenomena are occurring in the vicinity of sensitive military and governmental installations.

A catalog of observations, totalling 209 reports, was included with the Rees letter. It gives basic information about each sighting and the last of the catalog provides for an evaluation of each sighting. The evaluation is assigned a number—1, 2, or 3—with 1 being *Green Fireball Phenomena,* 2 being

"Disk" or Variation, and 3 being *Probable Meteor.* The FBI, at the request of the Air Force, censored out the evaluation number in each case when the catalog was released under the Freedom of Information Act. Obviously, this is to prevent the public from being aware that the Air Force concluded, at one time, that some sightings were evaluated as "Disk or Variation," that is, flying saucers.

Furthermore, a photo, labeled "Sighting No. 175" was included with the catalog. It shows a round, white object with a small trail behind and bears the following information:

> Photograph of Unknown Aerial Phenomena taken at Datil, New Mexico by Cpl. Lertis E. Stanfield, Holloman Air Force Base, New Mexico on 24 and 25 February, 1950. An analysis of the above photograph was made by Dr. Lincoln LaPaz, Head of the Institute of Meteoritics, University of New Mexico, Albuquerque, New Mexico, who reached the following conclusions:
>
> a. The angular diameter of the perfectly round luminous object Stafield observed was approximately ¼ of a degree.
>
> b. The angular velocity of the object in the sky was greater than half a degree per minute.
>
> Dr. LaPaz stated that on the basis of the results (a) and (b) above, the object seen by Stanfield was not the moon (for the angular diameter is too small), it was not Venus or any other planet (for the angular diameter was too large), and it was not a bright fixed star slightly out of focus (for the observed rate of motion is double that due to the diurnal rotation of the earth).
>
> The green fireballs and associated sightings remain unexplained to this day.

More interesting memos appeared during 1950. On March 22, a memo was sent to the Director, FBI, by Guy Hottel of the Washington Field Office. Title: "Flying Saucers—Information Concerning."

> An investigator for the Air Forces stated that three so-called flying saucers had been recovered in New Mexico. They were described as being circular in shape with raised centers, approximately 50 feet in diameter. Each one was occupied by three bodies of human shape but only 3 feet tall, dressed in metallic cloth of a very fine texture. Each body was bandaged in a manner similar to the blackout suits used by speed flyers and test pilots.
>
> According to Mr. . . . informant, the saucers were found in New Mexico due to the fact that the Government has a very high-powered radar set-up in that area and it is believed that the radar interferes with the controlling mechanism of the saucers.
>
> No further evaluation was attempted by SA (Deleted) concerning the above.

Not only was no further evaluation attempted, but no further information appears in the file. A spurious report or a top security matter? We don't know.

A flurry of reports suddenly burst into FBI files from Oak Ridge, Tennessee, during the fall of 1950. A summary of the events follows:

June 1947	Mr. W. R. Pressley photographed a flying object at Oak Ridge, Tennessee. The street in the foreground has been identified as Illinois Avenue, Oak Ridge, Tenn.
20 June 1949	At 1900 hours Mr. and Mrs. E. H. Anderson and Mrs. John A. White sighted three objects at Oak Ridge, Tennessee, similar to SUBJECT.
1–6 March 1950	Mr. Stuart Adcock reported peculiar readings on his "Ham" Radar Scope. These objects reappeared at approximately the same time of day which is similar to SUBJECT. (Refer: Summary of Information, Subject: Unidentified Objects Over Oak Ridge Vicinity, dated 6 March 1950.)
12 October 1950	2325 hours. Knoxville Airport Radar Unit indicated a series of unidentified targets over the "Restricted Zone" at Oak Ridge.
12 October 1950	2347. Fighter aircraft was at the position of the radar target and made three perfect interceptions but could see nothing.
13 October 1950	0000–0100 hours. Additional Radar plots as before.
15 October 1950	Approximately 1400 hours. Major L. E. Ronniger, accompanied by his daughter, heard intermittent noises.
15 October 1950	151? hours. Fighter plane made unsuccessful passes at a good radar target four (4) miles from the East Boundary (Kerr Hollow Gate).
15 October 1950	1520 hours. SUBJECT seen at Kerr Hollow Gate by Troopers Rymer and Zarzecki, Mr. Hightower, and Mr. Moneymaker.
15 October 1950	1520 hours. Radar scopes at McGhee-Tyson Airport indicate unidentified targets.
16 October 1950	1455 to 1530 hours. Objects seen by Troopers Isabell, Briggs, and Clark.
16 October 1950	1520 hours. Radar scopes at McGhee-Tyson Airport giving unintelligible readings.
16 October 1950	1956 to 2004 hours. NEPA Guards, Brown, Herron, and Davis report peculiar sounds.
20 October 1950	1655 hours. Visual sightings by Larry P. Riordan, Security Chief, X-10 Plant.
23 October 1950	1630 hours. Visual sightings made by Francis J. Miller. (Geiger counters in the vicinity had unexplainable readings at about this time.)
24 October 1950	1855 to 1900 hours. Visual sightings of a light by Major Dallveg, Mr. Frey, and the Radar Station.
24 October 1950	1823 to 1920 hours. Several small, slow targets appeared on radar scope.

26 October 1950   Robert W. Lassell and five others sighted objects from
                     the Knoxville Airport, Knoxville, Tennessee.
5 November 1950   1155 to 1200 hours. Visual sighting by Don Patrick.
25 May 1949   In the vicinity of Louden, Tennessee, a flat, metallic
                     object, accompanied by "a flapping noise," was seen
                     by five people living in that area.

Certainly something big was going on. Oak Ridge was the site of the old
Atomic Energy Commission's testing facilities. Unauthorized aerial craft in
this area would amount to a major security breach of very great concern
to the military.

A memo dated October 25, 1950 provided some details:

OBJECTS SIGHTED OVER OAK RIDGE, TENNESSEE

At 1655 hours, on 20 October 1950, Mr. Larry P. Riordan, AEC Badge
No. 522, Superintendent of Security at X-10 in the "Control Zone" at Oak
Ridge, Tennessee, while enroute from X-10 to the Oak Ridge residential
area, on Benton Valley Road, saw an object in the sky which appeared
to be directly over the University of Tennessee Agricultural Research Farm.
This object gave the general appearance of an aerial balloon which had
lost its "basket." In other words, the object was generally round; appeared
to come together at the bottom in wrinkles (rather indistinct), and something
was hanging below. The balloon was described as being from eight to
ten feet long; of a lead pipe or gunmetal color; and seemed to be approximately one-fourth (¼) mile from the observer, at a thirty (30) degree elevation above the horizon. The object was apparently stationary but since
the observer was in a moving vehicle, he did not verify that it was stationary.
As the vehicle in which he was travelling changed position, and went around
a curve, Mr. Riordan noticed that this object appeared to be thinner. He
concludes that by reason of his changing position, or the object changing
its altitude, he observed another angle of the object which appeared to
be thinner than upon his first sighting.

At the time of the observation there was adequate light and the object
was plainly visible. Mr. Riordan is a responsible person, as is indicated
by his position, and he has been aware of the many instances of reported
objects flying in the sky. He is also very familiar with the weather balloons
which are sent up hourly each day over Oak Ridge between 6:00 AM of
one day until 1:00 AM of the next day. The size of these balloons vary,
but generally they are similar to a circus balloon which is about twenty-
four (24) inches in diameter. Mr. Riordan is certain that the object was
not a weather balloon but his first impression was that this object was an
experimental "gab" being utilized by the University of Tennessee Agricultural Research Farm.

Mr. Riordan has been the Security Chief of X-10 since 14 July 1943. His
vision is normal except that he has negligible impairment of the right eye.
Like many of the Atomic Energy Commission officials, Mr. Riordan has
hoped for the opportunity to see one of these objects, and under the circumstances, he visualized it as accurately as possible.

At 1845 hours, on 24 October 1950, Mr. William B. Fry, Assistant Chief of Security, NEPA Division, Oak Ridge, Tennessee, while attending a Drive-in theater with his wife and child, at Oak Ridge, noticed an object in the sky North-Northwest of his position, at a thirty (30) to forty (40) degree elevation. This object was moving gently in a horizontal plane, back and forth, within thirty (30) degrees of his line of sight. This object emitted a glow, varying in color from red to green, to blue-green, to blue, and to orange. The variations were checked on the vertical window post of Mr. Fry's vehicle and were witnessed by Mr. Fry's wife. The attention of another observer, the Projectionist at the Drive-in theater, was also called to the object and verification of this sighting was made. The object disappeared from his sight at 1920 hours.

At 1855 hours, on 24 October, 1950, an Air Force Major, Lawrence Ballweg, NEPA Division, Oak Ridge, Tennessee, also saw from his residence an object which he described similarly. The object disappeared from the sight of Mr. Ballweg at 1920 hours, which coincides with the time of disappearance of the object from Mr. Fry's sight.

On 20 October 1950, at 1527 hours, aircraft No. AF-409, Pilot Wolf, 5th AW-Fighter Sqd., took off from the Knoxville Airport for a "local patrol." The Radar Unit at Knoxville Airport received readings on their Radar scope and sent the aircraft after these targets. The aircraft pilot was unable to identify any flying object in the vicinity of the said targets. All targets were between eighteen (18) and twenty-five (25) miles from the Airport at 320 degrees. The aircraft was landed at 1713 hours. (Attention is invited to the fact that these targets were sighted at approximately the same time, and locality, that was reported by Mr. Larry Riordan.)

On 24 October 1950, at 1823 hours, several small, slow targets were seen on the Radar screen at the Knoxville Airport Radar Site. These targets appeared in the Southeast sector of the "Restricted Flying Zone" and over the city of Oak Ridge. These targets moved from the city area to and along the East boundary of the area. At 1826 hours, the fighter aircraft was "scrambled" and proceeded to the area where it was vectored among the targets but the pilot reported no visual contact with said targets. At 1920 hours the targets disappeared from the Radar Screen and the fighter was vectored toward another target believed to be one of three (3) aircraft enroute from Andrews Field to Steward Field. (Note: 1920 hours is also the time that the object sighted by Mr. Fry and Major Ballweg disappeared from their view).

Sightings continued into December 1950 around Oak Ridge. On December 14, the following information was reported.

A. Location and Time of Sighting: From 1605 hours for about three (3) hours, on 14 December 1950, on the Radar Scopes of the 663rd AC and W Squadron, McGhee Tyson Airport, Knoxville, Tennessee.

B. Weather at the Time: At 1600 hours on 14 December 1950—"Ceiling–2100 feet; Broken overcast; Seven (7) miles visibility; temperature–37 degrees F.; and Wind–Southwest at thirteen (13) miles per hour.

C. Names, Occupations, and Addresses of Witnesses: Personnel of the 663rd AC and W Squadron, 30th Air Division, McGhee Tyson Airport, Knoxville, Tennessee, who were on duty at the time. Their occupations are Radar operators, Supervisors and experts.

D. Photographs of Objects, if available: No photographs taken. See "F" below.

E. Objects Sighted: A group of targets blanketed the Radar Scopes in the area directly over the government Atomic Energy Commission projects at Oak Ridge, Tennessee. These objects could not be identified from the radar image and a perfect fighter interception met with negative results.

F. Any other pertinent information: Lt. Robinson of the 663rd AC and W Squadron, McGhee-Tyson Airport, Knoxville, Tennessee took photographs of the scope readings with a personal, four (4) by five (5) Speed Graphic Camera, using Plus-X civilian procured film, a lens opening of F-2.5, and a shutter speed varying from twenty (20) to forty-five (45) seconds. The negatives were printed and forwarded to the 30th Air Division, Selfridge Air Force Base, Michigan, which installation printed the negatives and sent copies thereof to the 663rd AC and W squadron. The numerous targets can be readily identified from the permanent radar echos by comparing the photographs.

The Army sent a report to the FBI on a sighting by employees of the Nuclear Energy for Propulsion of Aircraft project (NEPA) at Oak Ridge:

On December 18, 1950, at sometime between 0820 and 0830, the following NEPA employees were riding in a vehicle on the Turnpike within the Controlled Area toward the NEPA Project approximately one mile short of the "Y" cutoff to White Wing entrance. The passengers, with the exception of . . . who did not attempt to participate in the viewing, observed a light emanating in the shape of a circle, of an intensity much greater than that of a bright moon, through the windshield of the vehicle. The viewers had the impression that there was form in connection with the light rather than merely a point source. The light was white in appearance and did not show any signs of refraction into a band or continuous spectrum. It appeared to be from 15 to 30 degrees elevated above the horizontal and on an azimuth between west and northwest, and appeared to be traveling in a northwesterly direction. The impression of it traveling is due to the fact that the object appeared to diminish considerably in size during the approximate thirty seconds during which it was viewed. The vehicle remained in motion and in following the course of the road, changed its relative position so that the object was viewed during the last few seconds from the side windows. As the vehicle proceeded down the road a nearby ridge obstructed the view of the object, and although the vehicle completed the turn toward K-25 at the "Y" intersection and the passengers had a relatively clear view at points along the road, the object was not viewed again. The observers were unable to estimate approximate size, speed, or vertical elevation; and, therefore, were not certain whether the object was over the Controlled Area or a considerable distance away. There was no vapor trail or any other visible condition within the vicinity of the object and there were no clouds which could have obscured it. The observers were unable to identify the object in terms of mass or shape, other than the circular appearance of the light. However, the circular area appeared to darken, starting at approximately 7:00 to 9:00 o'clock along the perimeter and continuing to darken along the perimeter and inner area until the light was concentrated in approximately 1:00 to 3:00 o'clock position of a very small diameter, at which point it appeared somewhat similar to a large star.

The observers were not in complete agreement as to whether the object
was moving at a speed which caused it to diminish in size or actually
was diminishing in size without any great velocity of travel due to the darken-
ing effect described above.

Another radar report was received on December 20 as follows:

Object sighted: The radar log of the 663rd AN and C Squadron, McGhee
Tyson Airport, Knoxville, Tennessee contained the following entry: "20 December 1950. 1247 hours. Small paint in area (Oak Ridge Controlled Area).
Very very slow. Made perfect intercept (with F-82 Fighter aircraft) and orbit
surrounding small smoke cloud.

A very cryptic teletype appears here as the final entry for 1950. Whether it
relates to the activity at Oak Ridge or elsewhere remains to be explained.
No other file has been found relevant to the information contained in it. It
is dated December 3, 1950.

RE flying saucers. This office very confidentially advised by Army Intelligence, Richmond, that they have been put on immediate high alert for
any data whatsoever concerning flying saucers. CIC (Counter Intelligence
Corps) here states background of instructions not available from Air Force
Intelligence, who are not aware of the reason for alert locally, but any
information whatsoever must be telephoned by them immediately to Air
Force Intelligence. CIC advises data strictly confidential and should not
be disseminated.

So, flying saucers, once again, upset the military to such an extreme that
an *"Immediate High Alert"* must be declared. This is hardly what to expect
from an illusion.

Most UFO information in the FBI files from this point on is sporadic
in nature. A number of unusual reports appear, however. This teletype is
dated May 26, 1952.

RE Flying Saucers, information concerning. Three women saw strange objects floating in sky over Ashland, KY. At eight fifty PM, EST, May twenty-
five last for two or three minutes. Objects described as looking like large
oysters with fishtails floating low like a cloud. They were oval in shape
and according to observers could have been balloons. They came in over
Ashland from the north, circled and went back in the opposite direction.
Above information for Bureau. No action here.

An important admission is made in the first paragraph of this July 29, 1952
memo:

SUBJECT: FLYING SAUCERS

Purpose:
To advise at the present time the Air Force has failed to arrive at any
satisfactory conclusion in its research regarding numerous reports of flying
saucers and flying discs sighted throughout the United States.

Details:

Mr. N. W. Philcox, the Bureau's Air Force Liaison Representative, made arrangements through the office of Major General John A. Samford, Director of Air Intelligence, U.S. Air Force, to receive a briefing from Commander Randall Boyd of the Current Intelligence Branch, Estimates Division, Air Intelligence, regarding the present status of Air Intelligence research into the numerous reports regarding flying saucers and flying discs.

Commander Boyd advised that Air Intelligence has set up at Wright Patterson Air Force Base, Ohio, the Air Technical Intelligence Center which has been established for the purpose of coordinating, correlating and making research into all reports regarding flying saucers and flying discs. He advised that Air Force research has indicated that the sightings of flying saucers goes back several centuries and that the number of sightings reported varies with the amount of publicity. He advised that immediately if publicity appears in newspapers, the number of sightings reported increased considerably and that citizens immediately call in reporting sightings which occurred several months previously. Commander Boyd stated that these reported sightings of flying saucers are placed into three classifications by Air Intelligence:

1. Those sightings which are reported by citizens who claim they have seen flying saucers from the ground. These sightings vary in description, color and speeds. Very little credence is given to these sightings in as much as in most instances they are believed to be imaginative or some explainable object which actually crossed through the sky.

2. Sightings reported by commercial or military pilots. These sightings are considered more credible by the Air Force in as much as commercial or military pilots are experienced in the air and are not expected to see objects which are entirely imaginative. In each of these instances, the individual who reports the sighting is thoroughly interviewed by a representative of Air Intelligence so that a complete description of the object sighted can be obtained.

3. Those sightings which are reported by pilots and for which there is additional corroboration, such as recording by radar or sighting from the ground. Commander Boyd advised that this latter classification constitutes two or three percent of the total number of sightings, but that they are the most credible reports received and are difficult to explain. Some of these sightings are originally reported from the ground, then are observed by pilots in the air and then are picked up by radar instruments. He stated that in these instances there is no doubt that these individuals reporting the sightings actually did see something in the sky. However, he explained that these objects could still be natural phenomena and still could be recorded on radar if there was some electrical disturbance in the sky.

He stated that the flying saucers are most frequently observed in areas where there is heavy air traffic, such as Washington, D.C., and New York City. He advised, however, that some reports are received from other parts of the country—covering the entire United States and that sightings have also recently been reported as far distant as Acapulco, Mexico; Korea and French Morocco. He advised that the sightings reported in the last classification have never been satisfactorily explained. He pointed out, however, that it is still possible that these objects may be a natural phenomenon or some type of atmospherical disturbance. He advised that it is not entirely impossible that the objects sighted may possibly be ships from another planet such as Mars. He advised that at the present time there is nothing to substantiate this theory but the possibility is not being overlooked. He stated that Air Intelligence is fairly certain that these objects are not ships or missiles from another nation in this world. Commander Boyd advised that intense research is being carried on presently by Air Intelligence, and at the present time when credible reportings of sightings are received, the Air Force is attempting in each instance to send up jet interceptor planes in order to obtain a better view of these objects. However, recent attempts in this regard have indicated that when the pilot in the jet approaches the object it invariably fades from view.

A memo dated October 27, 1952 states:

Air Intelligence advised of another creditable and unexplainable sighting of flying saucers. Air Intelligence still feels flying saucers are optical illusions or atmospherical phenomena but some Military officials are seriously considering the possibility of interplanetary ships.

Repeatedly, memos cite the "reliability" of information and the "creditability" of witnesses as very favorable. Yet, repeatedly, this high-quality information is lumped together with low-grade nonsense. Witness the following memo, dated September 7, 1956.

On August 31, 1956, . . . Street, St. Louis, Missouri, employed as an electrician, . . . St. Louis County, . . . appeared at the St. Louis Office to advise that he and a group of fellow workers have subscribed to a publication entitled "The A.P.R.O. Bulletin," which is published at 1712 Van Court, Alamogordo, New Mexico, and which contains articles about flying saucers.
. . . stated he and a group of fellow workers saw an advertisement concerning the above described publication in a magazine and they subscribed to this publication for one year at a cost of $3.00. . . . further stated this publication slurred and criticized the U.S. Air Force and officials of the U.S. Air Force and was in his opinion communistic.
A copy of this communication is being forwarded the Albuquerque Office for purposes of information.

Apparently, to some people, criticizing Air Force policy on UFOs is "communistic." The sad thing about this is that such a charge is allowed to perpetuate in a file for many years afterward without the knowledge of the accused.

The next story appeared in a memo dated November 7, 1957, regarding a wartime sighting:

In response to a letter directed by him to Mr. Robert Cutler, Special Assistant to President Dwight D. Eisenhower, reflecting that he "might have some information about the rocket in Texas," . . . Detroit, was interviewed November 7, 1957, and furnished the following information:
Born February 19, 1926 in the State of Warsaw, Poland, . . . was brought from Poland as a Prisoner of War to Gut Alt Golssen, approximately 30

miles east of Berlin, Germany, in May, 1942, where he remained until a few weeks after the end of World War II. He spent the following years at Displaced Persons Camps at Kork, Strasburg, Offenburg, Wilheim and Frei-burg and about a year was employed in a textile mill at Laurachbaden, Germany. He arrived in the United States at New York, May 2, 1951, via the "S.S. General Stewart" as a Displaced Person, destined to the Reverend . . . , Hamtramck, Michigan; his alien registration number— . . . .

Since May, 1951, he has been employed at the Gobel Brewery, Detroit.

New report of mysterious vehicle in Texas causing engines to stall prompted him to communicate with the United States Government concerning a similar phenomenon observed by him in 1944 in the area of Gut Alt Golssen.

According to . . . , during 1944, month not recalled, while enroute to work in a field a short distance north of Gut Alt Golssen, their tractor engine stalled on a road through a swamp area. No machinery or other vehicle was then visible although a noise was heard described as a high-pitched whine similar to that produced by a large electric generator.

An "S.S." guard appeared and talked briefly with the German driver of the tractor, who waited five to ten minutes, after which the noise stopped and the tractor engine was started normally. Approximately 3 hours later in the same swamp area, but away from the road where the work crew was cutting "hay," he surreptitiously, because of the German in charge of the crew and "S.S." guards in the otherwise deserted area, observed a circular enclosure approximately 100 to 150 yards in diameter protected from viewers by a tarpaulin-type wall approximately 50 feet high, from which a vehicle was observed to slowly rise vertically to a height sufficient to clear the wall and then to move slowly horizontally a short distance out of his view, which was obstructed by nearby trees.

This vehicle, observed from approximately 500 feet, was described as circu-lar in shape, 75 to 100 yards in diameter, and about 14 feet high, consisting of dark gray stationary top and bottom sections, five to six feet high. The approximate three foot middle section appeared to be a rapidly moving component producing a continuous blur similar to an aeroplane propeller, but extending the circumference of the vehicle so far as could be observed. The noise emanating from the vehicle was similar but of a somewhat lower pitch than the noise previously heard. The engine of the tractor again stalled on this occasion and no effort was made by the German driver to start the engine until the noise stopped, after which the engine started normally.

Uninsulated metal, possibly copper, cables one and one-half inch to two inches in diameter, on and under the surface of the ground, in some places covered by water, were observed on this and previous occasions, apparently running between the enclosure and a small concrete column-like structure between the road and enclosure.

This area was not visited by . . . again until shortly after the end of World War II, when it was observed the cables has been removed and the previous locations of the concrete structure and the enclosure were covered by water. . . . stated he has not been in communication since 1945 with any of the work crew of 16 or 18 men, consisting of Russian, French and Polish POW's, who had discussed this incident among themselves many times. However, of these, . . . was able to recall by name only . . . , no address known, described as then about 50 years of age and presumed by . . . to have returned to Poland after 1945.

In 1964, comment appeared about the now-famous sighting at Socorro, New Mexico, of an egg-shaped UFO on the ground by patrolman Lonnie Zamora on April 24th. The FBI maintained liaison with the military on the matter but conducted no investigation. (See also Chapter 9 for CIA treatment of Socorro.)

A 1974 incident in Milwaukee generated some FBI concern:

> At 12:07 A.M., 8/22/74, Security Patrol Clerk (SPC) . . . , Intelligence Division received a call via Command Center telephone from a Major . . . NMCC (National Military Command Center). Major . . . asked for any information the FBI might have concerning a report that an unidentified object which fell from the sky at Milwaukee, Wisconsin, had been recovered by local police and turned over to the Milwaukee Office of the FBI.
>
> No information available at Intelligence Division. Night Duty Supervisor . . . , called SPC . . . Milwaukee Office, who advised an unidentified object had been recovered by . . . at about 5:55 P.M., 8/21/74, but that it was still in possession of . . . . He said a . . . had called the Milwaukee FBI Office to report the recovery. Very little was known about the object which was described as about 13x8x5 inches, metallic in substance and color, jagged on one side and had an "internal heat source.". . . notified military locally.

Finally, in 1977, the last policy statement on UFOs by the FBI was released in connection with a query by presidential staff member Jody Powell on how the FBI handles UFOs:

> I advised him that as far as the FBI is concerned there appears to be no conceivable jurisdiction for us to conduct any inquiries upon receipt of information relating to a UFO sighting and, in the absence of some investigative jurisdiction based upon the information furnished, that information would be referred to the Department of the Air Force without any action being taken by the Bureau.
>
> He thanked me for the information and stated that if any further contact was necessary he would call back.

While the FBI's involvement in UFOs after 1947 could be considered half-hearted, it must be remembered that UFO investigation was not the function of the FBI. That job belonged to the Air Force and the FBI knew it. We are left with a rather compelling collection of data and in a future time it may contribute to the ultimate solution of the UFO enigma.

CHAPTER TWELVE
Ears of America

One other item that we did not mention in Chapter 9 relating to Victor Marchetti's *Second Look* article is the fact that another government agency seems to be in possession of significant amounts of UFO data. That another agency should have UFO data may not be a big surprise after reading through the first ten chapters of this book. (It is obvious that many had their fingers in the pie!) However, this new group deserves special treatment.

Marchetti related a highly placed rumor of how strange signals had been detected. Strange signals? By whom? By the National Security Agency (NSA)!

Acknowledging that many of the rumors that he heard about UFOs could not be verified independently, Marchetti regarded the NSA signal story as the most impressive. Why? Because he had been an NSA officer at one time and had also maintained contact with the NSA after he had joined the CIA. The signal story, according to Marchetti, was "treated with extreme caution even by normal SIGINT (signal intelligence) standards," meaning that it was a highly sensitive matter.

What is the NSA and how is it involved in UFOs? The National Security Agency/Central Security Service is responsible for performing highly technical activities in support of U.S. government efforts to protect its own communication systems and to acquire foreign intelligence data.

The NSA came into being on November 4, 1952, without fanfare and since that time has been generally regarded as the most secret agency in the United States, cloaked in an aura of top security. Very little is known about how the NSA performs its work except that it is quite efficient and productive in its duties. So much information is generated in NSA operations that it is said to shred forty tons of documents per day.

Based in Ft. Meade, Maryland, the NSA employs tens of thousands of people in a massive complex of buildings with a multibillion dollar budget. Their function is to collect and analyze international communications through a network of radio disk antennas, computers, listening posts, and satellites worldwide, thus the name the "Ears of America." The NSA can listen to virtually every telegram and phone conversation made internationally, not to mention domestically. The Central Security Service is responsible for code making and breaking, and its chief is also NSA's Director.

When the Freedom of Information Act appeared in the mid-1970s, UFO researchers recognized that an agency which collected information via electronic signals may have gathered a considerable number of UFO reports and information. Even with the FOIA, requesting data would be a difficult task. No law was ever enacted to cover NSA activities, so the agency might be regarded as virtually immune to scrutiny by any means.

Initial requests to the NSA were unproductive. They consistently denied having anything whatsoever on UFOs in their divisions. A February 20, 1976, letter, answering a request by UFO researcher Robert Todd, stated, "Regarding your inquiry about UFOs, please be advised that NSA does not have *any* interest in UFOs in *any* manner [emphasis in original]." The letter was signed by NSA's Information Officer.

This public policy on UFOs remained essentially intact until things began to turn around slightly in 1978. During litigation against the CIA for UFO data, it was discovered that a portion of the CIA's withheld data originated with another agency, the NSA. The CIA contacted the NSA on November 9, 1978, with a referral of fifteen documents for review towards possible declassification. This was followed by two more referrals on December 4, totalling three documents, or eighteen in all. The attorney for the plaintiffs against the CIA, Peter Gersten, was informed of the referrals by the CIA on December 14. Gersten filed a request with the NSA for copies of the eighteen documents on December 22. Therefore, through what amounted to a leak *by the CIA* of the fact that the NSA did actually have file material on UFOs, researchers had what was necessary to engage in a serious pursuit of NSA UFO data.

Admitting for the first time that they had files, NSA's Chief, Policy Staff, Roy R. Banner advised Gersten that the NSA records in the CIA's holdings were exempt from release under 5 U.S.C., Section 552 (b) (1), which covers national security, and three other regulations. Gersten appealed the decision to withhold in a January 29, 1979, letter to the NSA which was again denied for the same reasons.

A new tactic was employed by Gersten. On February 16, 1979, another FOIA request was filed with the NSA, this time requesting all documents in possession or under the control of the NSA relating to the UFO phenomenon. After a long delay, the tactic worked and Gersten hit paydirt. The NSA surprisingly released two documents under cover of a January 10, 1980, letter from Roy Banner. The letter advised Gersten that other documents existed within the scope of the FOIA request but that these, like the original eighteen, were exempt from release due to national security. It also stated that a total of *seventy-nine other documents,* originating with other federal agencies or components, were being referred to those agencies for review toward release.

Getting back to the released documents, this was the public's first real look at what the NSA thought of UFOs. And what did they think?

The first record is entitled "UFO's [remainder of title deleted]" consisting of three undated pages and a four-page appendix. The first three pages were censored down to about a page and half as follows.

2. Scientific Findings: Dr. Jacques Vallee famed communications science expert has studied thousands of cases where human beings have observed unusual phenomena. He has found that the human response to such observation is predictable and graphically depictable. Whether the person's psychological structure is being assaulted by the unusual and shocking brutality of a murder or the strangeness of a UFO sighting, the effect is the same:

   a. Initially as by a kind of psychological inertia, the mind records fairly objectively what the eye is reporting.

   b. But when it has realized the strange nature of the phenomena it goes into shock. The mind likes to live in a comfortable world where it feels it knows what to expect, and that is not too threatening either physically or psychologically. The unusual dispels the comfortable illusion the mind has created. This shock tears at the very mooring of the human psychological structure.

   c. To protect itself against such an intrusive and threatening reality the mind will begin to add imagination and interpretation to the incoming data to make it more acceptable. Since the mind is doing all this in haste some of the hurriedly added details and suggestions tumble over one another and contradict one another in a bizarre fashion (as any police officer interrogating murder witnesses will tell you). (See Chart A.)

   d. Once the mind has constructed a "safe" framework for the new information it may again peek out and collect some more objective data. If the data is still threatening it will again go into shock and the process starts all over again.

   e. If the data is at the highest strangeness level where it brings terror either:

      (1) The mind will pass out and go into amnesia burying the events perhaps permanently in the unconscious.

      (2) The personal psychological structure will collapse and the mind will reach down into its deepest place where "that which cannot be destroyed" is and it will abandon itself to this entity for survival protection. Encounter with this changeless inde-

structible entity is usually referred to as a religious experience. In the confusion and the shock, this experience is often attributed to the shocking event or object and that is why primitive peoples worship such bizzare things as airplanes or cigarette lighters.

f. The degree of strangeness of the phenomena dictates how many people the mind is willing and able to tell the event to. A mildly unusual or shocking event will be told to many people. A very shocking event of high strangeness will be told to few people or practically none at all. Occasionally the event is so shockingly unusual that it isn't even reported to the person's conscious mind but is buried in the unconscious of the person where it is only accessible to hypnosis or careful level six communication sharing with another person. (See Chart B.)

The appendix section includes two pages of historical examples of "Blindness to Surprise Material Causing Defect" such as Pearl Harbor, the Maginot Line, the Normandy Invasion, and the like, and the remaining two pages include a suggestion for a chart titled "The Pattern of Objective and Speculative Material During Observations of Unusual Data" and a chart with a "Strangeness Index."

The document deals with an individual's reaction to strange events, such as UFOs. What is amazing here is that a UFO event is being treated here as a *real* event of genuine strangeness in the same context as a brutal murder is real and something, visually, out of the ordinary. What type of UFO data may the author have based his conclusions upon in this draft report? Were there truly strange UFO sightings in NSA files? The answer to this question may lie in the reason for the drafting of the second NSA document released to Gersten titled "UFO Hypothesis and Survival Questions." The report was written by an NSA analyst in 1968. The NSA released this with a disclaimer that it does not represent NSA policy. Yet it is significant that the document has been kept in NSA files through the years:

UFO HYPOTHESIS AND SURVIVAL QUESTIONS

It is the purpose of this monograph to consider briefly some of the human survival implications suggested by the various principal hypotheses concerning the nature of the phenomena loosely categorized as UFO.

1. All UFOs Are Hoaxes. From the time when hoaxes were first noted in history, they were characterized by infrequency of occurrence and usually by a considerable restriction of their geographical extent. Rarely have men of science, while acting within their professional capacities, perpetrated hoaxes. The fact that UFO phenomena have been witnessed all over the world from ancient times, and by considerable numbers of reputable scientists in recent times, indicates rather strongly that UFOs are not all hoaxes. If anything, rather than diminishing, the modern trend is toward increased reports, from all sources. In one three month period in 1953 (June, July and August) Air Force records show 35 sightings whose nature could not

be determined. If UFOs, contrary to all indications and expectations, are indeed hoaxes—hoaxes of a world-wide dimension—hoaxes of increasing frequency, then a human mental aberration of alarming proportions would appear to be developing. Such an aberration would seem to have serious implications for nations equipped with nuclear toys—and should require immediate and careful study by scientists.

2. All UFOs Are Hallucinations. People, of course, do hallucinate. Although groups of people hallucinating is rare, it has been known to happen. Machines have their own form of hallucination; the radar, in particular, "sees" temperature inversions. But a considerable number of instances exist in which there are groups of people and a radar or radars seeing the same thing at the same time; sometimes a person and a gun camera confirm each other's testimony. On occasion, physical evidence of a circumstantial nature was reported to have been found to support witnessed sightings. A continuing high percentage of reports of unusual aerial objects are being reported by people in responsible positions in science, government, and industry. The sum of such evidence seems to argue strongly against all UFOS being hallucinations. In spite of all the evidence to the contrary, if UFOs did turn out to be largely illusionary, the psychological implications for man would certainly bring into strong question his ability to distinguish reality from fantasy. The negative effect on man's ability to survive in an increasingly complex world would be considerable—making it imperative that such a growing impairment of the human capacity for rational judgment be subjected to immediate and thorough scientific study so that the illness could be controlled before it reaches epidemic proportions. (For comments on mass hysteria and UFOs see source 8 below which contains a statement by Dr. Robert L. Hall, a social psychologist formerly with the AF Personnel and Training Research Center and the Program Director, Sociology and Psychology, National Science Foundation.)

3. All UFOs Are Natural Phenomena. If this hypothesis is correct, the capability of air warning systems to correctly diagnose an attack situation is open to serious question.

    a. Many UFOs have been reported by trained military observers to behave like high speed, high performance, high altitude rockets or aircraft. The apparent solidity and craft-like shape of the objects have often been subject to radar confirmation. If such objects can appear to trained military men as rockets or aircraft and if such objects should come over the Arctic from the direction of Russia on the United States, they could trigger "false reports of missile attacks."

    b. Many responsible military officers have developed a mental "blind spot" to objects which appear to have the characteristics of UFOs. Such an attitude is an open invitation to the enemy to build a replica of the phenomena in order to penetrate the "hole" in his adversaries' defenses—Was this the purpose of the lens-shaped reentry vehicle tested by the U.S. Air Force in 1960 and recently featured in the Washington, D.C. *Evening Star,* dated 24 September 1968, page A4?

    c. Sometimes the phenomena appear to defy radar detection and to cause massive electromagnetic interference. Surely it is very important to discover the nature of these objects or plasmas before any prospective enemy can use their properties to build a device or system to circumvent or jam our air and space detection systems—Any nation certainly could use a system or device to penetrate enemy defenses.

4. Some UFOs Are Secret Earth Projects. The above-referenced U.S. Air Force reentry vehicle and an often publicized Canadian "saucer" project leave little doubt as to the validity of this hypothesis. Undoubtedly, *all UFOs* should be carefully scrutinized to ferret out such enemy (or "friendly") projects. Otherwise a nation faces the very strong possibility of being intimidated by a new secret "doomsday" weapon.

5. UFOs Are Related to Intra-terrestrial Intelligence. According to some eminent scientists closely associated with the study of this phenomenon, this hypothesis cannot be disregarded. (The well documented sightings over Washington, D.C. in 1952 strongly support this view.) This hypothesis has a number of far-reaching human survival implications:

a. If "they" discover you, it is an old but hardly invalid rule of thumb, "they" are your technological superiors. Human history has shown us time and again the tragic results of a confrontation between a technologically superior civilization and a technologically inferior people. The "inferior" is usually subject to physical conquest.

b. Often in the past, a technologically superior people are also possessors of a more virile or aggressive culture. In a confrontation between two peoples of significantly different cultural levels, those having the inferior or less virile culture most often suffer a tragic loss of identity and are usually absorbed by the other people.

c. Some peoples who were technologically and/or culturally inferior to other nations have survived—have maintained their identity—have equalized the differences between them and their adversaries. The Japanese people have given us an excellent example of the methods required to achieve such survival:

(1) full and honest acceptance of the nature of the inferiorities separating you from the advantages of the other peoples,

(2) complete national solidarity in all positions taken in dealing with the other culture,

(3) highly controlled and limited intercourse with the other side—doing only those things advantageous to the foreigner which you are absolutely forced to do by circumstances,

(4) a correct but friendly attitude toward the other people,

(5) a national eagerness to learn everything possible about the other citizens—its technological and cultural strengths and weaknesses. This often involves sending selected groups and individuals to the other's country to become one of his kind, or even to help him in his wars against other adversaries.

(6) Adopting as many of the advantages of the opposing people as you can, and doing it as fast as possible—while still protecting your own identity by molding each new knowledge increment into your own cultural cast.

6. Comment: Although this paper has hardly exhausted the possible hypotheses related to the UFO phenomena, those mentioned above are the principal ones presently put forward. All of them have serious survival implications. The final answer to this mystery will probably include more than one of the above hypotheses.

Up until this time, the leisurely scientific approach has too often taken precedence in dealing with UFO questions. If you are walking along a forest path and someone yells "rattler," your reaction would be immediate and defensive. You would not take time to speculate before you act. You would have to treat the alarm as if it were a real and immediate threat to your survival. Investigation would become an intensive emergency action to isolate the threat and to determine its precise nature. It would be geared to developing adequate defensive measures in a minimum amount of time. It would seem a little more of this survival attitude is called for in dealing with the UFO problem.

Observations of chimpanzees while in a captive environment have shown that the animals tend to become confused and disoriented. Since they do not usually have adult chimps to teach them how to be good apes, they are not even sure of their behavior. Often their actions are patterned after human behavior and would have virtually no survival value in the wild. Lacking the challenge of environmental adaptation, the bodies of the animals atrophy and become subject to many diseases—mostly unknown in their wild counterparts. Reactions to stimulus usually become less responsive and suitable. Sex often becomes a year-long preoccupation instead of a seasonal madness.

Do the captivity characteristics of modern civilization cause a similar lessening of man's adaptive capability, of his health, of his ability to recognize reality, of his ability to survive?

Perhaps the UFO question might even make man undertake studies which could enable him to construct a society which is most conducive to developing a completely *human* being, healthy in all respects of mind and body and, most important, able to recognize and adapt to real environmental situations.

First the theory of UFOs being hoaxes is considered. What does the NSA analyst say? Since UFOs date back to ancient times and have been seen by reputable people, this "indicates rather strongly that UFOs are not all hoaxes."

Second, are UFOs hallucinations? The analyst says "The sum of such evidence seems to argue strongly against all UFOs being hallucinations."

Third, are UFOs natural phenomena? The analyst offers the argument that if UFOs are some form of natural event, our national defenses are seriously flawed. He refers to the "solidity and craft-like shape of the objects" and stresses that it is very important to investigate the subject. Are they secret earth projects (i.e., government experimental vehicles)? The analyst gives this possibility credence but the examples he cites are not and could hardly be mistaken for UFOs. Furthermore, if these are secret projects, testing such vehicles in public areas is foolish beyond belief.

Are UFOs extraterrestrial? The analyst clearly entertains this possibility based on the opinions of "eminent scientists closely associated with the study of this phenomenon." Reference is made to the Washington, D.C., UFO sightings of July 1952 as positive evidence in favor of this point. It is also strongly emphasized that the human race, as a whole, could be in serious danger if UFOs were proven to be the product of a superior civilization. It might be argued that if the analyst is correct, then UFOs are not extraterrestrial since we have not been conquered by the occupants. We get onto shaky ground when we try to ascribe motivation to something about which we hardly understand even the most basic things (i.e., What are they? Who's in them? Where do they come from?).

Nevertheless, the seriousness of the UFO problem is made expressly apparent in this document. It would have been easy for the NSA to release something which argued strongly against UFOs. The scientific community and the public at large would see this information, lose interest in UFOs and go on to other concerns. Why didn't they do this? Do people within the NSA want the public to know what is happening? More information would be needed.

On January 23, 1980, Peter Gersten filed an appeal with the NSA to release more material, but the NSA felt that they had given enough UFO data and issued a general denial on all points of the appeal on March 24. Soon after the denial, Gersten filed suit against the NSA in District Court, Washington, D.C., on behalf of Citizens Against UFO Secrecy (CAUS) to gain release of what the NSA admitted to be 135 UFO documents.

We should take this opportunity to explain the NSA's specific reasons for withholding their UFO documents, outlined in their public affidavit filed September 30, 1980. According to NSA official, Eugene Yeates:

The COMINT reports being withheld from the plaintiff are all based on intercepted foreign communications. The disclosure of these records would identify the communications that had been successfully intercepted and processed for intelligence purposes. No meaningful portion of any of the records could be segregated and released without identifying the communications underlying the communications intelligence report. Also disclosed would be the communications lines, channels, links, and system targeted and intercepted and NSA's capabilities to successfully process the underlying communications. These communications targets and the processing techniques are current intelligence sources and methods. Disclosing them would permit foreign intelligence officials to draw inferences and make assessments about this nation's COMINT collection and processing activities that would enable them to take countermeasures, as described above, to defeat the capabilities of NSA's intelligence gathering techniques.

The COMINT reports being withheld from the plaintiff are classified in their entirety to protect intelligence sources and methods. When originated, certain of the records were properly classified Top Secret pursuant to Executive Ordor 10501, Section 1 (a), providing for the application of that classification to information, the unauthorized disclosure of which could result in exceptionally grave damage to the nation, such as the "compromise of . . . intelligence operations . . . vital to the national defense." Other documents were properly classified Secret pursuant to Executive Order 10501, Section 1 (b), providing for the application of that classification to information, the unauthorized disclosure of which could result serious damage to the nation, such as by "compromising . . . information revealing important intelligence operations." The rest, which were originated after June 1, 1972, were properly classified Top Secret pursuant to Executive Order 11652, Section 1 (A), providing for the application of that classification to information, the disclosure of which could result in exceptionally grave damage to the national security, such as "the compromise of complex cryptologic and communications intelligence systems, or were properly classified Secret under Executive Order 11652, Section 1 (B), providing for the application of that classification to information, the unauthorized disclosure of which could result in serious damage to the national security, such as the revelation of significant intelligence operations. Each COMINT record was appropriately marked when it was originated. Each COMINT record and each portion thereof remains properly so classified.

Besides the public affidavit filed with the court, a twenty-one page, top secret *In Camera* affidavit was filed by Yeates. ("In Camera" means essentially that only the judge may see it, along with the government's lawyers, thus effectively omitting the plaintiffs, CAUS, from any participation in the decision-making process.) The *In Camera* affidavit explained the contents, in summary form, of the NSA's UFO holding and it remained a mystery throughout the legal battle. On November 18, 1980, the court issued its decision, granting summary judgment in favor of the NSA.

In his decision, Judge Gerhard Gesell said that the NSA's public affidavit, supported by the *In Camera* affidavit, caused him to find that "the claimed exemptions have been properly and conscientiously applied." Besides this, he felt that the release of this material "could seriously jeopardize the work of the agency and the security of the United States."

An appeal was filed on January 12, 1981, but the court reinforced its decision in a Per Curiam Judgment dated November 3, 1981. One last attempt to gain release of the NSA's UFO file was made early in 1982 when Attorney Peter Gersten filed a petition to have the Supreme Court hear the case of *CAUS* v. *NSA*. The eighty-four page petition argued against the NSA's sweeping classification of all UFO data, claiming that the NSA did not clearly justify its reasons for involving national security as a way to keep UFO files out of the public domain. It also questioned the actions of the court in not reviewing the documents firsthand, rather than relying upon a summary, prepared by the defendant, of what the files contain.

On March 8, 1982, amid considerable publicity, the Supreme Court decided not to hear the case. Headlines announced, "Court Rebuffs UFO Buffs" and "Supreme Court Dodges UFO Document Issue," but the lawsuit was effectively over and the NSA's 135 UFO papers still remained cloaked in mystery.

The key to the original suit, the appeal, and the Supreme Court decision rested entirely on one document, the twenty-one page top secret affidavit. It is amazing that while this document was prepared only for government lawyers and the judges involved in the cases, the original documents were seen by *no one but the defendants*. Therefore, if merely the *summary* is classified "Top Secret" and the judge can see this, what classification do the 135 UFO documents bear that the judge can't see? It seemed ridiculous to even try, but the authors decided to find out what would happen if a Freedom of Information request were filed for the twenty-one page affidavit.

On April 27, 1982, a request was filed with the NSA for all legal documents, memos, records, affidavits, notes, and the like used to prepare and argue U.S. District Court Civil Action No. 80–1562 CAUS v. NSA (the original suit) plus U.S. Court of Appeals Case No. 81–1042 CAUS v. NSA. Also included was a specific request for all or any portion of the twenty-one page top secret affidavit, even if only a title page could be provided. We requested that appropriate deletions be made of descriptions of electronic monitoring and interception techniques. We are not unpatriotic and would not wish any damaging information to be revealed that is harmful to the U.S. and helpful to hostile powers. The thrust behind the request was to obtain as much information about UFOs as possible without exposing the means used to get the information. (Remember, official U.S. policy has been that UFOs are no threat to national security.)

The request was received and processed under the FOIA and on May 18, the NSA's Director of Policy, Eugene Yeates, who authored the affidavit, responded that the "portion of the twenty-one page affidavit which is releasable is enclosed." And indeed it was! The full twenty-one pages was sent under cover of Yeates' letter. There was a slight problem, however. Out of the 582 lines in the report, 412 were either totally or partially blackened out and rendered senseless. What did the rest say?

Under a section headed "Relevant Documents," the NSA explains that a total of 239 documents on UFOs were located, of which 79 originated with other government agencies, leaving 160 documents originating with the NSA. Four documents had been either released in part or found not to be answerable to the original request. One of these involved an NSA employee's attendance at a UFO symposium. What remain are 156 UFO documents, not the 135 publicly stated.

According to the affidavit, "the remaining 156 records being withheld are communications intelligence (COMINT) reports which were produced between 1958 and 1979." They are in three groups of 115, 2, and 39 documents, the contents of which are almost completely censored, except that they are in either message or summary format. A message format consists of the verbatim text of a transmission preceded and followed by data about the sender and receiver, date, and time of transmission along with other technical data. A summary gives contents of a single message or several messages in brief with technical data.

Beyond this, a brief, tantalizing reference is made to a "1973 report" which is not described in any way. We have already seen a number of extraordinary reports of UFOs from 1973, so perhaps this might be related to one or several of them.

The affidavit ends by reiterating the reasons for the NSA not releasing its file. It was strange that the affidavit was *totally* withheld from the plaintiffs in three legal actions, yet with a quick letter from private citizens the affidavit was released; censored, yes, but released.

A further attempt was made to reveal more of the affidavit. In an appeal of the decision to deny portions of the text, the authors argued that two categories of information should be released: (1) the month and/or year of UFO incidents described, and (2) the nation where the incident occurred. The contention was that such information is of sufficient vagueness that no possible threat to national security would result. In fact, one date (1973) was already given. It was again stated that the appeal did not seek information which identified NSA personnel or operations, but it did seek very general information on the UFO phenomena which happened to have been noted by the NSA in its normal functions.

The NSA's reply was not unexpected. A few very minor deletions were lifted, mostly in reference to UFOs as "surprise material"; however, national security prevailed.

Once again, national security. We have seen the NSA's reasons for censorship. Are they legitimate? To a degree, yes. The security of the United States is vital to everyone. We, as much as anyone else who enjoys a democracy, would not wish any harm to come to the place we have lived all our lives. We know the NSA is trying to look out for our best interests. But the problem we raise is of universal importance. UFOs are seen everywhere by people of all races, creeds, and nationalities; it affects everyone. The UFO phenomenon is also centuries old. The only barriers thrown in the way of legitimate scientific study of the subject are political. If UFOs are a threat to our security, as has been shown quite distinctly, it is the public's right to know this.

The NSA shreds forty tons of documents per day in its operations, but 279 UFO documents are saved. Why? Certainly not for reference to NSA interception techniques and personnel. These are easily available to NSA personnel elsewhere within the agency. It is evident that these are saved for the UFO subject matter. Simple narrative accounts of UFO incidents will not be released by NSA under any circumstances despite our efforts to purge the documentation of any reference to NSA operations. Why?

Furthermore, NSA's monitors only choose the best sources of foreign intelligence. Why waste time on poor information? Foreign governments, just as the U.S., have said publicly that UFOs are a nonsense subject. Yet, they broadcast UFO data over their most important intelligence channels such that the NSA intercepts the broadcasts and retains the information under top security!

We also question why the NSA finds it necessary to withhold UFO information that is up to twenty-five years old and to use the excuse that disclosure of vital techniques of electronic interception would threaten our security. Surely, the methods of electronic interception have changed considerably since 1958. This justification for withholding of UFO sightings acquired through what are likely to be obsolete methods strains credibility. And we have already asked that these materials be deleted!

We have heard stories of nuclear accidents where a B-52 aircraft crashes with a load of nuclear bombs. One accident involved a nuclear weapon, dropped inadvertently, on which all but one of its safety features failed. This is public knowledge now and it was unmistakably a threat to national security at the time. We've survived though. National security is intact. Can UFOs be more important than this?

The way to knowledge and understanding is truth. In this age of communication, ignorance is no longer bliss. We urge that this data be released for serious study so that speculation and rumor can be put to rest.

CHAPTER THIRTEEN

David and Goliath:
The CAUS Battle

Early in the quest to obtain UFO files, concerned individuals recognized the need to band together into a unified group with specific goals. Good results had come from FOIA results, but the effort was fragmented and uncoordinated. The FOIA provides that each person filing receive a response to his or her request, but frequently, individuals would file requests with agencies that virtually duplicated requests by others. This resulted in a great deal of wasted time and money, both for the government and for UFO researchers.

Several times throughout this book, we have mentioned an organization called CAUS, or Citizens Against UFO Secrecy, as being involved in FOIA requests and court cases against federal agencies seeking to withhold UFO documentation from the public. What is CAUS, and why was it formed?

CAUS was created early in 1978 to battle government secrecy regarding UFOs and to raise the effort above the internal disputes that rage between UFO groups of varying philosophies, disputes which have hampered the anti-UFO secrecy efforts of the past. The intention of CAUS was to concentrate solely on UFO incidents which relate in some way to government involvement. All such evidence gathered would be relayed to the public through CAUS's official newsletter, *Just Cause*.

The group's officials in 1978 included: W. Todd Zechel, Acting Director; Steven Stoikes, Administrator; Brad Sparks, Director of Research; and Peter Gersten, Legal Consultant. Gersten had been involved in the original suit against the CIA by Ground Saucer Watch (GSW) of Arizona and served as consultant to both GSW and CAUS for a time. GSW was later forced to withdraw from further legal action against the CIA due to lack of funds, so Gersten became a consultant exclusively to CAUS. The group's focus in 1978 included continued pursuit of CIA files, along with the development of several interesting stories that had been sent to CAUS from correspondents.

An example of the difficulty that CAUS would experience in dealing with government agencies surfaced in clashes with NASA and the State Department. On April 26, 1978, Miles Waggoner, of NASA's Public Information Services Branch, responded to a CAUS request for information relating to a NASA report. The report, titled "UFO Study Considerations," was previously said by NASA to have been prepared in cooperation with the CIA.

Waggoner did an about-face, stating, "There were no formal meetings or any correspondence with the CIA." No explanation was offered for the earlier statements.

CAUS attempted to force the issue in a May 8 appeal of NASA's reversal, calling Waggoner's response "capricious and arbitrary." NASA's reply on May 23 came from Kenneth Chapman, Associate Administrator for External Relations, on behalf of NASA's Administrator, Robert Frosch. He explained that "UFO Study Considerations" was prepared "solely by NASA employees and not coordinated with the CIA or any other agency." Chapman adds, "We specifically queried the CIA by telephone to inquire as to whether they were aware of any tangible or physical UFO evidence that could be analyzed; the CIA responded they were aware of no such evidence, either classified or unclassified."

NASA Administrator Frosch had earlier advised White House Science Press Advisor Dr. Frank Press via a letter dated December 21, 1977, that NASA knew of no tangible evidence of UFO reality based on a check with the CIA (Waggoner letter, dated March 2, 1978).

Sounds confusing, doesn't it? Basically, NASA found it necessary to check twice with the CIA for guidance regarding whether tangible evidence of UFO reality existed. The CIA, true to form, stated the UFO policy line of "no evidence." What is puzzling is why NASA kept going to the CIA, *if the CIA had not been involved in UFOs since 1953.* Obviously, NASA wanted to make sure that they were not exposing the CIA's hand by making "unauthorized" or "unapproved" statements. The CIA's advice to NASA was to stay out of UFOs, which they did. Would NASA have stepped on someone else's toes if they did pursue UFO investigation? The lid came down fast on this, so fast that no further information was made available.

The State Department resisted attempts to gain UFO data also. CAUS filed a request on January 19, 1978, for classified UFO documents, including in the request the date/time information, transmit numbers, and message serial numbers—all essential to properly locating a document. The State Department's FOIA group replied that it could not locate the information despite repeated searches. The contents of the messages were known from an exposé in the *UFO Investigator,* a publication of the National Investigations Committee on Aerial Phenomena (NICAP). They describe sightings in Morocco during 1976 (see Chapter 6).

Additional information on the messages were sent to the State Department on February 2. A month passed and no reply was given to CAUS. In a phone conversation with a CAUS member, a State Department FOIA Center employee, Mary Spruell, stated that the messages had been found and sent along to the Department of Defense's Office of Security and Review for clearance. Two weeks passed with no word. Another phone call to the Office of Security and Review was made; their representative stated that no documents were received from the Department of State! Returning to the State Department, CAUS was asserted by Spruell that the messages were sent and she would check into the situation. Further delays occurred, and it was only after a photocopy of the NICAP article was sent to the State Department that the messages were ultimately released.

Obstacles abounded in CAUS's path of acquiring UFO documents, as it seemed that the only way to get documents released was to *have them in the first place* so that one could mail them back to the agency as proof that they existed.

One very strange series of incidents reported to CAUS involved a possible UFO crash and electromagnetic effects on aircraft. On March 27, 1978, during a nine-hour period, near San Diego, an F-14 Tomcat went out of control, making touch-and-go landings, an A-4 Skyhawk crashed into the Pacific 50 miles west of San Diego, and an S-3A anti-submarine plane from North Island Naval Air Station exploded and crashed into the sea six miles from the base.

The next day, a college art instructor and a shipping company owner (names withheld) were discussing business on the phone at 8:30 P.M. The local call between Laguna Beach and South Laguna was interrupted by another conversation on the line. At first the two men tried to talk over the interruption, but they soon began to listen instead, when one of the intruding individuals said, "footprints leading from the site but none to it."

The art instructor began taking notes on the curious conversation as follows.

March 27, 3:00 P.M.: in danger Geiger-counter readings.
Same footprints as before.
One spotting, Palm Springs, eight in three months.
They dug 8 feet down, everything in the area was dead.
There were footprints leading from the site but none leading to.
They had it on radar for less than 2 seconds to touchdown.
They don't know who they are or where they're from.
It seems impossible that they can live unless they eject before they hit.

> They told the news media that it was a meteor (and with some humor in his voice he told the general that they believed it). He also said that it couldn't have been a meteor because it moved too fast.
>
> Miramar lost three planes. Everything in the planes went haywire in the same part of the stratosphere.
>
> General Kelley is on his way out tomorrow.

From the gist of the conversation, someone was giving a briefing to a General, although the General could not be heard on the other end. The information discussed was to be relayed to Washington and a General Kelley.

Attempts by the two men to contact the media were rebuffed, because no one believed the admittedly unbelievable story.

They found the UFO Report Center of Orange County, run by Professor Alvin H. Lawson of California State University, an affiliate group of Dr. J. Allen Hynek's Center for UFO Studies. Lawson found the men to be sincere and launched inquiries into the events, using the art instructor's notes as a reference.

Needless to say, no agency admitted to having any knowledge of the details given in the phone conversation. CAUS located one of the downed pilots, Lt. Evan Chanik of the A-4 Skyhawk crash, who had been rescued and placed back on duty. Chanik did not allude to anything unusual with himself or the aircraft prior to the crash. He said that the accident was being attributed to "a malfunction unique to the Skyhawk." The case is still open if anyone can provide additional details.

An amazing development surrounding a decade-old report re-emphasized the strong national security nature of the UFO phenomenon. This report is the 1967 Cuban jet incident.

The story became known to CAUS in the form of a statement by a security specialist who was assigned to the 6947th Security Squadron centered at Homestead Air Force Base, a unit of the U.S. Air Force Security Service (AFSS). The specialist had attended a lecture in 1978 by nuclear physicist and UFO researcher Stanton T. Friedman and informed Friedman of the incident at the conclusion of the talk. Friedman asked for additional details, which were provided later in the form of a typed statement by the specialist.

The 6947th Security Squadron's mission was to monitor all Cuban Air Force communications and radar transmissions. One hundred of the squadron's men were assigned to Detachment "A," located at Key West Naval Air Station. This forward base against attack from Cuba was on Boca Chica Key, a tropical island in the Florida Keys, east of Key West and about 97 miles from the nearest Cuban coastline. Several of these units were scattered geographically to enable direction-finding equipment to locate fixed or mobile land-based radar sites and communications centers and to plot aircraft movements from flight transmissions.

One day in March, 1967, the Spanish-speaking intercept operators of

Detachment "A" heard Cuban air defense radar controllers report an unidentified "bogey" approaching Cuba from the northeast. The UFO entered Cuban
air space at a height of about 10,000 meters (about 33,000 feet) and sped
off at nearly Mach 1 (nearly 660 mph). Two MIG-21 jet fighters were scrambled to meet it.

The single seat MIG-21 UM E76 is the standard, top-of-the-line fighter
supplied to Soviet bloc countries such as Cuba (MIG stands for Soviet aircraft
designers Mikoyan and Gurevich). It is capable of Mach 2.1 (1,385 mph)
in level flight, service ceiling of 59,000 feet, and combat radius of more
than 300 miles on internal fuel.

The jets were guided to within five kilometers (three miles) of the UFO
by Cuban ground control intercept radar personnel. The flight leader radioed
that the object was a bright metallic sphere with no visible markings or
appendages. When a try at radio contact failed, Cuban air defense headquarters ordered the flight leader to arm his weapons and destroy the object.
The leader reported his radar was locked onto the bogey and his missiles
were armed. Seconds later, the wingman screamed to the ground controller
that his leader's jet had exploded. When he gained his composure, the wingman radioed there was no smoke or flame, that his leader's MIG-21 had
disintegrated. Cuban radar then reported the UFO quickly accelerated and
climbed above 30,000 meters (98,000 feet). At last report, it was heading
south-southeast towards South America.

An Intelligence Spot Report was sent to NSA headquarters, since AFSS
and its units are under NSA operational control. Such reports are standard
practice in cases of aircraft losses by hostile nations. NSA is required to
acknowledge receipt of such reports. But the 6947th's Detachment "A" did
not get one; so it sent a follow-up report.

Within hours, Detachment "A" received orders to ship all tapes and
pertinent data to NSA and to list the Cuban aircraft loss in squadron files
as due to "equipment malfunction." At least fifteen to twenty people in the
Detachment were said to be fully informed of the incident. Presumably, the
data sent to NSA included direction-finding measurements that NSA might
later combine with other site's data to triangulate the location and altitude
of the MIG-21 flight paths. If the AFSS equipment in Florida was sensitive
enough, the UFO could have been tracked by its reflection of the Cuban
ground and airborne radar.

Friedman sent the statement to Robert Pratt, a reporter who worked
for the *National Enquirer*. Pratt, in turn, sent the statement to Robert Todd,
CAUS Research Director, desiring to verify the accuracy of the story.

Todd sent information requests concerning the Cuban incident to the
Air Force, CIA, NSA, and the Navy between February and July of 1978,
all without success. On March 10, the CIA suggested that Todd "check
with the Cuban government for records on the incident." Todd notified both
the NSA and the Air Force, on July 14, that because neither agency wished

to cooperate, he would contact the Cuban government for further information. Since he thought both agencies hinted that he might have classified data, Todd asked that they "provide advice as to what information in the attached statement should not be transmitted" to the Cubans. Todd gave them a twenty-day deadline for replies, but he did not have to wait long.

On July 28, 1978, between 5:30 and 6:00 P.M., Todd's mother answered a knock at the door. Two men, one older than the other, asked for Todd. When Todd came downstairs, one of the men asked if he was Robert Todd. He replied, "yes." The men then flashed their identification cards. Todd knew what it was about as soon as he saw "FBI." Todd and the two agents went into the living room, while Todd's parents kept their St. Bernard dog occupied outside. The two men read Todd his rights and then asked him to sign a paper which said that this had been done. Todd waived his right to silence because he felt that he did not have anything to hide. One of the men then began to read the espionage laws, but Todd told them that he was already familiar with them. They told Todd that the laws carry a penalty of life in prison or death. Both agents hinted at the possibility some indictments would be issued.

Todd, who earlier advised the NSA and the Air Force he might write to Cuba for details of the violent MIG-21 encounter with the UFO, said the agents asked him if he had ever written to a foreign government. Todd said that he had written to the Soviet Union, but explained that it was an innocent query. The older FBI agent told Todd that the Bureau had been asked by the NSA to investigate this matter because NSA has no law enforcement functions.

The two agents sat on opposite sides of him as they conducted the interview. Todd told us that he felt like a ping pong ball; one of them took the hard line and the other took the soft line. They indicated that they knew or had copies of Todd's July 14 letter to the NSA with the attached security specialist's letter. They asked Todd to identify the source of the letter. Todd told them a researcher (Friedman) had obtained the statement and passed it on to a reporter, who, in turn, passed it on to Todd. The question was asked several times because the younger agent kept confusing the "researcher" with the "reporter." Todd eventually identified. They next pressed Todd about the researcher, and when Todd refused to identify him, the agents pressed him to reveal if he was on the East or West Coast. Todd told them the West Coast. One agent asked Todd if information in the source's statement was ever published. Todd said that it had not been published to his knowledge. At the time, he did not know that Friedman had released the story to UPI.

Todd was not without some questions of his own; he wanted to know if any information in the source's statement was classified and at what level. The older agent, who Todd said had a granite face and wore a white suit, replied, "Some of the information is classified. Most of it is bullshit."

The question of tapping Todd's phone arose. At one point, Todd told the agents that based on the information they had given him, it seemed they had sufficient justification for a wiretap on his telephone. They both smiled.

Todd told both agents that under the authority of the Freedom of Information Act, he was going to demand the FBI file on its investigation of him. Surprisingly, they said they couldn't send the information that Todd had just given them because it was classified! Todd told them, "I have read enough FBI documents to know they always refer to the subject by saying 'captioned as above.' " He wanted to know how they were going to caption this one: "Internal Security" or "Espionage"? One of the agents replied that it was neither; it would fall under "Counterespionage."

When the two agents were leaving, they met Todd's parents, who had been in the dining room during the last half hour of the session. Todd's mother asked if her son was in trouble. One of the agents said no, that Todd was the "man on the end of a string." In recounting the incident, Todd stated that the agent said it straight-faced, and he thought he meant every word. His mother told them, "You ought to get the top guy." A bemused Todd thought, "She was a big help."

Todd informed CAUS that he had been visited by the agents, so CAUS contacted Paul B. Lorenzetti, spokesman for the FBI field division in Philadelphia, on July 31. When questioned about the Todd visit by agents of the FBI, Lorenzetti stated, "I'm not aware of anything about the Todd investigation," but he added, "I'm not cleared to gain information in such investigations. I have very little contact with the security end of anything." Pressed for more information, Lorenzetti reiterated, "I just don't have any knowledge of any of this," and he suggested a "call back later after I have got security to look for it." On August 1, CAUS again called Lorenzetti, who put special agent Roger Midkiff on the line, but first explained, "I've already given him instructions, if there is a pending investigation, he is not to make any comments. That is the official policy of the Bureau, as far as the Attorney General's guidelines are concerned."

Agent Midkiff said that if there was an investigation, there might be some official statement on it when it was complete. CAUS also called FBI headquarters in Washington, D.C., and talked to spokesman John Perks, who stated that he, too, knew nothing about an investigation of Todd. "I don't have any knowledge of this; we're going to have to check," he said. Later that day, Perks' superior, Tom Coll, called CAUS and said, "We never confirm who we've talked to or who we haven't talked to. We never do that." Coll said near the end of his call, "Whether we have had agents talk to him or they haven't, I don't know. But even if I did, we wouldn't confirm or deny it."

CAUS called the NSA at its headquarters in central Maryland and talked to Charles Sullivan, spokesman for the NSA. Sullivan stated, "If the

FBI is involved, and I'm only knowledgeable of that because you have said so, I'm not going to be responsive to you at all." He explained, "You are not going to get anything from any government agency about another government agency. It's tough enough knowing what goes on in my own agency."

On August 4, Todd received a call from Air Force Major Gordon Finley who was Chief of the Torts and Freedom of Information Branch, Air Force Judge Advocate General's Office. He told Todd that he was calling because it was the last day of the twenty-day time limit that Todd put on his request for information in his July 14 letter. (It came out to twenty-one days on the calendar.) Finley said the statement on the Cuban incident, if true, included classified information. He asked Todd how many copies of the statement were in his possession, and Todd asked him why he wanted to know. Finley simply told him to seal all copies of the statement in an envelope and that "someone" may come by to pick it up. Todd refused. He asked what the classification of the information was. Finley seemed very reluctant to give that information. Todd told Finley about the FBI investigation and quoted the agent who had said "secret or above." Finley stated that "secret sounded about right." Todd asked if the Air Force was going to turn the matter over to an investigative agency. (He had the FBI in mind.) Finley indicated to Todd that the Air Force had given his letter a lot of thought. Todd argued that the Cuban incident had been so widely disseminated that the information was "compromised totally." Finley responded, "I'm not qualified to debate that point," and he said it was to be the center of debate during the next few weeks.

When Todd first mentioned that the NSA requested an FBI investigation, Finley is said to have remarked, "NSA is ahead of us." He said Todd might be contacted by some intelligence agencies. "He didn't specify which agencies, and I didn't ask," Todd said. He finally told Finley that he would lock the Cuban incident statements in his file cabinet. Finley thanked Todd and hung up. No one ever came for the data.

An attempt to defuse the suspicion created by these events was made by the NSA in an August 8 letter to Todd:

> This agency has located no record indicating that the incident related in the attachment to your 14 July 1978 letter in fact occurred. However, information contained in the attachment related to the alleged manner in which information about the incident was obtained and handled is classified since, as you assert, its origin is a former U.S. intelligence analyst and was presumably an unauthorized disclosure in violation of the law.

The NSA advised Todd that he was free to discuss the Cuban incident itself with whomever he pleased, including the Cuban government. However, information about U.S. government activities and the means by which data is gathered is protected from disclosure. The sighting would surely have never been released if it had not somehow leaked out. But it did, and the only way for the NSA to salvage the situation was to use what we will call the "ways and means" technique of reducing the impact; that is, the incident is unimportant, but the methods of receipt are classified.

Todd filed a request with the Air Force to obtain copies of his FOIA case file on the matter (all documents generated as a result of his requests). The Executive Officer of the USAF's Office of the Judge Advocate General, Col. James Johnson, replied in a September 14 letter stating:

> "You have requested confirmation of the classification of the 'statement' attached to your letter of 14 July 1978 addressed to Mr. Nelson. You are advised that the Air Force *can neither confirm nor deny the authenticity of this statement,* nor the existence of any records concerning the incident described therein [emphasis added]. However, if authentic, I am advised the statement would be classified Secret in its entirety."

Col. Johnson advised Todd that he could only have letters which Todd had sent and received, excluding the "security analyst's" statement, which Todd had anyway. Johnson finally proceeded to describe ten documents which related to Todd's request and were classified under the national security provisions of the FOIA. They are:

    a. Memorandum for Record on USAFSS/DAD (Air Force Security Service/ Directorate of Administration) letter of March 24, 1978.
    b. HQ USAFSS/CS letter, 5 May 1978 to HQ USAF/JACL (Air Force Judge Advocate General, Litigation Division).
    c. HQ USAF/JACL letter of 22 May 1978 to HQ USAF/SPIB (Air Force Security Police, Classification and Safeguarding Branch).
    d. HQ USAF/SPIB letter of 25 May 1978 to HQ USAF/JACL.
    e. HQ USAF/JACL letter of 19 June 1978 to the following Air Force offices:
        (1) Intelligence (IN)
        (2) Security Police (SP)
        (3) Judge Advocate General (JA)
        (4) Information (SAF/OI)
        (5) Assistant Vice Chief of Staff (CVA)
        (6) General Counsel (SAF/GC)
        (7) Administrative Assistant to the Secretary (SAF/AA)
    f. HQ USAF/JACL letter of 23 June 1978 to HQ USAF/IN (Air Force Intelligence)
    g. HG AFIS/INS (Air Force Intelligence Service, no translation available for "INS") letter of 28 June 1978 to HQ USAF/JACL.
    h. HQ USAF/JACL Memorandum of 29 June 1978.
    i. HQ USAF/JACL letter of 21 July 1978 to HQ USAF/IN.
    j. HQ AFIS/INS letter of 1 August 1978 to HQ USAF/JACL.

These events as described clearly indicate that the Cuban incident was most probably authentic, that Robert Todd and CAUS were onto a big story, and that the government experienced a knee-jerk reaction to the fact that the story got out. Todd honestly tried to follow up the original story as any intelligent person would, when having such a story virtually dropped into his lap. The inquiries were structured specifically to spare the government undue embarrassment. Yet the reaction was to "sic" the FBI on Todd with the purpose of scaring him out of his wits. Such tactics do not work well in a democratic society, and whoever decided to take this course was ill-advised. The story remains a baffling mystery, and one wonders how many more of these incidents lie in state in the NSA's files, among others.

Another bizarre affair involved a possible UFO crash in Bolivia around May 6, 1978. The CAUS newsletter, *Just Cause,* followed the situation closely beginning in the May, 1978 issue.

Crashed UFO in Bolivia?

As usual of reports coming out of South America, details are still sketchy on an incident involving the crash of a purported UFO in Bolivia. CAUS first heard about it through a brief article in a Madison, Wis., newspaper on May 16, 1978, in which a UPI story reported that NASA was investigating a physical evidence case involving a UFO which had "exploded" some-where in Bolivia.

On Thursday, May 18th, CAUS phoned NASA in an attempt to ascertain details of the incident. Curiously, there seemed to be a widespread attack of "Blue Flu" in the NASA Public Affairs Office, as spokesman after spokes-man was reported being "home sick." Finally, Debbie Rahn, an assistant to NASA Public Affairs officer Ken Morris, provided information about a message originated by the U.S. embassy in La Paz. The message, La Paz # 3804, date-time-group May 15/1920Z, was based on a Bolivian news-paper account reporting that an object had crashed near the Bolivia/Argen-tina border; the Bolivian Air Force would investigate to determine what it was and where it came from.

About UPI's allegation that NASA was in Bolivia investigating, Rahn said: "From what we have been able to determine, NASA has not sent anyone down there." Rahn labelled the UPI report "false." The La Paz message, she said, had NASA on the distribution because ". . . State Department wanted to know if anyone else knew anything." The object and the incident involved in sighting it were not described in any detail in the La Paz report, Rahn added, and then referred CAUS to a Colonel Robert Eddington in the State Department for further details.

CAUS contacted Col. Eddington; he said, "They (NASA) have had numerous inquiries and immediately contacted us." Eddington said his office was part of the "Bureau of Oceans, International Environmental and Scientific Affairs," and "kept track of launches." In regard to the purported crashed UFO, Eddington stated: "We have received communications from our peo-ple (in Bolivia) who have also seen newspaper accounts . . . What wo do not have is any first-hand information that, in fact, the object does exist . . . I have second-hand information that the newspaper accounts indicate an object some four meters in diameter."

Eddington added that the object was described in some accounts as "egg-shaped," and there was some indication it might be "solid." The Colonel speculated that if that were the case, the object might be ". . . some bit of tankage—a near spherical liquid oxygen/hydrogen tank from a booster . . . four meters is a big tank." He added that his department could not correlate the reported object with the reentry of any known space debris. CAUS asked to be kept advised of further developments and subsequently sent a FOIA request for all La Paz traffic related to the incident.

Was it a UFO or a metal tank from a rocket booster? A follow-up article in *Just Cause,* June 1978, added detail to the initial, brief report.

> CAUS recently spoke with Bob Pratt, the *National Enquirer's* UFO experl, who returned from Bolivia last week (second week of June). Pratt said he had spoken with a number of Bolivian witnesses who reported seeing the object execute a series of maneuvers (turns) before it exploded and apparently crashed. According to Pratt, there were two explosions: the first was tremendous and was heard 85 miles away; the second was much smaller. Pratt also said he had flown over the suspected crash site and had identified a recent landslide in which the rocks showed signs of searing (burning).
>
> Pratt was evidently all set to write a story stating that a UFO *had* crashed and was buried under the beforementioned landslide. CAUS suggested that it was strange the U.S. government was totally unaware of the witnesses Pratt said he had spoken to; that NASA and the State Dept. hadn't even heard about the purported explosion. Pratt said he was aware of the U.S. personnel who were investigating the incident in the border area; he blamed their lack of diligence as the reason they hadn't made the same discoveries as he had. The Bolivians, Pratt said, were about to hold an election and various candidates were hopping around the country in the government's only helicopters. Thus, a recovery attempt on the mountainside where the UFO was allegedly located was not possible until after the election—if ever.
>
> After speaking with Pratt, CAUS phoned Col. Eddington in the State Dept. and described the information Pratt had purportedly developed. Eddington seemed neither surprised nor concerned, and said he was confident his department had made a thorough check but had discovered nothing of the sort of information Pratt described.
>
> Subsequently, Pratt stated that as of Monday, June 19th, the Bolivian UFO crash story had been "killed"—an editor had decided not to run it. Pratt said he would attempt to rewrite it and submit it again.

With Pratt's observations entered into the record, confirmation was needed to back his story. The only source which could be considered reliable enough to substantiate the event at the time would be the State Department, since the report originated from them, not NASA. Did any records exist? *Just Cause* for August 1978 answered this:

> CAUS sent an FOIA request to the State Department on June 21, 1978, asking for all documents related to the Bolivian incident. Within a week, Mary Spruell of State's FOI Staff replied that unless the information sought was of interest to a broad segment of the public, rather than to a limited or specialized group, her office would charge search fees of $11 per hour. Spruell's statement apparently was a State Department interpretation of subsection (4)(A) of the amended FOIA, which reads: "Documents shall

be furnished without charge or at a reduced charge where the agency determines that waiver or reduction of the fees is in the public interest because furnishing the information can be considered as primarily benefiting the general public."

Spruell argued that CAUS's request "does not appear to fall into this category." CAUS vigorously protested that recent public opinion polls and the popular successes of "Close Encounters" and "Project UFO" clearly showed the information sought is of interest to a broad segment of the public.

Evidently, the rather pointed letter by CAUS Director Todd Zechel, in response to Spruell's refusal to waive search and copying fees, convinced State that UFO material appealed to a "broad segment of the public." On Sept. 1, 1978, Spruell wrote that: "A search of our files has revealed 6 documents relevant to your request. The enclosed 5 documents have been reviewed by the appropriate officials of the Department of State and there is no objection to their release. One document is still under review and will be the subject of further correspondence." No mention was made of search or reproduction fees; State obviously decided to waive them after all.

Of the five documents released, three originally were UNCLASSIFIED, one was classified CONFIDENTIAL, and the other was SECRET. The earliest of the messages was sent on May 15 at 1909Z (3:09 P.M. EDT) from the U.S. Embassy in La Paz to the Secretary of State, with the action copy to State's Bureau of Politico-Military Affairs and information copies to CIA, NSA, NASA, and other units inside and outside State. It carried an IMMEDIATE precedence, a designator reserved for situations "gravely" affecting the national security, intelligence "essential" or "vital" to the national security, etc., and it reads as follows:

"Subject: Report of Fallen Space Object. 1. The Bolivian newspapers carried this morning an article concerning an unidentified object that apparently recently fell from the sky. The papers quoted a 'Latin' correspondent's story from the Argentine city of Salta. The object was discovered near the Bolivian city of Bermejo (2245S-6420W) and was described as egg-shaped, metal and about four meters in diameter. 2. The Bolivian Air Force plans to investigate to determine what the object might be and from where it came. 3. Request the Department check with appropriate agencies to see if they can shed some light on what this object might be. The general region has had more than its share of reports of UFOs this past week. Request a reply ASAP. Boeker." (Note: Paul H. Boeker is U.S. Ambassador to Bolivia.)

State replied to Boeker on May 18, in an IMMEDIATE message, classified SECRET, and drafted by Col. Eddington of OES/APT/SA:

"Subject: Report of Fallen Space Object. Ref: La Paz 3804 (Note: Quoted above). 1. Preliminary information provided in referenced cable and FBIS (Note: Foreign Broadcast Information Service, a CIA unit that monitors foreign newspapers, publications, radio and Tv broadcasts) cables Panama 142357Z (Note: May 14 at 2357Z) and Paraguay 161913Z (Note: May 16 at 1913Z) has been checked with appropriate government agencies. No direct correlation with known space objects that may have reentered the earth's atmosphere near May 6 can be made. However, we are continuing to examine any possibilities. 2. Your attention is invited to State Airgram

A-6343, July 26, 1973 which provides background information and guidance for dealing with space objects that have been found. In particular any information pertaining to the pre-impact observations, direction of trajectory, number of objects observed, time of impact and a detailed description including any markings would be helpful. Vance." (State 126725.)

At about this time, Project MOONDUST got involved. MOONDUST is a foreign-space-debris analysis program of the Air Force Systems Command's Foreign Technology Division (FTD/SDM) at Wright-Patterson AFB, Ohio. FTD originated a CONFIDENTIAL NOFORN (means "No dissemination to Foreign Nationals," in this case Bolivians, it would seem) cable on May 19 that evidently referred to Latin American press reports and raised the question of MOONDUST involvement. (The FTD cable was not released to CAUS. We suspect it is the 6th document under State's FOIA review and we have sent a special request for it to FTD.)

On May 24, the U.S. Defense Attache Office (USDAO) in La Paz transmitted a CONFIDENTIAL NOFORN cable to FTD/SDM and to HQ USAF WASHDC/INYSA (Air Force Intelligence Science & Technology Branch, or AFINYSA for short), with info copies to DIA/DC-4B/DT-3B (Defense Intelligence Agency DC-4B is Guidance & Requirements Branch, Human Resources Division, Directorate of Collection Operations; DIADT-3B is Technical Data & Foreign Material Branch, Directorate of Scientific & Technical Intelligence), NORAD COC/DOFS (North American Air Defense Command Combat Operations Center/Aerospace Defense Command Space Operations Division), and the State Department. It read as follows:

"Subject: Moon Dust (U) (Note: "U" means subject title is unclassified). Ref FTD CONF NOFORN 191830Z May 78, subj, as above & SECRET State 126725 (Note: Quoted earlier). 1. (C/NOFORN) (Note: This begins CONFIDENTIAL/NOFORN part of cable) This office has tried to verify the stories put forth in references to the FTD msg and those which appeared in the local press. The Chief of Staff of the Bolivian Air Force told DATT/ AIRA (Note: U.S. Defense Attache's Air Attache) this date that planes from the BAF (Note: Bolivian Air Force) have flown over the area where the object was supposed to have landed and in their search they drew a blank. Additionally, DATT/AIRA talked this date with the Commander of the Bolivian Army and he informed the DATT that the Army's search party directed to go into the area to find the object has found nothing. The Army has concluded that there may or not (sic) be an object, but to date nothing has been found. 2. (U) (Note: Remainder of message UNCLASSIFIED) Will keep you informed if anything factual turns up. GDS 31 Dec 84." (Note: Under the General Declassification Schedule, this cable ordinarily would not have been declassified until Dec. 31, 1984.)

From what CAUS can determine, the May 24 USDAO message was based on an expedition of Bolivian Army soldiers and scientists that returned from the suspected impact area on May 21. CAUS has reliable information from an American source that this expedition did not get to Cerro Bravo (Bravo Mountain), the suspected crash site, because the slopes were too steep to negotiate.

After the first expedition returned, a young Bolivian astronomer, who had been part of that team, flew over Cerro Bravo in a BAF plane with a BAF pilot, making five or six passes to observe a rockslide he had noticed earlier from the ground. He became convinced something had struck the side of the mountain, causing the slide.

A second expedition consisting of three BAF officers and a guide set out on horseback on May 23, reaching the rockslide on foot on May 25. The officers told the American source they believe something crashed into the mountain but they could not find any debris. The officers reached this conclusion because: the rockslide appeared to be recent; it had created huge monolith-like boulders three meters (10 ft) tall and two meters (6 ft) in diameter; they found a 100-meter trench running parallel to the slide three to four meters (10–13 ft) wide at the top; some of the large rocks appeared to have been burned, having a whitish appearance as though seared by extremely high heat; and the grass around the sides and the top of the slide area was brown and withered for about 100 meters, whereas grass further away was green.

At present, it is not known if the information gathered by the second expedition—which returned on May 27—ever reached the U.S. Government. (The latest document released was dated May 26 and it merely promised to pouch on May 29 a copy of State Airgram A-6343 to Bolivia as requested on May 19.) Strangely, none of the State Department documents even alludes to the type of detailed and significant information given to CAUS by a reliable American source. Whether this denotes a coverup or a simple foulup is yet to be seen.

One of the very frustrating things in attempting to obtain documentation for incidents like the Bolivian crash is the extreme reluctance of government authorities to want to give a full accounting of *anything*. If this object were not a UFO but say, a Soviet spacecraft, much more cable traffic would have taken place, and some indication of this should have at least been alluded to in the messages. Yet, no positive identification is made. Furthermore, if an object caused the damage, where was it? It seemed to have vanished according to the later cables. If the Bolivian Army was correct, and no object was found because none may have existed, then again, what caused the destruction?

CAUS has come across many accounts of alleged secret projects which relate in one way or another to UFOs. In the event that readers who were once in the military may have detailed knowledge of one or more of these projects, we will list several by code name, along with a brief description of what is known about them:

Project Blue Paper—	Post-Blue Book UFO investigation.
Project Old New Moon—	Post-Blue Book UFO investigation.
Project Aquarius—	Secret UFO study. Late 1970s to early 1980s.
Project Whirlwind—	1949 M.I.T. UFO study.
Project Pounce—	UFO study proposed by Kirtland AFB, early 1950s.
Project Pinball—	Attempt in Alaska to track UFOs on radar.

Project Bluebolt—	Antigravity research project by the U.S. Air Force, early 1970s. (See Chapter 1.)
Project Redlight—	?

One of the few rumored secret projects that has been verified, along with the more well-known UFO projects, such as Blue Book, Grudge, and Twinkle, is "Project Saint," or "Sanctum," in some accounts.

"Saint" is an acronym for both Satellite Inspector and Satellite Interceptor. Initiated by the Air Force, Saint was to be a spacecraft designed to rendezvous with an unidentified object with the purpose of inspecting it with optical, infrared, and other radiation sensors. An advanced model of Saint would be capable of destroying the target if necessary. In effect, it was an early "killer satellite." The project lasted from 1959 to December 1962, when design difficulties and more advanced technological developments caused it to be cancelled.

Application of such a vehicle to UFO research is obvious, and we may wonder if present versions of Saint have pursued, photographed, or even shot down an unidentified object in space.

The previously-mentioned National Investigations Committee on Aerial Phenomena became a subject of intense government scrutiny. Long regarded as the most influential UFO group of the 1960s, NICAP began a gradual decline to virtual oblivion during the 1970s. CAUS uncovered a number of disturbing bits of evidence relating to NICAP that should cause other UFO groups considerable concern.

During NICAP's first year of existence under its original founder, T. Townshend Brown, several mysterious persons managed to fit themselves into NICAP's structure. One, named Nicolas de Rochefort, was a Russian immigrant who, among other jobs, wrote scripts in French and Russian for the Voice of America. He was also employed by the Psychological Warfare Staff of the CIA. De Rochefort became NICAP's Vice-Chairman, alongside Brown. Another NICAP staffer in 1956 was a man named Bernard J. O. Carvalho, a native of Portugal, who was also involved in CIA-owned companies (secretly owned, that is). Perhaps the involvement of two CIA employees was not all that mysterious. After all, T. Townshend Brown's leadership of NICAP was short-lived and, in fact, ended near the end of 1956.

Well-known UFO authority Major Donald Keyhoe took over NICAP in January, 1957. A strong believer in UFO reality, Keyhoe managed to beef up NICAP's prestige by looking for and appointing prominent people to NICAP's Board of Governors. One of the first board appointees was Vice Admiral Roscoe Hillenkoetter, a Naval Academy classmate of Keyhoe's and the first Director of the CIA, when it formed in 1947. Hillenkoetter made a number of positive statements on UFO reality, thus endearing himself to Keyhoe. This relationship reversed itself, however, when Keyhoe developed

NICAP into a fierce opponent of government secrecy and pushed for Congressional hearings in the early 1960s. Hillenkoetter abruptly resigned from NICAP, expressing the opinion that NICAP went as far as it could go, and no further criticism should be aimed at the Air Force for its handling of UFOs.

It can probably be surmised that Hillenkoetter was pressured out of NICAP by the CIA, since it was of considerable embarrassment to the CIA to have a former Director making pro-UFO statements.

Further evidence of CIA influence in NICAP developed during the period immediately before NICAP's decline. On December 3, 1969, Donald Keyhoe was ousted as NICAP's Director during a Board meeting. Who led the effort to remove Keyhoe? The Chairman of the Board, Col. Joseph Bryan, former Chief of the CIA's Psychological Warfare Staff (1947–1953). And who replaced Keyhoe? John Acuff, who was the head of the Society of Photographic Scientists and Engineers (SPSE), a frequent target of Russian spying attempts and a group that had many members involved in Defense Department intelligence units, including the CIA. His management of NICAP was financially "tight" (in the cheap sense) and totally inept in a research sense. Criticism of government UFO policy was gone, and NICAP merely served as a sighting collection center. Acuff's management drove loyal NICAP members away and ultimately led to Acuff's downfall in 1978.

Who replaced Acuff? None other than Alan Hall, a retired CIA employee, who accepted the position after a number of other CIA employees were offered the job. Support for Hall from the NICAP Board came from Charles Lombard, an aide to Senator Goldwater and a former CIA covert employee.

NICAP eventually became so ineffective that it was dissolved, and the group's UFO files were absorbed by the Center for UFO Studies in Evanston, Illinois.

There certainly seems to be a pattern behind NICAP's destruction. Is it a coincidence that so many ex-CIA people became deeply involved in the operation of NICAP? It is possible that the CIA wanted to influence NICAP activities for several reasons:

1) To gather intelligence through NICAP's investigators network.
2) To identify and plug leaks from government sources (NICAP was renowned for receiving military-oriented reports).
3) To monitor other hostile intelligence agencies (NICAP received several overtures from the Soviet KGB).

After Acuff's bungled management of NICAP, the CIA may have felt that NICAP's effectiveness as a "front" was gone and allowed it to be taken over by CUFOS.

Speculation? Yes, but not without justification, as one can clearly read.

A new question now arises. Would the same thing happen to another UFO group that became too effective and efficient? We can only watch for the signs.

The structure of CAUS underwent changes (not CIA-induced!) in the 1980s. Peter Gersten became its new Director, with Lawrence Fawcett as Assistant Director. A Board of Advisors was formed, containing well-known names in UFO research such as Raymond Fowler, Stanton Friedman, Dr. Bruce Maccabee, and others. The focus, to this day, continues to be the release of government documents on UFOs, although pressure by the Reagan Administration to restrict the Freedom of Information Act may hamper the work of CAUS in this area.

It is important that the public become involved in the search at this time. To prevent further dissolution of the FOIA, we urge citizens to write to their elected officials telling them to support the free flow of government information, particularly about UFOs. Use this book as a source of documented evidence. Make copies of the reports and send them to your Senators and Congressmen. CAUS has been effective in obtaining new data, but there is strength in numbers. The more support behind CAUS's efforts to inform the public, the better off both the public and CAUS will be.

CHAPTER FOURTEEN
Conclusion: Who Goes There?

What immediate observations can we draw from the information presented here? We have seen evidence that UFOs have posed an enormous problem for the international community over the last several decades. We've seen how military bases across the northern border of the U.S. were inundated with UFOs and strange helicopters in 1975, activity which to this day remains unexplained. Federal agencies have conducted secret probes on UFOs, details of which have been either partially or totally suppressed. The public has been deliberately and consciously misinformed by federal agencies in an effort to keep us ignorant of the fact that any probem exists at all. Aircraft have crashed or disappeared, and lives have been lost in UFO encounters. *According to the government,* the national security of the United States would be threatened by an open discussion of government UFO information.

Such statements are as unbelievable to us as they would be to anyone else. But we cannot ignore the weight of the evidence. Essentially, it has come from the horse's mouth!

It has been said that the UFO phenomenon cannot be real because it has been with us for so many years that it should have been solved by now. We are highly advanced technologically and recent breakthroughs in various branches of science are extensive.

A man has lived with a mechanical heart, a feat which would have been considered pure science fiction not too far in the past. Men have walked on the moon, photographed planets hundreds of millions of miles away, peered into the subatomic world. The very basis of biological life is beginning to be understood. Yet, UFOs are still unsolved; the controversy continues into its fourth decade without any apparent let-up.

The problem seems simple enough on the surface. This might be expressed in our definition of a UFO expert: that is, a person who knows everything there is to know about UFOs except what they are, who's in them, and where they come from!

Who, what, and where. Neat, concise, basic questions. But the nature of UFOs forbids the application of the usual methods of scientific research. Experimentation, observation, and reasoning don't work when the subject does not stay around long enough to be examined. For example, there is only so much that can be done with a physical trace left by a UFO such as a broken tree limb or a hole in the ground. The situation is comparable to placing a television set in a muddy field after a rainstorm and then removing it. Holes in the ground are left as evidence that the set was once there. However, we cannot determine anything about the nature of the set by the holes left by its legs. Perhaps we could tell if it were made out of wood or plastic, but it would be necessary for a piece of the set to break off in the hole, which as a rule would not be likely.

The objects that appeared over Loring, Malmstrom, Minot, Wurtsmith, and other air bases in 1975 caused a major security alert. After the overflights, the UFOs slipped away, evading all attempts to identify them. The problem was simple: intrusions by UFOs. An answer was impossible under the circumstances since the objects came and left, apparently leaving nothing behind as evidence of their visit.

But something was left behind. It was a sense of powerlessness and anxiety on the military's part to deal with the objects. In the K-7 incident in Chapter 3, we see evidence of tampering with our nuclear weapons by unidentified aerial objects, an event which should shake our sense of security right down to the roots. In fact, some sources informed us that as a result of these missile tamperings, an upheaval occurred by which the military found it necessary to test and examine other missiles to insure that they were in order. Is it possible that in 1975 a security problem of very high order developed due to the possibility that our nuclear weapons secrets were compromised by whoever buzzed the sites? It is unlikely that such an admission would ever be made, but it is worth thinking about.

Detractors of UFOs have expressed the idea that highly tense world events may somehow stimulate UFO sightings as a way for people to escape stressful news. As an example, it has been said that in 1973, Middle East tensions, which included an Arab-Israeli war and large oil shortages in the United States, contributed to the public's anxiety and resulted in the UFO wave of 1973. There is no real evidence to support this theory but could important news events have stimulated the 1975 activity?

September 10, 1975—   William Calley's 1971 conviction is reinstated after having been overturned previously.

September 18, 1975—   Patty Hearst is captured.

September 5, 1975 and
September 22, 1975—   Two failed attempts to assassinate President Ford.

October 1975—   Employment and production in the U.S. grows.

October 22, 1975—   Sara Jane Moore indicted for assassination attempt on President Ford.

Last week of
October, 1975—   President Ford denies financial aid to New York City.

One would hardly think that these events would cause military men to go bonkers and start seeing UFOs when nothing was there! Well, then, it must have been mass hallucinations! Sounds silly, doesn't it? But such explanations have been (and will be) offered to dismiss UFOs. The press carried a story at one time explaining UFOs as dust shaken loose from a returning Russian lunar probe. The dust, it seems, was somehow swirled into disc shapes by the eddies and currents in the upper atmosphere, and then the shapes were seen by people on the ground as mysterious, saucer-shaped craft. There are extremes on both sides of the UFO question, and it is sometimes tricky to strike a balance between the two.

Support for UFO reality has come from a number of surprising sources. Former Air Force Chief of Staff General Curtis Le May commented on UFOs after stating that he was not "quoting any classified information" and was "giving the straightest answers that I can give" in his autobiography *Mission with Le May* (Doubleday, 1965). He went on to report that while the bulk of UFO reports could be explained away as natural phenomena, some could not be dismissed so easily.

"There is no question about it," Le May said. "These were things which we could not tie in with any natural phenomena known to our investigators."

Le May proceeded to say that the Air Force was not involved in any effort to influence the public's attitude toward UFOs and expressed his dislike of stories that the Air Force was trying to muzzle the press. As the Air Force Chief of Staff, General Le May would understandably want to defend his men against such charges. The fact remains that these charges were true, and there is an enormous body of evidence to support it.

Le May ended his commentary on UFOs by reiterating, "There were some cases we could not explain. Never could."

No less than the late eminent Swiss analyst Dr. C. G. Jung expressed his opinion on government UFO secrecy in a letter to former NICAP Director Major Donald E. Keyhoe as follows:

If it is true that the AAF (American Air Force) or the government withholds telling facts, then one can only say that this is the most unpsychological and stupid policy one could invent. Nothing helps rumors and panics more than ignorance. It is self-evident that the public ought to be told the truth.

This sentiment has come from many sources within the government; sources that have seen and experienced the UFO phenomenon as well as those who have studied it. Five theses/research studies have been located, via the FOIA, at Maxwell Air Force Base, Alabama; in particular, at the Air University. These are:

"UFOs and Extraterrestrial Life," Captain D. Stanley, 1968
"The UFO Problem: Time for a Reassessment," Major J. King, 1968
"An Analysis of UFOs," Major R. Dutton, 1967
"The UFO Debate Is Still Alive," Major J. Stroh, 1971
"Should the USAF Reopen Project Blue Book?" Major W. Brummett and Captain E. Zuick, 1974

One's first impression might be that any mention of UFOs from within a military educational facility would be largely negative, echoing the usual policy line of no threat to national security and no evidence of reality. However, upon scanning the contents of the documents cited here, a different picture emerges.

The Stanley thesis concludes that UFOs are most likely real, material objects. Secret weapons are not considered a likely explanation. The extraterrestrial hypothesis is entertained as a distinct possibility, and Stanley advises that increased effort to study the subject is warranted.

The King thesis observes that while most UFO reports are misidentifications of conventional phenomena, some of the UFOs are space vehicles, extraterrestrial in nature and definitely intelligent. The possibility that covert contact with man has been made is stated in no uncertain terms. And the public pronouncements on UFOs by the government may hide a serious concern over implications for mankind if UFOs were to be announced as real.

The Dutton thesis takes a more conservative stance by stating only that a more detailed study of UFOs is necessary. No specific conclusions on UFO reality are given, but Dutton's opinion is that an open, scientific inquiry is the only way to deal with the subject.

The Stroh research study rejects the idea that UFOs should be studied intensively, because, based on prior investigations by the Air Force, no positive proof was found that UFOs are a threat to national security and no contribution to scientific knowledge was evident in UFO study according to the Condon Committee's investigations. It does advise the Air Force to monitor the phenomenon until either all sightings are explained by science or the Air Force is required to reassess its policy by whatever new information may come along, meaning proof positive of UFOs.

Finally, the research study by Brummett and Zuick concludes that the Air Force and Condon Committee investigations lacked credibility and that a new UFO project should be instituted under the wing of a Congressional subcommittee. A call is made for the development of a professional UFO group consisting of scientists and trained personnel.

So, out of five papers located at the Air Force's Air University, only one is largely negative about UFOs, but even this paper calls for, at the very least, an open monitoring of UFOs by the Air Force. The rest of the papers take remarkably anti-government UFO policy positions, recognizing what Dr. Jung saw as a far more serious threat to our national security: ignorance and biased negativism.

Who else went on record as believing that UFOs are something worthy of serious consideration?

—Dr. Clyde Tombaugh, the discoverer of the planet Pluto, who observed UFOs on two occasions, one of which was described as a large, elongated object with rectangular windows.

—President Jimmy Carter, who asked that NASA explore the possibility of conducting an investigation of UFOs.

—President Gerald Ford, who, as a Congressman from Michigan, called for Congressional investigations of UFOs after an enormous wave of sightings in 1966.

—Dr. Paul Santorini, Greek physicist and engineer influential in the development of fuses for atomic weapons and a guidance system for the NIKE missile. Santorini felt that UFOs were under intelligent control and that a "world blanket of secrecy" was put over the subject.

—Fifty-three percent of the respondents to an American Astronomical Society survey in 1977, who said that UFOs either certainly or probably deserve scientific study. Of the 1,356 surveys returned, 62 astronomers said that they had seen or recorded a UFO but only 18 ever reported their experience to anyone.

—Ex-astronaut Gordon Cooper, who has stated, "I believe that these extraterrestrial vehicles and their crews are visiting this planet from other planets." Cooper was witness to numerous UFO overflights in Europe during 1951, some of which involved jet chases.

—Sixty-one percent of respondents to an opinion poll of readers of *Industrial Research/Development,* who felt that UFOs probably or definitely exist. Eighteen percent of these felt they "possibly" or "definitely" had seen a UFO.

—Dr. Hermann Oberth, eminent German rocket expert generally regarded as the "father of modern rocketry," who was convinced that UFOs were most probably extraterrestrial vehicles of high technical design and ability.

—General Nathan Twining, head of the Air Force's Air Materiel Command and later to become Air Force Chief of Staff and Chairman of the Joint Chiefs, who wrote in a September 23, 1947, letter to the Commanding General of the Army Air Forces on the subject of "Flying Discs":

a. The phenomenon reported is something real and not visionary or fictitious.

   b. There are objects probably approximating the shape of a disc, of such appre-
      ciable size as to appear to be as large as a man-made aircraft.
   c. There is a possibility that some of the incidents may be caused by natural
      phenomena, such as meteors.
   d. The reported operating characteristics such as extreme rates of climb, maneu-
      verability (particularly in roll), and action which must be considered *evasive*
      when sighted or contacted by friendly aircraft and radar, lend belief to
      the possibility that some of the objects are controlled either manually, auto-
      matically, or remotely.

—U.S. Senator Barry Goldwater, also a general in the Air Force Reserves,
   who has repeatedly expressed his opinion that UFOs are real and who has
   been denied access to top secret UFO files at Wright-Patterson Air Force
   Base, Ohio, despite his status.

A curious set of regulations exists within NASA. Listed in the Code of
Federal Regulations since 1969, 14 CFR 1211, as they are known, provide
for the detention, examination, and decontamination of persons and things
that have come in direct or indirect contact with a person, animal, or other
form of life or matter that has "touched directly or come within the atmospheric envelope of any other celestial body."

Originally designed for our expeditions to the moon and, in fact, instituted only a few days before the first lunar landing, the regulations can be
applied to space voyages by vehicles *not originating from Earth,* according
to NASA's general counsel Neil Hosenball. Theoretically, anyone who sees
and approaches a UFO and, if lucky (?) enough, is able to touch the object,
may be liable for a $5,000.00 fine and/or a year in prison if he or she does
not submit to detention.

Now, we don't anticipate that such a thing will ever come down upon
a UFO witness. It would hardly be a way to reward someone with physical
proof of UFO reality! However, another problem surfaces and that is the
fact that when such stories are circulated in the media, a potential witness
could be frightened away from reporting a UFO encounter. The threat of
a fine and prison term for exposing the public to some as yet unknown
peril may be impetus enough to remain silent.

One witness involved in the following encounter had precisely this fear
in mind when he came forward to tell us what he had gone through.

Persistent stories had come out of England about an unidentified flying
object which had come down into the Rendlesham Forest near the American
Air Force Base at Bentwaters on December 30, 1980. Reports included radar
tracking from a civilian radar site, which later had been visited by U.S.
Air Force officers with the purpose of confiscating the radar tapes, and accounts by USAF personnel of a metallic craft and entities seen in a clearing
at Rendlesham. The stories, of course, were unverified and little else could
be accomplished unless more concrete data came forth.

Two British UFO investigators, Brenda Butler and Dot Street, followed
up on several of the stories and found substance to them. Reportedly, a

security sergeant saw entities associated with a dome-shaped UFO in the woods; another witness, an airman, saw marks in the earth characteristic of what he had heard about UFO landing marks. All witnesses desired complete anonymity, however, and while the story became more intriguing with the increase in the number of confirming witnesses, it still could not be considered a strong case by any means. Anonymous witnesses and scattered rumors are not convincing evidence of anything.

While we were putting this book together, a person came forward as a result of a UFO article he had read. Fascinated by the subject because of his experience, this individual was eventually put in contact with the authors and told a very interesting tale. His identity is known to us, but, by his request, we will change his name to Art Wallace.

Wallace was attached to Bentwaters Air Force Base as a security policeman. He had been assigned to the base for only a short period of time, when at 1:00 A.M. on a night either on or very near to December 30, 1980, his life took a strange twist. While he was on duty at the Bentwaters flight line, a jeep pulled up. Two men, a sergeant and a lieutenant, told Wallace to get in because they were going over to the motor pool. On the way over, Wallace noticed that many animals were running out of the woods nearby; something he had never seen before, even in the States. When they arrived at the motor pool, Wallace and the sergeant were told to get gas-powered "light-alls" (trailer-mounted lights used for illuminating large areas). The lights were attached to the jeep, and they proceeded to the Bentwaters main gate where they met other vehicles.

The convoy moved out toward the Rendlesham Forest a few miles away. Wallace heard radio chatter mentioning names of people he knew plus "OSI," most likely a reference to the Air Force's Office of Special Investigations. Wallace saw security police as well as members of the British military stationed all along the way.

They pulled onto a dirt road and drove about a mile into the Rendlesham Forest, stopping at what Wallace referred to as a "staging point." The men were ordered to check their weapons in since they would not be taking them along. Wallace went into the woods with four other men led by a captain who had met them at the Bentwaters motor pool. As they approached a clearing in the woods, they noticed a brightness in the distance and the sound of helicopters overhead. Wallace noticed an airman crying at the edge of the clearing with a medic attending him. This puzzled Wallace greatly as he couldn't imagine what might have been going on. The first thing the men noticed when they had a clear view was that large movie cameras had been placed surrounding a field in the clearing. Many military and plainclothes personnel were milling about watching something.

The "something" was an object, taking the appearance of a transparent aspirin tablet, hovering about one foot off the ground. Wallace estimated that the object was fifty feet in diameter and had a bright, pulsating, yellow mist inside. It did not move from its position. Wallace and some of the men approached the object to within about ten feet. Two cows in the field had come over to the object and according to Wallace, appeared to be just staring at it, oblivious to the security men in the area.

A radio call was heard over a field radio unit. A helicopter pilot said, "Here it comes." In the distance, a red light appeared, first behind a pine tree, then in front of it. The light quickly sped over to the aspirin-shaped object and hovered at a position about twenty feet above it. After maintaining this position for a minute, the red light broke up. No explosion occurred in the conventional sense. The light merely broke up into a shower of particles.

Suddenly, in the place of the red light and the aspirin-shaped object, another vehicle appeared. Wallace said it was a domed disc, bright white in color, with an intricately detailed surface much like the models used in movies like "Star Wars" and "Close Encounters." It had two appendages on the lower flange of the disc which seemed to be the beginning of delta wings but not quite. Shadows were cast on the surface of the disc by some of the raised-relief detail. Wallace and the men with him walked around the object and noticed an interesting effect. Their own shadows were cast onto the object, probably by the bright "light-alls" in the field. Not only did their shadows bend upwards at the head, but as they walked and then stopped, the shadows would appear to advance *one pace more* and then stop. Stunned and disbelieving of this effect, Wallace and the others walked and stopped several times, each time noticing the effect repeat itself. Additionally, the third time that they tried this, a light came over the head of a shadow and moved from one head to another.

Wallace recalled turning to say a few words to one of the men. The next thing he knew, he woke up in bed, fully dressed and muddy up to his knees. Wallace asked one of his companions in the barracks what time he had come in. He replied 4:00 A.M. At that point he did not remember what had happened that night. As he went about his usual duties, Wallace began to recall the events.

A phone call came later in the day. Wallace was summoned to his commander's office along with other security policemen who were at the scene of the UFO activity. Civilians were in the office also, giving Wallace the impression of being CIA personnel. The commander politely advised the men not to talk about the night's events to anyone. They were brought into another room where the civilians, much more stern and rude, reminded the men of their duty and ordered them never to discuss the matter with anyone. They were checked for radiation, debriefed for an hour, and made to sign forms which re-emphasized the high security nature of what happened. Wallace and others were put on a call-in schedule by which they would be required to phone a certain number daily at 11:30 A.M. as a check on their whereabouts and activities.

Wallace recalled being shown a film on UFOs in a room with other men for reasons which he still doesn't understand. The movie displayed film clips, some dating to World War II, of actual UFO activity in various places and times. Several of the sequences showed UFOs near what appeared to be fighter aircraft, and in one sequence from the Korean War, a disc-shaped object passed close to an MIG fighter, causing it to crash. Wallace was told they were being shown this so that they might better understand the need for secrecy on the events of the 30th.

Wallace said that versions of the story leaked to the British media detailing alien meetings in the forest and landing marks on the ground were deliberately contrived by the military to mislead the public. The false evidence was intended to be discovered by UFO investigators so that a negative evaluation would be ascribed to the story, thus preserving secrecy.

It is quite a story, and coupled with other accounts of the Rendlesham Forest events, we are inclined to think that something truly extraordinary may have happened.

What was the Air Force's official response to this? The authors filed a FOIA request with the 81st Combat Support Group at RAF Bentwaters to determine if documentation was on file at the base. A reply dated April 28, 1983, came from Col. Henry J. Cochran, Bentwaters Commander.

> Reference your letter dated April 14, 1983 requesting information about unknown aircraft activity near RAF Bentwaters. *There was allegedly some strange activity near RAF Bentwaters at the approximate time in question* but not on land under U.S. Air Force jurisdiction and, therefore, no official investigation was conducted by the 81st Tactical Fighter Wing. Thus, the records you request do not exist [emphasis added].

If no records exist, how did Col. Cochran know that something had happened near Bentwaters? He was not the Bentwaters Commander at the time. Furthermore, under the provisions of Air Force Manual 12–50, such records would either have been destroyed after a short period of time or they would have been passed along to a permanent storage facility for retention; that is, they would no longer be at the base. And the investigation was probably not conducted by the 81st Tactical Fighter Wing but by someone else (OSI?).

On May 7, 1983, CAUS Researcher Director Robert Todd filed an FOIA request with the Air Force's 513th Combat Support Group for information on the Rendlesham Forest affair. The 513th CSG provides document management services for the Headquarters of the Third Air Force in Europe, which covers the Bentwaters area. Our hopes were low for any positive results as it seemed that a tight ring of secrecy was placed around the story.

However, in a June 14, 1983, letter from Col. Peter Bent, Commander of the 513th CSG, an utterly stunning admission was made. Col. Bent said:

> It might interest you to know that the US Air Force had no longer retained a copy of the 13 January 1981 letter written by Lt Col Charles I. Halt.

The Air Force file copy had been properly disposed of in accordance with Air Force Regulations. Fortunately, through diligent inquiry and the gracious consent of Her Majesty's government, the British Ministry of Defence and the Royal Air Force, the US Air Force was provided a copy for you.

The January 13 letter was enclosed with Col. Bent's response. It was on the official letterhead of the 81st Combat Support Group at Bentwaters and signed by Lt. Col. Halt, who was the Deputy Base Commander. The title of the document is "Unexplained Lights," and it reads like science fiction:

1. Early in the morning of 27 Dec 80 (approximately 0300L), two USAF security police patrolmen saw unusual lights outside the back gate at RAF Woodbridge. Thinking an aircraft might have crashed or been forced down, they called for permission to go outside the gate to investigate. The on-duty flight chief responded and allowed three patrolmen to proceed on foot. The individuals reported seeing a strange glowing object in the forest. The object was described as being metallic in appearance and triangular in shape, approximately two to three meters across the base and approximately two meters high. It illuminated the entire forest with a white light. The object itself had a pulsating red light on top with a bank(s) of blue lights underneath. The object was hovering or on legs. As the patrolmen approached the object, it maneuvered through the trees and disappeared. At this time the animals on a nearby farm went into a frenzy. The object was briefly sighted approximately an hour later near the back gate.

2. The next day, three depressions 1½" deep and 7" in diameter were found where the object had been sighted on the ground. The following night (29 Dec 80) the area was checked for radiation. Beta/gamma readings of 0.1 milliroentgens were recorded with peak readings in the three depressions and near the center of the triangle formed by the depressions. A nearby tree had moderate (.05–.07) readings on the side of the tree toward the depressions.

3. Later in the night a red sun-like light was seen through the trees. It moved about and pulsed. At one point it appeared to throw off glowing particles and then broke into five separate white objects and then disappeared. Immediately thereafter, three star-like objects were noticed in the sky, two objects to the north and one to the south, all of which were about 10° off the horizon. The objects moved rapidly in sharp angular movements and displayed red, green and blue lights. The objects to the north appeared to be elliptical through an 8–12 power lens. They then turned to full circles. The objects to the north remained in the sky for an hour or more. The object to the south was visible for two or three hours and beamed down a stream of light from time to time. Numerous individuals, including the undersigned, witnessed the activities in paragraphs 2 and 3.

Outside of some small variation in detail, the story in the document is amazingly similar to what Art Wallace described. This letter was certainly part of a more detailed file, since it is clear that an official investigation *was* conducted. Looking back at Col. Cochran's April 28 response to our inquiry on Rendlesham, we now see that it amounts to nothing more than a gross attempt to mislead the public and constitutes a blatant violation of the spirit and the letter of the Freedom of Information Act.

What could be equally as mysterious as the events themselves is the reason why the letter was released in the first place. We probably would not have known about its existence had it not been given to us. And it surely doesn't help to make the Air Force's official stance on UFOs credible. Could there be a segment within the Air Force that wants us to have the facts on UFOs? It's a distinct possibility.

Our investigation into this most bizarre affair continues.

We have already discussed many of the agencies involved in collecting reports of UFOs domestically and internationally. One other potential source of UFO data has not been mentioned only because it has been relatively unknown until recently through revelations by the *New York Times.*

The National Reconnaissance Office (NRO) is an intelligence agency whose very existence has been classified top secret. It has an extraordinary budget of $2 billion per year and manages to hide this primarily in Air Forces operations. It functions in such a manner that nothing about it is subject to open scrutiny.

The NRO's mission is to monitor international communications (like the NSA) and to oversee the operation of the nation's spy satellite system. Government officials have even refused to discuss the agency's name if it were brought up. How might the NRO's operations relate to UFO research?

Photo-reconnaissance satellites have advanced to such a degree that even individuals can be specifically identified from orbits one hundred miles up. If strange aerial activity were to be detected in space as has been done in the past by NORAD (see Chapter 1), a photo-reconnaissance satellite could be expected to be pressed into duty by taking high-resolution photos of the UFOs. Significant strong evidence for UFOs may currently exist in the NRO's files but accessability would be virtually impossible under present security provisions. Such security could also protect an above-top secret version of Project Saint (see Chapter 13) in photographing UFO activity.

Let us summarize in detail our conclusions on the UFO subject. (We refer to the small percentage of total reports which are currently listed as genuine unknowns:

1) UFOs are a real, material, physical phenomenon, completely unidentifiable in conventional terms.
2) UFOs display intelligence of a very high order.
3) Granting that UFOs are real and intelligent, somebody is behind the phenomenon; that is, advanced biological life forms.
4) These life forms are here for a purpose. A "clear intent" has been demonstrated numerous times.

5) Their purpose at the present time is unknown but may be related to an extended surveillance of what might be termed a primitive, embryonic society.

6) The origin of the biological life forms is unknown, but the extraterrestrial hypothesis seems to be the most attractive explanation, although not the only one.

7) UFOs have overflown U.S. military and other government facilities since World War II, as evidenced by official U.S. document releases from a variety of federal agencies.

8) This activity has extended to other nations, as evidenced by official U.S. government document releases.

9) UFO activity over some U.S. military/governmental facilities has been of such a sensational, dramatic nature that a definite threat to U.S. national security is considered as fact within the highest levels of government. (This scenario also applies to foreign governments.)

10) Documented UFO reports of national security significance have been and continue to be withheld, under tight secrecy regulations, from all but the most highly-placed government officials.

11) Despite tight secrecy regarding release of UFO documents, government officials most closely associated with UFO data of national security importance probably do not have a definite "answer" to the UFO problem, but they monitor the phenomenon in pursuit of an answer.

12) The monitoring procedure probably includes the use of unmarked helicopters as convenient vehicles of transportation to and from scenes of UFO and other related activity.

Part of why this book exists is to urge people with any knowledge of the events discussed here to contact us and fill in the missing details. Other events related to the subject matter of the book, but not mentioned, would also be of great interest.

We would like to stress that no information is being sought other than UFO data. Sensitive material about the defense of the United States, military and government personnel, and the internal functions of federal agencies is not of interest to the authors. The protection of such details is fully and understandably recognized under the Freedom of Information Act. Since the government has declared many times that UFOs are no threat to national security, we feel fully justified in asking that data about UFOs be released and put out before the public for a fair and open-minded assessment of what is one of the most intriguing topics in recorded history.

In particular, we solicit any information on the existence of long-rumored movie films on UFOs—some in general documentary format, others showing actual footage of UFOS filmed by people on the ground and by pilots in the air, equipped with aerial cameras. Additionally, a document written in the summer of 1948 by Air Force Project Sign personnel entitled "Estimate of the Situation" is sought. Although the original document was supposedly destroyed in 1948, copies were known to exist years later.

The "Estimate of the Situation" is a curiosity of UFO history. The document concluded that UFOs were interplanetary, according to those few individuals who saw it, including the former head of Project Blue Book in the early 1950s, Captain Edward Ruppelt. Ruppelt stated that at least one copy, legal-sized with a black cover stamped "Secret," survived its original destruction order. Since then, all attempts to locate the document have failed. The Air Force's responses to such inquiries have been strangely contradictory.

One letter to a UFO researcher by the Air Force's Director of Legislative Liaison, Major General W. P. Fisher, said, "There has never been an Air Force conclusion that flying saucers were real and were interplanetary space ships. The alleged 1948 document mentioned in your letter is nonexistent."

Yet, in 1967, the Air Force's Chief, Civil Branch of the Office of Information's Community Relations Division, Lt. Colonel George Freeman, said:

> Regarding the 1948 "Estimate of the Situation" the late Captain Ruppelt in his book, *The Report on Unidentified Flying Objects,* provides the answer. The Top Secret Estimation was working its way up to the higher echelons of the Air Force. It got to the late General Hoyt S. Vanderberg, then Chief of Staff, before it was "batted down." The General wouldn't "buy" interplanetary vehicles. The report lacked proof and the Estimate died a quick death. Some months later, it was completely declassified and relegated to the incinerator. I am sorry, but we have no copies of this document.

The "Estimate" obviously survived destruction by several accounts. Knowledge of its location would be of great historical importance.

We have tried to give a rational assessment of UFOs. Old questions have been answered and new ones have been raised. To be sure, UFOs have not been given a fair day in court, which is why the subject remains cloaked in rumor and ambiguity. Some scientists are aware of the challenge placed before us, but the scientific community at large must shoulder some of the blame for the way the UFO phenomenon has been treated. Scholars have descended upon UFO enthusiasts in righteous indignation, accusing them of promoting pseudoscience and misinforming the public to an almost irreversible degree. Indeed, some of the criticism is well-deserved. Serious UFO researchers were, for some time, a small minority in a subject dominated by religious fanatics, pseudointellectuals, and a variety of space explorers, whose alleged trips to "lush, green Venus" and the marvelous cities on the far side of the moon titillated millions.

Inevitably, the wheat is separated from the chaff and the true nature of a mystery manifests itself. This is what present-day UFO logists are promoting—a serious look at real events, not a 1980s version of "Earth vs. Flying Saucers" or "Invaders from Mars."

The U.S. government is convinced that UFOs are a serious matter. It is only through a concerted effort by the world's braintrust that UFOs can be dealt with effectively, almost surely leading to the revelation of new truths.

For those wishing to obtain more information about Citizens Against UFO
Secrecy (Caus), please write to:

> CAUS
> c/o Mr. Lawrence Fawcett
> 471 Goose Lane
> Coventry, Connecticut 06238

Epilogue

As if the information related in this book is not enough to prove our contention that the U.S. considers UFOs a major security problem, the authors came across a startling file while in the process of putting the book together.

On November 14, 1982, the authors met at the home of Barry Greenwood to sort out documents for several chapters. We intended to spend the afternoon deep into the project, but as it turned out, we were interrupted by phone calls informing us that a UFO documentary would be on television. The program, entitled "The UFO Experience," came on at 2:00 P.M., and since we had a video recorder available, we decided to tape it for our records.

The show was rather good, but it told us nothing new. About forty-five minutes into the documentary, a segment on the government's UFO interest was shown. It was pretty familiar, except for one document which the producers flashed on the screen. The document concerned sightings of UFOs at Kirtland Air Force Base in New Mexico during August 1980. Various security personnel were involved in the reports, and the whole matter was apparently quite baffling. The report itself was stamped "Secret."

We watched this and looked at one another, wondering why we had not heard of this report. Here we are, the Assistant Director and a Board member of CAUS, looking at a government UFO document on TV and not knowing anything about it! Since the CAUS Director, Peter Gersten, had appeared on the documentary, we assumed that he had supplied the document to the producer, Ron Lakis.

Gersten told us later in a phone conversation that Lakis had shown him the document when they met to tape the show that summer. Gersten had not seen it prior to taping and admitted that he didn't pay too much attention to it as it had looked "too good." (We had run into sensational, but unsubstantiated documents many times). He had asked Lakis for a copy later, but never received it.

Since his curiosity was aroused once again, Gersten asked Barry Greenwood to follow up on the report, hoping that if it were for real, we could get a copy. How would this be done?

Fortunately, the program was on videotape. Greenwood ran over the segment several times to pick out pertinent data from the document as it was shown on TV. The most important portion needed to trace the story was the source, which turned out to be the Headquarters, District 17 of the Air Force Office of Special Investigations, based at Kirtland. On November 23, Greenwood filed a Freedom of Information request with OSI Headquarters in Washington, D.C. (Requests filed with OSI District Offices are automatically forwarded to Washington.)

OSI's Chief of the Information Release Division, Noah D. Lawrence, responded to the request on December 9. A flat denial was expected before the envelope was opened. Instead, the cover letter bore the astonishing news, "AFOSI is maintaining file 8017D93-0/29 identifiable with your request." Aside from a few minor deletions with personal information on witnesses, the file was intact and almost unbelievable in content. What did it say?

The file is seven pages long. The first two pages consist of an official OSI Complaint Form stamped "For Official Use Only." Dated 2–9 Sept., 80, it is titled "Kirtland AFB, NM, 8 Aug–3 Sept 80, Alleged Sightings of Unidentified Aerial Lights in Restricted Test Range." It relates that:

1. On 2 Sept 80, SOURCE related on 8 Aug 80, three Security Policemen assigned to 1608 SPS, KAFB, NM, on duty inside the Manzano Weapons Storage Area sighted an unidentified light in the air that traveled from North to South over the Coyote Canyon area of the Department of Defense Restricted Test Range on KAFB, NM. The Security Policemen identified as: SSGT STEPHEN FERENZ, Area Supervisor, AIC MARTIN W. RIST and AMN ANTHONY D. FRAZIER, were later interviewed separately by SOURCE and all three related the same statement; At approximately 2350 hrs., while on duty in Charlie Sector, East Side of Manzano, the three observed a very bright light in the sky approximately 3 miles North–North East of their position. The light traveled with great speed and stopped suddenly in the sky over Coyote Canyon. The three first thought the object was a helicopter, however, after observing the strange aerial maneuvers (stop and go), they felt a helicopter couldn't have performed such skills. The light landed in the Coyote Canyon area. Sometime later, three witnessed the light take off and leave proceeding straight up at a high speed and disappear.

2. Central Security Control (CSC) inside Manzano, contacted Sandia Security, who conducts frequent building checks on two alarmed structures in

the area. They advised that a patrol was already in the area and would investigate.

3. On 11 Aug 80, RUSS CURTIS, Sandia Security, advised that on 9 Aug 80, a Sandia Security Guard, (who wishes his name not be divulged for fear of harassment), related the following: At approximately 0020 hrs., he was driving East on the Coyote Canyon access road on a routine building check of an alarmed structure. As he approached the structure he observed a bright light near the ground behind the structure. He also observed an object he first thought was a helicopter. But after driving closer, he observed a round disk shaped object. He attempted to radio for a back up patrol but his radio would not work. As he approached the object on foot armed with a shotgun, the object took off in a vertical direction at a high rate of speed. The guard was a former helicopter mechanic in the U.S. Army and stated the object he observed was not a helicopter.

4. SOURCE advised on 22 Aug 80, three other security policemen observed the same aerial phenomena described by the first three. Again the object landed in Coyote Canyon. They did not see the object take off.

5. Coyote Canyon is part of a large restricted test range used by the Air Force Weapons Laboratory, Sandia Laboratories, Defense Nuclear Agency and the Department of Energy. The range was formerly patrolled by Sandia Security, however, they only conduct building checks there now.

6. On 10 Aug 80, a New Mexico State Patrolman sighted an aerial object land in the Manzano's between Belen and Albuquerque, NM. The Patrolman reported the sighting to the Kirtland AFB Command Post, who later referred the patrolman to the AFOSI Dist 17. AFOSI Dist 17 advised the patrolman to make a report through his own agency. On 11 Aug 80, the Kirtland Public Information office advised the patrolman the USAF no longer investigates such sightings unless they occur on a USAF base.

7. WRITER contacted all the agencies who utilized the test range and it was learned no aerial tests are conducted in the Coyote Canyon area. Only ground tests are conducted.

8. On 8 Sept 80, WRITER learned from Sandia Security that another Security Guard observed an object land near an alarmed structure sometime during the first week of August, but did not report it until just recently for fear of harassment.

9. The two alarmed structures located within the area contain HQ CR 44 material.

The source of the information is listed as Major Ernest E. Edwards, Commander, 1608 SPS (Security Police Squadron), Manzano, Kirtland AFB, New Mexico, and the form is signed by OSI Special Agent Richard C. Doty.

Remarkable information indeed! At this point, the plot thickens, however. The next part of the file is a two-page section on an OSI "Multipurpose Internal OSI Form" bearing the same title as the previous document, and dated 28 Oct. 80.

. . . On 24 Oct 80, Dr PAUL FREDRICK BENNEWITZ, Male Born 30 Sep 27, KS, Civ, SSAN: . . . Albuquerque, NM, contacted SA RICHARD C. DOTY through Major ERNEST E. EDWARDS, Commander, 1608 SPS, Kirtland AFB, NM and related he had knowledge and evidence of threats against Manzano Weapons Storage area. The threat was from Aerial phenomena over Manzano.

On 26 Oct 80, SA DOTY, with the assistance of JERRY MILLER, GS-15, Chief, Scientific Advisor for Air Force Test and Evaluation Center, KAFB, interviewed Dr. BENNEWITZ at his home in the Four Hills Section of Albuquerque, which is adjacent to the northern boundary of Manzano Base. (NOTE: MILLER is a former Project Blue Book USAF Investigator who was assigned to Wright-Patterson AFB (W-PAFB), OH, with FTD. Mr. MILLER is one of the most knowledgeable and impartial investigators of Aerial Objects in the southwest). Dr. BENNEWITZ produced photographs and over 2600 feet of 8mm motion picture film depicting unidentified aerial objects flying over and around Manzano Weapons Storage Area and Coyote Canyon Test area. Dr. BENNEWITZ has been conducting independent research into Aerial Phenomena for the last 15 months. Dr. BENNEWITZ also produced several electronic recording tapes, allegedly showing high periods of electrical magnetism being emitted from Manzano/Coyote Canyon area. Dr. BENNEWITZ also produced several photograhs of flying objects taken over the general Albuquerque area. He has several pieces of electronic surveillance equipment pointed at Manzano and is attempting to record high frequency electrical beam pulses. Dr. BENNEWITZ claims these Aerial Objects produce these pulses.

3. After analyzing the data collected by Dr. BENNEWITZ, Mr MILLER related the evidence clearly shows that some type of unidentified aerial objects were caught on film; however, no conclusions could be made whether these objects pose a threat to Manzano/Coyote Canyon areas. Mr MILLER felt the electronical recording tapes were inconclusive and could have been gathered from several conventional sources. No sightings, other than these, have been reported in the area.

4. Mr MILLER has contacted FTD personnel at W-P AFB, OH, who expressed an interest and are scheduled to inspect Dr. BENNEWITZ's data.

5. Request a DCII check be made on Dr BENNEWITZ.

6. This is responsive to HQ CR 44.

7. Command was briefed but did not request an investigation at this time.

This document is signed by Major Thomas A. Cseh, Commander of the Base Investigative Detachment. Bennewitz had apparently observed other UFO activity at the Manzano site and had managed to photograph the objects from his home close to the area. [He later revealed, in an interview with the Albuquerque, New Mexico *Tribune* on April 8, 1983, that the photos were taken on February 2, 1980.] Furthermore, the Air Force admitted on official documents for the first time that:

1) Since the closure of Project Blue Book, they have continued to investigate UFO signtings at Air Force installations, and

2) A civilian was investigated by the Air Force—something not to be done, according to previous Air Force statements.

3) The Air Force still employs the services of a former Blue Book investigator (Mr. Miller) who "is one of the most knowledgeable and impartial investiga-

tors of aerial objects in the southwest." Not was, but *is!* Present tense. And the data was scheduled to be inspected by "FTD (Foreign Technology Division) personnel at Wright-Patterson AFB, Ohio," the former home of Blue Book!

What is going on here? This information turns previous Air Force policy concerning UFOS on its ear. It is utterly amazing that this data was released with such statements. Yet, here they are.

Going further, another internal OSI form dated 26 Nov. 80 relates:

1. On 10 Nov 80, a meeting took place in 1606 ABW/CC Conference Room attended by the following individuals: BGen WILLIAM BROOKSHER, AFOSP/CC, COL JACK W. SHEPPARD, 1606 ABW/CC, COL THOMAS SIMMONS, 1606 ABW/CV, COL CRES BACA, 1606 SPGp/CC, COL FRANK M. HUEY, AFOSI Dist 17/CC, LTC JOE R. LAMPORT, 1606 ABW/SJ, MAJ THOMAS A. CSEH, AFOSI Det 1700/CC, Dr. LEHMAN, Director, AFWL, ED BREEN, AFWL Instrumentations Specialist and Dr. PAUL F. BENNEWITZ, President Thunder Scientific Laboratory, Albuquerque. Dr. BENNEWITZ presented film and photographs of alleged unidentified Aerial Objects photographed over KAFB, NM during the last 15 months. Dr. BENNEWITZ also related he had documented proof that he was in contact with the aliens flying the objects. At the conclusion of the presentation, Dr. BENNEWITZ expressed an interest in obtaining financial assistance from the USAF in furthering his investigation regarding these objects. DR. LEHMAN advised DR. BENNEWITZ to request a USAF grant for research. DR. LEHMAN advised DR. BENNEWITZ he would assist him in filling out the proper documents.

2. On 17 Nov 80, SA RICHARD C. DOTY, advised DR. BENNEWITZ that AFOSI would not become involved in the investigation of these objects. DR. BENNEWITZ was advised that AFOSI was not in a position to evaluate the information and photographs he has collected to date or technically investigate such matters.

3. On 26 Nov 80, SA DOTY received a phone call from an individual who identified himself as U.S. Senator HARRISON SCHMIDT, of New Mexico. SEN SCHMIDT inquired about AFOSI'S role in investigating the aerial phenomena reported by Dr. BENNEWITZ. SA DOTY advised SEN SCHMIDT that AFOSI was not investigating the phenomena. SA DOTY then politely referred SEN SCHMIDT to AFOSI Dist 17/CC. SEN SCHMIDT declined to speak with 17/CC and informed SA DOTY he would request that SAF look into the matter and determine what USAF agency should investigate the phenomena.

4. It should be noted that DR. BENNEWITZ has ALLEGEDLY had a number of conversations with SEN SCHMIDT during the last few months regarding BENNEWITZ'S private research. SEN SCHMIDT has made telephone calls to BGEN BROOKSHER, AFOSP/CC, regarding the matter since Security Police are responsible for the security of Manzano Storage Area.

Bennewitz had now been invited *onto the air base* to present his evidence, another first for an Air Force document to admit. Note the reference to Bennewitz being in "contact with the aliens flying the objects." One's first impression might be to dismiss this person immediately as a nut. It certainly is a wild claim. What did the Air Force do? The Director of the Air Force Weapons Lab advised Bennewitz to obtain an *Air Force grant* for further research!

OSI then suddenly did an about-face, and told Bennewitz that they would not get involved in further investigation. Why? We might speculate that OSI felt that if it became too deeply involved in this case, especially where a civilian was concerned, that such information would get into the open more easily. It worked for a while, but the dam finally broke.

The last document in the file is dated July 30, 1981, and involved a Congressional inquiry.

> On 30 Jul 81, the 1606th ABW IG contacted DO 17/BID and advised that Senator PETER DOMENICI desired to talk to SA RICK DOTY regarding the matter involving BENNEWITZ. After checking with Col HARVELL, Acting AFOSI/CC, it was agreed SA DOTY and DO 17/CC would meet with Senator DOMENICI. Senator DOMENICI was present in the IG's Office but departed immediately to meet with BENNEWITZ. A subsequent check with Mr. TIJE-ROS, Senator DOMENICI's Aide, in an effort to determine the Senator's specific questions, determined his sole interest was to know whether AFOSI had conducted a formal investigation of SUBJECT. Mr. TIJEROS was informed that no formal investigation of BENNEWITZ was conducted by AFOSI. Mr. TIJEROS stated that he assumed if any information were available, and was to be requested from AFOSI, it would have to be requested from our Headquarters. He was provided Col BEYEA's name and the Bolling AFB address of our HQ AFOSI in event he desired any further information. Mr. TIJEROS thanked us and indicated no further inquiries from the Senator regarding this matter are anticipated.

Thus, we now have a clearer picture of what happened at Kirtland AFB in 1980. Normally, with an FOIA request, specific queries are replied to by addressing the original request *very literally;* you get *exactly* what you ask for. In this case, the request for the Kirtland data focused on just the sightings between July 1 and September 10, 1980. The first document responded to this. But additional documents were provided with startling statements, falling well outside the time period requested. One document was dated nearly a year later! Strangely enough, if OSI hadn't volunteered the other documents, we wouldn't have known any better; the story about Bennewitz's involvement would still be safely locked away.

Bennewitz's claim to contact with UFO entities must be taken with a grain of salt (or maybe several grains!) without more than just a few of his brief comments. What is most significant at present is the Air Force's *reaction* to him. Have they experienced similar situations before? We think this is a distinct possibility since other accounts of such events have been related to us in confidence.

The Kirtland reaction was hardly one of disbelief and skepticism. They seemed to have wanted to encourage further developments *with funding,* perhaps to obtain clear photographs or better instrument readings. The list of personnel attending the November 10, 1980, meeting at Kirtland is impressive, and certainly implies that the UFO phenomenon must be serious if these individuals take time out of their schedules to participate.

"Significant" is hardly adequate to describe these events, but if this is what the public is being allowed to see, what else is being suppressed? To paraphrase Roy Neary in Steven Spielberg's *Close Encounters of the Third Kind,* "We just want to know what's going on."

APPENDIX A

Sample UFO Documents
from Government Files

Figure 1. Four pages from CIA files regarding a private UFO group, the National Investigations Committee on Aerial Phenomena (NICAP). The CIA shows an inordinate amount of interest in this group, considering that the CIA's function is *foreign* intelligence. NICAP's influence began to ebb shortly after the writing of the second two-page undated memo from the early 1970s.

UNITED STATES ░░VER░░ ░NT

Memorandum

-72-65

TO : Chief, Contact Division
Attn: ░░░░░░░░░░░░░░░░░░░░░░

DATE: 25 January 1965

FROM : Chief, ░░░░░░░░░░░░░░░

SUBJECT: National Investigation Committee on Aerial Phenomena (NICAP)
Case ░░░░░░

    1.   This confirms ░░░░░░░░░░░░░ conversation 19 January 1965, at which time various samples and reports on UFO sightings procured from NICAP were given to ░░░░░░░░ for transmittal to OSI. The information was desired by CSI to assist them in the preparation of a paper for ░░░░░░░░░░░░░░░ on UFO's.

    2.   In accordance with ░░░░░░░░░ request, we met on 19 January 1965 with Mr. Richard Harris Hall, Acting Director of NICAP. Though Major William Kehoe, founder of NICAP, is still listed as Director of the organization, we gather that he is present on the premises at 1536 Connecticut Avenue, N. W., only infrequently.

    3.   The material which was given to us on loan by Mr. Hall is representative of the type of information available at NICAP. Their past and present correspondence from all over the US relative to UFO sightings is voluminous. They have slack periods, as was the case in December 1964, thus there were no "Investigator's" reports immediately available for the month of December. NICAP has active Committees scattered throughout the US. Investigators active with these committees call upon the sources of reported UFO sightings to obtain first hand, eye witness accounts of the sightings. A printed form, prepared by the Air Force for NICAP's use, is utilized during the interview, and submitted to NICAP headquarters along with the source's eye witness account as told to the investigator. It was our understanding that copies of these reports go directly to various Air Force bases. There apparently is a strong feeling on the part of NICAP officials, i.e., Kehoe and Hall, that the Air Force tends to downgrade the importance of UFO sightings because they(the Air Force) does not care to have too much made of the sightings by the US press. We were told by Mr. Hall that there have been instances where the Air Force has attempted to intimidate witnesses and get them to sign false statements relative to UFO sightings.

APPROVED FOR RELEASE
DATE ...16. Nov. 7.

/1)

÷ ⅁- (#,

4. The most recent UFO sighting of considerable interest
to NICAP was the series of pick-ups of UFO's on the radar screen
of the Patuxent Naval Air Station between 1500 and 1530 on 19
December 1964. This incident was reported in the press as a
single sighting, a UFO approaching Patuxent at speeds up to 3800
miles per hour. The Air Force a day or so later stated in the
press that the blip was caused by faulty radar equipment.
Actually, according to Hall, who talked with an unidentified
person close to the situation, there were three separate sightings:

> (a) Two UFO's about 10 miles apart, southeast of Patuxent,
> approaching at a high rate of speed, disappeared from the
> screen;
> (b) A single UFO picked up 39 miles southeast of Patuxent,
> altitude estimated somewhere between three thousand and 25
> thousand feet, approaching base at estimated speed of six
> thousand miles per hour. UFO lost from screen about 10 miles
> out;
> (c) A single UFO eight miles northeast of Patuxent, approach-
> ing at high rate of speed, made 160° turn, and dropped off
> the screen.

The Federal Aviation Agency (FAA) station at Salisbury, Maryland,
was contacted to determine if any reported UFO's; a radio operator
had received a message from a US Coast Guard ship reporting "visual
objects sighted" in same locale at approximately the same time
of day. Hall did give us the name of one of the radar operators
at Patuxent--a Chief Pinkerton.

5. There was another UFO sighting reported in the area by
the Washington Post within the last week or 10 days. Several
men watching from the windows of the old Munitions Building on
Constitution Avenue watched several UFO's on the horizon traveling
at high rates of speed. They have promised to fill out NICAP's
sighting questionnaire, which Hall says we are welcome to see when
available.

6. ▮▮▮▮▮▮▮▮ informed us that she is requesting a security
clearance on Mr. Hall predicated upon biographic information provided by ▮▮▮▮▮▮▮▮▮▮▮▮

National Investigations Committee on Aerial Phenomena (NICAP)

Appears to be a fairly loose structure but rather efficient. Stuart Nixon (background in investigative journalism) is currently Executive Director. He along with John Acuff and Charles Miller (backgrounds unknown) make up the organizations Editorial Review Board which is responsible for policy, including the newsletter, press and other media relations as well as special reports and programs.

This board relies heavily on both a loosely structured advisory group and a fairly well developed and well placed network of investigators. The advisory group is made up of experts in many disciplines including physics, astronomy, anthropology, medicine and psychology. This group also includes some ex-CIA and Defense Intelligence types who advise on investigative techniques and NICAP / Government relations. There does not seem to be any logical or systematic program by which these advisors are chosen, but rather the procedure seems to be to simply offer one's services to the organization through either Nixon or the Review Board. Often the advisors simply joined NICAP(a rather easy task since all it takes is a specified membership fee) found something out about the organization and then made their qualifications known to the Review Board.

The system of investigators is a good one. Nixon has divided the country into regions and has established "investigators" in each of the regions. Any member of NICAP is encouraged to request a form by which one can apply for this position. The requirements for the position include a minimum age of 25, formal training or experience in some branch of science, or other specialized background applicable to systematic collection of information, the ability to cover an area of at least 50 miles in diameter or one hour of driving time. As of a few months ago some 35 investigators were located throughout the country, with NICAP in the process of establishing even more. A breakdown of their backgrounds looked like the following: 7 PhDs, 2 MAs or MS, 23 BAs or BS, 1 AA and 2 with college training but no degrees. Occupationally they included 4 physical scientists, 13 engineers, 3 college profs, 13 specialists, including doctor, technician, computer programmer and businessman. Five of the 35 are pilots. Also utilized as " legmen" for the investigators are investigator assistants. All investigators carry credentials identifying them as investigators for NICAP.

NICAP currently operates on a $40,000 yr. budget
and has 3,500 dues paying members. Both the membership
and the budget may be expected to increase ~~substantix~~
substatially due to the recent UFO flap.

A computer project codenamed "Project Acess" is currently
in the mill. An effort is being made to develop some
sort of pattern analysis out of the 15, 000 or more raw
reports reportedly in NICAP's files. This apparently
will take the following form:

       1.   event- including time, place, terrain, weather,
                  speed, color, ~~ix~~ shape and other
                  information

       2.   principals-including data on all witnesses
                      and others involved in reports
                      such as bio data, medical
                      info and psychological aspects

       3.   investigation- including evaluation of
                      reports and special
                      notes from the regional
                      investigator on witness
                      discrepancy in testiony etc...

The following is apparently the ~~xs~~ organizational structure and
relationships within NICAP:

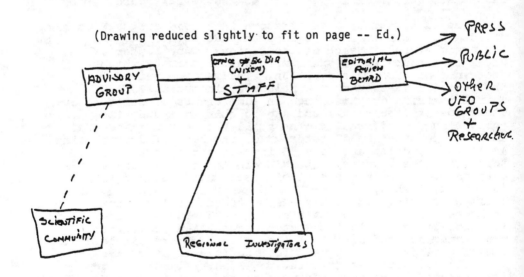

(Drawing reduced slightly to fit on page -- Ed.)

Figure 2. Two pages from the National Security Agency's twenty-one page Top Secret affidavit.

~~TOP SECRET~~ ██████████

UNITED STATES DISTRICT COURT
FOR THE DISTRICT OF COLUMBIA

CITIZENS AGAINST UNIDENTIFIED)
FLYING OBJECTS SECRECY,)
)
Plaintiff,)
v.)
)
NATIONAL SECURITY AGENCY,)
)
Defendant.)
_____)

Civil Action No.
80-1562

IN CAMERA
AFFIDAVIT OF EUGENE F. YEATES

County of Anne Aruñdel)
) ss:
State of Maryland)

Eugene F. Yeates, being duly sworn, deposes and says:

1. (U) I am the Chief, Office of Policy, of the National Security Agency (NSA). As Chief, Office of Policy, I am responsible for processing all initial requests made pursuant to the Freedom of Information Act (FOIA) for NSA records. The statements herein are based upon personal knowledge, upon my personal review of information available to me in my official capacity, and upon conclusions reached in accordance therewith.

2. (U) This affidavit supplements my unclassified affidavit executed on September 30, 1980 regarding all documents which have been located by NSA pursuant to plaintiff's FOIA request but which have been withheld wholly or in part by NSA. I submit this affidavit in camera for the purpose of stating facts, which cannot be publicly disclosed, that are the basis for exempting the records from release to the plaintiff.

3. (S-██ At the beginning of each paragraph of this affidavit, the letter or letters within parentheses designate(s) the degree of sensitivity of information the paragraph contains.

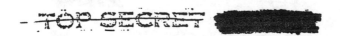

~~TOP SECRET~~ ██████████

c. ████████████████████
██
███████████████████████████████████████
████████████████████████████████████ —7
██████████████████████████████████████
██
███████████████████████████████████████
██████████████████████████████████████
██████████████████████████████████████
██████████████████████████████████████
██████████████████████████████████████
██████████████████████████████████████
██████████████████████████████████████
██████████████████████████████████████
██████████████████████████████████████
██████████████████████████████████████
██████████████████████████████████████
██████████████████████████████████████
██████████████████████████████████████
██████████████████████████████████████
██████████████████████████████████████
██████████████████████████████████████
███████████████████████████████████
███████████████

d. █████████████████████████████████
██████████████████████████████████████
██████████████████████████████████████
██████████████████████████████████
███████████████████████

11

Figure 3. One page. A March 1, 1967, memo from the Air Force Assistant Vice Chief of Staff alluding to reports of mysterious individuals intruding upon the privacy of UFO witnesses. These individuals have become more commonly known as the "men in black" over the years, due to their manner of dress and their peculiar behavior.

DEPARTMENT OF THE AIR FORCE
OFFICE OF THE CHIEF OF STAFF
UNITED STATES AIR FORCE
WASHINGTON, D.C. 20330

REPLY TO
ATTN OF: AFCCS

1 March 1967

SUBJECT: Impersonations of Air Force Officers

TO:

ADC	AFSC	HQCOMD USAF	SAC
AFCS	ATC	CAC	TAC
AFLC	AU	MAC	USAFSS

Information, not verifiable, has reached Hq USAF that persons claiming to represent the Air Force or other Defense establishments have contacted citizens who have sighted unidentified flying objects. In one reported case an individual in civilian clothes, who represented himself as a member of NORAD, demanded and received photos belonging to a private citizen. In another, a person in an Air Force uniform approached local police and other citizens who had sighted a UFO, assembled them in a school room and told them that they did not see what they thought they saw and that they should not talk to anyone about the sighting. All military and civilian personnel and particularly Information Officers and UFO Investigating Officers who hear of such reports should immediately notify their local OSI offices.

HEWITT T. WHELESS, Lt General, USAF
Assistant Vice Chief of Staff

Figure 4. A February 26, 1942, memo sent to President Roosevelt by General George C. Marshall regarding an incident known as the "Battle of Los Angeles." An extensive investigation failed to identify the aerial craft involved in the overflight and the event still ranks as the earliest instance of a government-investigated UFO sighting.

OCS
GCM

SEC____

OCS 21347-86

February 26, 1942.

MEMORANDUM FOR THE PRESIDENT:

The following is the information we have from GHQ at this moment regarding the air alarm over Los Angeles of yesterday morning:

"From details available at this hour:

*1. Unidentified airplanes, other than American Army or Navy planes, were probably over Los Angeles, and were fired on by elements of the 37th CA Brigade (AA) between 3:12 and 4:15 AM. These units expended 1430 rounds of ammunition.

*2. As many as fifteen airplanes may have been involved, flying at various speeds from what is officially reported as being 'very slow' to as much as 200 MPH and at elevations from 9000 to 18000 feet.

*3. No bombs were dropped.

*4. No casualties among our troops.

*5. No planes were shot down.

*6. No American Army or Navy planes were in action.

"Investigation continuing. It seems reasonable to conclude that if unidentified airplanes were involved they may have been from commercial sources, operated by enemy agents for purposes of spreading alarm, disclosing location of antiaircraft positions, and slowing production through blackout. Such conclusion is supported by varying speed of operation and the fact that no bombs were dropped."

DECLASSIFIED
E.O. 11652, Sec. 3(E) and 5(D) or (E)
OSD letter, May 3, 1972
By ____ NARS Date ___ 4-9-74

(Sgd) G. C. MARSHALL

Chief of Staff.

21347
86

mkn

Orig. dispatched to Pres.

Figure 5. One page. An Army helicopter/UFO encounter.

DISPOSITION FORM

For use of this form, see AR 340-15; the proponent agency is The Adjutant General's Office.

ERENCE OR OFFICE SYMBOL	SUBJECT
	Near Midair Collision with UFO Report

Commander
83D USARCOM
ATTN: AHRCCG
Columbus Support Facility
Columbus, Ohio 43215

FROM Flight Operations Off   DATE 23 Nov 73   CMT 1
USAR Flight Facility
Cleveland Hopkins Airport
Cleveland, Ohio 44135

1. On 18 October 1973 at 2305 hours in the vicinity of Mansfield, Ohio, Army Helicopter 68-15444 assigned to Cleveland USARFFAC encountered a near midair collision with a unidentified flying object. Four crewmembers assigned to the Cleveland USARFFAC for flying proficiency were on AFTP status when this incident occurred. The flight crew assigned was CPT Lawrence J. Coyne, Pilot in Command, 1LT Arrigo Jezzi, Copilot, SSG Robert Yanacsek, Crew Chief, SSG John Healey, Flight Medic. All the above personnel are members of the 316th MED DET(HEL AMB), a tenant reserve unit of the Cleveland USARFFAC.

2. The reported incident happened as follows: my Helicopter 68-15444 was returning from Columbus, Ohio to Cleveland, Ohio and at 2305 hours east, south east of Mansfield Airport in the vicinity of Mansfield, Ohio while flying at an altitude of 2500 feet and on a heading of 030 degrees, SSG Yanacsek observed a red light on the east horizon, 90 degrees to the flight path of the helicopter. Approximately 30 seconds later, SSG Yanacsek indicated the object was converging on the helicopter at the same altitude at a airspeed in excess of 600 knots and on a midair collision heading. Cpt Coyne observed the converging object, took over the controls of the aircraft and initiated a power descent from 2500 feet to 1700 feet to avoid impact with the object. A radio call was initiated to Mansfield Tower who acknowledged the helicopter and was asked by CPT Coyne if there were any high performance aircraft flying in the vicinity of Mansfield Airport however there was no response received from the tower. The crew expected impact from the object instead, the object was observed to hesitate momentarily over the helicopter and then slowly continued on a westerly course accelerating at a high rate of speed, clear west of Mansfield Airport then turn 45 degree heading to the Northwest. Cpt Coyne indicated the altimeter read a 1000 fpm climb and read 3500 feet with the collective in the full down position. The aircraft was returned to 2500 feet by Cpt Coyne and flown back to Cleveland, Ohio. The Flight plan was closed and the FAA Flight Service Station notified of the incident. The FSS told CPT Coyne to report the incident to the FAA GADO office a Cleveland Hopkins Airport MR. Porter, 83d USARCOM was notified of the incident at 1530 hours on 19 Oct 73.

3. This report has been read and attested to by the crewmembers of the aircraft with signatures acknowledging this report.

FORM
1 FEB 62 2496 -   REPLACES DD FORM 96, EXISTING SUPPLIES OF WHICH WILL BE
ISSUED AND USED UNTIL 1 FEB 63 UNLESS SOONER EXHAUSTED.   ☆U. S. GPO: 1972 – 473-663 P.O. 1

239

Figure 6. Two pages. Sighting on September 8, 1973 at Hunter Army Airfield, Georgia, filed as a "Serious Incident Report" (SIR).

DATE – TIME | MONTH | YR

DESK NO — MESSAGE HANDLING INSTRUCTIONS

FROM:

(1) Involvement: Witness

TO:

(2) Name: MURRAY, Alexander S., JR. .

(3) Grade: E-5

(4) SSN: 370-58-0744

(5) Race/Natinnality/Ethnic Gp: Çau

(6) Position:- Military Police Desk Sergeant

(7) Security Clearance: c. None

(8) Unit/Station of Assignment: 2nd PLT, 298th MP Company, Hunter Army Airfield, Ga.

(9) Duty Status: On duty

8. Publicity: Widespread publicity, including national news agencies has occurred.

9. Summary of Incident: At approximately 0220 hrs, 8 Sep 73, an unidentified flying object was sighted by two military policemen, SP4 BURNS and SP4 SHADE at Hunter Army Airfield while in the course of a routine patrol of the installation perimeter. When in the vicinity of Cobra Hall they noticed an "object" traveling at what appeared to them to be a high rate of speed traveling east to west at approximately 2000 feet altitude and crossing the post perimeter. Approximately ten (10) minutes later they resighted the "object" when it appeared at "treetop" level and made an apparent dive at their vehicle seemingly just missing the vehicle. There was no damage to the vehicle.

DRAFTER TYPED NAME, TITLE, OFFICE SYMBOL, PHONE & DATE | SPECIAL INSTRUCTIONS

TYPED NAME, TITLE, OFFICE SYMBOL AND PHONE

SIGNATURE | SECURITY CLASSIFICATION

The "object" again reappeared at another location and came to
a hover for approximately fifteen (15) minutes in front of them.
The unidentified object appeared to have brilliantly flashing
lights, blue, white, and amber in color. They then returned to
the main post area and were "followed" by the unidentified object
50 to 100 feet away at tree top level until it finally veered off
and visual contact was lost. The "object" made no noise. The
alleged UFO was described as round or oval in shape and between
35 and 75 feet across. SGT Murray and SP4 Burns reported that
at approximately 0430 hrs, 9 Sep 73, while sitting in their
vehicle at the end of the airfield at Hunter Army Airfield,
Ga., they observed what they first believed to be the red
light of an aircraft some distance away. The light then moved
rapidly and disappeared into the woods.

10. Remarks: The above information is based upon information
furnished by the above witnesses.

11. XCommander reporting to HQDA: Frank L. Dietrich, Colonel,
Infantry, Commanding, HQS, Ft Stewart, Ft Stewart, Ga.

12. Prot. mark. excl. from auto. term. (Para 13, AR 340-16).

The following information was provided in response to query concerning alledged sightings of UFO's by 3800 ABG security police personnel.

Each statement was prefaced with a statement "the Air Force no longer investigates UFO sightings."

"At 2340 a security policeman radioed his office that he had seen what he believed to be a UFO in the eastern sky. He related seeing bright pulsating white light with intermittent red and blue lights in the east-northeast sky. He related the object appeared to be moving west and moving up and down. After two to three minutes, the lights disappeared.

A second security policeman also radioed he saw the same object.

At 0110 security policeman radioed and related seeing another object which resembled the object in the first entry northwest of Maxwell. Furthe stated the object disappeared at 0115.

A security policeman also radioed he saw the same object at 0114. The object was west of the base.

Four security policeman took up positions at different locations and tracked the object which was heading west from the base.

Contact was made with RAPCOM who related having a target in the west and it seemed to land near Prattville.

The object disappeared from sight at 0147.

This information was provided by Lt. Boyd to:

WLWI
WBAM
AlaNet
WABT
WHHY
WDJC - BIRMINGHAM - JOHN SIDES

Figure 8.   One page. Conflicting statements by the Rand Corporation, a U.S. government "think tank," concerning a 1968 Rand UFO document *UFOs: What to Do.*

1-20-75

Ref: Req. dtd. 1-10-75

"UFO's: What to Do" is an internal RAND document and not

available for external distribution. we are unable to

identify any available RAND publications on the subject.

RECEIVED JAN 2 5 1975

The Reports Department

8-8-69

Ref: Letter Dtd 8-1-69

RAND has done very little research on the subject of UFO's: therefore,
no publications have been written on the subject.

Figure 9. A December 6, 1980, US Army cable, obtained from the CIA, detailing sightings of UFOs over Czechoslovakia. Coincidentally, this report occurred during the same month as the Dayton, Texas, and Rendlesham Forest, England incidents. (See Chapters 7 and 14.)

```
--------------------------------------------------------------------
80 5498352                                                NC 5498352
                        TOR: 060901Z DEC 80
--------------------------------------------------------------------
PP RUEA:IA
DE RUEKJCS #9390 3410859
ZNY CCC:C
P 060852Z DEC 80
FM OJCS4C WASHINGTON DC
INFO RUEAMCC/CMC CC WASHINGTON DC
RUEAHQA/CSAF WASHINGTON DC
RUENAAA/CNO WASHINGTON DC
RUEADWD/CSA WASHINGTON DC
RUEAIIA/CIA WASHINGTON DC
RUEHC/SECSTATE WASHINGTON DC
RUETIAH/NSA WASH DC
P 051335Z DEC 80
FM CDR511THMIBN NUERNBERG G E //IARPE-N-BFO//
TO AIG 7104
DIA WASH DC
BT
E21:
C O N F I D E N T I A L
E22:
SUBJ: I1 2 212 2570 80 (U)
THIS IS AN INFO REPORT, NOT FINALLY EVALUATED INTEL.
1.  (U) CTRY: CZECHOSLOVAKIA (CZ)
2.  (U) TITLE: BORDER AREA SIGHTINGS, ACTIVITIES (U)
3.  (U) DATE OF INFO: 801127
4.  (U) ORIG: 511TH MIB 66TH MIGIS(P) IAGPE-OI-M  APO NY 09108
5.  (U) REQ REFS: U-GEC-G9044
6.  (U) SOURCE: SCI 22121748/ORIGINAL SOURCES WERE LEGAL TRAVELLERS
7.  (C) SUMMARY: THIS REPORT DETAILS CZECH BORDER AREA OBSERVA-
TIONS, TO INCLUDE AN UNIDENTIFIED FLYING OBJECT (UFO) SIGHTING,

8A. (C) DETAILS:
    (T)(C) UNIDENTIFIED FLYING OBJECTS:  BETWEEN 1715A AND 1745A,
NUMEROUS RED SIGNAL FLARES WERE FIRED NEAR VOLARY IN THE AREA OF
VQ2018.  THE LONG BURNING RED SIGNAL FLARES WERE FIRED FROM 30 SEC-
ONDS TO ONE MINUTE INTERVALS. AT 1745A, A LUMINOUS UFO FLEW FROM
THE AREA OF VIMPERK (VQ1034) IN A WESTERLY DIRECTION, THEN TRAVELLE
A REAR BORDER AREA LOOP AND CONTINUED FLIGHT IN AN EASTERLY DIRECT-
ION. FLIGHT ALTITUDE ESTIMATED AT 500 TO 1000 METERS, DISTANCE FRO
ACTUAL BORDER WAS EIGHT TO TEN KILOMTERS , AND APPROACH FIGURED AT

A 40 TO 50-DEGREE ANGLE. AROUND 2010A, IN THE AIR CORRIDOR OVER
VOLARY (VQ1818), TWO SIMILAR LUMINOUS UFO WERE SIGHTED. THESE TWO
UFO CAME FROM AN ESTERLY DIRECTION, TRAVELLING AT APPROX ONE MINUT
INTERVAL, KEPT A CONSTANT ALTITUDE OF 800 TO 1000 METERS, AND
CONTINUED FLIGHT IN A NORTHERLY DIRECTION.  THE UFO WERE ONLY VISI
BLE FOR A COUPLE OF SECONDS AND NO FLIGHT SOUNDS WERE AUDIBLY.
WHETHER THE UFO AND SIGNAL FLARE ACTIVITIES ARE RELTATED IS UNKNOW
```

APPENDIX B
NORAD UFO
Sighting Report Forms

Contrary to what the public has been told about UFOs by the Air Force, sightings by civilians and military personnel are investigated. Here is the evidence in 6 pages from the North American Aerospace Defense Command.

I. WHEN NOTIFIED OF A POSSIBLE UFO:

   A. OBTAIN THE FOLLOWING:

      (1) CALLER'S IDENTITY _____

                        NAME   ADDRESS   PHONE NUMBER

      (2) CALLER'S LOCATION: _____

                       WHERE CALLING FROM

      (3) OBJECT LOCATION: _____

                     WHERE OBJECT SIGHTED

      (4) OBJECT DESCRIPTION: _____

                     SHAPE, SIZE, LOCATION

      (5) OBJECT CHARACTERISTICS: _____

                     MOVEMENT, NOISE, LIGHTS, HEIGHT

      (6) WEATHER AT TIME OF OBSERVATION: _____

                     CLEAR, CLOUDY, RAINY, DUSTY

      (7) TIME AND DURATION OF OBSERVATION: _____

                     TIME/HOW LONG UNDER OBSERVATION

   B. HAVE ASO/RICMO ATTEMPT TO LOCATE USING HF/SEARCH RADARS. (IF OBJECT WITHIN 26NR).

   C. NOTIFY NORAD,   ; STANDBY FOR CONFERENCE; WHEN NORAD IS READY, RELAY INFORMATION.

   D. NOTIFY IO,   . DUTY HOURS OR   * AFTER DUTY HOURS.

      * DO NOT RELEASE HOME PHONE NUMBER.

   E. NOTIFY   \ OR   THROUGH THE WILLIAMS AFB OPERATOR). (NORMAL DUTY HOURS ONLY)

   F. LOG INFORMATION IN SD LOG.

   G. REPORT LOG ENTRY ON SD SHIFT REPORT.

UNKNOWN TRACK REPORT *(All times are Zulu)*			REGION			TRACK NUMBER

I. IMMEDIATE

1. TIME UNKNOWN	2. COURSE	3. SPEED	4. ALTITUDE

5. NO. OF OBJECTS	6. REASON UNKNOWN

7. POSSIBLE IDENTIFICATION

8. GEOREF AND LATITUDE/LONGITUDE AT TIME UNKNOWN

9. WPNs COMMITTED *(Number and type)*	10. SCRAMBLE BASE	11. SCRAMBLE TIME

12. RECEIVED		13. PASSED		
TIME	INITIALS	TO	TIME	INITIALS

II. IDENTIFICATION

14. TIME		
IDENTIFIED/RECLASSIFIED	FADED	

15. TYPE AIRCRAFT	16. TRACK IDENTIFICATION

17. HOW IDENTIFIED/RECLASSIFIED

18. RECEIVED		19. PASSED		
TIME	INITIALS	TO	TIME	INITIALS

III. FINAL ACTION

20. INTCP ABN TIME	21. COURSE	22. SPEED	23. ALTITUDE

24. MISSION RESULTS	25. MODE 4 INTERROGATED *(US Military only)* ☐ YES ☐ NO *(Explain in remarks)*

26. REASON FOR MISSED INTERCEPT

27. GEOREF AND LATITUDE/LONGITUDE AT TIME IDENTIFIED

28. GEOREF AND LATITUDE/LONGITUDE AT TIME FADED

29. FLIGHT PLAN *(Include departure and destination)*

30. VIOLATION RECOMMENDED *(Explain in remarks)*   ☐ YES   ☐ NO

31. RECEIVED		32. PASSED		
TIME	INITIALS	TO	TIME	INITIALS

IV AIRCRAFT OF FOREIGN REGISTRY

33. COUNTRY	34. INTERCEPT TIME

35. SERIAL NUMBER/MARKINGS	36. INTERCEPT RANGE/AZIMUTH

37. RECEIVED		38. PASSED		
TIME	INITIALS	TO	TIME	INITIALS

REMARKS *(Continue on reverse)*

h. WEATHER AND WINDS ALOFT CONDITIONS AT THE TIME AND PLACE OF SIGHTING

    (1) OBSERVERS ACCOUNT OF WEATHER CONDITIONS_____

_____

    (2) REPORT FROM NEAREST AIR WEATHER SERVICE OR U.S. WEATHER BUREAU OFFICE OF WIND DIRECTION AND VELOCITY IN DEGREES AND KNOTS AT: (IF AVAILABLE

    SURFACE_____

    6,000'_____

    10,000'_____

    16,000'_____

    20,000'_____

    30,000'_____

    50,000'_____

    80,000'_____

    (3) CEILING_____

    (4) VISIBILITY_____

    (5) AMOUNT OF CLOUD COVER_____

    (6) THUNDERSTORMS IN AREA AND QUADRANT IN WHICH LOCATED_____

    (7) TEMPERATURE GRADIENT_____

i. ANY OTHER UNUSUAL ACTIVITY OR CONDITION, METEOROGICAL, ASTRONOMICAL, OR OTHERWISE, WHICH MIGHT ACCOUNT FOR THE SIGHTING_____

j. INTERCEPTION OR IDENTIFICATION ACTION TAKEN (SUCH ACTION MAY BE TAKEN WHENEVER FEASIBLE, COMPLYING WITH EXISTING AIR DEFENSE DIRECTIVES)_____

k. LOCATION APPROXIMATE ALTITUDE, AND GENERAL DIRECTION OF FLIGHT OF ANY AIR TRAFFIC OR BALLOON RELEASES IN THE AREA WHICH COULD POSSIBLY ACCOUNT FOR THE SIGHTING

_____

_____

1. POSITION TITLE AND COMMENTS OF THE PREPARING OFFICER, INCLUDING

HIS PRELIMINARY ANALYSIS OF THE POSSIBLE CAUSE OF THE SIGHTING _____

_____

m. EXISTENCE OF PHYSICAL EVIDENCE, SUCH AS MATERIALS AND PHOTOGRAPHS

_____

_____

(3) ANGLE OR ELEVATION AND AZIMUTH OF OBJECT UPON DISAPPEARANCE _____

(4) DESCRIPTION OF FLIGHT PATH AND MANEUVERS OF OBJECT _____

(5) HOW DID THE OBJECT DISAPPEAR (INSTANTANEOUSLY TO THE NORTH, ETC.) _____

(6) HOW LONG WAS THE OBJECT VISIBLE (BE SPECIFIC: 5 MINUTE, 1 HOUR, ETC.)

e. MANNER OF OBSERVATION:

(1) USE ONE OF ANY COMBINATION OF THE FOLLOWING ITEMS: GROUND-VISUAL, GROUND-ELECTRONIC, AIR-ELECTRONIC. (IF ELECTRONIC, SPECIFY TYPE OF RADAR)

(2) STATEMENT AS TO OPTICAL AIDS (TELESCOPE, BINOCULARS, ETC) USED AND DESCRIPTION THEREOF_____

(3) IF THE SIGHTING IS MADE WHILE AIRBORNE, GIVE TYPE OF AIRCRAFT, IDENTIFICATION NUMBER, ALTITUDE, HEADING, SPEED AND HOME STATION_____

f. TIME AND DATE OF SIGHTING:

(1) ZULU DATE/TIME GROUP OF SIGHTING_____

(2) LIGHT CONDITIONS (USE ONE OF THE FOLLOWING TERMS: NIGHT, DAY, DAWN, DUSK

g. LOCATION OF OBSERVER: EXACT LATITUDE AND LONGITUDE, AND/OR GEOGRAPHICAL POSITION_____

THE FOLLOWING WILL APPLY WHEN REPORTING UNIDENTIFIABLE OBJECTS.

   a. CIRVIS REPORT

   b. IDENTIFICATION OF REPORTING AIRCRAFT OR OBSERVER _____

   c. OBJECT SIGHTED. BRIEF DESCRIPTION CONTAINING THE FOLLOWING ITEMS.

     (1) SHAPE _____

     (2) SIZE COMPARED TO A KNOWN OBJECT (USE ONE OF THE FOLLOWING TERMS: HEAD OF A PIN, PEA, DIME, NICKEL, QUARTER, HALF DOLLAR, SILVER DOLLAR, BASEBALL, GRAPEFRUIT OR BASKETBALL) HELD IN THE HAND AT ABOUT ARM'S LENGTH _____

_____

     (3) COLOR _____

     (4) NUMBER _____

     (5) FORMATION, IF MORE THAN ONE _____

     (6) ANY DISCERNIBLE FEATURES OR DETAILS _____

     (7) TRAIN OR EXHAUST INCLUDING SIZE OF SAME COMPARED TO SIZE OF OBJECT

_____

_____

     (8) SOUND. IF HEARD, DESCRIBE SOUND _____

_____

     (9) OTHER PERTINENT OR UNUSUAL FEATURES _____

_____

   d. DESCRIPTION OF COURSE OF OBJECT.

     (1) WHAT FIRST CALLED THE ATTENTION OF OBSERVER TO THE OBJECT _____

_____

     (2) ANGLE OR ELEVATION AND AZIMUTH OF OBJECT WHEN FIRST OBSERVED _____

_____

Glossary of Acronyms

AAC Alaskan Air Command

AAF Army Air Force

ADC Aerospace Defense Command

AEC Atomic Energy Commission

AFB Air Force Base

AFGWC Air Force Global Weather Control

AFIS Air Force Intelligence Service

AFOC Air Force Operations Center

AFR Air Force Regulation

AFSS Air Force Security Service

AMB Ambassador

ANG Air National Guard

APRO Aerial Phenomena Research Organization

ARPA Advanced Research Projects Agency

ASD Applied Science Division (CIA)

AST Atlantic Standard Time

ATIC Air Technical Intelligence Center (Air Force)

BMW Bomb Wing

CAUS Citizens Against UFO Secrecy

CFS Canadian Forces Station

252

CGS   Coast Guard Station
CIA   Central Intelligence Agency
CIC   Counter-Intelligence Corps
CINC/NORAD   Commander-in-Charge, NORAD
COMINT   Communications Intelligence (NSA)
CP   Command Post
CSC   Central Security Control (Air Force)
DATT   Defense Attache (U.S. Embassy)
DCD   Domestic Collections Division (CIA)
DCSOPS   Deputy Chief of Staff for Operations and Plans (Air Force)
DDO   Deputy Director for Operations (Air Force)
DIA   Defense Intelligence Agency
DMZ   Demilitarized Zone (Vietnam)
DO   Duty Officer
FAA   Federal Aviation Administration
FBI   Federal Bureau of Investigation
FOIA   Freedom of Information Act
GCI   Ground Control Intercept
GMT   Greenwich Mean Time
GSW   Ground Saucer Watch
INYSA   Assistant Chief of Staff, Intelligence, USAF (Science and
    Technology Branch, Directorate of Response Management)
INZ   Aerospace Intelligence Division (AFIS)
INZA   Editing, Debriefing, and Continuity Branch (AFIS)
JACL   Judge Advocate General, Litigation Division (Air Force)
JANAP   Joint Army Navy Air Force Publication
JCS   Joint Chiefs of Staff
KISR   Kuwait Institute for Scientific Research
KM   Kilometer
LCF   Launch Control Facility (Air Force)
NAVSPASUR   Naval Space Surveillance System
NCOC   National Combat Operations Center
NEPA   Nuclear Energy for the Propulsion of Aircraft
NICAP   National Investigations Committee on Aerial Phenomena
NM   Nautical Mile
NMCC   National Military Command Center
NORAD   North American Aerospace Defense Command
NPIC   National Photographic Interpretation Center

NRL   Naval Research Laboratory
NSA   National Security Agency
NSF   National Science Foundation
OAM   Operation Animal Mutilation
ONI   Office of Naval Intelligence
OSI   Office of Special Investigations (Air Force)
OSI   Office of Scientific Investigation (CIA)
RAPCOM   Radar Approach Communications
RAPCON   Radar Approach Control
RCMP   Royal Canadian Mounted Police
SA   Special Agent
SAC   Special Agent in Charge (FBI)
SAC   Strategic Air Command
SAC/HO   Strategic Air Command Office of History
SAFOI   Secretary of the Air Force Office of Information
SAO   Smithsonian Astrophysical Observatory
SAT   Security Alert Team
SIGINT   Signals Intelligence (NSA)
SPADATS   Space Detection and Tracking System (NORAD)
SPS   Security Police Squadron
SSB   Soft Support Building (Air Force)
TIA   Temperature Inversion Analysis
USAF   United States Air Force
USG   United States Government
Z   Zulu (Universal Time)

Bibliography

Adams, Tom. *The Choppers and the Choppers: Mystery Helicopter and Animal Mutilations*. Paris, Tex.: Project Stigmata, 1980.

"Air Force, N.S.A. and F.B.I.: Egg on the Face Over Cuban Incident—Robert Todd: A Frightened UFOlogist." *Just Cause,* September 1978, pp. 4–6.

Berliner, Don. "Air Force UFO Spokesman Describes Personal Sighting." *MUFON Journal,* February 1978, pp. 3–4.

"Bits, Straws and Blips." *Newsweek,* July 1, 1968, p. 38.

"Bolivian Documents Released By State Department: Mystery Continues." *Just Cause,* August 1978, pp. 8–15.

Brummett, William, and Ernest Zuick. *Should the USAF Reopen Project Blue Book*. Research Study, Air Command and Staff College, Air University, Maxwell Air Force Base, Alabama, May 1974.

Bryant, Larry. "UFO Secrecy Update." *MUFON Journal,* October, November, 1979; February, March, November, 1980; January, July, October, 1981; March, 1982.

Carpenter, Donald G., ed. *Introductory Space Science,* Vol. II, USAF Academy, 1968.

Catoe, Lynn, *UFOs and Related Subjects: An Annotated Bibliography*. Washington, D.C.: U.S. Government Printing Office, 1969.

Claflin-Chalton, Sandra, and Gordon MacDonald. *Sound and Light Phenomena: A Study of Historical and Modern Occurrences*. McLean, Va.: MITRE Corporation, November 1978.

Code Names Dictionary. Detroit, Mich.: Gale Research Company, 1963.

Condon, E. U. *Scientific Study of Unidentified Flying Objects*. ed. Daniel S. Gilmor. New York: E. P. Dutton and Co., Inc., 1969.

Crain, T. Scott, "Aircraft Accidents and UFOs," *Search,* Winter 1982–83, pp. 54–60.

"Crashed UFO in Bolivia?" *Just Cause,* May 1978, pp. 10–12.

"Cuban Jets Incident," *Just Cause,* July 1978, pp. 11–12.

"Cuban Jets Pursue a UFO and the F.B.I. Pursues Its Researcher." *International UFO Reporter,* September 1978, pp. 11 13.

Davidson, Leon. *Flying Saucers: An Analysis of the Air Force Project Blue Book Special Report No. 14,* 4th ed. Clarksburg, W. Va.: Saucerian Publications, 1970.

Dutton, Ronald. *An Analysis of Unidentified Flying Objects (UFO's).* Thesis, Air Command and Staff College, Air University, Maxwell Air Force Base, Alabama, June 1967.

Emenegger, Robert. *UFOs Past, Present and Future.* New York: Ballantine Books, 1974.

"F.B.I. Interrogates UFO Researcher: Government May Confiscate Documents." *Just Cause,* August 1978, pp. 4–6.

Flammonde, Paris. *The Age of Flying Saucers.* New York: Hawthorne, 1971.

———. *UFOs Exist.* New York: G. P. Putnam's Sons, Inc., 1976.

"F.O.I.A. Yields Pilot Sighting." *MUFON Journal,* May 1979, pp. 14–16.

Fowler, Raymond E. *The Andreasson Affair.* Englewood Cliffs, N.J.: Prentice-Hall, Inc., 1979.

———. *The Andreasson Affair: Phase Two.* Englewood Cliffs, N.J.: Prentice-Hall, Inc., 1982.

———. *Casebook of a UFO Investigator.* Englewood Cliffs, N.J.: Prentice-Hall, Inc. 1981.

———. *UFOs: Interplanetary Visitors.* Englewood Cliffs, N.J.: Prentice-Hall, Inc., 1979.

"Fred Valentich: The Missing Australian Pilot." *International UFO Reporter,* December 1978, pp. 2–10.

Fuller, John G. *Incident at Exeter.* New York: G. P. Putnam's Sons, Inc., 1966.

Gatti, Art. "The C.I.A. File on UFO's: Preventing the Public From Seeing The Light," *Gallery,* February 1980, pp. 67–69, 100–101.

Gersten, Peter. *What the Government Would Know About UFO If They Read Their Own Documents.* Evanston, Ill.: Center for UFO Studies, 1982 (text of speech presented at the 1981 MUFON International Symposium, Cambridge, Mass., with document reproductions).

Gross, Loren. *The Mystery of the Ghost Rockets,* 2nd ed. Scotia, N.Y.: Arcturus Book Service, 1982.

Hall, Richard. "C.I.A. Documents Show UFO Interest." *MUFON Journal,* April 1980, p. 16.

———. "Military Secrecy: Sailors, Soldiers and Airmen." *MUFON Journal,* November 1980, pp. 4–5.

Hall, Richard A., ed. *The UFO Evidence.* Washington, D.C.: National Investigations Committee on Aerial Phenomenon (NICAP), 1964.

Heflin, Woodford. *The United States Air Force Dictionary.* Washington, D.C.: U.S. Government Printing Office, 1956.

Hendry, Allan. *The UFO Handbook.* New York: Doubleday and Co., Inc., 1979.

Huyghe, Patrick, "Interview with Arthur C. Lundahl." *MUFON Journal,* February 1980, pp. 3–5.

————. "UFO Files: The Untold Story." *New York Times Magazine,* October 14, 1979.

Hynek, J. Allen, *The UFO Experience.* Chicago: Henry Regnery Co., 1972.

Hynek, J. Allen, and Jacques Vallee. *The Edge of Reality.* Chicago: Henry Regnery Co., 1975.

Jacobs, David M. *The UFO Controversy in America.* Bloomington, Ind.: Indiana University Press, 1975.

Kerr, Richard. "East Coast Mystery Booms Mystery Gone But Booms Linger On." *Science,* January 19, 1979, p. 256.

Keyhoe, Donald E. *Aliens from Space.* New York: Doubleday & Co., Inc., 1973.

————. *Flying Saucers: Top Secret.* New York: G. P. Putnam's Sons, Inc., 1960.

————. The Flying Saucers Are Real. New York: Fawcett Publications, Inc., 1950.

————. *The Flying Saucer Conspiracy.* New York: Henry Holt and Company, 1955.

————. *Flying Saucers From Outer Space.* New York: Henry Holt and Company, 1953.

King, John. *The UFO Problem: Time for a Reassessment.* Thesis, Air Command and Staff College, Air University, Maxwell Air Force Base, Alabama, June 1968.

Kinney, A. J. *Air Force Officers Guide.* Harrisburg, Pa.: Stackpole Books, 1981.

Klass, Philip J. *UFOs Explained.* New York: Random House, 1974.

————. "UFO Proponents and the C.I.A.: Conspiracy Theorists Rise Again." *Skeptical Inquirer,* Winter 1981–82, pp. 6–7.

————. "UFOs, the C.I.A. and the *New York Times." Skeptical Inquirer,* Spring 1980, pp. 2–5.

Lear, John. "The Disputed C.I.A. Document on UFO's." *Saturday Review,* September 3, 1966, pp. 45–50.

LeMay, Curtis, and MacKinley Kantor. *Mission With LeMay.* Garden City, N.Y.: Doubleday and Company, Inc., 1965.

Lore, Gordon, and Harold Deneault. *Mysteries of the Skies: UFOs in Perspective.* Englewood Cliffs, N.J.: Prentice-Hall, Inc., 1968.

Maney, Charles, and Richard Hall. *The Challenge of the Unidentified Flying Objects.* Washington, D.C., privately published, 1961.

Marchetti, Victor. "How the C.I.A. Views the UFO Phenomenon." *Second Look,* May 1979, pp. 2–5.

Marchetti, Victor, and John Marks. *The CIA and the Cult of Intelligence.* New York: Dell Publishing Co., Inc., 1980.

McCarthy, Paul. *Politicking and Paradigm Shifting: James E. McDonald and The UFO Case Study:* Doctoral Thesis, University of Hawaii, December 1975.

Menzel, Donald. *Flying Saucers.* Cambridge, Mass.: Harvard University Press, 1953.

Menzel, Donald, and Ernest Taves. *The UFO Enigma.* Garden City, N.Y.: Doubleday and Company, Inc., 1977.

Menzel, Donald, and Lyle G. Boyd. *The World of Flying Saucers.* Garden City, N.Y.: Doubleday and Company, Inc., 1963.

National Archives. *The United States Government Manual 1981–82.* Washington, D.C.: U.S. Government Printing Office, 1981.

Naval Research Laboratory. *NRL Investigations of East Coast Acoustic Events, 2nd December 1972–15th February, 1978.* Washington, D.C.: Naval Research Laboratory, 1978.

Neumann, Mary. *Washington Information Directory, 1981–82.* Washington, D.C.: Congressional Quarterly, Inc., 1981.

"NI-CIA-P or NICAP." *Just Cause,* January 1979, pp. 5–13.

"1975 Flap Over SAC Bases and Missile Sites." *Just Cause,* July 1978, pp. 2–4.

Oberg, James E. *UFOs and Outer Space Mysteries.* Norfolk, Va.: The Donning Company, 1982.

Olsen, Thomas. *The Reference for Outstanding UFO Sighting Reports.* Riderwood, Md.: UFO: RC, 1966.

Ruppelt, Edward J. *The Report on Unidentified Flying Objects.* Garden City, New York: Doubleday and Company, Inc., 1956.

Sachs, Margaret. *The UFO Encyclopedia.* New York: G. P. Putnam's Sons, Inc., 1980.

Sagan, Carl, and Thornton Page. *UFOs: A Scientific Debate.* Ithaca, N.Y.: Cornell University Press, 1972.

Satchell, Michael. "UFO's vs USAF, Amazing (but True) Encounters." *Parade,* December 10, 1978, pp. 8–11.

Saunders, David R., and Roger R. Harkins. *UFOs? Yes! Where the Condon Committee Went Wrong.* New York: World Publishing Company, 1968.

Schuessler, John. "Cash Landrum Radiation Case." *MUFON Journal,* November 1981, pp. 3–6.

———. "Pentagon Investigates Cash Landrum Case." *MUFON Journal,* October 1982, pp. 3–6.

Shapley, Deborah. "East Coast Mystery Booms: A Scientific Suspense Tale." *Science,* March 31, 1978, pp. 1416–17.

Shea, David. "The UFO Phenomenon: A Study in Public Relations." Thesis, University of Denver, 1972.

Sheaffer, Robert. *The UFO Verdict.* Buffalo, N.Y.: Prometheus Books, 1981.

Shields, Henry (Captain). "Now You See It, Now You Don't." *MIJI Quarterly,* Third Quarter, 1978.

Stanley, Darrell. *UFOs and Extraterrestrial Life.* Thesis, Air Command and Staff College, Air University, Maxwell Air Force Base, Alabama, June 1968.

"Stonewalling at USAF's OSI." *Just Cause,* September 1979, pp. 2–3.

Story, Ronald. *The Encyclopedia of UFOs.* Garden City, N.Y.: Doubleday and Company, Inc. Dolphin Books, 1980.

———. *UFOs and the Limits of Science.* New York: William Morrow and Company, Inc., 1981.

Sturrock, Peter A. *Report on a Survey of the Membership of the American Astronomical Society Concerning the UFO Problem,* SUIPR Report No. 681, Stanford, Calif.: Institute for Plasma Research, January 1977.

Stringfield, Leonard H. *Retrievals of the Third Kind.* Rome, Ohio: UFO Information Network, 1979.

Stringfield, Leonard H. *UFO Crash/Retrievals: Amassing the Evidence.* Published by the author: 4412 Grove Ave., Cincinnati, Ohio 45227, 1982.

Stringfield, Leonard. *The UFO Crash/Retrieval Syndrome.* Seguin, Tex.: The Mutual UFO Network (MUFON), 1980.

Stroh, Jerry. "The UFO Debate Is Still Alive." Research Study, Air Command and Staff College, Air University, Maxwell Air Force Base, Alabama, May 1971.

Tacker, Lawrence. *Flying Saucers and the U.S. Air Force.* Princeton, N.J.: D. Van Nostrand Company, Inc., 1960.

"UFO's Just Will Not Go Away." *Science,* December 16, 1977, p. 1128.

"The UFO Papers." *Saga's UFO Report,* August 1979 (special issue devoted to the C.I.A.'s UFO files).

"Update on the Ground Saucer Watch (GSW) Lawsuit Against the C.I.A." *International UFO Reporter,* July 1978, p. 8.

"U.S. Agencies Scratch Heads Over Bolivian Incident." *Just Cause,* June 1978, pp. 10–12.

U.S. Air Force. *Projects Grudge and Blue Book Reports 1–12.* Washington, D.C.: NICAP, 1968.

U.S. Congress, House of Representatives Armed Services Committee. *Unidentified Flying Objects Hearing.* 89th Congress, Second Session, April 5, 1966.

Aids to the Identification of Flying Objects. Washington, D.C.: U.S. Government Printing Office, 1968.

Vaeth, J. Gordon. *200 Miles Up.* New York: The Ronald Press Company, 1951.

Vallee, Jacques. *Anatomy of a Phenomenon.* Chicago: Henry Regnery Company, 1965.

————. *Challenge to Science.* Chicago: Henry Regnery Company, 1966.

"Washington Whispers." *U.S. News and World Report,* April 18, 1977, p. 11.

Willcox, P. J. *The UFO Question (Not Yet Answered).* Roslyn Heights, N.Y.: Libra Publishers, Inc., 1976.

Wood, Derek. *Jane's World Aircraft Recognition Handbook.* London: Jane's Publishing Company Ltd., 1982.

Index